Date Due

The
Female
Frontier

THE FEMALE FRONTIER

A Comparative View of Women on the Prairie and the Plains

GLENDA RILEY, 1938–

University Press of Kansas

© 1988 by the University Press of Kansas
All rights reserved

Published by the University Press of Kansas (Lawrence, Kansas
66045), which was organized by the Kansas Board of Regents and is
operated and funded by Emporia State University, Fort Hays State
University, Kansas State University, Pittsburg State University,
the University of Kansas, and Wichita State University

Library of Congress Cataloging-in-Publication Data

Riley, Glenda, 1938–
    The female frontier / Glenda Riley.
      p. cm.
    Bibliography: p.
    Includes index.
    ISBN 0-7006-0354-9
    1. Women pioneers—Great Plains—History. 2. Women pioneers—
Middle West—History. 3. Frontier and pioneer life—Great Plains—
History. 4. Frontier and pioneer life—Middle West—History.
5. Prairies—Middle West—History. I. Title.
HQ1438.G75R55 1988
305.4'2'0978—dc19   87-32447
                                                                   CIP

British Library Cataloguing in Publication Data is available.

Printed in the United States of America
10 9 8 7 6 5 4 3 2

To Richard S. Kirkendall
for his unflagging encouragement and support

Contents

Acknowledgments

The evolution of this study has been a long one, and I have incurred many debts along the way. Richard S. Kirkendall, Henry A. Wallace Professor of Agricultural History at Iowa State University, has been particularly helpful and highly encouraging to the development of the concept of the female frontier, as well as aiding in the research and other detailed work needed to bring the idea to fruition as a book.

Other people also assisted me in various ways. Botanist Marshall Sundberg of Louisiana State University helped immensely with my development of definitions of the prairie and the Plains. Historian John L. Eiklor of the University of Northern Iowa combed book sales and collected an invaluable assortment of women's guidebooks, which he donated to the project. And archivist Greg Koos of the McLean County Historical Society in Bloomington, Illinois, enhanced the study by giving freely of his time, his ideas, and his own work.

The archivists and staffs of many other libraries and historical societies were also extremely helpful. These included the Barker Texas History Center at the University of Texas in Austin, the Denver Public Library, the Historical Society of Iowa in Iowa City, the Illinois State Historical Library in Springfield, the Iowa Museum and Archives in Des Moines, the Kansas State Historical Library in Topeka, the Minnesota Historical Society Archives in St. Paul, the Montana State Historical Society Library in Helena, the Montana State University Library Special Collections Department in Bozeman, the Nebraska State Historical Society Library in Lincoln, the Newberry Library in Chicago, the South Dakota State Historical Resource Center in Pierre, the State Historical Society of Missouri Library in Columbia, the State Historical Society of North Dakota in Bismarck, the University of Missouri Western History Manuscript Collection in Columbia, the University of Northern Iowa Library in Cedar Falls, the University of Oklahoma Western History

Collection in Norman, the Wyoming American Heritage Center in Laramie, and the Wyoming State Archives in Cheyenne.

Two energetic young women acted as research assistants and "gofers." Karmen Berger helped during the early stages of the project, and more recently, Rebecca L. Wheeler contributed much, including statistical materials, to the volume. The excellent and thorough typists of the manuscript were Judith M. Dohlman and Patricia L. Murphy, both on the staff of the University of Northern Iowa.

The work was aided by grants from the National Endowment for the Humanities and the University of Northern Iowa, each of which funded a summer of research and writing time.

And finally, my thanks to the University Press of Kansas for patiently encouraging the research and writing of this study for several years, to Elliott West of the University of Arkansas at Fayetteville for improving its substance, and to the editorial staff of the press for enhancing its style.

It is my hope that the usefulness of the book, which all of these people so generously supported, will be great and that any errors or omissions that I may have introduced into it will be few.

Glenda Riley
University College, Dublin

The
Female
Frontier

W. D. Koerner's 1921 painting "Madonna of the Prairie" presents a common and enduring image of frontierswomen. Courtesy of the Buffalo Bill Historical Center, Cody, Wyoming.

1
The Female Frontier:
Definitions, Interpretations,
and Images

Until the mid 1970s, frontierswomen appeared in histories of the American West only as one-dimensional stereotypes or not at all. When Frederick Jackson Turner delivered his now-famous address "The Significance of American History" to the American Historical Association in 1893, he clearly was talking about a male frontier. He stated: "The wilderness masters the colonist. . . . It takes him from the railroad car and puts him in the hunting shirt and the moccasin . . . he shouts the war cry and takes the scalp in orthodox Indian fashion." Nearly three decades later, another western historian, George F. Parker, offered a similar definition of frontier settlers to the Mississippi Valley Historical Association when he declared: "I define the American Pioneer as the man who . . . crossed the mountains from the thin line of Atlantic settlement. . . . To me, this man reflects the character of the most effective single human movement in history."[1]

One might reasonably raise the question, "But were there no women in this grand historical event?" A few historians asserted that women were indeed present. Some of these argued that it was women who actually bore the brunt of the hardships involved in opening the West. In 1921, historian Emerson Hough claimed: "The chief figure of the American West . . . is not the long-haired fringed-legged man riding a raw boned pony, but the gaunt and sad-faced woman sitting on the front seat of the wagon, following her lord where he might lead. . . . That was the great romance of all America—the woman in the sunbonnet."[2] In 1937, Everett Dick explained that women on the Great Plains (hereafter Plains) became leathery, stooped, and lifeless figures who either begged to return home or persevered until they were broken entirely.[3] Numerous other historians presented western women in brief cameo appearances as Gentle Tamers, Pioneers in Petticoats, Saints in Sunbonnets, Madonnas of the Prairies, Pioneer Mothers, Light Ladies, Calamity Janes, Fighting Feminists, and Reluctant Pioneers.[4] Only during the past decade have a number of historians begun to refute these puerile stereotypes by establishing a picture of frontierswomen's contributions as both important and complex.

My intention in this study is to demonstrate not only that women did play highly significant and multifaceted roles in the development of the American West but also that their lives as settlers displayed fairly consistent patterns, which transcended geographic sections of the frontier. Further, I maintain that these shared experiences and responses of frontierswomen constituted a "female frontier." In other words, frontierswomen's responsibilities, life styles, and sensibilities were shaped more by gender considerations than by region. Men's lives, on the other hand, often took form as a result of their physical setting and its resources. The activities, interests, and attitudes of a male settler who was a rancher diverged in important ways from that of a frontier merchant, while those of a farmer assumed far-different configurations from those of a miner. Yet, because women's lives focused upon domestic production, childbirth and childcare, family relationships, and other "female" tasks, the mothers, wives, daughters, and sisters of these men were touched only marginally by the resources of the area and by the resulting occupations of their menfolk. Even unmarried women and married women who worked outside the home usually found their employment opportunities limited by their gender. Also, they were expected to participate fully in domestic duties, whether for themselves, their parents, and other families with whom they lived or for their own husbands and children.

Because gender was the key factor in determining their duties and interests, frontierswomen pursued a similar list of activities in every frontier setting. Not only did they manage their households and families; they were also charged with preserving family, religious, and ethnic traditions; and they served as family historians, producing family Bible records, quilts, and such "women's" artwork as wedding or mourning pictures. Those who held paid employment before, in addition to, or in place of marriage were typically limited to such "acceptable" female occupations as milliners, shop clerks, domestic servants, teachers, and nursemaids. Women's leisure time was dictated by gender as well in that they could "appropriately" attend school and church functions, join women's organizations, participate in family-centered social activities, and ride horseback sidesaddle, rather than astride. Women were also expected to be the prime movers in the establishment of schools, churches, and other cultural institutions while initiating a broad spectrum of social reforms. Even their dress reflected their status as females, rather than as frontier settlers; and more than one hoop-skirted frontierswoman lamented the singeing of her long skirts while she was cooking over an open fireplace.

The lives of frontierswomen were affected only secondarily by the occupations of the men in their families. A ranchwoman might learn how to pull a calf or take in orphan calves to be hand-suckled and warmed by her stove, and the merchant's wife or daughter might spend some time clerking in the family store. A homesteader's daughter might learn to dig potatoes, and a mining-camp woman might learn to sift and weigh ore. There is no doubt that numerous women worked in fields, helped with cattle roundups and drives, and aided in running inns and other family businesses, both while the men of the family were present and while they were absent. But in almost every case, the primary focus of women's lives, whether they were married or single, was supposed to be, and usually was, domestic. While the mineral, soil, timber, or other resources of a region highly influenced men's occupations, activities, and ideas, they marginally affected those of women.

Frontierswomen were also touched less by era than were the men. Technology, for example, affected men's and women's lives to different degrees. As their financial situations began to improve, ranchers, storekeepers, farmers, and miners turned to such technological improvements as refrigerated and cattle railroad cars, cash registers, McCormick reapers, windmills, barbed-wire fencing, gas- and electric-powered machines, and hundreds of other implements for help in their daily work. Despite a prevalent myth to the contrary, similar labor-saving tools were very slow to appear inside the home. Usually, first priority was given to the business; and second, to the home. In addition, women who had been schooled in nineteenth-century principles of domesticity were hesitant to abandon the practice of personally investing their own energies in their work in favor of some impersonal machine. Thus, women whose men threshed with the newest machinery frequently cooked for those men on wood-burning stoves. When women did have mechanical helpers, they often lacked the support technology that was needed to make the machines truly effective. Generations of women carried buckets of water to newfangled washing machines, because their homes lacked indoor pumps, and carried the dirty water away in the same manner, because no indoor drains existed. For later generations of women, rural electrification passed them by, although their fathers, brothers, husbands, and sons might be driving the latest gasoline-powered tractors. Although frontierswomen frequently noted the gradual appearance of economic, housing, and other types of improvements over the decades, their lives still exhibited strong elements of sameness and continuity that often outweighed the changes occurring in them.

Clearly, region and era created some differences in women's lives. A female settler on the Plains faced greater difficulty in obtaining water for washing clothes than did her counterpart on the prairie. And a woman of 1900 might use a machine to wash her clothes, whereas a woman of 1820 did not have that option available to her. But the point is that women, whether on the prairie or on the Plains, early or late, were charged with the task of either doing the laundry or seeing that it was done. Even such factors as social class, ethnicity, race, religion, education, and marital status did not substantially alter the gender roles and the expectations of women on the prairie and on the Plains.

Of course, many women resisted the dictates and the limitations of the female frontier. Some regularly engaged in "men's" work, wore pants, and rode astride. Others, like "Mountain Charley" Guerin and Elizabeth C. ("Bill Newcom") Smith emulated men in many ways.[5] Many young women defiantly threw their protective sunbonnets over their shoulders and let their faces become sun-tanned and freckled. And thousands more expanded their "domestic" sphere to encompass the yard, barn, fields, wilderness, and local communities. But when women's own words, as recorded in diaries, daybooks, journals, letters, memoirs, reminiscences, and oral-history interviews are collected and compared, it is apparent that resistance tended to be random and intermittent. Such deviation from female norms frequently engendered criticism, rejection, and other forms of social control. Consequently, even as they expanded their horizons, most women used traditional female values as their guides. Thus, women's lives were generally more alike than they were varied. Despite locale or era, women's experiences exhibited a remarkable similarity, which was shaped largely by gender and its associated concept of "women's work."[6]

The concept of the female frontier indicates that the usual ways of defining frontier areas have been male in orientation. The very notion of a western region as a fur, farming, mineral, or lumber frontier reflects an overwhelming interest in the economic pursuits of its Euro-American male settlers. In 1949, Ray Allen Billington's now-classic *Westward Expansion: A History of the American Frontier* promoted the idea of subdividing the West into zones on the basis of their resources and the male occupations that they attracted.[7] Billington's scheme inspired other historians to produce a huge number of books that reconstructed and analyzed almost every aspect of economic life in each district.[8] Two outstanding studies of this kind were Rodman W. Paul's investigation into the mining frontier and Gilbert C. Fite's examination of the farming frontier,[9] both of which took as their central issues economic activities that were primarily male, rather than a broader vision of frontier society as a unified whole.

Numerous other organizing themes for the definition and study of frontier belts appeared in subsequent years. In 1959, Richard C. Wade, in *The Urban Frontier,* argued that pioneer life in such cities as Pittsburgh, Cincinnati, Lexington, Louisville, and St. Louis deserved to be examined.[10] In 1964, Oscar O. Winther, in *The Transportation Frontier,* offered a new perspective on the Trans-Mississippi West between the end of the Civil War in 1865 and the penetration of most regions by some form of transportation by 1890.[11] Winther's volume was part of a series called Histories of the American Frontier, edited by Billington, that took as its crucial limits the economic, political, and time factors. In addition to Paul's study of mining and Fite's work on farming, mentioned above, topics that were covered by the series included the Spanish borderlands and the Canadian, northern-colonial, revolutionary, and early-national frontiers.[12]

The attempt to assess the larger meaning of the American West and its various regions also has been heavily influenced by viewpoints that seem relevant to endeavors and concerns that have customarily been associated more with men than with women. When Frederick Jackson Turner first argued for the great significance of the frontier to American society as a whole, he noted the frontier's economic and political contributions. To Turner, the West was especially important for its spirit. It encouraged men to rebel against eastern conservatism, particularly by shaping new policies on land, banks, and tariffs, and to liberalize their political views in support of democracy.[13] Other historians concentrated upon economic elements. Bernard De Voto, for instance, insisted that the geography of the West was its primary gift. In his view, the rivers, mountains, lakes, soils, and climate of the West were what allowed extensive and abundant agriculture, caused straight axe handles to become curved, and forced the men who conquered it to become innovative and resilient workers.[14] More recently, Henry Nash Smith and Richard Slotkin have analyzed the physical aspects of the frontier and the intellectual constructs that developed from the promises of growth and progress that the region seemed to offer.[15]

Historians were not alone in looking at the frontier in male-oriented terms; the reports of contemporary observers also concentrated more upon the political and economic features of the West than on the establishment of home, family, and culture in a new land. As scores of travelers, explorers, novelists, poets, and social commentators focused their attention on the prairie regions that ran along both sides of the upper Mississippi River, they reported first upon the region's native inhabitants but then quickly began to assess the opportunities that the area offered for farmers, fur trappers, merchants, and other entrepreneurs. Such accounts ranged from the romanticized view of James Fenimore Cooper to the homespun simplicity of Edward Eggleston and eventually to the realism of Hamlin Garland. As the American Indians of the Middle West were rapidly displaced by settlers who established farmsteads, businesses, and towns, Garland chronicled the rapid settlement that caused the prairie to be "blackened by the plow" and farming to pervade the land.[16]

Because it was an unusually harsh frontier area, the Great Plains and any economic opportunities that it might offer were an even greater source of concern for commentators than the prairies had been. As early as 1810, the publication of the journal of Lt. Zebulon M. Pike firmly implanted his negative view of the Plains as being little more than a vast desert. In a letter written shortly before the appearance of his soon-to-become-famous "Great American Desert" statement, Pike had suggested that the United States government would be wise to return all the lands that it owned west of the Mississippi River to Spain in exchange for Florida.[17] In subsequent years, many other travelers, explorers, and commentators confirmed Pike's interpretation of the Plains. In 1866, Gen. John Pope declared that the Plains were both unproductive and uninhabitable and urged the United States government to settle the Indian problems there so that Euro-Americans might cross it safely on their way to the more promising mining districts of the Far West.[18] Because population advanced beyond the ninety-sixth meridian onto the Plains during the mid 1860s, this pessimistic picture soon came under scrutiny from those who were determined to either settle the Plains themselves or to see it developed by others. Proponents of the theory that "rain would follow the plow" and advocates of such technological advances as railroads, windmills, and barbed wire argued for a more optimistic outlook.[19]

Of course, the many words that were expended on the political and economic aspects of the American West during the nineteenth century reflected the intense interests of men who were, after all, charged by society with the primary conduct of political and economic matters. Those who desperately wanted to escape restrictive governments, black slavery, high taxes, and religious prohibitions were concerned with the political climate of the area that they hoped to call home. Potential settlers who had to earn a living, once they had relocated in the West, were compelled to explore its occupational possibilities. The presence of plentiful fur-bearing animals, rich soil, vast grazing lands, abundant mineral resources, or thick forests was crucial information to thousands of Euro-Americans who looked to the West as a source of sustenance for themselves and of future economic opportunities for their children. In addition, the many people who hoped to realize a profit on the frontier—for example, land and railroad companies, merchants, mine and factory owners, ranchers and bonanza farmers, and state governments—were exceedingly interested not only in determining what financial gains the frontier might offer them or their organizations but also in apprising possible customers of them as well.

As a result of the widespread need either to learn about economic opportunities in the West or to convince others that the chances of success there were great, there was an explosion of promotional materials that reinforced the customary focus on political and economic factors. Frequently referred to as boomer literature, these advertising attempts extolled the virtues of towns, areas, and states, often with little respect for veracity. Weekly newspapers soon became key promoters of frontier enterprise. Commonly established to stimulate land booms and to print the proving-up notices that were legally required as part of the homesteading process, these newspapers were often funded by land or railroad companies or by town-site promoters.[20] State governments also enthusiastically publicized the advantages of advertisements, as did promotional agents, boards, and societies.[21] But railroad companies were probably the most prolific producers of boomer materials. The Illinois Central developed its promotional techniques to such a sophisticated state that other railroad companies sent observers to learn from it. Pamphlets, broadsides, free trips to a frontier area, professional touring lectures, guidebooks, and promises of low shipping rates were among the methods that railroad companies used.[22]

These exaggerated promotional attempts also featured men, resources, and occupations, giving only passing mention to homes, schools, churches, and related subjects. In 1837 the *Iowa News* (Dubuque) proclaimed that in its area of the West, "one remarkable characteristic of matters and things is perpetual excitement." Describing the mushrooming towns, the throngs of emigrants, and the rapidly burgeoning economy, the paper asserted, "It is seldom that a person who has resided for some years here, can ever content himself to return and live in the east."[23] Promises of rewards that guaranteed to out-distance even the wildest dreams were held out to those who would migrate, multiply, and work hard. In 1855 the *Eddyville* (Iowa) *Free Press* vowed that migrants had only to come with "strong minds and willing hands to work" and they would be "abundantly blessed and rewarded."[24] During the early 1880s an advocate of Plains development claimed that Kansas contained un-surpassed richness, the Dakotas offered many "flattering inducements to im-migration," and Colorado had so many enticements that it was the fastest growing of all western areas.[25] Others insisted that Wyoming was one of the most flourishing western territories because of its incredibly productive land and its unsurpassed mineral wealth. By the late 1880s the boom town of Lara-mie was receiving energetic support from promoters. The rhetoric that they marshaled is a good indication not only of the heights of eloquence and the inaccuracies that were reached in boomer literature but also of its male bent:

> Every element to make a most rich and prosperous commonwealth is here. . . .
> No place offers more inducements for men who are willing to work. . . . If
> the eve of our prosperity has been a glorious one, with the sunlight of the
> new dawn beginning to warm and glow in the sky . . . , Laramie will be a
> place in which the rich and indolent will come to repose . . . and the sterling
> soul to build up an inheritance.[26]

These elaborate advertising efforts to attract men to the West began to ex-tend beyond the boundaries of the United States during the late 1850s and early 1860s. In Iowa, a variety of handbooks began to be printed in 1858 which were aimed at potential settlers from Canada and Europe. In 1870 a group of Iowa business people and promoters formed one of the first state boards of immigration.[27]

Promotional efforts that were directed at other countries received a warm welcome from people who had long seen America as a New World in both political and economic terms. As Americans pushed into westward regions, the interest and curiosity of Europeans intensified. Such observers as Isabella Bird, Fredrika Bremer, Charles Dickens, Mary Austin Holley, Alexis de Tocqueville, Friedrich von Raumer, and scores of others poured out a torrent of essays and books describing and assessing the American West. A common theme was concern with farmland; other concerns were mineral and timber resources, abundant food, and the ability to own land. The need that many Europeans felt to free themselves from restrictive political and economic systems led them to the easy acceptance of an image of the American West as a cornucopia of plenty.[28]

The promotional and other literature about the American West was overwhelmingly concerned with political and economic issues of more direct relevance to male roles and responsibilities than to those imputed to females by nineteenth-century ideas. But did commentary on the western frontier always speak, as the pieces discussed here, only of men and never of women? The answer is no. Writers on the West, including journalists, travelers, explorers, novelists, poets, social commentators, and promoters, occasionally considered women and issues that are traditionally associated with them, such as home, family, culture, education, and religion. Because women were usually seen as ancillary to economic activities, they were assigned their own specialized functions and roles in writings about the frontier. While men were cast as the breadwinners, women were portrayed as the maintainers and protectors of the home, the family, and the society. Thus, women most commonly appeared as helpmates to men and as the civilizers of the new, raw western societies. Probably because the helpmate and civilizer functions were seen as important but definitely secondary, representations of these roles lacked depth and soon became little more than stereotypes. Helpmates and civilizers soon became mythologized figures who either triumphed over the wilderness or suffered greatly as a result of its harsh conditions. Western women who did not fit the helpmate and civilizer images, such as prostitutes, suffrage proponents, and pseudo-men, were essentially dismissed by being reduced to outright caricatures.[29]

As the veil of myth that came to shroud frontierswomen was being woven, many types of people contributed to its creation. Journalists often wrote about western women, usually favoring the hardy and staunch characterization. In 1880 a female writer for *Lippincott's Magazine* claimed that women both loved the West and worked assiduously to civilize it.[30] A few years later, two male writers supported this view by pointing out that women brought civilization both to crude western men and to the new environment that these men had chosen.[31] As the twentieth century progressed, such wide-selling periodicals as *Life Magazine* repeated the idea that frontierswomen were "fabulous." These "brave, strong-minded, and gay ladies helped tame the pioneers," with the term *pioneers* presumably meaning men.[32]

Dime novelists, who originally tended to present their heroines as fair maidens in need of the protection of men, soon came to support the concept of the plucky frontierswoman so touted by journalists. For instance, one maidenly heroine of the 1890s who cried out for a "real man" to save her from the unwanted attentions of a bully was duly saved by a stalwart hero who proclaimed that he "never hesitated to face death in defense of a woman." But in a later tale of daring, a courageous and very able young woman threw sandbags out of a hot-air balloon onto the heads of Sioux Indians; then she brandished the revolver that she always carried as a further deterrent to her pursuers. She capped her unladylike performance by returning to camp, where "with several of the females of the settlement" she "engaged in making coffee for the men." Other versions of this audacious and hardy protagonist later appeared in the comic strips of the 1940s and 1950s in such reincarnations as Prairie Kate and Buckskin Bell. Tough, competent, and gutsy, these women were capable of wringing the ultimate praise from men: "Yuh're as good as two men!"[33]

Depictions of frontierswomen by novelists and poets are much more difficult to summarize because so many of these writers tackled the topic. Here, too, the helpmate and civilizer not only abounded but ranged from those who triumphed over the frontier to those who were defeated by it. As historian Sandra L. Myres has pointed out, "Concomitant with the image of the weary and forlorn frontier wife, a sort of helpless heroine, is the stereotype of the westering woman as sturdy helpmate and civilizer of the frontier."[34] During the early years of the nineteenth century, such popular writers as William Gilmore Simms and James Fenimore Cooper presented their readers with women who were heroic, skilled with weapons, and even tough.[35] This early tradition of strong frontierswomen was expanded during the twentieth century by such writers as Willa Cather, Vardis Fisher, Mari Sandoz, and Bess Streeter Aldrich, through their representations of women who displayed great stamina and ingenuity.[36] During the early decades of the twentieth century, this longstanding trend to picture frontierswomen as able and self-reliant received a serious challenge from the works of two writers who had little experience with the West and its women. One of these was Ole E. Rölvaag, who himself never homesteaded, and Hamlin Garland, who had fled the Middle Border area for the city at an early age. Yet, with their heartrending lamentations concerning women's work loads, hostility to the frontier, and tendencies toward insanity, these two writers etched the picture of a helpless, hopeless drudge into the minds of generations of American readers.[37]

The authors of captivity narratives also drew heavily upon the theme of the weak and unfortunate woman who was destroyed by the frontier. Although these tales claimed to be factual accounts of the experiences of women while they were living with American Indian captors, they actually incorporated large doses of fiction and maudlin sentiments designed to boost sales. Captivity narratives by women, especially those that included inferences of sexual mistreatment, appealed to a wide market from the time they first appeared during the American colonial period. One of the earliest was *The Narrative of the Captivity and Restoration of Mrs. Mary Rowland-son*, which first appeared in 1682. By the mid-nineteenth century the prairie region of the trans-Mississippi West supplied the setting for these horrifying and titillating dramas. In 1857 the abuse of frontierswomen by American Indians in the so-called Spirit Lake Massacre in Iowa was told in terrifying detail by a survivor, Abbie Gardner-Sharpe. In 1862, Minnesota's New Ulm Massacre received similar treatment at the hands of Mary Renville. The scene for captivity dramas soon moved to the Plains. As late as 1892, with most native Americans destroyed, dispersed, or on reservations, Emeline Fuller achieved best-seller status with her saga of the torture that was imposed on defenseless white women, which she claimed to have witnessed on her way to Oregon.[38]

Writers who drew upon the West and its women for their themes were not the only contributors to female stereotypes. Western artists often overlooked the presence of women entirely, but when they did include women, they usually portrayed them in the civilizer role. Moreover, these women were genteel civilizers; that is, as passive figures protected by men, they triumphed over the strange land by virtue of their gentility and their ethereal natures. An outstanding example of the genteel frontierswoman was W. H. D. Koerner's "Madonna of the Prairie," an engaging portrait of a dewy-eyed, naive eastern woman perched on a wagon seat, with the bow of the covered wagon forming a halo around her head. With her lace collar and a delicate brooch at her throat, she is the picture of innocence and daintiness. Even as ideas concerning women and their roles began to broaden around the turn of the twentieth century, the figure of the prairie madonna persisted in the works of most western artists. One commentator described the dominant artists' representation of western women as a "frozen goddess" whose idealization continued in the face of an opposing reality. The artists' refusal to reflect the reality of western women in their work was later continued by makers of western films, who, until the last few years, cast women as the good woman, the schoolmarm, the kindhearted prostitute, and in other limited characterizations.[39] With such stereotypical depictions of western women holding sway for so many years, it is not surprising that the reality of frontierswomen's lives is only beginning to come to light. Fortunately, as a result of a few early dissident voices and vigorous scholarship during the past decade, these images currently are being replaced by a more realistic and complex picture of women's participation in the westward movement.[40]

As details concerning the experience of frontierswomen emerged, they showed a striking similarity from one region to the next, no matter what its economic base and predominant occupation. For several years, I have believed that these similarities constituted a female frontier. In 1981, I wrote that most commentators had concluded that "there was no one frontier; rather, there were many frontiers, such as a cattle frontier, a farmer's frontier, and an urban frontier, among others." But the existing definitions excluded a frontier that pertained to women. In my view, it was only by reconstructing the female frontier in all its reincarnations that we could ever attain "an understanding of the full implications of women's participation in America's westward movement."[41] Since that time, I have pursued the female frontier slice by slice; in Iowa, South Dakota, Illinois, and, eventually, in all the other prairie and Plains states. These investigations have confirmed my belief that the female frontier was every bit as real and coherent as, for example, the mining frontier was. Both the female and the mining frontiers displayed their own modes of operation, cultures, and value systems.

To demonstrate the existence of a female frontier and to illustrate its usefulness as a concept, this study compares in detail the lives of female settlers on the prairie and the Plains frontiers. Women's roles and concerns are largely reconstructed from women's own words, as recorded in their diaries, daybooks, journals, letters, memoirs, reminiscences, and interviews. The authors of these sources include the barely literate to the educated, young and old, single and married, white and black, native-born and non-American-born. These women's materials are supplemented by census data; legal codes and proceedings; listings in city directories; newspaper accounts; genealogies; family, local, and county histories; essays; sermons; novels; works of art; photographs; and interpretations of artifacts. I begin by establishing who the prairie women and the Plains women were in terms of marital status, age, social class, race, ethnicity, and religious affiliation. I then reconstruct in detail their lives at home, in the realm of paid employment and income production, and in the larger community. The chapters are paired, so that prairie women's and Plains women's experiences as domestic practitioners, paid workers, and community participants parallel each other.

As the term *frontier* in the title of this study suggests, I do not examine the role of American Indian women. The study is concerned with frontierswomen: the women who settled the prairie and the Plains regions. American Indians are, however, touched upon slightly in discussions of women's adaptation to prairie and the Plains areas.

For the purposes of this study, the prairie and the Plains regions have been determined on the basis of a combination of geographical, cultural, and political features. A purely physical conception of the prairies and the Plains is extremely problematic. On the prairie frontier the savanna regions of tall grasses and relatively few trees were often intermixed with forest and hilly districts. Although the physical traits of the Great Plains were more consistent than were those of the prairie, historian Frederick Luebke has argued that defining the area only by its geography, as did the Plains historian Walter Prescott Webb, who used aridity, treelessness, and flatness as his criteria, is a form of environmental determinism that ignores other significant factors.[42] One of these factors was the culture that characterized and unified a region despite its geographical profile. Nebraska and Kansas, for example, reflected more of what might be called a Plains mentality than one of prairie, even though they encompassed both types of terrain. These cultural zones were reflected and reinforced by the political units of state governments that derived from other aspects than just the physical ones.

Taking the geographical, political, and cultural factors and their attendant complexities into account, I define the prairie region as western Indiana, central and northern Illinois, southern and western Minnesota, all of Iowa, and western and northern Missouri. The Plains include the Dakotas, Nebraska, Kansas, northern Oklahoma, western Texas, eastern Colorado, and most of Wyoming and Montana.[43]

Although the prairie and the Plains juxtapose each other geographically, they differ in many respects. The prairie is generally characterized by rolling grasslands and forested zones, while the Plains tend to be level and treeless. Soil on the prairie is good to very rich, notably the grade-1 soil in parts of Iowa, but that of the Plains varies more in its productivity, ranging from sparse grasslands that are suited for the grazing of cattle and sheep to fields that produce rich stands of wheat. Prairie land has yielded such minerals as limestone and coal, whereas parts of the Plains were once rich in gold. Another contrasting resource is the adequate to plentiful rainfall on the prairie, as opposed to the arid condition of most of the Plains.

As a consequence of these differences, it was possible for settlers to "break" and develop the prairie with such relatively simple tools as the breaking plow. On the Plains, settlers were forced to rely upon more advanced technology, which included windmills, barbed-wire fencing, and increasingly sophisticated reapers and harvesters. This situation, in turn, demanded more capital and more knowledge from those who were attempting to subdue the Plains.

The differences in the two regions and in the technology needed to conquer them resulted in two eras of settlement. Thus, the time period considered here begins in 1815, when the effects of the War of 1812 combined with other factors to propel westward migration into prairie regions. It ends a century later, in 1915, when most of the Plains districts contained too many people to continue to be considered frontier zones by the United States Bureau of Census. Although examinations of prairie areas begin in 1815, they do not end at one single time. The analysis of Iowa, for example, lessens after 1870, when the U.S. Census Bureau declared its frontier closed, but continues in Minnesota well into the 1890s because of the persistence of frontier conditions in many places. Similarly, some attention is paid to early settlement on the Plains during the 1850s, but the primary emphasis begins in the mid 1860s, with the first significant wave of settlers to push into the Nebraska and Kansas areas. Trends, changes, and national events that occurred during the one hundred years between 1815 and 1915 are referred to in topical discussions throughout the study and in citations that suggest a range of possibilities for further reading and investigation.

The conclusion offers a summary view of the existence and significance of the female frontier. It draws upon women's lives on the prairies and on the Plains as illustrations of the shared experiences that constituted the female frontier. By establishing such a comparative view of women on the prairie and the Plains and by introducing the idea of a female frontier, I hope to supply perspectives that will lead to a fuller understanding and an enhanced appreciation of the contributions of the millions of women who helped to open, settle, and develop the American West.

2

A Profile of Frontierswomen
on the Prairie and the Plains

For most people the term *frontierswomen* is definitive and crisp. The image of the frontierswoman that still prevails is that of a slender, pale-skinned woman wearing a long-skirted dress and a sunbonnet with pasteboard slats. One of her hands clasps the tiny fingers of a child; her other arm cradles a rifle or perhaps presses a baby against her breast. She is wife, mother, helpmate, and intrepid pioneer personified.

In spite of recent scholarship to the contrary, this stereotype, along with its many variations and typologies that have been created by generations of writers, historians, and artists, continues to exert wide appeal, especially outside the academic community. This assertion is based upon a series of interviews that I conducted between 1985 and 1987 with scholars, students, and lay people. Scholars were the most critical of the traditional image of frontierswomen, students were less so, and lay people were the most accepting of it. The stereotype has numerous manifestations. As a saint in a sunbonnet, a helpmate, or in historian Everett Dick's phrase, "the homesteader's consort," the frontierswoman put up a hardy and formidable front; faced all challenges, whether beast, climate, or American Indian; completed endless domestic chores; and helped with men's work as well.[1] As the pioneer in petticoats, she retained her feminine ways yet remained undaunted by the vast frontier. As the gentle tamer, she brought culture, schools, and churches to the unbridled land. As the pioneer mother, she suffered extensively while raising her family and helping to break a farm under the most primitive of conditions.[2]

Such depictions, however compelling and sentimentally appealing they may be, are not adequate representations of the thousands of women who helped to settle the prairie and the Plains regions of the United States. They would have us believe that frontierswomen were wives and mothers, young, of no particular social class, but definitely of white American stock. In reality, these

14

women were a highly diverse lot, whose ranks included the single and the married, young and old, lower- and upper-class, white and black, American- and non-American-born, and Catholic and Jew. If any one generalization can safely be offered regarding prairie and Plains women, it is that they brought a myriad of backgrounds, statuses, values, and beliefs with them to the frontier area that sprawled from Illinois to Wyoming.

Because marital status has long been such an important element of the archetypal female settler, it in particular deserves extensive discussion and examination. Although an awareness of variations in marital state is growing among researchers of western women, a still common image is one that equates frontierswoman with wife. This is an understandable interpretation, given the fact that nineteenth-century American society expected women to marry and that the majority of them did so sometime during their lives. In addition, in an economic system in which men were the primary breadwinners and women were expected neither to take paid employment seriously nor to be paid fair wages when they did work, marriage provided necessary financial support for women and their dependents.

Population imbalances in both the prairie and the Plains regions intensified the pressure upon women to marry. During the early years of settlement, the number of men outdistanced the number of women in most regions. This relative scarcity of women became national news upon more than one occasion. For example, in 1837 the *Philadelphia Ledger* promised young single women that "every respectable young woman who goes west, is almost sure of an advantageous marriage, while, from the superabundance of her own sex in the east, her chances for it are not greater than those for a disappointment."[3] A few years later, the following story in a national magazine, although probably apocryphal, embodied the prevailing attitudes toward young single women, who were assumed to desire marriage at any cost, and the ripe situation for the unmarried women on the prairie:

> . . . the arrival of 41 ladies, all at one time, in Iowa has caused "a sensation." We think it should. But the manner of "paying addresses" and getting "hitched" is what we want to come at. It is said to be done in a business-like way. . . . When a steamboat-load of ladies is coming in "at the wharf," the gentlemen on shore make proposals to the ladies through trumpets, something like the following:—"Miss with blue ribbon on your bonnet, will you take me?" "Hallo thar gal with a cinnamon-colored shawl! if agreeable we will jine." The ladies in the meantime get ashore and are married at the "hotel," the parties arranging themselves as the squire sings out, "Sort yourselves! Sort yourselves!"[4]

Some years later, an Iowa writer reinforced this image by remarking that "it would be an act of humanity if scores of the young maidens who are pining away in the eastern villages for somebody to love would set their faces

(Above) Although most frontierswomen were white, some were black, like this Dodge County, Minnesota, pioneer, photographed with her husband circa 1905. Courtesy of the Minnesota Historical Society, St. Paul. (Right) The pose used in this wedding photograph suggests a somewhat egalitarian relationship. Anna Belle and William Steintemp, 20 February 1881. Courtesy of the Minnesota Historical Society, St. Paul.

(Left) Although many frontierswomen were native born, a huge number, like this unidentified immigrant woman, photographed shortly after her arrival in Minnesota in the late 1900s, came from other countries. Photograph in the author's possession. (Below) Most frontierswomen married at some time in their lives. Mr. and Mrs. James Sullivan, circa 1870, in the studio of photographer E. H. Train in Helena, Montana. Courtesy of the Montana Historical Society, Helena.

at once toward Iowa." Another commented: "According to this last census, the number of males exceeds that of females some 16,000. Let the Yankee girls take the hint when they see these figures."[5]

Census data demonstrate the existence of high ratios of men to women during the early years of a region's settlement; they also indicate that in most areas the discrepancy diminished rather quickly.[6] Some observers, however, maintain that the closing of the gap was not as orderly and linear on the Plains as in prairie zones, because of such factors as drought, floods, and grasshopper invasions that created waves of settlement, retreat, and resettlement, with attendant imbalances in the population. This was exacerbated by the tendency of non-American-born groups, which had large numbers of males, to migrate to the Plains.[7]

Even during the years when female:male ratios were fairly well balanced, single women were in great demand as mates. Often in desperate need of a business partner to help them establish a farm or other enterprise, men avidly sought women who would be wives, mothers, and co-workers. They believed, as one writer put it, that "married persons are generally more comfortable, and succeed better, in a frontier country, than single men; for a wife and family, so far from being a burden to a western farmer, may always prove a source of pecuniary advantage in the domestic economy of his household."[8] Accordingly, women were encouraged to make themselves more marketable by honing their domestic skills and to "think less of fashion than of kitchen duties."[9]

By the time they reached marriageable age, women were rated as workers in the same way that the men were graded as providers. One observer of frontier marriage concluded: "The choosing of a mate on the frontier was a matter of economic necessity far and above individual whim. Good health and perseverance were premium assets while the charm and ability to entertain that one values so highly in a society of mechanization and leisure time was only of tangential significance . . . the woman who could not sew nor cook had no place on the frontier."[10]

Yet in spite of the tremendous pressure to marry, a significant number of women chose to do so only relatively late or not at all. Because census takers did not record marital status until late in the nineteenth century, figures for the prairie regions are not available. Census data on single women in the Plains states, however, show considerable numbers of single adult females in residence after 1890.[11] These single women sometimes lived alone, but more typically they lived with another adult, a group of adults, or a group of adults and children. The Dakota territorial census of 1885 revealed that excluding the population at Fort Buford, white households were organized as follows: approximately 49 percent were composed of single males, 2 to 3 percent were single females, and 3 percent had single heads with children present. Another 13 percent of the households were multiperson groups of related or unrelated persons, while only about 33 percent were based upon married couples.[12]

While census data do not include women who never married, case studies indicate that such women did exist. A case in point was Eleanor Gordon, who dropped out of Iowa State College after a year because of financial problems, taught in rural schools, and continued to educate herself through night courses. She was determined not to marry, even though in the early 1870s "the outlook for the ambitious American young woman was dreary enough" in her view. Justifying her decision to remain single, she remarked: "I had two hands, a brain of my own. No one should dictate as to ways and means." Eventually, her dedication was rewarded by her being elected as assistant principal of Centerville (Iowa) High School, then as principal of the Humboldt (Iowa) Public Schools, and by a fulfilling life as an unmarried woman.[13]

A sizeable body of anecdotal evidence suggests that in any grouping of women, some chose marriage while others did not. Variety of choice seemed to prevail. A young single woman who joined her family in Dakota Territory in 1885 shortly returned to her Minnesota home wearing an engagement ring, while another woman who joined her family in Wyoming in 1887 remained single and undertook a variety of economic pursuits to support herself.[14]

The many women who came to the prairie and the Plains as teachers and nurses included a large number who forswore marriage entirely. These were the women religious who frequently established schools and hospitals. An early group was the Sisters of St. Joseph's, whose members in 1853 built the first hospital in the St. Paul area; it was soon followed by other teaching and nursing orders.[15] These included the Sisters of Charity, more commonly known as the Grey Nuns because of their somber black and grey garments, who came to the Dakota Territory from Montreal in 1872. A particularly energetic group was the Sisters of the Presentation of the Blessed Virgin Mary, whose members first arrived in Dakota Territory in 1880, where they devoted their lives to improving educational and health facilities for native groups.[16]

Yet other teachers and missionaries to the Indians chose to marry. One of the most widely known of these because of her writings on behalf of Indians was Elaine Goodale, who went to the Great Sioux Reservations in Dakota Territory in 1886. Here, in 1891, she married a Sioux physician named Charles A. Eastman. One of Goodale's co-workers, Thisba Hutson Morgan, also spent a number of years teaching the Oglala Sioux people and eventually wed a non-Indian spouse.[17]

The so-called girl homesteaders constituted another group of women on the Plains who were divided on the question of singlehood versus marriage. Encouraged to take up farm claims by the Homestead Act of 1862, which offered 160 acres to unmarried adults and to heads of households, and later by the Kinkaid Act of 1904, which increased the stakes to 640 acres, some women homesteaders retained their single status, whereas others combined their lives and claims with those of men.[18]

The numerous diaries, letters, and other writings of women homesteaders frequently comment upon their varied marital statuses. In a letter written in South Dakota, Myrtle Yoeman commented to a friend: "There are the most old maids out here holding down claims that a person must wonder where they all come from." One such woman was Elizabeth Corey, or "Bachelor Bess," as she was known to her family, who both homesteaded and taught school in early-twentieth-century South Dakota. In her brother's commentary on her letters he noted that she "fended off many suitors" in order to pursue the freedom and happiness that she found in living on the Plains. Similarly, Edith Eudora Ammons (later Kohl) homesteaded near Pierre with her sister Ida Mary around the turn of the twentieth century. By the time they had proved up their claim, they found that they no longer wanted to return to the city, as they so long had planned to do. Edith Kohl explained that the hardships of frontier life "were more than compensated for by its unshackled freedom. . . . The opportunities for a full and active life were infinitely greater here." When Ida married, Edith moved on to Wyoming.[19]

As the story of the Ammons sisters suggests, some women homesteaders did marry. There is the well-known story of Elinore Pruitt Stewart, who, while homesteading in southwestern Wyoming, wed a fellow homesteader. As might be expected, this was a familiar tale. Adelaide Skinner, single and twenty-eight years old, took up a claim in Nebraska in the 1880s; shortly thereafter she married the holder of the adjoining claim. Some years later, a teacher from Alberta homesteaded in Montana, where she raised flax and married a neighboring homesteader. The diaries and memoirs of scores of other women homesteaders such as Abbie Bright indicate that they left their claims after proving them up and returned to their homes, where they married.[20]

Thousands of females spent one segment of their adult lives as married women and other parts as single women because of divorce or the desertion of a spouse. Tantalizing glimpses of these women occur in newspapers, as brief references in someone else's account, or in their own letters, diaries, and memoirs. As early as 1824, for example, the *Missouri Intelligencer* (Franklin) carried a notice that Reuben Warson of Howard County had left his wife and disclaimed any responsibility for her debts. Interestingly, Warson concluded the notice with some fascinating advice to his wife: "When thou readest this, suppress thy sobs, sue out a divorce, and set thy cap for another and a more happy swain, while I roam through the world sipping honey from the bitter or sweet flowers that chance may strew in my path." That this divorce was not an isolated event was demonstrated a few years later by another announcement in the same newspaper, notifying an absent husband that his wife was going to court to divorce him from her "society, fellowship, and company" as well as from the "bonds of matrimony."[21]

Many documents by women also mentioned divorce and desertion. One of these was written by Caroline Phelps in Illinois in 1833. Phelps briefly referred to her sister, who fled from her husband with her young daughter, claiming that her husband was a "disapated" man "who was not providing a decent living" for her and her child. Another woman wrote a poem to tell her story about being deserted by and divorced from her alcoholic husband. In 1831, this determined woman moved eight boys under the age of twenty-one by wagon to La Salle County, Illinois, where they farmed and raised sheep for wool.[22] Among women homesteaders, thousands of separated and divorced women often worked their claims alone in order to support themselves and their children, rather than to accept offers of marriage or seek a new spouse.[23]

Although current generations often view the nineteenth century as an idyllic age of happy families and virtually no divorce, this picture is not accurate. Territorial and state legislatures, almost from the day they came into being, regularly granted divorces. Law records and codes were peppered with "acts of divorce" granted to individual applicants. Divorce provisions also made their appearance during the early decades of the nineteenth century. The Fourth General Assembly of the state of Illinois passed "An Act Respecting Divorces" in 1819 and liberalized it in 1825. The amended act permitted divorce in cases of "impotency in either of the parties," adultery, absence of two years or more, "extreme and repeated cruelty," and "constant and habitual intemperance for two years."[24] When Iowa Territory was formed in 1838, divorces were granted by district courts on the basis of impotency, adultery, extreme cruelty, and willful desertion of three-years' duration. In 1842 and 1843, bigamy, committing a felony or "infamous" crime, drunkenness, and the imposition of personal indignities upon a spouse were added as grounds.[25]

Trans-Mississippi regions soon gained a widespread reputation for their broad-minded—some would say decadent—divorce codes. In 1867, one commentator upon the western scene remarked that "the divorce laws of all our new States and Territories are practically very liberal; seldom compelling men or women to remain in marriage bonds which they wish severed." More women than men availed themselves of these divorce provisions. When Iowa was still part of the territory of Wisconsin in 1836, for example, more divorces were granted to women than to men by the territorial legislature. These divorcing women frequently met with favorable treatment in their divorce decrees. In 1838 a Burlington, Iowa, woman received custody of her child, not a common provision anywhere in the United States at the time. Another woman kept her children and her property. By the 1860s, public opinion pushed divorce courts in the direction of regularly awarding children to their mothers, rather than fathers. Yet in the eastern states during these years, such women as author and lecturer Frances Wright and actress and author Frances Kemble lost both their property and their children to their spouses in divorce actions.[26]

As a result of progressive divorce provisions, first the prairie and then the Plains area became havens for those seeking divorces. As early as the 1850s,

Indiana was widely known as a divorce center. By the late 1860s, Illinois (particularly Chicago) and Iowa gained similar notoriety.[27] In Iowa between 1870 and 1880 the divorce rate jumped from forty-nine to sixty per hundred thousand of population. The rates in Illinois were slightly higher during these years, while Minnesota ranked somewhat lower than Iowa.[28] Increasingly, popular sentiment supported women and men who wanted to escape loveless, abusive, or otherwise troubled unions. Combined with other factors such as liberalizing religious beliefs, varied ethnic and racial values, and disruptively high rates of migration, prodivorce views supported a steadily rising divorce rate on the prairie and the Plains throughout the 1800s. By the latter part of the century, North Dakota and Oklahoma had become the nationally known centers for divorce.

Another sizeable group of women who returned to single status did so through the death of their spouses. Matilda Peitzke Paul described how her widowed mother constructed the family's long-planned new home by using bricks that had been prepared by her recently deceased husband; she hired bricklayers but put her older sons to work as carpenters and laborers. An Illinois widow, left with twelve children to provide for, spun and wove cloth and sent the older girls out to work as domestics and the older boys as laborers. Other widows turned to friends, family members, and neighbors for help.[29]

Many widows soon remarried, sometimes two or three times if necessary. Yet, not all widows were anxious to give up their new-found autonomy. Given the ratio of females to males, it is difficult to believe that these women could not have found mates had they so desired. Instead, they chose to support themselves in a variety of occupations, ranging from farmer to journalist. A Missouri woman who routinely ran the family inn and post office while her husband was involved in political and military activities away from home continued to do so after he was killed in the Second Seminole War in 1837. She raised nine children on the proceeds from her business ventures, supplemented by a meager widow's pension of thirty dollars per month for five years. When she died in 1870 at the age of seventy-nine, she left an estate valued at $17,000.[30] Numerous other widows continued to work homestead claims after their husbands had died.[31]

A strange kind of temporary "widowhood" occurred when husbands went farther west in hopes of finding gold, locating better land for the family farm, or establishing some other type of business. Termed "women in waiting" by a recent study, these wives and often mothers ran families, farms, and businesses, frequently handing back an ongoing enterprise to their husbands when they eventually returned, but in other cases refusing to accept the wanderer back into the household at all. Another study has suggested that this not uncommon separation of spouses created a "maritarchy"—that is, a marital relationship in which either spouse functions as a surrogate for the other. In other words, numerous married women actually lived and functioned as if single, in the process often taking on the duties and responsibilities usually assigned to men.[32]

While marital status is an important and complex characteristic of women settlers on the prairies and the Plains, other significant features must be considered as well. One of these is age, for although it is commonly assumed that the frontier primarily attracted the young, demographic analyses have disproven this idea. Settlers did tend to be younger than people living in settled areas, but not overwhelmingly so, as is often thought. Historian Allan G. Bogue has described the typical migrant to prairie regions as "between the ages of twenty-five and forty-five," with a family already started before westward migration. Another investigator has claimed that in frontier counties in general, younger couples who were just starting out tended to be slightly more numerous than middle-aged couples with children.[33]

Census data show that female settlers both on the prairie and on the Plains ranged in age from the newborn to those in their sixties and seventies. Although the bulk of women usually fell in the categories "under 20" and "20 to 39," older women existed in significant numbers. In Iowa in 1840, for example, a date early in the area's development, about one-tenth of white females were aged forty to sixty or older, while in Kansas in 1870, at a comparable point in its settlement, about 15 percent exceeded forty years of age. Clearly then, various age ranges were represented by female settlers.[34]

Gradations in social classes also existed. Although the popular mythology of the time promoted the prairie as "the paradise of the poor," many social classes were actually represented.[35] At the lower end of the class scale were domestic servants, hired help, and various kinds of female laborers. These were largely non-American-born or black women who, although they had migrated to the prairies to improve their economic opportunities, often found themselves employed as washerwomen, nursemaids, and field help. Middle-class women on the prairie frontier were generally those who lived in cabins and sod huts. Although they might have endured want during the early years of settlement, these women usually experienced an improvement in their economic and social status within two or three years. At the top of the social scale were women from families that had sufficient wealth to provide them with "proper" eastern-style homes, domestic servants, and some leisure time.[36]

Class mobility was a reality in most prairie locales. As a frontier area evolved into a settled community, a log cabin often became a two-story cabin and eventually a frame or brick house with its share of store-bought luxuries. Many women who began prairie living in one-room cabins ended it as mistresses of solid, respectable farmhouses. Abbie Mott Benedict, who made twenty-one moves during her first twenty years of marriage, was one such woman. Benedict spent her last years both financially stable and physically comfortable, having moved up the social-class ladder through her own hard labor and that of her family. Other women improved their class status through education. After her marriage, Druscilla Allen Stoddard continued her teaching career. In 1858 she was appointed head of the Woman's Department at Iowa Central College in Pella, a prestigious and respected position.[37]

A similar progression occurred on the Plains. Historians generally agree that life there was neither for the very poor, who did not have the necessary capital to make the long trip, buy the land, and plant seed, nor for the very wealthy, whose money would buy little in the way of position or material goods on the frontier. Once on the Plains frontier, social class was frequently obscured by a situation that reduced everyone to primitive living conditions, at least during the early years. As one woman remarked, "Debt was no disgrace . . . everybody was in debt; everything was mortgaged."[38]

As the Plains frontier developed and people occasionally prospered, a class system emerged, especially in urban areas. An "upper class" of large farmers and ranchers, successful shop owners and miners, professional people, and others began to appear. The women of this class often joined literary and service clubs, worked on behalf of local churches and schools, and sought better educational opportunities for their children than they themselves had enjoyed. At the other end of the scale were the poor folks: those on unproductive land, migrant blacks and non-English-speaking foreign-born peoples who were struggling to get a toe hold on the Plains, and destitute widows and others who were not able to support themselves. The women of this class sometimes accepted charity or pushed themselves to their limits working to improve a seemingly impossible situation.[39]

Racial background was yet another factor that differentiated women on both the prairie and the Plains frontiers. Although most female settlers were of Caucasian stock, other groups migrated to both regions, particularly Mexicans, Orientals, and blacks.[40] Mexican and Oriental women were so few in number that they received only occasional mention in newspapers or such personal documents as letters and diaries. In addition, census takers usually lumped them into a catchall category "women of color" or sometimes "people of color" that included both women and men. The presence of black women can be more easily documented because they were numerous enough to have been frequently enumerated in a separate category by census takers.[41]

Census data occasionally combined enumerations of blacks with some basic data concerning them. The Cooper County, Missouri, census of 1850 not only counted free blacks but also noted their age, gender, occupation, and place of origin. Here, in a county of over one thousand families, there were 16 free blacks, 5 of whom were female, 2 being cooks and 3 not having paid occupations. In that same year in McLean County, Illinois, the population totaled 1,594: 777 white females, 777 white males, 17 black females, and 23 black males. Among the black females were cooks, servants, and a twenty-year-old schoolteacher who had been born in Kentucky.[42]

Other documents that reflect the presence of blacks on the prairies range from personal writings to county records. One Missouri woman recollected that her town during the early 1850s had less than three hundred people, including "negroes." While her memoir demonstrates the existence of blacks, it unfortunately does not go on to describe the composition of the black population or black occupations and life styles. The letters of Anna Ramsey of St. Paul, Minnesota, give slightly more information concerning her black domestic servant Martha. Ramsey occasionally commented upon Martha's duties as well as her esteem for Martha. County records also documented the presence of blacks but contained minimal additional information. The Howard County, Missouri, registry for free blacks between 1836 and 1861 listed approximately ten women and twenty-nine men.[43]

On the prairie, black settlers composed a smaller proportion of the population than did blacks in settled areas, yet some scholars argue that they were numerous enough to deserve more attention than is usually accorded to them.[44] Blacks migrated into prairie regions very early. In Mickilimacknac Parish, Minnesota, a marriage between Jean and Jeanne Bonga, both black, was recorded on 24 June 1794. Some years later, a black man named York traveled with William Clark and Meriwether Lewis on their expedition in 1804/5 to explore the newly acquired Louisiana Purchase. Other black women and men filtered into the area during those early years as well, and by 1818 there were an estimated two thousand to three thousand blacks in the upper Louisiana country.[45]

The highest concentration of black people on the prairies was in Missouri, which was admitted to the Union as a slave state in 1821 as part of the Missouri Compromise; its admission thus balanced that of the free state of Maine. Pioneer settlers seeking better land and improved opportunities were thus encouraged to migrate from southern states to frontier Missouri. For example, in 1822 a party of settlers from Virginia included four white men and their four black valets, as well as "Mammy," a black woman servant who was ensconced in the cook and supply wagon. This family spent its first years in a log cabin and broke the prairie sod with the help of black slaves. Another party from Virginia made the trip to Missouri in 1841 accompanied by sixty slaves, to be utilized as laborers once it had arrived in Missouri. Slave labor was not only used on the land, but during the pre–Civil War years, numerous white women relied upon black women for help in raising their families, doing domestic chores, and running inns and other family businesses.[46]

All of the other prairie areas—Iowa, Indiana, Illinois, and Minnesota—prohibited slavery both under territorial and state governments. Antislavery sentiment ran high in sections of these locales, and the underground railroad, the antislavery organization that aided runaway slaves in reaching free soil, sometimes flourished.[47] This is not meant to suggest that other prairie areas were totally free of slavery. In defiance of the Ordinance of 1787, which outlawed slavery in the Northwest Territory, and the Missouri Compromise of

1820, which declared the territory above latitude 36°30' (except Missouri) to be free, early trappers, traders, soldiers, miners, and settlers brought slaves to such prairie areas as Iowa. As a result, although Iowa did not legally countenance slavery, the census of 1840 listed ten female and six male slaves. Although no slaves appeared in the Iowa census after 1840, means were devised to circumvent the law. One method was to hold black slaves as indentured servants. As late as 1850, an advertisement in the *Burlington* (Iowa) *Tri-Weekly Telegraph* asked for the return of one such servant. Described as black, thirteen or fourteen years old, and with five years left to serve on her indenture, the girl was said to have been "decoyed" away by some "meddling person." Her owner claimed that "it would be an act of charity . . . could she be restored to him."[48] And throughout the pre–Civil War years, mention of slaves appeared in various documents, especially in Iowa and Illinois. Female slaves served as cooks, nursemaids, and domestic servants.[49]

The presence of strong proslavery sentiment on the prairies at least partially explains why these districts were not as amenable to the entry of free blacks as some had expected or hoped that the supposedly equalitarian frontier areas would be. Predictably, Missouri was intolerant of free blacks, requiring them to register with the county governments and submitting them to numerous other restrictions upon their lives. Understandably, in a slave state the presence of free blacks caused problems. The willingness of some white employers to hire free blacks at "liberal wages" and the ability of some free black men to buy fiancées, wives, and children out of slavery could have done little but add to the dissatisfaction that most slaves already felt.[50]

Moving north to Minnesota for contrast, the situation concerning free blacks was less volatile, perhaps because the black population was very small. When Minnesota was organized as a territory in 1849, its population included 40 blacks, 30 of whom lived in St. Paul. By 1860, blacks numbered 259, and by 1870, only 759. Still, the 1860 Minnesota Legislature did consider a bill to prevent the migration of free blacks into the state. By 1868, sentiment had liberalized enough to allow the legislature to amend the state constitution by granting the right of suffrage to male blacks.[51]

In Minnesota the black population was concentrated in St. Paul and Minneapolis. Here, black males held employment as laborers, porters, waiters, cooks, and barbers; and black females worked as domestics, nursemaids, washerwomen, and cooks. The occupation that allowed the most upward mobility for black males and their families seems to have been barbering, for a number of successful black barbers counted many prominent white Minnesotans among their customers, and they provided their wives with enough leisure time to participate extensively in church and other benevolent activities.[52]

Wherever blacks lived on the prairies, they tended to form their own communities. During the 1840s, for example, Brooklyn, Illinois, was founded across the river from St. Louis. Whether in a separate town or a community within a larger town, members of black enclaves clung to their own culture and value systems and established their own schools, social-service agencies, and churches, which often became a focus for black women. One example is the Pilgrim Baptist Church, organized in St. Paul in 1866, the oldest predominately black church in the prairie region.[53]

It is extremely difficult to assess the role of black women in prairie locales. Not only have source materials for these black women been neglected, but because of their relatively low numbers both before and after the Civil War, black women have received little attention from historians and other scholars of the region. Furthermore, the stereotyping of black females and males in popular literature and media during the nineteenth century obscured the realities of their lives on the prairies and elsewhere. It is evident, however, that black women had serious disadvantages in the postwar migration from the South, because they had been trained primarily as field hands and domestic servants throughout the ante-bellum period. Thus, they most often worked as domestics, washerwomen, and day laborers for white prairie families. It is also clear that enough black women existed on the prairie frontier to destroy the notion that prairie women were uniformly white.[54]

Black settlers arrived on the Plains later and as a result of different circumstances than did most prairie blacks. During the 1870s, thousands of southern blacks traveled up the Missouri River and along other routes in an attempt to escape the evils of sharecropping, tenant farming, and antiblack sentiment. Seeking a better life and the "promised land," they sought employment in the cities or on farms, homesteaded individually, or created both rural and urban all-black communities.[55]

The best-known of the black migrations to the Plains were the so-called Exodusters of Kansas. Under the leadership of Benjamin ("Pap") Singleton, one group of migrants founded the all-black colony of Nicodemus in 1877. Black communities also sprang up in such cities as Atchison, Kansas City, Lawrence, Leavenworth, Topeka, and Wyandotte. In 1870, blacks in Kansas numbered 17,108; by 1880 this figure had risen to 43,107. Because the black migrants arrived in large numbers and destitute condition, they were frequently the butt of harsh resistance efforts on the part of white settlers, as well as the recipients of private and state aid in the late 1870s.[56]

Many individual white Kansans did attempt to help the black migrants. Anne E. Bingham explained that in 1880 she and her husband hired a family of six black Exodusters—two adults and four children—to help on their farm. Anne recalled that the two adult Exodusters were diligent workers, and she was particularly glad to have the woman's services as a washerwoman. "She would carry a pail of water on her head with one hand to steady it," Bingham later recalled, "and something in the other hand, and carry the clothes basket that way, too." The Binghams were very sorry when the family of Exodusters "got lonesome and finally went to town."[57]

Other discouraged blacks moved to Colorado and Oklahoma.[58] In most other Plains areas, blacks and black communities were transient and few. Black men sometimes worked as cooks and deck hands on steamboats, porters on passenger trains, "buffalo" soldiers, and drovers and cooks on cattle drives, while black women often worked as servants, laundresses, and nursemaids. Those who tried to settle on the land seldom achieved permanence; they soon moved to towns and cities. In North Dakota, for instance, around 1910 a group of black homesteaders attempted to establish a farm community near Alexander in the southwestern section of the state. At its peak, it had approximately ten families; but within a decade, they had all dispersed, many to the towns and cities of North Dakota, leaving little in the way of either material goods or historical evidence behind them.[59]

The story of the roles that women played in the black migration to the Plains is yet to be written. Evidence of black women's trials and contributions is found in a few tantalizing diaries, letters, and memoirs by them. One of these is the newspaper account about Williana Hickman, an Exoduster to Kansas in 1878. After a long rail journey from Kentucky, her husband pointed to "various smokes coming out of the ground and said, 'That is Nicodemus.'" She explained that "the families lived in dugouts." Her response to the Plains resembled that of many of her white counterparts: "The scenery to me was not at all inviting, and I began to cry." Another newspaper account told about a Nicodemus woman who, in the same year that Hickman arrived, taught a class of forty-five children in her dugout.[60]

The letters of a black woman whose family settled in Cherry County, Nebraska, in 1885 offer another perspective on black plainswomen. Ava Day's letters dramatically illustrate the significant role that the factor of race can play in a human experience; at the same time they demonstrate that both white and black settlers shared many similar circumstances as a result of their environment. Day spent her childhood in the Nebraska Sandhills, where her family raised cattle, brood mares, and mules, and her adolescence in South Dakota, where she eventually married a black South Dakotan. She later recalled that her grandfather was white and her grandmother black. She explained: "Color never made a difference to Grandpa. You were a person and a man and a lady." Day added that the family's neighbors in the Sandhills felt much the same, for they were very friendly and helpful: "Everybody asked did you need anything from town—& brought it back by your house or left it at your gate."[61]

Some years later, Era Bell Thompson of North Dakota recorded a similarly positive view of her white neighbors. She claimed that when her family had moved to the Plains shortly before World War I, they had encountered little prejudice. Thompson later wrote, "I was very lucky to have grown up in North

Dakota where families were busy fighting climate and soil for a livelihood and there was little awareness of race." She recalled that her family was befriended by neighbors, particularly a Norwegian family who brought supplies at critical times. She felt that since North Dakota was a miniature melting pot, settlers tended to look upon each other as equals. She explained that in 1910 the majority of the population was categorized as either "native white of foreign parentage" or "foreign white," with only 28 percent being classified as "native white of native parentage." In Thompson's opinion, this situation led to the easy acceptance of the few black families who did migrate to North Dakota.[62]

A slightly different view was given by Sudie Rone of Cheyenne, Wyoming, in a 1979 interview. Describing the founding of the black women's Searchlight Club in 1904, Rhone noted that it was the only service group in Cheyenne for black women at that time. She explained that black women could have joined the white women's clubs if they had chosen to do so; but she also admitted that widespread prejudice and nonacceptance of blacks effectively kept the two groups of women segregated.[63]

While race was an important and distinctive differentiating feature of female settlers on the prairie and the Plains, place of origin was also important. Women who migrated westward within the United States represented a large and diverse number of regions. When historian Allan G. Bogue used selected census figures to determine the prairie settler's places of origin, he discovered that they came from the Ohio Valley states, the South, the Middle Atlantic states, New England, and from other countries. Bogue's findings substantiated historian Frank Herriott's earlier contention that migration did not follow latitude lines from east to west, as was so often assumed. Several other investigators have confirmed Bogue's and Herriott's findings by identifying significant numbers of southerners in prairie districts. Neither were prairie settlers' journeys a direct line from place of origin to their new home; they often included several other stops first.[64]

Manuscript sources by prairie women validate both their varied points of origins and their multiple moves. The Archer family, for example, moved from Ohio to Waterloo, Iowa; next they lived in Jones County, Iowa, for a short time; then they briefly tried Missouri and Illinois; finally they settled in Lee County, Iowa. The Welch family was originally southern-based, leaving South Carolina for Richmond, Indiana. After a short time they decided to move again, to Van Buren County, Iowa, and finally to Jefferson County, Iowa. The Lacey family, originally from the Middle Atlantic states, settled first in Illinois, then in Chester, Iowa, and finally in Storm Lake, Iowa. Influenced by the fact that Missouri was a slave state, both the Dyers and the Vanarsdales moved directly from Virginia to Missouri. A very different factor, the free state status of Minnesota, drew blacks Thomas Neal from Tennessee, Charley Jackson from Georgia, and Emily O. Goodridge Grey from Pennsylvania.[65]

The Plains also attracted women from numerous areas of the United States. The adjustment was particularly severe for well-born southern women. Fannie Forbes Russel settled in Montana in 1864 with her former slaveholding family. Here she learned to conduct domestic duties without the help of black slave women. After a year of living on the Plains, Forbes wrote that Montana "looked barren." She added: "We had left our homes with the cut glass pendants on the chandeliers and with stone porticos to come and live in a one room log cabin made by men not trained in manual labor. We had come to hundreds of miles of prairie that grew bunch grass and sage-brush. . . . We had left behind us reconstruction in a war ravaged land, we had left hatred and strife. I wonder how many of us would have willingly returned to it."[66]

Settlers on the prairie and the Plains also came from Canada and from northern- and central-European nations. Fleeing from countries that were torn by political conflict, religious disputes, oversupplies of people, droughts, famines, and other problems, they were seeking a more promising environment. When the first sizeable numbers of these Canadian and European immigrants reached the United States during the 1840s, many of them chose to settle on the prairies. Although they were fewer in number than the native-born settlers in most areas, these immigrants were often farmers who deeply influenced farm techniques, crops, and rural industries where they settled. According to historian Theodore Saloutos, "Farm techniques, seeds, life styles, and limited quantities of capital brought from the home country and put into American farmlands added to the growth and development of American agriculture."[67]

In the years after the American Civil War, thousands of non-American-born migrants chose homes on the Great Plains. Unlike their predecessors on the prairie, they often formed the numerical majority of settlers in many Plains regions. In 1870, 25 percent of the population of Nebraska had been born in other countries. When counted with the second generation, these non-American-born people composed 54 percent of the white population of the state. In 1900, immigrants and children of immigrants accounted for 47 percent of Nebraska's population. These immigrants also tended to be farmers, who contributed much to agricultural development in their new lands.[68]

Despite their usefulness, both as settlers and frequently as farmers, non-American-born migrants were not highly regarded by those who claimed native birth. Consequently, nativist sentiments held by American-born settlers frequently retarded serious efforts to recruit non-Americans as settlers until after the Civil War. Although hundreds of "emigrants' manuals" were produced by towns, counties, land and transportation companies, entrepreneurs and promoters, and emigrants' associations, few were designed for distribution in other countries. State boards of immigration, organizations of business people and professional promoters, did not begin to appear until the late 1860s and the early 1870s. Gradually, these boards issued promotional pamphlets in many languages, sent emigration commissioners to meet incoming ships and to tell newly arrived immigrants about the prairie and the Plains districts, and supported agents in such countries as Germany, the British Isles, Belgium, Holland, and Scandinavia.[69]

Interestingly enough, literature that was aimed at potential settlers from other countries often made a special appeal to women. Such topics as coeducation, female occupations, and women's rights were discussed in glowing and sometimes misleading terms. One brochure noted: "Under the laws of Iowa no distinction is now made between husband and wife in the possession and enjoyment of property. One-third in value of all the real estate of the husband, in case of his death, goes to the wife as her property in fee-simple, if she survives him." It then added: "For the information of the ladies especially it may be well to state, also, that the last General Assembly of our State took the first step necessary for amending the Constitution so as to confer the right of suffrage upon women." Despite the implication that the right to vote was about to be extended to women, this did not occur until 1920, with the passage of the Nineteenth Amendment to the United States Constitution.[70]

In spite of these special appeals to non-American-born female settlers, little attention has been paid to immigrant women, either in their own time or by succeeding generations. As with black women, immigrant women's experiences on the frontier are just beginning to be studied. Yet from the pages of the diaries, letters, and memoirs that these women left emerges a picture of the lives of women who were trying to adjust to America and frontier conditions at the same time. Because the ethnic pattern of settlement was slightly different on the prairies and on the Plains, the ethnicity of available writings by women are also slightly different, yet the feelings and experiences that they contain are remarkably similar.

On the prairies, Scandinavian peoples formed one of the most significant groups of settlers. A Minnesota woman of the 1850s recalled that the Scandinavian population, "astounding in growth, grew from 12 to 12,000 in ten years."[71] The Swedes were one of the earliest Scandinavian groups to arrive on the prairies, particularly in Illinois, Minnesota, and Iowa, beginning around 1840.[72] Arriving in family units, the Swedes tended to found their own communities, such as New Sweden in Iowa and Chicago Lake in Minnesota.[73] A much-larger Scandinavian group was made up of the Norwegians, who founded prairie settlements in the Fox River valley of Illinois in the mid 1830s, at Sugar Creek, Iowa, in 1840, and along the Mississippi River in southeastern Minnesota during the 1860s. Norwegians particularly flourished in Minnesota, where they became the third-largest ethnic group in the state.[74]

A fuller picture of the lives of Norwegian women on the prairies can be established than of any other group of ethnic women because of the relative abundance of Norwegian women's documents that are available. One of the most complete accounts is that of Elisabeth Koren, who arrived in Decorah, Iowa, in 1853 with her husband, who was to serve as minister to the Norwegian settlers in the area. As an educated middle-class woman, Koren was often taken aback by the crude living conditions and the lack of time for reading, contemplating, and writing. At one point, she noted in her diary that her "wish to have a cultured person to talk to" became almost overwhelming. Yet, once she had made the transition to her adopted land, she felt great affection for it and its people. Another interesting tale of a Norwegian woman is the life story of Johanna Tatley of Hawley, Minnesota. Born in 1850 in Leksvik, Norway, Tatley migrated to southern Minnesota with her parents in 1866. In 1877 she married a Norwegian immigrant named Knute Roadhl and, after Roadhl died, another Norwegian immigrant named Martin Landsem. This energetic woman bore seven children, all of whom carried the name of Tatley, which she apparently convinced both of her husbands to use in conjunction with their own.[75]

In addition to the Swedes and the Norwegians, Danes also migrated to the prairies, but later and in smaller groups. One early Danish settlement was established in 1853 at St. Ansgar, Iowa, and another in 1863 at what later became Clarks Grove, Minnesota. Unfortunately, because the number of Danes was relatively small and they were often absorbed into larger Norwegian communities, writings by Danish women on the prairies are not easily obtainable. It is known, however, that they played a significant role in the development of Danish dairy cooperatives in Minnesota.[76]

Although Scandinavian people were numerous and important on the prairies, many other groups settled extensively, making their own contributions to the development of the region. Settlements established by immigrants from the British Isles began to dot the prairies by the middle of the nineteenth century. Efforts had begun as early as the mid 1840s to entice English settlers to take up prairie lands. In 1849 the Englishman George Sheppard helped to organize a colony of immigrants who arrived in De Witt, Iowa, in 1850. In that year there were 3,785 English people in Iowa, more than half of the state's total non-American-born population. In 1879, William, Frederick, and James Close established a major English colony at Le Mars, Iowa; and during the 1880s, they founded several more in southern Minnesota. Not all of the English settled in colonies; many farmers and laborers came to prairie farms and towns as single persons or in individual family units.[77]

Unlike their Scandinavian neighbors, the English, especially those of the middle and upper classes, seemed to experience great difficulties in adapting to the prairies. Writings left by English female settlers on the prairies described the hardships that they faced and their despair over what Rebecca

Burlend, an Englishwoman who came to Pike County, Illinois, in 1834, termed "limited opportunities" for the cultivation of one's mind. Similarly disappointed, Lucy and Marianne Rutledge, who made the crossing to arrive in Davenport, Iowa, in 1848, could do nothing but "weep and bemoan" the necessity to live in a "squalid" one-room cabin. Expectations concerning servants also created additional adjustment problems for some Englishwomen. Margaret Marston, who settled in Illinois in the 1850s with her family, commented that they were thrown into upheaval when their servants refused to work because "only negroes did so in this country." Other Englishwomen, however, seemed to adjust with relative ease to life in a log cabin, even if they had come from a fairly comfortable background.[78]

Women from other parts of the British Isles—Scotland, Wales, and Ireland—seemed to have a relatively easy time accommodating themselves to the frontier. The Iowa settler Janette Murray complimented Scotswomen for their many skills as frontierswomen and their ability to blend old customs with new ones. That Welsh and Irish women were similarly creative and adaptable was demonstrated in many cases, not the least of which was Helen Ross Hall, an Irish immigrant to McLean County, Illinois, during the 1860s. Hall bore her fourteenth child at the age of forty-nine and lived in good health and continuing productiveness until she was eighty-two.[79]

Another significant group of prairie settlers were the Germans, who fanned out across the prairies particularly during the mid-nineteenth century. In Iowa, many Germans settled, for example, in Davenport during the late 1840s because they were disgruntled with limited civil rights in their homeland. And in 1855 a pietistic German group founded the Amana colonies in the rich farmlands of Iowa in an attempt to find religious and economic freedom. Despite widespread anti-German sentiment, these and other German immigrants established communities in every prairie state and gave such cities as Milwaukee, St. Louis, and early St. Paul a distinctively German flavor.[80]

Many extant writings by German women describe their lives on the prairie. One writer was Louise Sophie Gellhorn Boylan, whose family migrated to Ackley, Iowa, in 1868. Here, her crippled mother was continually "knitting and sewing and baking and browning, and in summer working in her garden." Boylan remembered with awe that her mother supplied the entire family with hand-knit stockings, two pairs a year for each of the ten family members, while she also "made all our clothes, did all the baking and cooking, and nearly always had a baby at her breast." Another German woman who settled in Minnesota in 1856 bore ten children, produced food and household goods without the aid of hired help, was active in her church, and, according to her granddaughter, "seemed to exude a cheerful atmosphere in her home that all her family reflected."[81]

Although this brief discussion of non-American-born immigrants to the prairies gives some idea of the tremendous ethnic diversity of prairie women, it should be added that many other nations were represented as well. Immigrants from the Low Countries—Holland, Belgium, and Luxembourg—spread into all areas of the prairie. Still other groups were the Czechs, the Hungarians, the Swiss, and the Russians.[82]

The ethnicity of settlement differed slightly on the Plains. Here, Germans formed the most numerous group. Heavily concentrated in Nebraska and South Dakota, German groups tended to settle in enclaves where they often clung to their own ways and ideas. Of the many German groups to come to the Plains, the Germans from Russia are especially notable both because of their introduction of Turkey-red wheat, a hard winter wheat, and their ongoing efforts to retain their cultural heritage. These Germans, who had migrated to Russia in the late 1700s in hopes of acquiring free land and who now settled largely in Kansas, North Dakota, and Nebraska, tended to use their own language and to build distinctive homes in their customary style, while the women continued to wear their long black woolen dresses and kerchiefs on their heads.[83]

One of the few accounts of a German-Russian family that has been published paints an unattractive picture of women's lives and roles. The family came to North Dakota by railroad in 1909 and spent its first winter living in a boxcar, subsisting largely on fat meat and bread, and tolerating inevitable but unusually harsh family conflicts. Gradually, through their own labor and the help of neighbors, the family established a homestead. For the mother of the family the experience was marked by difficult pregnancies, incredibly hard work in their crude home and in the fields, and, worst of all, demeaning words and punitive actions from her husband. Whether this woman's experience was typical or not will be known only when additional similar documents become available.[84]

Other German-speaking peoples who migrated to the Great Plains were the Swiss, the Austrians, and the Alsatians. These people were not numerous, nor did they found colonies of their own. Rather, they usually dispersed widely across the Plains. For instance, Austrians Agness Kratochvil and her husband, Vaclav, migrated to Montana to take up a homestead. Although she missed the support of family and friends, Kratochvil gradually came to like her neighbors, garden, homestead, and the nearby town of Pompeys Pillar. Fifty-five years later, she looked back at her life on the Plains with fondness: "Montana has been good to us and we hope we were as good to Montana."[85]

The second-largest group of immigrants on the Plains consisted of English-speaking peoples, including the Irish, the English, the Welsh, the Scottish, and the English Canadians. Of these, the Irish Catholics were the most numerous. Although their poverty made it necessary for most of them to settle in urban areas on the East Coast, some did establish such farm colonies on the Plains as O'Neill, Nebraska. Still others were drawn to the Plains by jobs in railroad construction.[86]

The story of the Feeney family was typical of the Irish who came to the Plains. First, young Andy migrated to work as foreman of the railroad crew that was building the Chicago and North Western Railroad to Pierre, South Dakota. After his father's death, his mother, a sister, and two brothers joined him in Pierre in 1882. Here, his sister married an attorney and helped her new husband take up a homestead, thus finding a life for herself that was far different from the one that she had known in Ireland.[87]

The English formed the second-largest group of English-speaking peoples. Although they sometimes settled in such colonies as Runnymede and Victoria, Kansas, they more often spread out over the Plains. Early English settlers tended to be men who were interested in land and cattle investments. Occasionally, wealthy English gentry tried to found baronies, while other young Englishmen sought independence and fortune on the Plains. Later English settlers often immigrated in family units. An example of this was the Ashton family, who joined a number of other family members in Oneida Township, South Dakota, in 1883. Here, they developed a school and a Sunday School with other members of what was described as a "closely knit family group."[88]

Compared to the Irish and the English, the Welsh and the Scots came in relatively small numbers. The Welsh settled primarily in Kansas, while the Scots scattered over the Plains. Often homesteaders, the women of these groups remarked about their difficulties in learning to use corn as a staple in their cooking. Unaccustomed foods, such as pumpkins, squash, and melons, also sometimes caused them initial problems, as did the picking up of "cow chips" to use as fuel for cooking.[89]

The English Canadians did not usually have as many cultural shocks as did members of some of the other English-speaking groups. Because they frequently came from farms, sometimes on the Canadian Plains, and had already heard much about the American Plains, they had some idea of what to expect. Still, occasionally a Canadian woman felt that her life in Canada left her unprepared for what one called the "territorial experience" in the Dakotas. Another Canadian woman who settled in the Dakotas explained that even if one was dismayed by the reality of life on the Plains, it was easy to hang on because the land was so beautiful and "things got more comfortable every year."[90]

In addition to the German- and English-speaking peoples, many Scandinavians also made their way to the Great Plains. Of these, the Norwegians were the largest group. Primarily farmers, they were also known as hard workers and strict adherents of the Lutheran faith. Because they consciously attempted to preserve their heritage, an unusually large amount of writing by Norwegian plainswomen is available. One example is the detailed reminiscence of Lettie Brandt, a pastor's wife in Dakota Territory during the 1880s and 1890s. Another interesting memoir is that of a Norwegian woman who lived in Nebraska and described her feelings regarding a new language, strange foods, and farm work.[91] Letters exist as well, such as that of a South Dakota woman to her stepdaughter in Norway, describing women's work in a soddie.[92]

Norwegian women's documents offer particularly good accounts of migration techniques. Frequently the men of a family went first, taking stock, farm machinery, seed, and household goods with them by covered wagon or immigrant railroad car. The women and children then arrived by railroad or river steamboat. Norwegian families, along with Lutheran churches and local Ladies Aid societies, cushioned the immigrants' adjustment to the new environment, culture, and language.[93]

Although women from Norway showed great interest in preserving family ties and Norwegian traditions, they also generally showed themselves to be anxious to fit into their new land. They worked hard, often "working out" as domestic helpers or doing such men's work as plowing and hauling hay for wages when necessary. They became skilled in cooking American foods, and they learned to speak English. Some Americanized their family names, not, as one woman said, that they "were ashamed of their Norwegian names and heritage," but rather "as a matter of convenience" and as a sign of "belonging."[94]

Norwegian women demonstrated a very strong interest in education of all sorts, both for themselves and for their families. Mothers taught their daughters not only household skills but also how to read, write, and speak English and Norwegian. Women formed literary circles, book discussion clubs, community-advancement associations, and church-related organizations wherever possible. And they pursued education in every form, whether self-teaching, high school, or college. One woman commented that although her grandmother had little formal schooling, she "availed herself of every opportunity and learned to speak and write the English language as well, mostly by studying and reading by night."[95]

Next to the Norwegians, the Swedes constituted the second-largest group of Scandinavian immigrants to the Plains. Primarily migrating to Nebraska, the Swedes tended to settle in communities. Once established in colonies on the Plains, Swedes often vigorously urged their friends and family members in Sweden to join them. One energetic young woman even went back to Sweden to marry a particular man and bring him to the Plains.[96]

Like the Swedes, the Danes located the majority of their settlements in Nebraska. The story of Bertha Josephson Anderson is representative of many Danish women. Trained as a dairymaid in Denmark, she worked at her trade and married a promising young farmer there. Because they were disappointed with the poor quality of their land, Bertha and her husband responded enthusiastically to the letters sent by her brother in Montana and soon decided to migrate to the Plains themselves. The couple's voyage in 1889 was marred by Bertha's seasickness and the resultant lack of milk for her nursing infant. When they finally reached Glendive, Montana, they soon settled into a two-room log shack. They bought milk cows and, utilizing Bertha's skills, began to produce milk, butter, and cheese. Their early years were rough ones, marked by their struggle to learn English and the necessity of accepting help from their neighbors during lean times. Bertha began to raise chickens, wash clothes for pay, and help her husband plow in the fields, at the same time bearing several more children.[97]

As their situation gradually improved, the Andersons forgot about their plans to return to Denmark and began to think of themselves as permanent residents of the Plains instead. In 1895 they filed on their claim and took out citizenship papers. Then, although Bertha had seven of her own children to care for, fourteen of her relatives came to her home from Denmark in hopes of finding their own homesteads. After a stillbirth and a miscarriage, Bertha bore her last baby at the age of forty-two. Recalling her silver-anniversary party, Bertha summed up her life as an early plainswoman in a touching sentence: "We were happy and gratified to be a real part of the lives of the community, but there was also regret that the pioneer days were over." On her golden anniversary she said simply, "Yes, we are Americans."[98]

Slavic groups also took up the challenge of life on the Plains. The two that settled in significant numbers were the Czechs and the Poles, mostly in Nebraska. Of the two groups the Czechs (Bohemians) were the most numerous. Like so many other immigrants, Czechs found the American language and culture confusing. One Czech pioneer in Dakota Territory, W. H. Elznic, recalled that in his home only Czech was spoken, a practice that upset the children's teacher, who was determined to teach English to her students. The teacher threatened anyone who spoke Czech on the school grounds with the forfeit of their recess, an admonition that forced the children to speak some English at school. The writer also clearly recollected that there was spirited dancing to the music of an accordion. Elznic concluded that despite the Czechs' differences from their neighbors, a "neighborly, cooperative and jovial spirit" prevailed among the farmers in the vicinity.[99]

The letters of the Czech immigrant Marie Stritecky offer further insights into the lives of Czech people on the Plains. Migrating to South Dakota in 1921 to escape religious persecution, political unrest, and compulsory military service, members of the Stritecky family were confronted with new values and practices at almost every turn. Like other Czechs, their adjustment was cushioned by such social organizations as Sokols and the Western Bohemian Fraternal Association, first organized in Omaha in 1897 for women and men of Czech extraction. At the same time, the Striteckys maintained strong ties with their families, sending them financial aid, helping them to sell their property in the homeland, and giving them detailed news about family members.[100]

The Dutch also settled on the Plains, largely after 1880. Settling mostly in farm colonies in Dakota Territory, they joined other immigrants in using sod to build their homes and churches. Their Reformed or Christian Reformed churches helped to keep the Dutch culture and religion alive, as did the Dutch-language newspapers that were published in virtually every Dutch community. Dutch women clung to traditional clothing, methods of preparing food, and house decoration, thus contributing their own unique customs to the ethnic mosaic of Plains' society.[101]

A very small number of Mexicans settled on the Plains. They came relatively late, motivated by the chaos of the Mexican Revolution of 1910 and by the possibility of finding jobs in the sugar-beet fields or with the railroads and meat-packing plants on the Plains. Because their skins were darker than those of most settlers on the Plains and because they did not easily surrender their language, Mexicans were often not well received. The daughter of a railroad worker who arrived in Laramie shortly before the beginning of World War I remembered "a lot of discrimination," a circumstance that she and her family found very distressing.[102]

Besides varied ethnic backgrounds, the complexity of female settlers was further heightened by their wide range of religious beliefs. On the prairie these included affiliations to many Protestant sects, including Methodist, Baptist, and Congregationalist. There were also a number of Catholics, particularly among German and Irish immigrants. Quaker and Amish farm settlements were scattered over the prairies; Mormon settlements also existed. The Mormons left their mark as they blazed the Mormon Trail across Iowa, founding such outposts as Garden Grove and Mt. Pisgah in Iowa, and creating Mormon communities in Nauvoo, Illinois, and Independence, Missouri.[103] The Plains were, and still are, known for a religious diversity that encompassed Catholic, Congregational, Dutch Reform, Episcopalian, Hutterite, Jewish, Lutheran, Mennonite, Methodist, and Presbyterian groups, to name some of the best known.[104]

Although religious beliefs might isolate people somewhat from their neighbors, churches often served as a unifying factor within a group. Churches were important for women, who commonly used their churches as emotional, social, spiritual, and psychological advisors and outlets. Because women, especially those in rural areas, had fewer support systems and sources of information than did men, who could relate to other men at the local shop, the livery stable, the grain elevator, the stockyard, or in the fields, women often turned to their churches. Here, they were also able to participate in the charitable activities that were widely thought to be part of a woman's duties. In case after case, women wrote about the importance in their lives of establishing and supporting a church. One woman's description of her grandmother could have been applied to thousands of others: "[She] loves God's Word, her church and its mission program."[105]

For Jewish settlers, however, their religion often seemed to create more difficulties than cushioning. Early Jewish migrants to the prairies were often single men who worked as peddlers, entrepreneurs, and laborers, often finding themselves suspect or at least curious to others who did not understand their culture and beliefs. As women joined them on the prairies, small Jewish enclaves formed. For example, by the 1850s, enough Jews lived in St. Paul to hold Jewish services and to organize the first Jewish congregation, Mount Zion, in 1857. The writings of these Jewish women poignantly describe the difficulties that were created for wives and mothers by a land devoid of established synagogues, kosher food, and Jewish schools. For instance, Florence Shuman Sher, a Minnesotan who was also a Lithuanian Jew, recalled her mother's continuing grief concerning her children's lack of a Jewish education and her own inability to preserve traditional religious beliefs within her home.[106]

On the Plains, Jewish settlers often formed agricultural communities of their own people. The Jewish Colonization Association and the Hebrew Emigrant Aid Society, among other groups, formed in order to help the immigrants with loans, advice, and supervision. Some of the early Jewish agricultural colonies that resulted from this "back to the land" movement were Painted Woods (1882) and Iola (1886), North Dakota, and Beersheba (1882), Kansas. Although their members found considerably less discrimination than had plagued them in other places, they did not achieve economic security. Jewish men took jobs with railroad companies to help their colonies survive, and on more than one occasion, the Jewish Agricultural and Industrial Society gave relief to beleaguered farm families. Gradually, most Jewish people left the land to move to cities, especially Omaha, Nebraska, Grand Forks, North Dakota, Seattle, Washington, and Portland, Oregon, where they established businesses and communities that could supply them with rabbis and other similar religious needs.[107] Not all Jewish farmers abandoned their homesteads, however. In south-central North Dakota, one Jewish man owned twelve farms in North Dakota and Canada by the World War I period. In Ramsey County, North Dakota, several Jewish farm families remained active until the 1920s. In Morton County a Jewish family farmed until the 1940s. But in most of the North Dakota counties in which there were Jewish settlements, not one Jewish farm family remains.[108]

The stories of the Jewish women who were part of these agricultural experiments do not appear either in collections devoted to the writings of pioneer women or in histories of Beersheba and other colonies. Nor do these women's tales seem to have been collected since the demise of the colonies.

Certainly, the lives of Jewish rural women must have resembled those of other immigrant women on the Plains in some respects and must have dramatically differed from them in others, because of the context of Judaism in which these women lived. But this has not been proved, for although some records of the activities of Jewish urban women have survived, little seems to be known about their rural counterparts.[109]

Clearly a wide range of variables contributed to the make-up of each individual woman on the prairie and on the Plains. A particular combination of marital status, occupation, education, age, social class, race, ethnicity, and religion often distinguished one female settler from another. Although many women fit the common images and stereotypes of the frontierswoman as an American-born and English-speaking wife and mother who dressed in calico and a sunbonnet while helping to "break" a homestead to the plow, many others did not fit. Some who did not conform to the image chose to remain unmarried for part or all of their lives or perhaps held paid employment; others had been born in another land, spoke a language other than English, and dressed in the traditional clothing of their own lands or religions.

The differing characteristics of plainswomen is unequivocally indicated by an examination of one rural Plains county in the census year 1870. In Hall County, Nebraska, women demonstrated a variety of marital statuses, number of children, household arrangements, ages, and ethnic backgrounds. An analysis of the census data shows that among Hall County women over the age of sixteen, 53 were single (including divorced and widowed) and 177 were married. The married women had from zero to seven children, with the majority having between one and four children. Virtually all of the single women lived in multiple-person households, which included their own children, parent or parents, grandparent or grandparents, siblings, other relatives, or women friends. A number of the single women lived in boardinghouses, and those who worked as domestic servants or nursemaids often lived with the family they served.[110]

Other variables also differed greatly among the females of Hall County in 1870. Their ages ranged from less than one to eighty, with more females under forty than over. The birthplaces of Hall County women who were older than sixteen also showed a great deal of variation. Of the eighty who had been born in the United States, seventeen were from New York, sixteen from Ohio, seven each from Indiana and Iowa, six from Pennsylvania, five each from Vermont and Virginia, four from Illinois, three each from Michigan and New Hampshire, two from Connecticut, and one each from Kentucky, Maine, Massachusetts, Missouri, and Wisconsin. Of the women who had been born in countries other than the United States, eighty-nine had come from Germany, twenty-seven from Ireland, thirteen from Prussia, nine from Denmark, three each from Canada and England, two each from Scotland and Wales, and one each from Italy and Luxembourg.[111]

It is evident from the disparate characteristics of Hall County women that female settlers, even within one rural county, exhibited a wide diversity in their make-ups. How, then, can early women of the prairie and the Plains be fairly portrayed? Or can they be summed up at all?

If there is any one truth about these women, it is that they were not homogeneous. Like their male counterparts, they were many things at many times and different things at different times. Perhaps the terse comment of one woman regarding the legendary and ubiquitous sunbonnet can serve as an appropriate maxim for those who are seeking to categorize or define such women. She remarked that sunbonnets were "an obstruction to sight and an impediment to hearing."[112] And so it has been with the image surrounding the women who wore those sunbonnets. The image has achieved little more than the impairing of accurate sight and hearing. Only by moving beyond the myths will we be allowed further exploration and understanding of the realities.

3
Home and Hearth on the Prairie

Because they were nineteenth-century women, female settlers on the prairie heard much during their lifetimes concerning the issue of domesticity. From observations of their own and other families, it was clear to them that home, marriage, and children were the focal point of women's lives. From speeches, newspaper articles, ladies' magazines, household guidebooks, and other sources, they learned about the high standard to be aimed for in their domestic and family endeavors.[1] At the same time, only infrequent notice was paid to men's roles as husbands and fathers, and none was given to their possible responsibilities as homemakers. Rather, men were counseled to think of "breadwinning" and to plan the ways and means of achieving financial success. As settlers, women and men not only carried these well-learned lessons with them to the prairie, but they also continued to adhere to them in the new environment.

For most prairie women, the standards of domesticity that they sought were often difficult to achieve. While there is no doubt that home and family provided the center for the majority of prairie women's lives, these women played their domestic roles on an ever-changing stage, one that imposed various conditions and challenges upon them depending upon the season and the era. Although their shifting and demanding environment never obviated the necessity for home and family to take precedence in their lives, it did affect the ways in which prairie women pursued their domestic and family responsibilities.

The prairie climate placed great demands upon female settlers. The onslaught of winter brought bone-chilling cold, piercing winds, and life-threatening blizzards. One young Iowa woman recalled two consecutive winters of frequent and frightening storms: "There were days when we could see only a few feet away because of blinding snow; and often the cold was so intense that people were frozen to death out on the prairie."[2]

42

Harsh winters were often followed by heavy rains in the spring, which placed another burden on the endurance of female settlers. According to Matilda Peitzke Paul, her mother, in order to keep the family's beds dry, used every pot and pan she owned to catch water that dripped through the roof during the spring rainy season. Dangerous floods were even more difficult to manage. In 1832, Caroline Phelps watched as high water and ice blocked up the river below her Illinois home, causing flood waters to rise. Hesitant to desert her home, she finally agreed to do so when "the water burst through the back of the chimney" and "the floor was all swimming." Caroline, after sending her sister ahead with the baby, tried to salvage some household goods; but when she was trapped by the rising water, her husband had to carry her out of the cabin on his shoulders.[3]

Many women feared the vagaries of the prairie climate. Eliza Farnham, who pioneered in Illinois during the early 1840s, claimed that these spring storms and ensuing floods "seemed to blight the country." She became so terrified of such events that for years afterward the sound of thunder produced a temporary faintness and nausea in her.[4] Tornadoes caused terror in many other women. One recalled that a four-mile-long tract near her Iowa home was ravaged by a tornado during the late 1840s. According to her, "not a house of any kind was left standing, all the stock killed but not so many people as it being Sunday alot were away from home . . . great beams from houses were driven in the ground."[5]

When summer arrived, it brought with it oppressive and inescapable heat, as well as the constant threat of prairie fires. After arriving in Minnesota from Norway in 1862, Gro Svendsen wrote to her family that it was a "strange and terrible sight to see all the fields a sea of fire."[6] Despite the plowing of firebreaks around homes and the setting of backfires to cause approaching prairie fires to change course, conflagrations often persisted and destroyed all that lay in their paths. A young woman who was living in the Minnesota Territory during the 1850s recalled a huge fire that roared toward her home, filling the air with bunches of burning grass. As the fire was driven on by furious winds, her family fled into their home. They and the house were saved by covering a few feet of ground with clay, but the fire came so close that the windows were too hot to touch for hours afterwards. She notes that the fire left a "black stretch of country as far as the eye could reach," and she remembered her mother's relief when, a few months later, the snow covered it from her sight.[7]

In addition to the prairie climate, various insects and animals also bedeviled homemakers. Grasshoppers were particularly feared. A Norwegian woman in early Minnesota described them as a "plague" that came in dense swarms that obscured the sun, devoured everything green in their paths, and invaded homes.[8] Because there were no screens, homes and cabins were open to insect invasions of all kinds. Flies and mosquitoes regularly feasted on a family's dinner, as well as on family members. Paul explained that flies were so dense that her family "used a little limb, thick with leaves, to keep them off food while we ate" and that mosquitoes were so pesky that at night the family burned a smudge of chips from the woodpile so everyone could sleep relatively unmolested. To her, these pests were "too terrible to dwell on."[9] A Norwegian woman who lived in Minnesota during the 1870s similarly remembered that she suffered from mosquitoes, flies, fleas, and "bugs of all descriptions" that "pestered us night and day." She added that in addition to the flying tormentors, "wherever we planted our feet there would be a toad, snake or a viper of some kind."[10]

That snakes were one of the most feared of all pests was attested to by such women as Svendsen, who wrote home that she was "horribly afraid of them, particularly the rattlesnake." According to Sarah Welch Nossaman of Iowa, "it was not an uncommon thing to get up in the morning and kill from one to three snakes, but they were of garter snake variety, but we would rather they had stayed out if it had suited them as well." Paul recalled many types of snakes: "the little green snake, hoop snake, spotted water snake and worst of all the poisonous rattle snake which sometimes killed people." Another prairie woman noted that all snakes were "very much dreaded by women and children." According to her, they got into the shallow wells so that before water could be drawn, the snakes had to be dipped out.[11]

Skunks, wolves, and other animals were also annoying to prairie women. Nossaman quipped, "We treated skunks very kindly until they were out of the shanty." On a more serious note, she said that she never learned to sleep soundly through the howling of the wolves and the screeching of the owls that sounded so eerie during the otherwise quiet prairie nights. Other women feared wolves who brazenly howled in close proximity to cabins at night and raided their pigsties and chicken houses.[12]

Many women were far more intimidated by American Indians than they were by weather, insects, or beasts. Fears of native peoples often ran rampant among female settlers, who had heard many titillating and terrifying stories about rapes, captivity, and child stealing. Captivity narratives—popular and often fictionalized accounts of women who had been taken captive by Indians—encouraged prairie women to fear the worst when they encountered their first Indians.[13] Consequently, women often shielded their children from contact with Indians, turned their homes into forts or fled from their homes for other shelter, encouraged their menfolk to join companies of frontier guards, and took other protective measures. Predictably, rumors and alarmism were rife across the prairies. Stories about Indian "depredations" and "atrocities" multiplied with alarming speed, and forts that were never attacked were hastily constructed in times of panic.[14]

Of course, prairie women had a number of very real reasons to fear the Indians. Native women and men who begged or threatened harm to get food, clothing, and other resources from female settlers endangered the latter's often meager stores of supplies.[15] Some women meekly bowed to the demands of Indians, believing, as one Minnesota woman put it, that "no one crossed an Indian for fear of exciting his anger."[16] Other women fought back by shouting, stamping their feet, and brandishing fireplace pokers and other household weapons, often with good results in that the Indians then obligingly deserted the kitchens and yards.[17]

Actual outbreaks of violence between whites and the natives were even more overwhelming to prairie women than were incursions into their homes by the natives. In Missouri, for example, early Quaker settlers were attacked by Indians in 1808. Rebecca ("Patsy") Cox was reportedly taken hostage and held captive until she managed to escape. After her marriage some years later, Patsy's husband was killed by Indians, leaving her a widow with a baby to raise until she remarried in 1819.[18] In Illinois, perhaps the most famous outbreak of white-Indian problems was the Black Hawk War of 1832.[19] In Iowa, too, conflicts occurred between the native inhabitants and the white settlers. These ranged from the little-known Teagarden "massacre" of 1843 to the much more widely publicized clash at Spirit Lake in 1857.[20] And in Minnesota, results of the hostilities at New Ulm in 1862 were that women fled from their homes with their children, were widowed and taken captive, and donned weapons as part of their regular attire.[21]

In spite of repeated occurrences of violence between settlers and natives, many prairie women had pleasant experiences with American Indians. Even in strife-torn Minnesota, women formed friendships with Indians, exchanged medical and child care with them, visited their camps and homes, and hired them as domestic workers.[22] Similar interchanges occurred in other embattled prairie areas, including Indiana, Illinois, and Iowa. Caroline Phelps, for instance, remarked about the many native women who had befriended her; the Indian doctor who had treated her young daughter for burns; the native ceremonies, dances, and parades that she had attended; and the grief that she had felt when John, their Indian helper and nursemaid, was killed in an accident. After his death she wrote: "We felt his loss very much, my children cryed for poor John as we called him, as much as though he had been a relative. He was their friend truly they missed his singing, he used to fix a drum and then sing and drum and have them and the little papooses dance."[23]

Another volatile situation, which in this case was based on differences of opinion between the northern and southern states, also caused prairie women a good deal of consternation. During the years immediately preceding the Civil War, women's lives were frequently disrupted by disputes concerning runaway slaves, crusades by abolitionists such as John Brown, and actual fighting between antislavery and proslavery factions. Missouri was especially torn by a series of border wars—guerrilla warfare along the state's western border with Kansas and, to a lesser extent, along its northern border with Iowa.[24] After the Civil War had broken out in 1861, prairie women lost fathers, sons, brothers, and husbands to military service. The swift departure of so many men compelled many prairie women to radically alter their life styles. According to Mary Livermore, an agent for the Sanitary Commission in the Midwest, numerous women began to labor at "planting, cultivating, and harvesting," in addition to their usual domestic duties.[25]

The war brought a host of other troubles to prairie women. A crushing loneliness and anxieties about money were constant themes in women's wartime correspondence.[26] Women were financially squeezed, not only by the lack of monetary contributions from their husbands, sons, fathers, and brothers, who had to use their meager pay to purchase their own supplies, but also by rising wartime prices. In 1861, Julia McCormick of Missouri penned a heartrending lament to her father: "Times are very hard harder than I ever seen them you cannot get any money at all and nothing to do only fighting plenty of that to do as we live on the line of Missouri."[27]

Women who were just beginning to cope with the exigencies of the frontier economy now had to dredge up even more ingenuity and energy to deal with the wartime economy as well. Simultaneously caught in the throes of wartime and frontier conditions, prairie women had to tackle a myriad of new roles, functions, and problems. In a representative case, Louisa Jane Phifer's letters to her husband brimmed with descriptions of her efforts to raise crops, lay in a wood supply, and generally keep the family farm running until his return. Another Illinois woman claimed that women gained a new strength by taking on such duties; she maintained that this caused them to bury their sorrows in their work.[28]

The prairie frontier, then, was not a particularly hospitable one for women. Given the nineteenth-century role expectations that, on the whole, women's lives would be domestically oriented, women were often disappointed with the setting and the resources that were offered to them by the prairie. Some of them returned to their former homes. As one woman pointed out, "some liked the new country, but others . . . returned to their native states."[29] Others took a stoic approach to the scene that lay before them. Arriving in Illinois, one early female settler remarked, "When we got to the new purchase, the land of milk and honey, we were disappointed and homesick, but we were there and had to make the best of it."[30] Still others derived solace from their hopes of a better future for themselves and their families.

In assessing what the demanding prairie setting would mean to their female roles and responsibilities, some women had only themselves to worry about. A number of ambitious unmarried women, whether by choice or because of the death or desertion of a spouse or divorce, headed for the prairie frontier as laborers, missionaries, and teachers. Catharine Beecher, who listed, among her reform causes, women as teachers, particularly encouraged young single women to migrate westward, both to seize employment opportunities there and to act as civilizing forces in the new society. Gazetteers, almanacs, and emigrants' guidebooks also suggested that unmarried women of any age were welcome as dairymaids, seamstresses, and dressmakers and in a variety of other "female" occupations.[31]

Most women, however, had a domestic establishment involving a number of people to consider. In fact, even unmarried women were usually attached to a family or a group of single people living together. The need for family labor on farms and the prevalent belief that the large family was virtuous in itself were rallying cries for land promoters. Consequently, the trails to prairie regions were traveled by more families and by higher proportions of women and children than were the routes leading to nonagrarian areas. The familial nature of the caravans was apparent to contemporary observers, one of whom wrote, "So far as I could learn no person in all that multitude traveled alone, or unattached to a family; and the very few unmarried men among them each was usually, if not in every case, a member or a near relative of the family to which he was attached."[32] Census data confirm that most people were connected with a family and that few people lived alone. They also show that migrants settled in households averaging five to six members, with a ratio of four men to three women.[33]

Yet, women had little say in the choice of the location of the new family homestead that they would manage. Often, the men of the family went ahead to procure suitable land. Because women were charged with the care of children and because travel conditions were harsh, it was not usually feasible for women to serve as advance agents. Instead, it was left to the women to prepare the men for the journey by providing food and clothing and perhaps by sewing a band inside that clothing to hold land warrants or cash with which to purchase land.[34] Land might also be paid for at the time of arrival. When the Shutes family arrived in Iowa in 1862, young Mary Alice was surprised to see her father pull "a canvas sack from somewhere" and count out "one thousand dollars in gold to pay for the land and some more to pay the Judge for legal fees."[35]

Many women found themselves establishing a new home where family members or friends had chosen to settle. Thousands of letters from prairie settlers pleaded for the company of family and friends and did not hesitate to wheedle and beg. More than one group responded to what one woman terms "letters of entreaty."[36] Often, migrants not only were met by family members and friends upon arrival but also lived with them for a time in their homes or in multiple-family dwellings.[37] When the migrants established their own households, families and friends typically settled in clusters, often building their houses within a quarter mile of each other.[38]

A family, once it had settled on the prairie, continued to be the focus of most women's lives. At some time during their lives, the majority of prairie women married, and many remarried two and three times. Although the courtships that led to these marriages occasionally fit the traditional image that frontier courtships were hasty, most followed a stylized ritual, just as in settled areas of the United States or other countries. The man usually came to a woman's home, paying a formal call on her and her family. Other courting opportunities were provided by husking and similar kinds of work bees, sleighing parties and sporting events, lectures and literary clubs, dances and parties, candy pulls, and church services, socials, and clubs.[39]

The postal service and the press also played a role in many courtships. Letters between potential mates, whether in New Hampshire or Norway, pledged affection. In 1853 an Illinois woman was assiduously courted by a young man who declared: "I love to think of thee and think that thare is a day a coming when wee will be happy together . . . I live a lonsom and desolate life."[40] Such entreaties frequently led to a man's returning home to marry or a woman's journeying to the prairie to do so.[41] In other cases, couples were brought together by classified advertisements, such as this one, which appeared in a Waterloo, Iowa, newspaper in 1860:

> A young lady residing in one of the small towns in Central New York, is desirous of opening a correspondence with some young man in the West, with a view to a matrimonial engagement. . . . She is about 24 years of age, possesses a good moral character, is not what would be called handsome, has a good disposition, enjoys good health, is tolerably well-educated, and thoroughly versed in the mysteries of housekeeping.[42]

On the editorial page the editor recognized the importance of women in frontier development when he remarked that this notice presented "a rare chance for a young man to obtain that useful and essential article of household furniture—a wife."[43]

Newspapers and magazines also took an active role in advising prairie women about the proper ways to conduct a courtship, desirable qualities to be sought in a potential mate, and methods for achieving a happy marriage. Sometimes the advice was contradictory in that women were told on the one hand to accept a proposal when offered, as another might not ever be tendered, but on the other hand to extend their love slowly and with great discretion.[44] The latter position seemed more popular, as women were often counseled to observe men's leisure habits, shunning those who indulged in "gaming" or other idle amusements. Susan Vanarsdale of Missouri took this advice to heart: when she learned that the object of her affections liked to play cards, she judged him to be of deficient character.[45] For their part, women were to display industry, economy, intelligence, morality, and honesty. According to one advisor, potential wives should demonstrate that "you would be willing to begin at the beginning in life with the man you would consent to marry."[46]

That women were not usually in their early teens when they married, as is often believed, is illustrated by census data. One student of Missouri census figures concluded that women married between sixteen and twenty-three years of age and that the average was nineteen for women and twenty-four for men.[47] Despite their adulthood, engaged couples frequently sought consent from a parent or guardian.[48] In those cases in which permission was not granted by the family, couples often took matters into their own hands. When Caroline Phelps of Illinois married her intended, both families boycotted a wedding of which they disapproved. Another young Illinois woman, who eloped in 1857, was confined to her room by her parents and was held there under lock and key, away from her new husband.[49]

Most weddings, however, occasioned ceremonies and celebrating. For wealthier families, these included elegant weddings, gifts of china and silver, and honeymoons to such towns as St. Louis.[50] Even if a family was poor and its resources were limited, its members did what they could to provide a dinner or a party of some sort for the marrying couple. An Illinois woman who married in 1873, when she was twenty-four and her fiancé was thirty, explained that they were married in her family's small home and could thus invite only a few of their most intimate friends. Although the wedding was small, she still insisted on a "proper" wedding gown of white organdy, with a train and a tulle veil.[51] Other prairie brides similarly attired themselves in white-satin bonnets and ruffled gowns.[52] Unlike twentieth-century gowns, these were not always white. One Illinois bride was delighted with a dress that she had made for herself out of black-and-white plaid silk trimmed with black-velvet ribbon.[53]

Prairie weddings were sometimes followed by additional parties. One of these was a bran dance, during which the feet of the dancers released oil from kernels of bran into the unseasoned wood floor of the couple's new home. Another popular celebration was the charivari, an informal and often raucous party, held immediately after a wedding or within the next few weeks. At one of these charivaris during the 1840s, "cow-bells, whistles, horse-fiddles, drumming on tin pans enlivened the neighborhood until morning."[54]

Having married, most prairie women expected to bear children. This expectation was reinforced by popular literature, which assured women that motherhood was a highly desirable achievement.[55] Children usually appeared with great regularity. A study of patterns of childbirth in Missouri during the pioneer period indicates that a child was born every two to three years in most families.[56] An Illinois woman bore out this statistic by remarking that both she and her sister had babies regularly every two years.[57] According to one investigator, an average of ten children per family is a conservative estimate.[58] Anecdotal evidence supports the contention that families of ten, twelve, and even fourteen children were common on the prairie. As a case in point, Helen Ross Hall of Illinois, an Irish Episcopalian, bore fourteen children between 1870 and 1895.[59] A Minnesota woman of the same era bore her tenth child in 1876 at the age of forty-five, much to the disgust of her eighteen-year-old daughter, who thought that her mother had had enough children.[60]

Although the production of children was one of the most important social and economic functions of prairie women, it taxed women physically and often left women's bodies with evidence of its difficulties. Yet, birth-control information was not widely available. Popular lectures on anatomy and physiology for women seemed to ignore the subject; and physician's reference books might include some information on the treatment of miscarriages or stillbirths but nothing on birth control itself.[61] Nor did gynecology help women who had medical problems related to reproduction, for this area of medical practice was struggling with ignorance and nineteenth-century standards of modesty. Rather, female ailments, complaints, weaknesses, diseases, and problems, as they were called, were widely accepted as part of woman's lot in life.[62]

As a result of such attitudes and beliefs, prairie women obtained little reliable information regarding birth control, abortion, and "female" ailments. When they did approach a medical practitioner with their ills, they might be examined discreetly, swathed in a gown, or be asked to describe their complaints, using a small female doll, rather than their own bodies, to do so. Treatment routinely included the cauterization of the womb with a hot poker, or even a clitoridectomy.[63] It is little wonder that many women turned to "mail-order" doctors for help with their problems. One of these was a Dr. LaCroix of Albany, New York, whose book *Physiological View of Marriage* was advertised in prairie newspapers. At a cost of twenty-five cents, this 250-page guide promised to provide women with a "confidential medical adviser in regard to any interesting complaints to which their delicate organization renders them liable."[64]

Prairie women also turned to patent medicines for relief both from their maladies and from frequent pregnancies. Based on morphine, quinine, or alcohol, these remedies were supposed to relieve menstrual pain, female diseases of all sorts, and problems associated with childbearing and birth. These drugs ranged from Yellow Dock Sasparilla and Henry's Invigorating Cordial to Dr. Duponco's Golden Periodical Pills for Females and Morrell's Electro Magnetic Fluid.[65] The subtle wording of many advertisements suggests that the medicines they promoted were actually intended to act as abortants. James Clarke's Celebrated Female Pills claimed to be a "Remedy for Female Difficulties and Obstructions from any cause whatsoever" and of special appeal to "Married Ladies," for whom they would "bring on the monthly period with regularity." Similarly, Judson's Mountain Herb Pills pledged to "remove obstructions of all kinds," while Dr. Chesseman's Pills would correct "all irregularities, painful menstrations, removing all obstacles."[66] These medicines probably did little more than create profits for their manufacturers, but the significant point is that thousands of women spent hard-earned money in hopes of purchasing salvation from yet another pregnancy. When the United States Congress passed the Comstock Law of 1873, birth-control information and devices, as well as information regarding abortion, became illegal. Thus were women left to devise home potions and remedies to the best of their abilities.

Given this lack of birth-control and related information, it is not surprising that not only married women, but unmarried prairie women as well, endured unwanted pregnancies. Numerous unmarried women "fell by the way," as a German woman of the 1870s phrased it. She remembered that in her neighborhood, one young unmarried woman had a baby when she was sixteen, and another participated in a "rush marriage," with a baby boy being born about five months after the wedding.[67] In LaSalle County, Illinois, the 1881 case of *Caverly* v. *Canfield* also concerned the birth of a child by an unmarried mother. Here, seduction of the mother was charged, and claims were made that she was not only drugged but was also so innocent as to have no knowledge whatsoever of the implications of the proceedings between her and the father.[68]

Understandably, prairie women exhibited a wide variety of attitudes toward the children they bore. Unwanted pregnancies, both inside and outside of marriage, caused consternation and grief. Large numbers of children, who consumed a woman's time, were often resented. As one unhappy Minnesota woman lamented, her time as a young wife was "mostly taken up with the children."[69] Others, however, were delighted with their children, even in large quantities. They doted upon them, describing them as great blessings.[70]

Frequent births often led to matter-of-fact attitudes regarding birth itself. Women often saw birth as a casual matter, demanding only the assistance of some other woman, perhaps a midwife. A Missouri woman's taciturn remark regarding the birth of her first born was simply, "The baby was born with the help of a mid-wife on October 25, 1888."[71] Gradually, patent medicines entered the scene. Such cures as "The Mothers' Companion," a liniment, offered help with problems associated with childbirth and the nursing of a newborn child.[72] And as male doctors became more numerous on the prairie, they began to claim, like their counterparts in the East, that they had the latest word in delivery and postnatal care. But unlike midwives, who often worked free or for payment in kind, doctors usually charged cash for their services. In 1868, an Iowa man's diary tersely documented a representative story:

Feb. 25, 1868—Tacy, my wife, had a new daughter this a.m. at 6-1/2 o'clock. Sat. March 7th—I went to Salem and paid Dr. Siveter $10.00. I had expected him to charge only $5.00. Sun. May 3—Baby died![73]

Women did not take the loss of a child easily. One woman kept a dead child's miniature rocking chair in the living room of her home for forty years after the child had died.[74] Women spoke of their children's deaths as trials, seasons of sorrow, and a source of great loneliness.[75] After the death of her baby in 1852, Elizabeth Black of Springfield, Illinois, recorded a poignant thought in her diary: "I was cast into the very depths of despair—I felt as though I could not live longer seperated from him—in bitter anguish I cried unto the Lord to prepare me for death & then take me from this world of suffering."[76]

Child care was also complicated by the frequency and numbers of births, as well as by the rigors of life on the prairie frontier. Women devised ingenious solutions to their need to carry on domestic tasks while caring for infants and children. As Matilda Peitzke Paul hauled water from the well, she kept her baby tied in her apron, so that the child would not be "trampled on by the thirsty cattle." When she worked in the fields, Paul took the baby along, putting her "in a large box where she could play." When inside the house, Paul also combined work and childcare. She explained that, "I done all my washing by hand rubbing every garment, and often stood on one foot while rubbing and rocking the baby's cradle with the other foot." Kitturah Belknap followed a similar procedure. She placed her new baby and her one and a half year old in opposite ends of the same cradle, which she rocked with her foot while performing other chores.[77]

As children grew, it was women's duty to train and oversee them as laborers. People who lived in settled areas of the United States during the nineteenth century may have been beginning to see children as individuals to be enjoyed, played with, and educated, but on the prairie frontier they were also regarded as laborers.[78] Thus, acting as managers and supervisors, mothers initiated their children into the tasks of food processing, candle making, soap making, spinning, weaving, knitting, and other tasks. During their early years, both girls and boys took part in all household jobs, including knitting, spinning, piecing quilts, and scouring pots and pans with sand.[79] As children advanced in age, boys assumed more of the outdoor chores and girls more of the indoor ones. Boys were often sent to fetch fuel and water, to help with planting and the care of the stock, and to labor in the fields.[80] Girls engaged in the production of food, soap, and candles and helped with the care of the younger children of the family.[81]

Of course, the girls' domestic labor not only contributed to the household; it also provided an apprenticeship for them. An early female settler of the 1830s in Illinois learned the fine art of making tallow-dipped candles from her mother and also became adept at food processing and clothes production.[82] During the 1860s, Ellen Strang of Correctionville, Iowa, performed a bewildering range of domestic duties, which included chinking the walls of the cabin, caring for the sick baby, and dipping candles. Occasionally she was expected to remain home from school to participate in seasonal tasks, such as making molasses and maple sugar. Even when she became a teacher herself, Strang's domestic obligations continued. On a May day in 1867 she noted in her diary:

"Got up at quarter past four made the beads, picked up the clothes to wash, switched out and comed my hair. After breakfast worked at sundries and got to school in good season."[83]

These sex-role divisions could become flexible when there were not enough males to perform the outdoor labor. Females were then looked upon as a reserve labor force. Girls therefore often joined boys as stock herders, following the sound of a bell that was hung around a lead cow's neck and persuading what one Minnesota girl described as the "stubborn beasts" to return home for milking.[84] In one German family, both the girls and the boys herded the cows, but the girls were responsible for milking them.[85] In other families, the girls rode horses that were pulling a binder, shocked grain, and helped to thresh wheat. They also hunted and trapped wild game. The 1865 diary of an Illinois girl disclosed that she worked in the garden, helped with haying, stacked wheat, cut oats, drove horses for haying, picked apples, stripped sugar cane, dug potatoes, picked corn, carried wood, tended cattle, and hunted.[86]

Given the freedom of many young girls and given their ability to tackle what was usually considered men's work, it is not surprising that many of them became tomboys. One Minnesota girl, who cared for the family's stock because her father considered her more able than her brothers, came home from school one day with the triumphant announcement that she had beaten every boy in school at walking on the top rail of the fence.[87] A Quaker girl who lived in early-day Missouri could ride, swim, and shoot a gun as well as, or better than, most men.[88]

Some mothers graciously accepted the boylike ways of their daughters, while others were horrified. One Illinois woman of the 1840s, who watched her daughter work and play like her sons, simply said to her, "If you are bound to be a boy put on these pants."[89] Other mothers, despairing that their daughters were losing every semblance of civilized womanhood, commanded their daughters to sit primly, wear sunbonnets when outdoors, and use ladylike language. A particular struggle ensued over horseback riding. Although many girls and women did ride, there was constant pressure for them to use sidesaddles. Although it might be acceptable for women equestrians to gallop or to herd cows on horseback, it was considered unseemly and improper for them to do so astride—a proscription that some women avoided whenever possible.[90]

Mothers looked to prairie schools for help in training and socializing both their daughters and their sons. Early schools were held in churches, in people's homes, or in frame buildings and log cabins built for the purpose.[91] They were usually subscription schools; that is, the students paid tuition to attend. In 1825, for example, a Troy, Missouri, subscription school cost $1.25 per student for a four-month term held either during the summer months, between planting and harvest, or during the winter months, between harvest and planting.[92] These prairie schools were almost always coeducational. Thus, when boys headed for the one-room schoolhouse, they were accompanied by their sisters. In fact, girls frequently obtained more schooling than the boys did, because the girls were able to remain in school while the boys worked in the fields.[93]

Given their limitations, prairie schools offered much. Ellen Strang noted that she and her brother studied "McGuffeys fifth reader, McGuffeys spelling book, Rays Arithmetic second and third part, Pinneo's Grammar, Michels Geography and practice writing." She also became the "editress" of the school's semimonthly newspaper and attended a "Geography School" in the evening at "$1.00 for a schollar" for twelve evenings.[94]

For secondary education, many young women attended the private academies and seminaries that quickly began to dot the prairie. In Iowa, for example, the census of 1840 showed that two academies existed. One of these was the Dubuque Seminary, a secular coeducational institution that was chartered by the territorial legislature in 1838 and had a "female department." Other schools soon followed. In 1853 the Dubuque Female Seminary was organized, under the patronage of Catharine Beecher; and the Iowa Female Collegiate Institute was established in Iowa City. Such schools offered a "good English education," as well as instruction in ornamental needlework, pianoforte, and other nineteenth-century female "accomplishments."[95]

Parents who were concerned about the effects of frontier living on their daughters took advantage of early schools when they could afford to do so. A particularly relevant example was the Illinois girl whose mother had told her to wear pants when she attended a one-story frame schoolhouse during the 1840s but in 1855 sent the girl to a Professor Wilkinson's school in Bloomington and then to a "select school for girls" in the same town, where it was hoped that she would learn feminine graces.[96]

Apparently, women did not forsake the ideals of domesticity and femininity when they relocated on the prairie. Instead, they attempted to transplant their known ways and life styles to the new land. Rather than leave behind aspects of life that they regarded as civilized, women tried to recreate them on the prairie. Women tried to reestablish what they thought of as civilization, not only in child rearing but also in every other aspect of their lives.[97]

Housing must have been a particularly difficult hurdle for women who were intent upon converting a new land into a civilized one as quickly as possible. While their contemporaries in settled regions were beginning to consider their homes as places of serenity, tranquility, and stability, prairie women were confronted with crude, small, and inadequate dwellings.[98] It was up to them to convert these structures into homes for their families and into work places for themselves. It was in these homes that women had to function as domestic artisans, converting the produce of the fields into usable goods for their family's consumption. It was here, too, that they would practice whatever degree of domesticity they could attain under the circumstances.

The most readily available source of housing was the wagon that had carried the migrants to the prairie. Thousands of families began frontier life using covered wagons as their first homes. One Grinnell settler of the 1850s remarked on the prevalence of such housing: "There was not a shed, or fence, or even a hitching post on the prairie, all horses being tied to wagons, in many of which people were still living."[99] Wagons were also used as spare bedrooms for children or perhaps for bachelor uncles, as pantries for kitchen equipment and food, as root cellars for supplies of meats and vegetables, and as storage sheds for clothing and tools.[100]

Other quick sources of housing included renting or buying houses that had been left vacant by settlers who had moved and sharing another family's home. Some families utilized both of these options. Kitturah Belknap, her husband George, and her in-laws settled on a claim that boasted a two-room house made of hewn logs. Kitturah set up housekeeping in one room, while her mother-in-law and father-in-law crowded into the other room. Being young and practical minded, Kitturah made the best of the awkward situation. "We unloaded and commenced business," she recalled; "made us some homemade furniture and went to keeping house."[101] Other not-so-fortunate settlers took up residence in abandoned corncribs, stables, sheds, and outbuildings. When the Willis family moved into an "utterly desolate" structure, young Mary could understand why her mother, "remembering the pretty little white house back in Ohio, sat down and wept."[102]

Such primitive shelters were intended only as temporary homes, which the settlers on the prairie usually planned to replace as soon as possible with sturdier houses of logs or sod, sixteen by eighteen feet, with floors made of packed dirt or hand-hewn puncheons (split logs with smoothed surfaces) and perhaps with a root cellar underneath. All family members, and frequently friends and neighbors, participated in raising one of these homes. The men performed the heavy labor, the children lugged and carried, and the women provided the food, as well as assuming tasks such as building fireplaces and digging cellars, which would have been considered unwomanly in settled communities. The Hendrix cabin, built in Blooming Grove, Illinois, in 1822 by the first white settlers in McLean County, was representative of such efforts. It was a one-room pole-log cabin, about fourteen feet square. Covered with split shingles that were held in place by weight poles, it had a door made of split boards hung on wooden hinges. The only window was a small opening with a shutter, and the walls were chinked and daubed with a mixture of mud and clay.[103]

Because of the treeless nature of some prairie regions, other women became mistresses of sod huts, instead of log cabins or frame houses. Particularly in western Iowa, many settlers lived in "soddies." Abbie Mott Benedict explained that wood had to be hauled from twelve miles away for the frame of her fourteen-by-twenty-foot hut. Her husband used a prairie breaking plow to cut the untouched sod on their land. He cut strips of sod into lengths of two and one-half feet and then laid them up around the wall supports, like slabs of concrete block. He added a thatched roof of slough grass, a board floor, and a trap door to a small cellar. Benedict maintained that their first home on the prairie was not only inexpensive to construct but was also warm in winter and cool in summer.[104]

These early homes offered few facilities to homemakers. They usually lacked both kitchens and bathrooms. Cooking was done in a corner of the main room or out in the yard. A lean-to kitchen was often the first improvement added to a prairie home. Early "outhouse accommodations," as one woman called them, were simply, according to her, "the thick brush or a couple of fallen tree-trunks; one for men, one for women."[105] When women finally got sick of following what one of them described as the "western fashion" of personal hygiene, they urged that proper privies be constructed.[106]

It is significant that numerous women saw these rudimentary homes on the prairie in a positive light. They spoke of them as looking like playhouses, diminutive palaces, and fairyland houses. When Mary Burns, a northern Minnesota woman, entered her little cabin for the first time in 1892, she could not have been more delighted with it. She exclaimed about "the tiny oven of our doll-house sort of stove" and stated that the simplicity of her housekeeping was like "taking part in a fascinating play of make-believe." She created a chair out of a soap box and hand-embroidered burlap. Her pillows were gunnysacks filled with pine needles. Her tablecloth was a newspaper, and her dishes were made of tin. From this comfortable nest, this ingenious woman created cards and letters, written on thin sheets of birch bark, which she sent to admiring friends in the East.[107]

As demonstrated by Mary Burns, an individual woman's creativity was often the key to the successful conversion of a primitive structure into a comfortable home. Women made and upholstered furniture, hung blankets and calico curtains as walls, papered solid walls with newspaper or whitewashed them with lime, filled bedticks with slough grass or wild hay, which they jokingly referred to as prairie feathers, converted dry-goods boxes into cupboards, pounded pegs into the walls upon which to hang clothing, and even used corn-cobs as rolling pins. What they could create was augmented with treasures brought from home: rocking chairs, whatnots, bookshelves, clocks, curtains, kitchen utensils, and other precious items.[108]

Converting these dwellings into effective work places presented a great challenge to prairie women. Because the women had to perform a myriad of domestic functions in these homes, it was absolutely necessary that the homes be functional as well as comfortable. A prairie home was essentially a factory in which the women acted as domestic artisans. If the home/factory was inadequate, it hampered a woman's domestic production and threatened the welfare of her family. Especially during the early years of settlement in any locale, when such products as foodstuffs, candles, soap, textiles, and medicines were not generally available, families depended upon their female artisans to provide these essential commodities.[109] The importance of this domestic production by women was widely recognized by the print media, which stressed prudence, thrift, economy, and industry as crucial characteristics of a prairie woman.[110] Certainly, the women themselves recognized the importance of domestic production in their lives, for their diaries and letters are filled with recitals of their many skills and tasks.[111]

Of all the items that women manufactured, foodstuffs required the most attention. Production of the raw materials was the first step that women engaged in by planting kitchen gardens, digging "taters" in the fields, raising chickens, milking cows, and gathering wild fruits, nuts, roots, and herbs. Combined with the products of the fields and farm animals, this produce gave women a variety of materials that could be processed into usable and often appetizing foods. Most women soon became experts at processing food, using such techniques as salting, drying, and smoking. They transformed milk into butter and cheese, cabbage into sauerkraut, hogs' heads and feet into souse (pickled meat), fruits into jellies and jams, hops into yeast, and corn into hominy and meal.[112]

During the initial periods of settlement in a prairie area, women's best efforts often resulted in meager stocks of dried fruit, salted meat, and preserved vegetables. During those first years, women produced literally everything, including their own sugar, sorghum, and maple syrup.[113] One Illinois woman maintained that the first five years she had spent on the prairie during the 1820s were the hardest of her entire life because of the dearth of supplies. Another Illinois woman, who settled in LaSalle County during the 1830s, remembered that her family ate mostly salt pork and corn dodger during their first winters there. And in 1856, Iowan Mary Ellis mentioned a meal of "punkin flap jacks" and a few slices of venison, then grumbled, "We don't have anything but 'taters' and punkin here."[114]

As the years progressed, women had more resources available, and they made more products from them. In relatively settled regions, the end of the fall season saw most cellars filled with supplies for the coming year. Amelia Murdock Wing of Iowa remembered that sod-house soup was replaced by food from her mother's well-stocked cellar: "A barrel of kraut was made in the fall; chunks of pork were salted down; fruit was canned and kept in long, heavy wooden boxes. . . . There was a large cupboard whose tin doors had holes for ventilation, and this was where the milk, cream and butter was kept."[115]

After food had been produced and processed, the women prepared it for consumption, often with the most rudimentary of kitchen equipment. Common utensils included a black-iron kettle, suspended on an iron crane that could be swung in and out of an open fireplace; a flat-bottomed pot with an iron lid, called a Dutch oven; a long-handled frying pan, sometimes known as a spider skillet; a spit made of twisted string, which slowly unwound, turning the meat over an open fire; a triangular tin oven, known as a reflector; an iron teakettle or coffeepot; and a johnny-cake board, which was spread with corn dough and was turned to the fire until the bread was evenly browned.[116] Cookbooks—or receipt books, as they were called—were rare and, when they did exist, contained extremely basic directions, which were usually given only in terms of a pinch and a handful.[117]

Despite the limitations, early cooks concocted varied and nutritious meals. Not only did they produce perfectly browned johnnycakes on a board, but they baked tasty sourdough and yeast breads. Cakes, pies, and biscuits also graced their tables, along with stewed and fried chickens and other meats, potatoes and other vegetables, and a wide array of fruits. One Christmas during the early 1840s, Kitturah Belknap prepared a holiday dinner for twelve people that would tax the ability of a modern cook. Her bill of fare, as she called it, was elegant and extensive: "Firstly, for bread, nice light rolls; cake, doughnuts; for pie, pumpkin; preserves, crab apples and wild plums; sauce, dried apples; meat first round; roast spare ribs with sausage and mashed potatoes and plain gravey; second round: chicken stewed with the best of gravy; chicken stuffed and roasted in the Dutch oven by the fire."[118]

In addition to food, women manufactured many types of domestic goods. Soap and candles were two of the most time-consuming products. Soap making involved three separate processes: collecting grease, fat, and tallow from meat in drip pans and from the rendering of animals; saving wood ashes for lye; and boiling the two together to create lye soap. Candles also took a good deal of work. These were of two basic types: the tallow dip and the molded candle. Women collected tallow from meat fats, bought the wicking and iron molds, and supplied the labor and skill themselves. Both soap making and candle making were done outdoors in the yard, with the assistance of the children of the family. By the time the work was completed, candles and bars of soap, carefully wrapped in straw, joined the stored foodstuffs in the cellars.[119]

The production and care of clothing constituted another intricate and demanding area of women's expertise. During the early years, commercially produced yard goods were not available, so women began with plants, such as flax, and with animals, such as sheep, to get the fibers that they would make into thread, cloth, and finally clothing. The women prepared raw flax by throwing the fiber over an iron-toothed hackle, and they carded wool with an instrument resembling a currycomb. They then spun these fibers into thread on a spinning wheel. Next came hours at a loom, weaving flax into linen cloth, wool into woolen cloth, and flax and wool into linsey-woolsey. The fabric was colored with dyes that the women extracted from such plants as indigo and red sumac, which they kept in a dye pot near the fireplace. Finally, the cloth was laboriously handstitched into garments.[120] This clothing was also taxing to care for, once it had been produced. Washing was done in wooden tubs, on washboards; was whitened with bluing and was starched; and then was hung either indoors or outdoors to dry. Finally, the clothes were ironed with heavy flatirons made of solid iron, which were heated in the fireplace or on the stove.[121]

Although women's working conditions improved as regions became more settled and stable, an enduring continuity existed in their work. As young Lula Gillespie was growing up on two Illinois farms during the 1880s and 1890s, she observed her mother and other women laboring at the same tasks, and often in the same ways, as generations of early Illinois settlers had done. Gillespie described her mother's raising bees for honey to serve as sweetening, churning milk into butter, making lye soap, working at a spinning wheel and loom, weaving blankets, filling bedticks with straw, stocking the cellar with foodstuffs that she had preserved herself, and cooking huge and complex meals with only basic equipment.[122] According to the *Prairie Farmer,* labor-saving devices did appear on the prairie during the nineteenth century, but their spread and adoption was slow and uneven. It added that even in 1941, rural electrification and home machinery had reached only a relatively small number of prairie farms.[123]

Technology came slowly to the hands of prairie women, largely because of the ongoing struggle in regard to the division of limited resources between the field and the home. Decisions about whether to buy reapers for the men or sewing machines for the women were omnipresent ones. In 1864 the new McCormick Reaper and Mower cost $155 and "upwards."[124] During that same time period, a sewing machine ranged in price from $25 to $110.[125] Often, the reaper or other farm machine won out, while the purchase of the domestic machine was deferred. The decision to acquire technological aid for men's work before women's assumed that only the fields supported the family, a fallacious viewpoint that overlooked the many crucial contributions of women's domestic production. Women themselves lamented this inattention to the proper equipping of their homes. In 1868 a woman who was writing for the Illinois State Agricultural Society implored farm men to recognize the suffering that the lack of technology was causing their womenfolk. She argued for such labor-saving machinery as washing machines and wringers, improved stoves, and indoor pumps. Much as reformer Catharine Beecher did, she called for the professionalization of domestic labor and its acceptance as an honorable and significant occupation.[126]

Although technology came slowly to the prairie home, it did gradually appear in certain forms. By the 1850s, in some homes, the spinning wheel was beginning to lose its place of honor to the treadle-powered sewing machine. While the extravagant claims that appeared in advertisements for Singer, Raymond's, Weed's, Wheeler and Wilson's, and other sewing machines exaggerated the revolution that they had brought in the domestic manufacture of clothing, such machines did relieve women of hundreds of wearying hours of handsewing.[127] Woman after woman remarked upon her new sewing machine and the excitement of the neighbors as they flocked in to see the marvel.[128] Only gradually did women learn that the more complex fashions that were made possible by the machines created almost as much work as the machines saved. Alice Money, a young girl who did all the sewing for her family during the 1860s, treadled hundreds of miles as she produced muslin undergarments, with yards of ruffles and tucks, and calico dresses that were lined and trimmed with more ruffles, tucks, and bias bindings. Her early model of a Wheeler and Wilson sewing machine was said to have "made a noise like a threshing machine and ran almost as hard."[129]

Other technological innovations included stoves, washing machines, wringers, flatirons with clip-on handles, and even crude dishwashers.[130] However, women still had to supply the energy to power the machines. Because of a lack of such support technology as pumps and water heaters, the women lugged water in from wells, heated water and flatirons in fireplaces and on stoves, and hauled wood for those fireplaces and stoves.

Another form of assistance—manufactured goods—was offered to prairie women by the peddlers and merchants who proliferated along rivers, in small towns, and eventually in sparsely settled areas. Sometimes within months of settlement a peddler with a pack of goods would appear, or an enterprising settler would begin a store in her or his cabin.[131] Gradually, merchants offered many goods as supplements to what the women produced. As early as 1819 a Missouri newspaper carried a notice of the opening of a grocery, bakery, and confectionary store that promised to sell bread, crackers, cakes, biscuits, and candies, as well as brandy, rum, gin, whiskey, and claret.[132] Prairie grocers also catered to the appetites of migrants who were hungry for delicacies that they had enjoyed in their former homes. In 1850 a St. Paul newspaper announced a shipment of fresh oysters, to be sold at $1.00 per quart.[133] In January 1855 the *Iowa Sentinel* (Fairfield) advertised a shipment of raisins, figs, and Baltimore peaches.[134] By the 1870s, after the railroad had extended into most prairie regions, a German woman who was living in Minnesota explained that a wide variety of goods could now be purchased, including salt, baking powder, yeast, pepper, cinnamon and other spices, chocolate, vanilla, rolled oats, corn meal, rice, tapioca, sugar, tea, and coffee. Her family also carried its vinegar and molasses jugs to the grocery store, to be filled from the spigots of large wooden barrels. Bluing and starch for laundering, wicks for oil lamps and homemade candles, and kerosene were other items that they regularly purchased.[135]

Dry-goods stores also spread across the prairie, offering women yard goods, sewing equipment, bed and table linens, and even some ready-made garments. As early as 1836 the *Dubuque* (Iowa) *Visitor* advertised ready-made clothing and "Calicoes, ginghams, Muslins, Cambricks, Laces, Ribbands" and "Sattinettes, Cassimeres and brodd cloths." Other area newspapers of the time carried advertisements for ready-made clothing from New York, as well as boots and shoes, hats and bonnets, and "Rich Fancy Goods." By the 1850s, dry-goods establishments in the Mississippi River towns regularly offered for sale needles, thread, lace edging, calico, gingham, silk goods, and gloves and mitts.[136] Not to be outdone, merchants in interior towns also carried a varied line of goods. According to one woman, in 1844, Bloomington, Illinois, alone boasted four general and dry-goods stores.[137] By the late 1840s and early 1850s, merchants in towns across the prairie regularly advertised stocks of calico, gingham, ribbons, laces, bonnets, dresses, importations of French and English dry goods, and polka slippers.[138]

Women's writings indicate that the prices for these foodstuffs, dry goods, and other products varied greatly, depending upon the region and the era. In 1853, Sarah Ann Davidson of Illinois recorded her "expences" as follows: one hundred pounds of flour, $2.25; one yard of gingham, $0.30; one neck ribbon, $0.23; one gallon of molasses, $0.60; eight pounds of "shugar," $0.50; five spools of thread, $0.15; and one pair of girl's shoes, $1.50.[139] A few years later, an Iowa woman listed three yards of calico for $0.37 in 1856, five yards of calico for $0.37 in 1857, a calico dress for $1.25 in 1858, and another calico dress for $1.60 in 1860.[140] In 1861, before the Civil War drove prices up to an inflated wartime level, a Missouri woman noted that she had paid $0.50 for a bag of flour, $1.00 for a bag of sugar, $1.00 for a bag of coffee, and $1.00 for butter.[141] In 1881, Lydia Scott of Minnesota paid $1.33 for a calico dress with lining and buttons. She listed five pounds of butter at both $0.80 and $1.44, two spools of thread at $0.10, one pound of butter at $0.50, an unspecified quantity of sugar at $0.50, and a barrel of salt at $1.75.[142] Given the inexact quantities that are listed and given the lack of prices for consecutive years in any one region, it is difficult to draw any conclusions about relative costs. What is apparent from these lists is that prairie women could increasingly count upon manufactured goods to relieve their own heavy work loads.

A number of women were fortunate enough to get even more help with their household duties by hiring servants, usually white or free-black women wageworkers. But hired helpers were not numerous enough to meet the demand. Again and again, women lamented the lack of domestic help. An Illinois woman of the 1830s wrote to her family: "The truth is there is no such thing as getting hired help here, which is a great inconvenience." A Minnesota woman laughed when her father-in-law, newly arrived from Holland, told her to hire a maid to assist with the extra work.[143] Servants were often reported as being hostile and troublesome when they did exist. During the 1840s, Clara Dodge of Burlington, Iowa, wrote to her absent husband about the troubles she was having with the serving girl.[144] Evidently, so many other opportunities existed for young women that household labor was not very attractive to them.[145]

Despite the various forms of assistance that gradually aided prairie women in their domestic roles, women's work loads remained so heavy and menial that family members were frequently enlisted as helpers. Children, of course, routinely assisted with all types of household jobs. But men helped too. The husband of one Minnesota woman aided her in planting the garden, while the brother of another one performed similar duties. In 1874 a northern-Minnesota man spent two days traveling forty miles to bring his wife supplies that would alleviate her work load, while other men took turns loading wagons with women and taking them into town for supplies.[146]

Writings by women indicated that there were many more women who helped the men with their work than who got assistance from men. Because both the women and the men believed that the work of the farm or other business that supported the family had to come first, they accepted the idea that women should "help out" whenever necessary. Helping included a wide range of tasks. Caroline Phelps of Illinois aided her trader husband in loading and transporting furs. Other women assisted with planting corn, sowing and threshing grain, and a host of other farm jobs. An Illinois woman helped to run the hotel that her husband had purchased in Metamora, while a Missouri woman assisted first with a hotel and then with the general store that her husband had bought. Scores of wives of army officers aided their husbands in building and operating the rough forts that were strung out across the prairie. Thus, men's occupations did shape women's lives and work to some extent. Living on a fur frontier meant one kind of additional work for Phelps; on a farm frontier, other duties for other women; on a military frontier, still other responsibilities for yet other women.[147]

But in the final analysis, the core of women's lives was home and family. Although their "helper" role to men might marginally affect their activities, women seldom abandoned the domestic role as the focus of their lives. This statement held true for women in a variety of categories.

The lives of black women, for example, were very much like those of white women in that they were primarily domestic in orientation. One representative case was that of Emily O. G. Grey, who in 1857 joined a growing black enclave in St. Anthony, Minnesota, soon to be named Minneapolis. Like many white women, this black pioneer had a home that was a converted barn, and her bureau was a packing-box covered with calico. As the wife of a successful barber, she was able to devote her full energies to domestic duties, to her family, and, eventually, to participation in a number of civic activities and women's clubs.[148] Another similar example from a later period was Amanda Jennie Lee Bell, who married a St. Paul barber in the mid 1880s. As a full-time wife and mother, she cared for her home, reared her family, engaged in church work, and folded towels for her husband to take to his shop.[149] Unfortunately, very few papers of black prairie women are available. From the limited sources, it appears that although race may have shaped black women's experiences on the prairie in a divergent way from that of white women, it did not drastically alter the domestic focus.[150]

Living in a town or city also created a slightly different situation for urban prairie women, but it did not make any radical difference in the domestic dimension of their lives.[151] Although some women found towns attractive because of fine homes and a rich social life or because of the opportunity that town living offered them to escape the drudgery of farm work, others quickly realized that the rough, bustling scenes that they encountered would pose a whole panoply of difficulties for them as domestic practitioners.[152]

In Illinois, for example, the towns seemingly had little to recommend them, according to women who lived in them. In 1832, fifteen-year-old Sarah Aiken wrote to a teen-age friend that Peoria consisted of fifty to sixty families, principally log houses, and absolutely no "society."[153] Three years later, another young woman characterized Peoria as a crude and bustling steamboat town that in time would undoubtedly become an important city.[154] Springfield also received its share of criticism, with female inhabitants objecting to the many wagon teams, mud streets, and ever-present dirt and dust.[155] Smaller towns, such as Carlinville, were also indicted for poor housing, lack of service, and muddy streets.[156] And urban areas, such as Chicago, drew a huge amount of disapproving commentary. An English immigrant of the 1850s described Chicago as "a rough ragged town, built on a swamp with everything rudimentary and unclean." She found herself overwhelmed by homesickness as she looked at the "nasty ugly town" that seemed to her to be the "end of all things, the veritable jumping off place."[157] Other women complained less about the physical environment than they did about the immorality and the dissipation of frontier Chicago.[158]

Women who took up residence in a prairie town or city often made a quick adjustment to their new environment, especially as they observed the rapid changes that were taking place about them. A Bloomington, Illinois woman recalled that despite her tremendous disillusionment when she had arrived there as a bride in 1836, she had adapted and soon had become "really attached to the place and the people."[159] In 1840, Mary Todd Lincoln noted the great progress that was taking place in Springfield, Illinois, when she wrote to a friend: "Springfield has improved astonishingly, has the addition of another bell to the Second Church. . . . The State House is not quite completed, yet sufficiently to allow the Legislature to meet within its walls."[160]

Despite their growth, prairie towns continued to present challenges to women who tried to establish homes, rear their children, preserve morals, and retain their equanimity in difficult situations. Women in frontier Chicago struggled with inadequate housing, garbage in the streets, woefully inadequate sanitation facilities, and prevalent drinking and crime. The letters of two St. Paul, Minnesota, sisters reveal that they, too, witnessed drunkenness and crime and suffered a number of near-accidents as a result of the crowded

Mrs. Ted Pope, circa 1900, probably in Slope County, North Dakota. Courtesy of the State Archives and Historical Research Library, Bismarck, North Dakota.

(Top) Many frontierswomen lived in homestead shacks after marriage. An
unidentified couple near Terry-Fallon, Montana, probably 1890s. Courtesy of the
Montana Historical Society, Helena. (Bottom) Some women lived and worked in
frame homes with lean-to kitchens. The B. A. Benson farm, Morton County,
North Dakota. Courtesy of the State Archives and Historical Research Library,
Bismarck, North Dakota.

(Top) Unidentified immigrant women in North Dakota, boiling their wash outdoors around 1890. Courtesy of Fred Hulstrand Collection, North Dakota State University, Fargo. (Bottom) Zoe Greenough washing clothes in a stream near Fort Pierre, South Dakota, in 1911. Courtesy of the South Dakota State Historical Society, Pierre.

Women strained their limited resources to re-create customary rituals and celebrations in their new homes. Unidentified children in Presho, South Dakota, in 1909. Courtesy of the South Dakota State Historical Society, Pierre.

An unidentified woman cooking in her frame homestead in Montana, circa
1900. Courtesy of the Montana Historical Society, Helena.

(Top left) The Sears, Roebuck catalog tempted women with the latest in cooking technology. 1908 Sears, Roebuck catalog. (Top right) The Sears, Roebuck catalogs increasingly offered frontierswomen a variety of treadle-powered sewing machines. 1897 Sears, Roebuck catalog. (Bottom) Ada Blayney sewing outside her minuscule claim shack near Oelrichs, South Dakota, circa 1909. Courtesy of the Nebraska State Historical Society, Lincoln.

Women used all the resources and creativity at their command to turn their humble soddies into "elegant dugouts," circa 1909. Courtesy of the South Dakota State Historical Society, Pierre.

streets and the heavy traffic. They also had difficulty in obtaining such necessary items as milk.[161]

Although the problems might have been somewhat different for urban women, their daily lives, like those of rural women, still revolved around home and family. In Chicago in the early years, women frequently produced soap and candles, clothing, and foodstuffs, while the Fuller sisters of St. Paul spent their time cooking, baking, washing, cleaning, and even raising chickens in their backyard.[162]

Clearly, then, domestic life was the prevalent theme in the life of nearly every prairie woman. Despite the demands and exigencies of the prairie environment, most women pursued their family roles and responsibilities first and foremost. The fact that these women operated in what today is seen as a very restrictive sphere, while adapting that sphere to the demanding prairie frontier, has led to a widespread assumption that prairie women were a discontented and disillusioned lot. That is an important judgment to explore, because existing evidence suggests that it is an invalid generalization. While it is true that obstacles abounded and that certain domestic standards were hard to re-create on the prairie, it is also true that a huge number of prairie women brought creativity, ingenuity, and inner strength to the situation. Some were indeed miserable, others collapsed physically and psychologically, and still others returned to their former homes; but thousands more clung to their prairie homes, their families, and their sanity, and derived a measure of satisfaction and happiness from their new lives.

Especially during the early years of a region, women's diaries and letters did chronicle the women's discontent, loneliness, and homesickness. Some women wrote of depression and sick headaches. And some went insane, although it is debatable whether life on the prairie was the cause.[163] A close look, however, reveals that many unhappy prairie women were negative only during the early stages of their lives on the frontier and that their outlooks often brightened as time passed.[164]

Many other women were positive in their outlooks, even at the outset. One Iowa woman was very matter-of-fact, simply stating that if one liked "seclusion this is the place." At another point, she referred to the area as "a perfect garden of Eden."[165] Because family and friends tended either to settle near each other or to join others, isolation was usually short-lived. Some women, like one from Minnesota, claimed that they never felt lonely, while others maintained that they liked their new homes better than the old ones and never regretted their moves.[166]

The gradual adjustment of female settlers was eased by the fact that they were often farm women by background. Schooled in coping with arduous tasks, rudimentary equipment, and adversity, they had the necessary experience and skills to establish new homes on the prairie. They expected to make the best of whatever awaited them. One plainly stated: "I never thought about its being hard. I was used to things being hard." Even though her heart sank when she saw the new farm, she thought, "We had bought the farm and there we were."[167] A particularly revealing comment came from the woman who had initially been disillusioned when she had arrived in "the land of milk and honey." "Oh, how content we were," she later asserted, "I did not think it hard."[168]

In addition, in adapting to the prairie, most women did not find high standards of domesticity to be an insurmountable problem. Such standards were often more ideal than real. Although millions of words were spoken and written extolling the virtues of planned kitchens, professionalized homemaking, and the latest training in the domestic arts, not many women, eastern or western, actually achieved these goals. It is very likely that much of the talking and writing on behalf of domesticity was intended as an antidote to an opposing trend. That is, more and more women were widening their domestic sphere to include additional interests and activities, as well as paid employment. Reformers Margaret Fuller, Sarah and Angelina Grimké, and Susan B. Anthony were among those who argued for the expansion of woman's prescribed sphere. At the same time, editor Sarah Josepha Hale and writer Lydia H. Sigourney provided outstanding models of women who successfully combined motherhood and careers. Thus, as historian Julie Roy Jeffrey has pointed out, "Domesticity described the norms and not the actual conduct of American women." Jeffrey has suggested that perhaps frontierswomen were even paid for the slighting of domestic ideals by deriving great satisfaction from other roles that prairie society offered to them, such as being shapers of culture.[169]

Certainly, the role of prairie women as cultural conservators and initiators was a significant one. Their activities in this realm both aided their own adjustment to the frontier and gave them a sense of purpose as settlers. The artifacts and the material culture that women brought with them from their former homes were particularly important. A checkered tablecloth and silverware that had been carried from Ireland graced the holiday dinner table of an early Illinois settler.[170] The first piano that was hauled into McLean County, Illinois, by Laura Bradner's father, gave family members hours of pleasure. The Dresden cups that Dutch immigrants had brought from Amsterdam to Minnesota reminded Gertrude Vandergon's relatives of their homeland, while a wooden tea caddy and three tin containers assumed a place of honor in the home of English settlers in Minnesota during the late 1850s.[171]

Other women used holidays and family rituals to reestablish a homelike aura and to conserve known cultural patterns. One Iowa woman fondly remembered Christmas holidays as the times when her family celebrated its Swedish heritage. She explained: "It was not easy on that farm in Iowa to make such a transformation. Lutefisk herring, lingonberries, and cardamom seed—all must be ordered at least a month in advance from the big city of

Ft. Dodge." Yet her mother managed to produce a smorgasbord of traditional dishes, as well as to play Swedish carols on her small parlor organ and to create a number of presents that were reminiscent of the homeland.[172]

Re-creating certain social institutions and patterns of behavior was another way in which women both cushioned their adjustment to the prairie and attempted to make it a more amenable place in their own eyes. Objecting to living in what one female settler termed an "infidel neighborhood," women helped to organize churches, Sunday Schools, and Ladies Aid societies.[173] When Fort Snelling opened in Minnesota in 1821, the first officers' wives gathered the children together in the officers' quarters for a prayer service on Sunday afternoons.[174] Other prairie women worked on behalf of schools, including German and other ethnic ones; sewing groups; literary societies; and a wide range of other organizations.[175] Other women enforced long-accepted ideas of proper demeanor through their personal actions. In Illinois in 1839, one determined woman from New Hampshire refused to compromise herself just because church services were held out of doors. Dressed in a green silk dress, a high poke bonnet, and gloves, she accepted a ride from a man on horseback, and when she arrived at the service, she felt that she received at least as much attention as the minister.[176]

Another factor that softened the frontier experience for prairie women was their bonding with other women.[177] A common complaint in the personal writings of female settlers was the absence of other white women during the first months of their arrival and their great joy as other women moved into an area. They also reached out to family members and friends in their former homes through letters. In 1830, Lucinda Casteen begged her mother's forgiveness for not having written sooner, saying, "It is our duty to give each other all the Sattisfaction in this way we can."[178] As an area became more settled, women also formed groups to help incoming women with the personal disruption that migration entailed. For instance, in Minnesota in 1857 the feeding of the crew that built Sarah and Elknanah Davis's cabin was accomplished entirely by a local ladies group.[179] Sewing and quilting bees, along with wool pullings and other work parties, were also examples of women's groups that offered fellowship, support, and assistance with necessary tasks.[180]

Another important way that women bonded to and helped one another was during times of childbirth, illness, and death. Women commonly attended each other during birth, while neighbors and friends came into a new mother's home to prepare meals, to care for the other children, and to nurse the mother and the baby.[181] Using their extensive knowledge and experience as nurses, apothecaries, and herbalists, women also treated one another's families for illnesses and injuries. An 1864 handwritten notation in a Missouri woman's recipe book prescribed "16 grains of quinine in a half a teacup of Whisky" for a sore throat, chills, and fever, and a tincture of opium, red pepper, rhubarb, peppermint, and camphor for cholera.[182] To supplement their home remedies, women utilized some of the hundreds of patent medicines on the market, which ranged from "Worm Confections" for children at twenty-five cents a box to Dr. Christie's Ague Balsam, which was guaranteed to end fever and ague (flu).[183]

Women also eased the harshness of prairie living by turning to men for companionship and support. Although there were women who thought that prairie men were hard on their women or that their own men were not "doing quite right" by them, many also complimented their husbands.[184] The women spoke of their husbands as industrious in the fields, helpful in the home, and loving as fathers. The women enjoyed the men's company, lamented their absences, and missed them terribly when accidents or illness took their lives.[185]

Kinfolk, friends, and neighbors were yet another source of strength for prairie women. A Minnesota woman maintained that it was a "great event" to visit her mother's relatives, even though it meant traveling fifteen miles by ox team.[186] Another woman fashioned a pair of skis for herself, so that she could visit friends during the snowbound Minnesota winters.[187] Others spoke of frequent visitors and resulting dinners, talks, and songfests, to the accompaniment of guitar or piano.[188]

It must also be remembered that the harsh and demanding conditions of the first years of settlement did not stretch on infinitely. Towns, stage routes, and eventually railroads followed lines of settlement, so that few frontierspeople were isolated for long. One woman cogently described the rapid settlement in her neighborhood before the Civil War: "We saw the country change almost overnight, it seemed, from raw, unbroken prairie to a settled community with schools and churches. We saw the coming of the railroad, the building of roads and bridges, and the growth of a nearby county seat from a scraggly village to a thriving, up-to-date town with all the improvements of a city."[189] Some women felt that they became reasonably comfortable within two or three years, while others spoke in terms of a dozen. Rebecca Burlend, an English settler in Illinois who heartily regretted her family's move during the first few years, later admitted that "means of comfort" were now within its reach. She had seen a "neighborhood rise around us; and ... where at our first coming, everything appeared in its native wildness, small villages have now begun to rise."[190]

Along with change and progress came a rich social life. Religion formed the basis for social interaction on many occasions. Church services, weddings, Ladies' Aid meetings, singing schools, musical groups, socials, and camp meetings—all provided fellowship. Christmas was the cause of many gatherings, while the Fourth of July meant picnics, speeches, and fireworks. Dances, balls, and dinner parties occurred year round. Gradually, professional entertainments began to appear as well. Perhaps the most exotic of these were the numerous circuses that crisscrossed the prairie, bringing animals, equestrians, and other delights to settlers for as little twenty-five cents per person.[191]

Women's personal documents indicate that life was far from boring in many sections of the prairie. As early as 1819 an English settler in Illinois wrote to her uncle that although they had "expected to lead a very retired life in the backwoods of America," they were constantly busy and had never entertained half as many people at home as they "received in these humble little cabins." A few years later, her sister exclaimed, "We had a good deal of dancing and sleighing here last winter and were really quite gay and fashionable— in our particular way."[192] A Missouri woman of the time recalled parties and dances that drew guests on horseback from as far as fifteen or twenty miles away. They arrived, she said, with their "dresses in bandboxes hung on the pommel of the sadle." Although those dances often began in the afternoon and lasted most of the night, the guests frequently participated in a vigorous fox hunt or other activity on the following day.[193] Prairie towns also offered a huge variety of entertainments, ranging from vaudeville theaters to "bowling saloons."[194] By the 1860s and 1870s, women found that the "society" offered in such towns as Burlington, Iowa, and Springfield, Illinois was filled with balls, masquerades, church suppers, baseball games, and many other diversions.[195]

Although not debilitating or dull, the lives of prairie women had definite limits. Unlike their menfolk, who had little direct responsibility for the domestic sides of their lives, women focused their energies on homes and families. At the same time, their husbands, brothers, and fathers engaged in a wide spectrum of "breadwinning" and other "public" activities.

The perusal of hundreds of women's and men's diaries and other writings clearly reveals the differences between the activities of the two sexes. While daughters, wives, and widows wrote primarily about domestic matters, men recorded travels, education, political achievements, military experiences, work activities, and plans for their futures. Only occasionally did these men mention home and family concerns.[196] Thus, while the prairie frontier offered diverse opportunities to men, women retained home and hearth as the centers of their lives.

4

Home and Hearth
on the Plains

Like their counterparts on the prairies, plainswomen focused their primary attention upon matters associated with home and hearth. The welfare of their families and the maintenance of the homes in which they lived served as the organizing principle for most of these women's lives. As young girls, they served as apprentices to their mothers and other women in learning domestic skills. As adults who had not yet married, they helped to care for their family's homes and prepared to become mistresses of their own. Once they had married, they became the chief figures in the domestic operation of their newly created families. And as women who chose not to marry or who faced the termination of a marriage through divorce or death, they cared for themselves, while perhaps rearing children or helping to rear grandchildren.

Plainsmen, on the other hand, pursued a wide variety of callings and activities. As in virtually every region of the United States, numerous men wrested livings from the soil or ran businesses, but the Plains also offered them the opportunity to mine gold and other minerals, to herd cattle and sheep, to man frontier outposts, and to participate in scientific expeditions and the development of railroads. The chance to rise in public office or to succeed as an entrepreneur also existed. While their women's lives exhibited a pervasive sameness despite the locale, men's lives were often expanded by it.

What the Plains did give to women was a particularly difficult environmental setting in which to practice their domestic calling. There is no dearth of evidence to show that the Plains area was rigorous and demanding in terms of climate, insects, native inhabitants, and political upheaval. Although the Plains was presented as a region of unlimited opportunity in "boomer" and other promotional literature of the nineteenth century, later historical accounts depict its settlement as an ongoing struggle against numerous drawbacks.[1]

Until recently, however, few observers have noted the effects of the Plains environment upon women's work. Early in this century, Louise Pound of the University of Nebraska remarked that Plains conditions were especially trying to women. In the early 1970s, historian Mary W. M. Hargreaves maintained that the Plains frontier was considerably more difficult for women than other frontier areas had been. More recently, other scholars have added their voices to the growing case concerning the hardships endured by women settlers on the Plains.[2]

Of course, women themselves often recorded the adversities that disarranged their homes and families. For instance, drought and the resulting lack of water created problems for men, but women's writings dramatically illustrate the impact that scarce water had on domestic labor. Women wrote about carrying water supplies over long distances in pails attached to neck yokes and in barrels on "water sleds," buying water, making wash water by melting snow in kettles on the stove, using the same water several times for different tasks, and using sal soda to "break" water that was too hard for cooking or washing because of its alkali content. Women actively participated in seeking solutions to the water problem; this included hiring water diviners and digging wells. Often, a man who was digging a well worked in harmony with a woman, who pulled dirt and stones up out of the hole; or a woman descended into a hole to dig her own well.[3]

Another scourge described by plainswomen were the terrifying fires that resulted when homes, outbuildings, and fields became overly parched. These fires posed a menace to crops, stock, buildings, homes, and children. In 1889, one North Dakota man cried aloud when he saw his barn and horses destroyed by fire, while his wife fought in vain to save her cows and chickens.[4] Many women recounted their constant dread of prairie fires during the spring and fall, describing them as huge conflagrations that turned the sun red, whipped the wind into a deafening roar, and sent blinding billows of smoke over the land.[5]

Rain and snow storms unsettled women as well. Torrential downpours, floods, and blizzards often caught women in homes or schoolrooms, with small children to protect. In October 1880 a freak three-day blizzard trapped a South Dakota woman in her farm home with her four small children, while her husband was working away from the farm. Neighbor men came to help her, and they saved the cow, but her pig smothered to death in its pen.[6] Other women wrote about rain, hail, snow storms, and cyclones that knocked down stove-pipes, broke windows, caused roofs to cave in, flooded houses and ruined furniture, destroyed gardens, killed chickens, quickly reduced scanty stocks of food, and even froze to death their brothers, husbands, sons, and grandfathers. Yet others added that even when storms were not in progress, dampness and cold were facts of life. One Norwegian woman claimed that her kitchen was so cold all winter long that she "put on overshoes and tied a scarf over my head before preparing breakfast," while another set tin pans on her children's beds to catch the rain water that dripped through her soddie's roof.[7]

Insects and various animals also created their share of problems for plainswomen. Mosquitoes, bedbugs, lice, and snakes presented challenges to women who tried to prevent them from invading their homes and infesting family members. But the worst insect pests were the grasshoppers, which came in regular waves every decade or so. This scourge formed a "cloud so dense that the sun was obscured and the earth was in darkness."[8] It not only ate crops to the ground; it also threatened homes. Grasshoppers ate clothing and bedding, gnawed away woodwork and furniture, consumed the mosquito netting on windows and doors, destroyed stored foodstuffs, chewed gardens down to the bare ground, and laid their eggs in cracks and crannies of houses. During the 1870s, in order to save a few garden vegetables, Luna Kellie of Nebraska frantically fought the feeding grasshoppers, which to her sounded like "a bunch of hogs chanking." As she tried to flee from them, she discovered that her clothes were covered with "hoppers" and that the entry to the house was so filled with them that they had to be shoveled out. Grasshoppers also tended to lie in drifts around houses and, despite measures to combat them, managed to get inside. In her despair after the grasshopper plague hit Kansas during the 1870s, Anne Bingham complained that it had been "droughty Kansas, the state of cyclones, the state of cranks, the state of mortgages—and now grasshopper fame had come!" In their wake, the grasshoppers left destruction, disillusionment, and massive public relief efforts, designed to help the women and men who had been hurt by them.[9]

Women were further frightened and discouraged by American Indian peoples, who, the women expected, would be wary of white people at best and violent toward them at worst. Many women lived in fear, exacerbated by omnipresent scare stories, that Indians would steal their precious stocks of food, destroy their homes, carry off their children, rape them, and kill the men of the family. Despite frequent rumors that local Indians were "on the warpath," women slowly came to realize that Indians actually were more interested in attending governmental issues of beef, in procuring desperately needed food and clothing, and in performing their traditional dances and rituals than in waging war. Gradually, women learned that American Indians, in spite of the destruction and pain that they had suffered at the hands of white people, usually would not do more than annoy settlers with petty pilfering, aggressive begging, or staring in their windows out of sheer curiosity concerning white ways. Moreover, many plainswomen learned that they could form friendships with Indians, hire them as helpers, and turn to them as guides in learning techniques for survival on the Plains.[10]

In addition to the continuing fear of native Americans, repeated political upheavals added more trouble to plainswomen's lives. These began early for Kansas women. In 1856 the episode of violence known as "Bleeding Kansas" erupted when both proslavery and antislavery factions tried to push Kansas toward their own point of view. The writings of early Kansas women were punctuated with accounts of bloodshed and with descriptions of unsavory "Border Ruffians," who caused the women to fear for the safety of their own homes and families. A Lawrence woman, Sara Robinson, was not only continually terrorized by "street broils" but eventually had to endure her husband's imprisonment as a consequence of what she called the "reign of terror" in Kansas. In her view, the country had fallen upon "evil times," because those who spoke out against slavery and in favor of free labor were punished by "prisons or instant death by barbarians."[11]

In the words of another Kansas woman, this political convulsion was followed by "the great struggle between Freedom and slavery," the Civil War, which affected a wider slice of the Plains than just Kansas. Like many plainswomen who saw their men go off to military service, she believed that her father had given up his chance for wealth and had left his family to live "in the saddle for three years and a half . . . escorting trains and hunting out bushwackers."[12] Another Kansas man took up arms in response to the governor's appeal for volunteers after Quantrill's Raiders mounted a surprise attack on Lawrence in 1863.[13] As men left their farms and businesses to join the war effort, the care and maintenance of these enterprises fell increasingly to women.

The chaos of the Civil War was followed during the late 1860s and early 1870s by the problems of Reconstruction and the entry of thousands of black Exodusters into the Plains states, especially Kansas. Then, during the 1880s and 1890s, recurring economic dissatisfaction and disagreements over governmental policies erupted in Populist agitation across the Plains. The ensuing disputes regularly disrupted homes, families, and daily life.

Given all these crushing problems, why did women stay on the Plains? Of course, many did not stay; both women and men left to return to their former homes or try their luck somewhere else. Yet, a number of factors encouraged women to hang on. Many had come from a demanding environment, whether an eastern mill or a midwestern farmstead, so they were accustomed to hard times. As Laura Ingalls Wilder remarked, settlers saw the rigors of the Plains as "a natural part of life." In addition, they expected times to improve within the immediate future. As one woman explained, "We didn't mind the hard things because we didn't expect them to last."[14] And, in many cases, times did improve, and conditions did get better. Technology and agricultural knowledge both improved, thus helping to conquer this arid land; the economy experienced some boom times; the Indians were confined to reservations; and more settlers flocked into the Plains regions. Although some people were "busted," others found that their lives grew more comfortable every year. A Norwegian minister's wife wrote about the late 1880s, "As time passed people's circumstances improved."[15]

Another crucial reason that women stayed on the Plains derived from the strong family orientation of their lives. Women often persevered because of their hopes of improved health for a family member, the promise of a better future for their children, or, above all, the chance to obtain inexpensive or free land that might ensure financial security and happiness for their families. The aims of advancing the welfare of their families and of enhancing their life styles were often uppermost in these women's minds. In fact, family was omnipresent in the lives of plainswomen; it dominated their concerns for most of their lives.

The Plains family was generally a nuclear one. According to a revealing study conducted by geographer John Hudson, a family—consisting of "husband, wife, and children—was a basic part of the social fabric beginning with the first effective occupation" of the Plains. This view is certainly supported by such notations as it was "a happy day because we are alone once more," made by a woman when friends or relatives who had been living with her until they could establish themselves had moved out or when the woman herself and her family were the ones who finally had a place of their own.[16] These nuclear families were formed by women who averaged almost twenty-two years of age at the time of marriage and men who averaged a little over twenty-six. Contrary to the image of early marriage on the frontier, a study of census data from 1850 for northeastern Texas and a sample from the Dakota Territorial Census of 1885 indicates that marriage at an early age was more a myth than a reality.[17]

Of course, not all women gained their association with families through marriage. Both the Texas and the Dakota figures reveal the continuing presence of single female heads of households. Although women who remained single for their entire lives commonly have been overlooked by historians, they did exist.[18] By 1900 the number of plainswomen who had never married was slightly higher than the national figure of 10 percent. One investigator has speculated that some women went to the Plains with the intention of bettering themselves in ways other than marriage.[19] Here they formed family groupings, however, by living with friends or with members of their own or other families.

Another group of unmarried women consisted of widows. According to census data, the majority did not remarry, as has so widely been assumed. Evidence further indicates that the number of widows on the Plains was increased by an influx of widowed women from other regions or countries who moved to the Plains in order to support themselves or to join their families who were already living there.[20]

Other single women were divorcees. The number of Plains marriages that ended in divorce had already begun to rise noticeably by the turn of the twentieth century, slightly outdistancing the national average of one out of twelve. Despite the stigma attached to divorce, plainswomen increasingly chose it as an alternative to an unsuitable marriage.[21] In 1889, Emma Henries Plaisted, the daughter of a Methodist minister, left her husband in Dakota Territory to live in Massachusetts, where she gave music lessons to support her children.[22] Another woman of the same time period left a wealthy husband for a life of poverty with her children.[23] For some women—for example, the Montana woman who shot her divorced husband in the street in 1903— divorce did not buy them freedom from enmity, only from the shackles of the marriage itself.[24]

Certainly, legislation in the Plains regions hastened to catch up with the rising divorce rate. The liberalization of divorce judgments, which began in Montana as early as 1865, resulted in a transformation in divorce law during the early twentieth century. According to historian Paula Petrik, these reforms "included a liberal provision for mental cruelty, the catch-all clause that would provide an avenue out of unhappy unions for twentieth-century women in Montana."[25] By the 1890s the Dakotas and Oklahoma had nationally become known as havens for divorce seekers because of their short residency requirements for divorces, a development that undoubtedly inflated the divorce rate on the Plains. Profit-minded Oklahoma attorneys even advertised in major newspapers throughout the United States until the state legislature responded to widespread outrage concerning this practice by slightly extending the residency requirements.[26] These trends do indicate, however, that increasing numbers of women lived and often raised their children without the presence of a husband.

Still, it must be noted that the vast majority of women on the Plains were married for most of their lifetimes. They became wives through personally choosing a spouse, through arrangements made by their families, or as "mail-order" brides who came from another country to the home of a previously unseen husband. That many women married because of economic pressure is apparent, but social pressure was also great, especially from other women who were perhaps afraid of their single sisters. One married Montana woman of the 1880s told a single teacher that "it's kind-a queer you have been running around this country all this time and have not found a man." After the teacher replied that she had not been looking for one, the wife dourly stated, "It's about time you were." The teacher followed this advice and soon married.[27]

A woman's marriage often involved a wedding celebration shaped by local, ethnic, or racial customs and traditions. Weddings sometimes lasted for several days and included serenades, dancing, and infares, or charivaris. A wedding supper, or "feast," as some called it, could feature several meats and as many as five kinds of cake. And of course the bride's attire was a matter of serious discussion for weeks or months before the event.[28] Whether gala or simple, weddings were sometimes followed by honeymoons that were occasionally full-blown wedding trips, undertaken in a "traveling dress" and ranging as far afield as New Orleans.[29] For other plainswomen, honeymoons either were nonexistent or were very humble affairs. One Nebraska woman commented that her honeymoon consisted of a "sixty mile ride in a lumber wagon loaded with things I was taking from home."[30]

Once they had married, most women hoped to have children, an expectation that was widely supported by prevailing societal views of women as primarily being wives and mothers. Some women wanted large families, one saying that she thought twelve would be good but fifteen would be better.[31] Actually, the average family size among Plains families was comparable to the national birth rate. On the Plains, it ranged from approximately four children among American-born women to nearly eight among non-American-born ones during the later decades of the nineteenth century, a rate that began to decline after 1900.[32] Of course, this is an average, and some women bore as many as eighteen children, while others remained childless. Some further enlarged their families by caring for children from previous marriages, by taking the children of relatives into their homes, or by adopting children.[33]

Many women recognized the desirability of limiting the size of the family. After the Civil War, women living in the United States generally sought abortions, birth-control information, and contraceptive devices. They were encouraged by proponents of "Voluntary Motherhood," as the idea of controlling family size was then called. This position was strongly opposed by people who felt it was women's responsibility to bear many children, who feared the physical complications of abortion, and who were apprehensive that the nation's population would be depleted. The widespread appeal of anti-birth-control ideas resulted in the United States Congress passing the Comstock law in 1873, an act that banned "any article or thing designed or intended for the prevention of conception or procuring of abortion" and the "advertisement of such contraband."

On the Great Plains women avidly discussed the issue of birth control, offered advice to each other, and purchased the various devices that were still occasionally advertised and marketed in defiance of the Comstock Law. In 1885 a woman advised a friend who was about to be married to seek a "Pessairre," a "female preventative" that sold for $5.00. She added that perhaps it was not sold in the friend's area and, in a tongue-in-cheek fashion, commented that the only "sure prevenative" was for her to sleep in one bed and her husband in another.[34] Women also turned for help to unreliable home remedies. More than one woman who thought she was "safe" as a result of such aids and potions was dismayed to find herself pregnant again. A Kansas woman who wrote to members of her family in 1885 that "there is no prospect of babies at our house" told them less than a year later that she was "aiming to have a girl this time."[35]

When writing to one another, women shared news about whether they had made it safely—that is, without a pregnancy— through another month or had been "caught" and were thus preparing for yet another birth. They talked about "being in the soup" or, conversely, of being "all right" or "sick" (menstruating). They shared information, most of which was inaccurate, concerning pills, tonics, potions, advice books, and recipes, in tones of desperation and such an intense fear of discovery that they implored one another to write about these topics on a separate sheet of paper and to refrain from reading their letters aloud. Sometimes, however, they wrote to each other about these weighty matters with a touch of humor. In 1895, one woman who told her friend that she dreaded the thought of another pregnancy also wrote: "Oh say I have got another remedy now. I bet you will laugh. Tell how much faith you have in it. Just blow on your wrist."[36]

Despite the improved obstetrical techniques that were becoming available in eastern states, childbirth on the Plains was usually a matter of, in the words of a North Dakota woman, "allowing nature to take its course." A common anesthetic, if any was used at all, was whisky.[37] And the usual attendant, if one was available, was a female midwife, because doctors were scarce in most areas of the Plains. That these midwives worked hard and asked for little in return is illustrated by a family story that a Nebraska woman told regarding her own birth: "I was born in a sod house July 25, 1894, in Norton County, Kansas. The thermometer reached a high that day of 133 degrees, with a 55 mile per hour wind. The green corn was burned to a crisp. No doctors were nearby so a midwife was sent for. Father asked what he owed her and she asked for a used saddle of his."[38]

Women's writings, with their frequent mention of stillborn children and infant deaths, suggest that the infant mortality rate was high. Women attributed infant deaths to a variety of causes, including typhoid, smallpox, cholera, diphtheria, pneumonia, drowning, and other fatal accidents. Because of widespread absence of morticians, family or neighbor women made coffins and laid out the dead children. One woman of the early 1900s remembered plain pine caskets, lined with white muslin or "sheets that could be spared from the scanty supply"; but another recollected "fixing a box half full of shavings, covering it with a piece of white satin, and making a pillow with bits of lace."[39]

Childcare posed its own challenges on the Plains. Diapers were scarce and had to be washed by hand. Babies' and childrens' clothes were made by hand, sometimes from as simple a fabric as flour sacks, or were borrowed from family members and neighbors.[40] Wooden boxes and inverted trunk lids served as cradles, and toys were usually homemade, perhaps a toy wagon created by nailing four spools to a board, or a doll made from rags. Children played with dogs, cats, bears, birds, and other pets or with other children, including American Indian children.[41] As the children grew older, their social lives revolved around school, picnics, dances, card playing, home talent plays, candy pulls, roller skating, sledding, and holiday celebrations.[42]

Then as now, children were fascinated by the schools, where they spent so many of their hours. Terms were usually of three months' duration in many areas, even during the opening decade of the twentieth century. Sessions were held during the winter and the summer, to avoid conflicts with planting and harvesting, and were often preceded and supplemented by having mothers instruct the children at home. In their writings, children of the Plains devoted many paragraphs to fond memories of one-room schoolhouses, subjects studied, spelling bees and other contests, games played, and evening and weekend social events held in the schoolhouse. They remembered their friends, the presence of "breed" (Indians of mixed parentage) children in class, and teachers, whom they tended either to love or to hate.[43]

Life was not all play or schooling for Plains children, because they were generally regarded as workers in their own right.[44] Within the home, plains-women commonly trained and relied upon their children as domestic laborers. One Kansas woman recalled that during her childhood in the 1880s and 1890s,

> chores for the young ones were many. . . . Candle and lamp wicks needed trimming, the chimney to be cleaned and polished. Cobs from the bin by the corn sheller in the granary were brought to use for fuel along with wood and coal for the big kitchen range. A turkey wing was used to brush up around the fireplace. Preparing vegetables, setting table, dusting, watering the house plants in parlor and living room—there seemed to be no end to the helpful errands.[45]

Providing fuel for the cookstove was perhaps the most commonly assigned task; it consumed many long hours in twisting bundles of straw or long slough grass into "logs" or picking "buffalo chips" or "cow chips" from the fields.

The jobs that children carried out not only reduced the work load of adult family members but also trained the children themselves for their future duties. For girls and young women, work within the family home served as a training program for future domestic endeavors. Beginning at an early age and continuing until they left home, young women sewed, cooked, baked, cleaned, washed, ironed, gardened, canned, and executed many other tasks. An 1891 diary entry by a nineteen-year-old woman was typical: "I sprinkled clothes, watered the cow, mixed bread, made fire, ironed, baked, took a bath and got things ready for supper."[46] A 1911 diary kept by eighteen-year-old Della Todd of Montana indicated not only the complexity of her domestic duties but her apparent awareness of their training function as well: "This has seemed like a long day. I went to the garden and picked peas for dinner, made a pie, cleaned the milk-room. After dinner I swept the house, done some mending, made cookies. I have begun to believe in the old saying: 'Experience is the key that unlocketh many a door.' "[47]

These young women's repeated diary notations regarding baking, washing, ironing, and other household chores suggest that women's work knew no age limitations, because girls as young as ten years of age performed extensive domestic labor. Todd noted: "I got up at 5 this morning, got breakfast over, mopped dining-room, kitchen and Laundry-room. Made Lemon pie for dinner. Got dinner, then swept upstairs. I pressed Clyde's suit. Baked a cake." This indicates heavy chores for a young woman.[48]

Some girls managed at least partially to escape from the rigorous and exhausting domestic routines by doing outdoor work and joining in "men's" activities instead. More than one commented that they, a sister, a cousin, or a friend preferred the outdoors to staying in and learning women's skills and duties. A Kansas teenager's diary for 1896 revealed that while she washed, ironed, cleaned, sewed, and so on, she also fished, plowed, hunted, and went on expeditions into the surrounding countryside.[49] As respite from domestic and other cares of young womanhood, others rode horseback, often dashing "just as hard as the horses can go."[50]

Sometimes these escapees from domesticity maintained female values by riding sidesaddle and by wearing a proper riding habit.[51] According to a Kansas woman who was writing about the 1890s: "The skirt was long to cover the rider from the waist down while seated in a sideways position on the horse. A short jacket and a small hat completed the costume." Whenever possible, many young women wore something other than this cumbersome outfit, including skirts that were seamed up the middle to resemble pants. Some even scandalized their families by wearing boy's pants and riding astride.[52]

Mothers were often either outraged or cast into despair by such behavior on the part of their daughters. Anxious that their daughters learn not only the domestic arts but womanly values and behavior as well, mothers engaged in recurring struggles with their more liberal daughters. The sunbonnet was often the focus of the contest between the two generations. Daughters who threw the awkward headgear back over their shoulders ended up with freckled and sun-tanned faces, a scandalous condition to mothers who had been raised with ideals of beauty that emphasized clear and pale skin. Mary Raymond, who migrated to Nebraska in 1868, complained that not only had her mother dressed her in "the world's ugliest calico bloomers, 3¢ per yard," but had also subjected her to the wearing of "great large" sunbonnets "stiffened with cardboard slats" and "as uncomfortable as a football mask." Her mother's reason was a common one: the wind and sun of Nebraska would make her daughter as "freckled as a turkey egg" if she did not protect her face adequately. Evidently, first-generation plainswomen, especially those from a conservative non-American culture, clung to a number of expectations that were soon rejected by their female offspring.[53]

Often, intense conflict ensued between mothers and daughters as a result of the younger women's attitudes toward marriage. After experiencing the relative freedom of the Plains, particularly around the turn of the twentieth century, when attitudes toward women were liberalizing in much of the United States, many young women declared that they did not intend to marry. One of those who doubted that she would ever desire marriage also proclaimed, "It is wonderful how free and easy people become in this country."[54] Another who announced that she was "having too much fun to get married" finally did so at the advanced age of twenty-eight.[55] Others, who found their marriages distasteful in some way, chose to terminate them through divorce. While a mother usually persevered in a painful marriage, a daughter, confident in her ability to support herself and rejecting the idea that women could not manage their lives without the help of men, might choose divorce instead.[56]

The maintenance of traditional female values and practices was difficult for women on another front, the home itself. But here, mothers and daughters seemed to be more in harmony about maintaining certain standards. Plainswomen of all ages and eras filled their diaries and journals with lamentations concerning the keeping of a "proper" home environment in the crude housing that most of them were forced to cope with, at least during their first years on the Plains. They were often shocked by their first sight of the huts and shacks in which they were to live and work. One young woman was aghast at the filthy appearance of the family's sod hut. Her father unsympathetically replied, "Well, it is dirty looking because it is made of dirt." She remarked that she had thought a sod house would be "kind of nice . . . green and grassy," but "the sight of the first one sickened me."[57] Some women were so disgusted with these primitive dwellings that they lived in town during the winter or refused to live in them at all, thus forcing their husbands to commute.[58]

Generally, the housing that so upset women fell into three types: the log cabin, the wood or tarpaper-covered shack or house, and the sod house. Variations upon these basic forms sometimes derived from the availability of other building materials, which included adobe or grout (concrete); brick, usually manufactured by German groups; and stone and boulders cleared from fields and used for housing. Other distinctive features came from various ethnic groups who attempted to continue their familiar ways of building. The Germans-from-Russia were known for their long, narrow houses, one-room deep. The rooms were connected in a line; the walls were made of clay brick or stone; and the roofs were made of shingles and had gables at the ends. The Norwegians and Swedes, on the other hand, tended to build rectangular homes, with frame walls, ramp roofs, and porches.[59]

Because of the limitation of building materials, the first homes were more temporary and rough than any of these just discussed. It was not uncommon for a woman to set up housekeeping in a tent while a more permanent home was being built. Some lived in tents for a number of years, including one Wyoming woman of the early 1900s who did so for four years. She recalled

that the tent had no floor, just "scraps of canvas laid on the ground." Here
her two children were born, without a doctor.[60] Other families used tents for
living space and wagons for bedrooms, or lived entirely in all types of wagons
ranging from Conestogas to sheep wagons.[61] Those who came during the latter part of the nineteenth and the early part of the twentieth century, after
the railroad had penetrated most Plains regions, spent their first months living in the railroad "immigrant" car that had transported them, their goods,
and their stock to the frontier.[62]

Most families moved into more substantial homes within the first year. Log
cabins and wooden shacks and houses were popular wherever wood was locally
available or could be hauled in at a reasonable cost. Typically, the first cabin
or shack was 10 by 12 feet with only one room. Within a short time, such
additions as a sleeping loft or attic above, a storage cellar, and a lean-to kitchen
might be added. Because log cabins and lath shanties were vulnerable to
the weather, the cracks between the logs were chinked with mud, while
shacks often were covered on the outside with tar paper battened on with
laths or were lined on the inside with newspaper, blankets, or, after the beginning of the canning industry in the 1890s, with sheets of tin made from flat-
tened cans.[63] The dirt floors were kept in condition by sprinkling them with
water or by regularly dousing them with sudsy water, a process that eventually produced a hard-surfaced floor.[64] Insects and snakes were combatted
with kerosene sprays and oil and were attacked with a variety of weapons.
In Wyoming, a woman who was disgusted that her house was a "habitat for
pack rats," which entered through the holes between the logs, placed a .22
rifle in her lap at night, waited for one of the "curious little animals" to appear, and soon killed a rat or two.[65]

Another common structure was the sod hut, or soddie, built where lumber
supplies were scarce or nonexistent. The soddie could be a freestanding structure made of slabs of sod cut by a plow, or it could be a dugout partially bored
into the side of a hill or into the ground. Roofs were made of sod, and cactus
was planted on them to keep animals from digging in them. Sometimes, the
roofs were seeded with flowers, which bloomed in the spring and gave the
soddies a colorful appearance. The frames of the few windows and door were
made of scraps of wood. The first windows were usually of isinglass; glass
was a later improvement. With their natural and effective insulation, soddies were said to have been cool in the summer, warm in the winter, and im-
pervious to fire. And the price was certainly right, for a sod hut could be built
for a few dollars. An 1886 Nebraska soddie cost all of $13.75, which paid for
lumber, a roll of tar paper, and nails. Yet soddies had their drawbacks, especially for housekeepers. Insects, snakes, and small animals continually invaded, while the sod roofs dribbled dirt and dust on all below unless they
were covered with muslin, which had to be removed and washed twice a year.
In rainy weather these sod roofs tended to leak, and then, according to a Mon-

tana woman, "when the dirt was thoroughly soaked, it would drip for days in the house, after it quit raining outdoors."[66]

Although determined women were often dismayed by the limitations of such housing, they showed tremendous creativity in coping with their crude homes, frequently turning their interiors into comfortable dwelling places that sometimes even boasted a touch of elegance. Women installed rag rugs; wallpapered the sod walls with newsprint; curtained wooden-box cupboards, which were also frequently papered; and crocheted dainty covers for wash bowls and slop jars. To produce a homelike and livable environment, they often added house plants and flowers, in crocks or tin cans; family portraits and Bibles; framed cross-stitched mottoes or hair wreaths that they had made; and occasionally a canary.[67] By supplementing wooden homemade furniture with treasures brought from former homes, such as rocking chairs, knick-knack shelves, hanging or other types of kerosene lamps, embroidered throws, flowered carpets, and books, these homemakers expressed their contempt for the rigors of Plains living. And by transporting a precious clock or perhaps a uniquely styled dresser all the way from Norway or some other country, they preserved a small part of their ethnic heritage.[68]

Perhaps most importantly, women established a "proper" home as a symbol of their intent and ability to bring civilization and culture to the raw Plains. Making a home out of a hovel was their way of serving notice that the stabilizing force of family had arrived. Oddly enough, curtains seemed to be a particular mark of civilization to thousands of plainswomen who took great pride in having them hanging at the few windows they had. Undaunted by the lack of resources, the women fashioned curtains from newspaper, muslin, cheesecloth, and old sheets. An early Montana woman adorned her cabin's windows with shades that she had made from oiled red calico and covered them with lace curtains that she had preserved from her southern plantation home. Curtains were so important that some women sacrificed dresses for them, and in one case, a precious white cambric wedding petticoat ended up gracing a soddie window.[69]

Besides converting these rough houses into homes, women had to turn them into work places as well, if they were to fulfill their functions as domestic artisans. Working within the confining dimensions of these structures and using the adjoining yard as an additional work space, women performed household labor and practiced domestic skills that were a critical element in the survival of most families. Women's recitals of complex and innumerable domestic jobs document the critical nature of their work in maintaining homes and in providing such goods as food, clothing, and medicine for family members. In reading women's diaries, one is also struck by the repetitive nature of such tasks, or what might be called the "dailiness" of them. Women had little relief from the work and worries of running a domestic organization, even on Sundays, during illness, or immediately after childbirth.[70]

The preparation and preservation of food in particular was a constant concern of the Plains homemaker. Women spoke of what one of them described as "plain, substantial food, with few desserts, and practically no candy."[71] Despite their simplicity, these foods required a good deal of handling. Fresh and dried fruits and vegetables, especially corn, had to be grown, cooked, and preserved. Beef, pork, chicken, and turkey required raising, butchering, rendering, and dressing. The production of bread consumed one day a week. Milk and the butter and cheese that were made from it all involved time-consuming and tiring processes. It is to their credit that these women's culinary skills often resulted in well-stocked pantries and root cellars. One Kansas woman remembered that her grandmother's storage cellar was filled with bins of vegetables; jars of jam, jellies, catsup, and pickles; barrels and "great earthen jars" of pickled pork, corned beef, and kraut; bundles of herbs; and piles of potatoes.[72]

Given the work involved in food preparation, it is remarkable how many people the women often served at one sitting. They fed not only family members but also boarders, guests, travelers, cow hands, and threshers. A North Dakota woman described her mass feeding of threshers in the 1880s: I would start to bake two days ahead; bread, cake, doughnuts, cookies, and some pies, so when they came I had just the meats, vegetables, and pies to bake. We would always have a fat hog to kill and that would all be used up in three days . . . and we would have beef from town every day."[73]

Producing clothes and caring for them were other essential functions carried out by women. They knitted clothes, often from wool that they had produced themselves, handsewed a large variety of other garments, or treadled away on a foot-powered sewing machine to provide family clothing. They mended, darned, and repaired these clothes, also by hand. Washing clothing and linens was also tedious; it involved the home production by women of wash soap, the hauling and heating of water, scrubbing by hand on a wooden or zinc washboard or laboriously cranking a washing machine, hanging clothes out to dry, starching, and pressing them with heavy sad irons, heated on the stove.[74]

Gradually, women got a measure of help with their endless household duties. But as on the prairies, technology was purchased for the family business first and the home second. "Improved" stoves that burned kerosene or corn cobs allowed women to can foods instead of salting, drying, and pickling them. Eventually, sewing machines made their debut in various areas of the Plains. The first sewing machine in a family was a cause for celebration by women who found that it, along with the invention of paper patterns by the Buttericks in the late 1860s, lightened their work to a certain extent. Improved washing machines helped, too, although they were hand-powered, still required that boiling water be carried to them and dirty water hauled away, and could not adequately clean very soiled garments. Recalling her washdays during the 1880s, a South Dakota woman described her new washing machine as "a rectangular galvanized tank with a dome shaped cover" whose cylinder was turned by a hand crank. A Kansas woman remembered that her grandmother's washing machine consisted of a cradle tub, which was operated by a handle that necessitated a good deal of "hard work."[75]

Still, technology in the home never kept pace with the adoption of technology in the field, shop, or store. Although throughout the nineteenth century, Catharine Beecher and other domestic reformers called for the adoption of home technology, especially in the kitchen, it was slow to be embraced by women who had been socialized by the mystique of domesticity to believe that the old way was the best way. Another obstacle was the high cost of home technology. Historian Mary Hargreaves has argued that the cost of such domestic technology as indoor plumbing and electricity was prohibitive for most Plains settlers through the "lean years," which did not abate until 1940.[76]

Even when home technology was adopted, it usually only enabled a woman to do a more thorough job rather than cutting down the actual hours that she spent in doing it. And although new technology lightened the physical work of women, it did not alter the gender orientation of the tasks. In other words, water pumps made it easier to draw water, but it was still a chore performed by women; the operation of the new sewing machines were assigned to women; and the crude washing machines were used almost exclusively by women. Also, more was expected of women who had machines. One proud possessor of a sewing machine found herself making dresses for neighbors who "thought it a treat to have a machine made dress" and producing shirts and overalls for sale in her brothers' store. Technology did not extricate women from the domestic sphere, the importance of which was much undervalued by society in general, nor did it improve the status or prestige associated with that sphere.[77]

Many women also turned to hired help and domestic servants for assistance with household chores. These were often hired only for a short period of time, to help a woman through childbirth, threshing, or some other demanding period. White girls and women, black women, and American Indian women, men, and children—all worked as cooks, clothes washers, dishwashers, and general helpers. Women's writings contain frequent mentions of Indian helpers, servants, and nursemaids. And the wives of army officers noted that they, too, hired Indians as domestics and nursemaids, had enlisted men as servants, or, in a few cases, even brought their own servants with them from home. There were also instances, more numerous in well-settled areas, of women, usually upper-class and urban, who were relieved of most household labor by a retinue of domestic servants.[78]

Another source of help for plainswomen in their domestic endeavors were the traders and peddlers that soon appeared in every settled area. The first of the traders were often American Indians, who came to women settlers with foodstuffs, moccasins, buffalo hides and robes, antelope and elk clothing, baskets, and beadwork for barter or sale.[79] White women also purchased produce from black women who, barred by discrimination from many jobs, seized this opportunity to earn much-needed cash.[80] Itinerant peddlers were common as well; they sold tree seedlings, washing machines, clothing, pins, needles, buttons, thread, yard goods, and other necessities. At first carrying their goods in packs on their backs and later traveling by buggy and railroad car, these peddlers were usually a welcome sight to the Plains homemaker. Some, such as the Watkins Medicine Man, the Singer sewing-machine representative, or a Chinese vegetable man, specialized in certain products. Others tended to offer a wide variety of personal and household items.[81]

Shops also appeared rather quickly. The earliest ones were established in a cabin, but they were soon supplanted by separate shops and stores. At first these were all-purpose shops that stocked groceries, clothing, and hardware; but within a few years in the life of most towns, bakers, butchers, dressmakers, milliners, and dry-goods stores appeared. In these last stores, plainswomen could buy yard goods, sewing supplies, and ready-made underclothing, nightwear, and other garments.[82]

By the latter decades of the nineteenth century, plainswomen began to rely heavily upon the new mail-order houses. Montgomery Ward and Sears, Roebuck particularly reached into the Plains states with a remarkably complete line of goods, which included stoves that burned corn cobs; kitchen utensils; sewing machines; supplies for milking, butter making, and chicken keeping; and of course, clothing, shoes, and often-elaborate bonnets. Wyoming ranch wife Nannie Alderson stated that she got the Montgomery Ward catalog from 1885 on and that it was "impossible to exaggerate the importance of the part played by this book of wonder" in the lives of herself and her family.[83]

Naturally, prices that plainswomen paid for foodstuffs and other goods varied greatly, depending upon the era, the stage of development of a frontier area, the state of the national economy, and numerous other factors. In 1861 a Nebraska woman recorded the price of corn as $1.50 per bushel; flour, $0.06 a pound; and dried buffalo meat, $0.20 a pound. An 1874 Kansas account book showed that butter cost $1.50; oysters, $0.50; and calico, $1.50; but the amounts of each were not recorded. A few years later in Kansas, a similar listing showed that one pound of butter cost $0.25; calico, $0.10 a yard, and kid gloves, $1.25 a pair. In South Dakota in 1880, thread was $0.15 a spool, needles were $0.07 each, and cambric was $0.09 a yard. In Wyoming in 1890, butter was $0.25 a pound, eggs were $0.10 per dozen, and potatoes were $3.00 per hundred-weight. And in 1899 in Nebraska, one woman paid $0.14 a yard for calico and $1.50 for a pair of shoes. Women's account books showed not only prices but also the wide range of goods that had become available to them. Lists of purchases often included cologne, face powder, hair pins, curling irons, ribbons, lace, pearl buttons, corsets, hoop skirts, bustles, hats, gloves, stockings, shoes, books, paper, ink, post cards, and postage stamps.[84]

Plainswomen, in addition to turning to shopkeepers and such artisans as dressmakers for help with their tasks, also received sporadic assistance from their fathers, brothers, husbands, and sons. Men helped with cooking, washing dishes, scrubbing floors, churning, and washing clothes, often in their own fashion. Luna Kellie of Nebraska remarked that there were only two meals a day when her husband cooked and that her brother, who helped her wash by bringing and emptying the water and hanging out the clothes, sometimes took clothes "down to the lagoon and washed and dried them there to suit himself." She concluded that "men don't like to be bossed around when they have to do women's work."[85]

More commonly, a woman expanded her own list of duties by helping the men with their work. Kellie, for example, reciprocated for her husband's and brother's assistance by working at the corn harvest when no hired man could be found. Although she had recently borne a child, she wrapped it in a quilt and took it into the field with her. Other farm women drove planters, reapers, harvesters, and hay wagons; planted seed; dug potatoes; fished; hunted; helped to construct houses and henhouses; built fireplaces; dug wells and cellars; and crafted furniture and cabinets. Townswomen clerked in their family's stores, cooked in their husbands' hotel or inn, fulfilled all the duties connected with parsonages and churches, ministered to Indians on agent-husbands' reservations, and entertained in a governor's mansion or in a frontier fort.[86]

It was through their "helper" role that the domestic focus of plainswomen was modified somewhat by the occupations that the men of their families pursued. Although women's prime concerns continued to revolve around home and family, they were occasionally drawn into such other activities as field work or clerking in a store. Clearly, women participated in "men's" work partly because of the scarcity of hired labor. It might also be hypothesized that the caretaker role of women within the home could easily be widened in both women's and men's minds to include the care of chickens, cows, and other animals; to serving customers, clients, and patients; and in general, to "helping" the menfolk.

Army women were one type of plainswomen whose domestic arrangements were affected by the economic pursuits of their fathers, husbands, brothers, or other male relatives. Army women might be post cooks, laundresses living on "Soapsuds Row," or housekeepers in tents if their men were enlisted personnel; or they might have a slightly more refined but still difficult existence if their men were officers.[87] After bouncing across the Plains from post to post in army ambulances or traveling vast distances by railroad to join their men, the women who were attached to officers attempted, upon arrival, to establish homes in shacks, barracks, and officer's quarters. Although their domestic tasks were often lightened by a "striker," an enlisted man who served as a domestic servant and was assigned to them by the post commander, they still had many home-maintenance and child-care responsibilities. Their leisure time was devoted to worrying about their men's safety, fearing Indian attacks or visiting with "friendly" Indians, riding and picnicking around the fort, quilting with other women, and joining in fort balls, dinners, and other social events if they were fortunate enough to live in a reasonably sophisticated command.[88]

Like most other plainswomen, army wives, daughters, and sisters fulfilled their domestic tasks and duties under difficult conditions. Despite minimally furnished kitchens and limited provisions from the fort commissary, they often not only cooked for their own families but also carried out the entertaining, baking, and charity work that was expected of them among the poorer families in and around the fort.

Of all women's jobs, child care was probably the most challenging in the midst of the dangers and privations of a frontier fort. Women served as children's mothers, nursemaids, playmates, and teachers. As a result of the lack of children's services, particularly schools, many army women returned to their family homes when children reached school age, so that the children could receive formal schooling.[89] These women, although their lives were shaped in some ways by the military occupations of the men in the family, still struggled with the customary women's issues of domestic labor and child care.

Other factors besides the men's occupations affected the plainswomen's domestic practices and concerns. One of these was living in an urban rather than a rural setting. Plains towns were usually organized around an economic function, such as supplying farmers, ranchers, and miners or serving as a railhead. People were drawn to these towns at a rate that accelerated throughout the nineteenth century, so that by 1900 almost 30 percent of Plains dwellers were urban dwellers. Some settlers chose town living when they arrived on the Plains, while others moved to towns only after having tried rural life. They later came to town for a number of reasons: to obtain schools for their children, to find a more lucrative source of family income, to practice a profession or trade, or to escape the demanding labor of a farm or ranch.[90]

Women were not always pleased with what they found in a Plains town. Their descriptions usually reveal that raw frontier towns lacked the simplest of amenities. Such phrases as "roaring town," "tough town," and "hell on wheels" were used in reference to them, especially during the early days of settlement. Many towns developed too rapidly for planning to occur. A young woman of the 1880s observed that when the first train came through Aberdeen, South Dakota, in 1881, it "became a town almost over night." The result was chaos: "dozens of false-front store buildings rubbed elbows with tar paper shacks and sod shanties." In 1905 a Wyoming woman scoffed that Worland consisted of only a few frame buildings and a hotel that was only a "little log cabin shack." A South Dakota woman who reached Fort Pierre in 1909 was even more outraged by it, calling it a "rotten town" where "a full length photograph of a naked woman fell out of a man's pocket" and fourteen year old girls had babies. "It isn't safe for an unprotected woman outside the house at night," she lamented.[91]

Women were confronted with many problems in Plains towns. Alkali water was inadequate, the sanitary facilities were scarce. Moreover, many women were alarmed by crime—ranging from petty theft to murder—prostitution, dance halls, hurdy-gurdy houses, vaudeville theaters, numerous saloons, and heavy drinking. Mud streets made walking impossible for a long-skirted woman, while the lack of night lamps made it too dangerous for her to go out without an escort. In addition, the noise, dirt, and crowding that was caused by numerous carriages, freight wagons, other vehicles, and railroad lines created unsafe and unpleasant streets; and prices tended to be outrageously high.[92]

On the other hand, Plains towns did offer advantages to women. There were job opportunities; shops that offered a variety of goods and services; readily available hired help; a number of women's clubs and organizations; schools, normal schools, and sometimes even colleges; and a lively social life. According to a Pierre woman of the 1880s, the town had an intriguing side: "The social columns of the newspapers told of the gay life, ladies afternoon teas and elegant evenings, ladies and gentlemens' parties in full dress," and hotels that were said to be elegantly arranged and equipped. Similarly, a Topeka woman of the 1890s wrote about shopping trips, singing lessons, streams of visitors, parties and receptions, balls, card parties, and teas. It must be remembered, however, that such entertainments were usually only within the reach of middle- and upper-class women, while their poorer sisters were left to struggle with the negative aspects of town living.[93]

In addition to the locale, the factor of race influenced the way in which plainswomen actually carried out their domestic functions. Unfortunately, it is difficult to reconstruct the lives of minority women on the Plains because of the paucity of source materials. Occasional mentions of Orientals as salespeople, as cooks on ranches and in restaurants, and as washerwomen in towns and forts document their existence but offer little information concerning their lives.[94] Mentions of black women are more frequent and suggest that they lived on the Plains as wives and mothers, slaves, domestic servants, cooks, prostitutes, madams, interpreters, and farmers.[95]

The documents of a few black women offer some additional data regarding their experiences as Plains settlers. Typically, black women's diaries, letters, memoirs, and other sources contain comments that are almost identical to those of white female settlers, for they describe housing, food preparation, clothing, children, medical care, and other domestic matters in detail. Like their white counterparts, black frontierswomen wrote about their desire to begin "civilized" housekeeping in the new land. To that end, they carefully carried choice bits of chinaware or other treasures to their new homes on the plains. The letters of Ava Day, a black homesteader in Nebraska during the 1880s, and an interview with Era Bell Thompson, a black homesteader in North Dakota about 1910, demonstrate that black women shared the daily concerns of plainswomen first and black women second.[96] The women in the family of Helen Johnson Downing are other examples. During the early 1900s in North Dakota, they followed traditional work patterns for girls and women, relied on books to ease their isolation, and resorted to the same tactics to offset hard times that white women used.[97] This is not to minimize the special difficulties faced by black women. Many black plainswomen did meet with prejudicial treatment, which undermined their effectiveness as homemakers and mothers and circumscribed their employment opportunities. Thompson, in fact, finally fled to Chicago to escape the prejudice that seemed to grow as settlement increased. The significant point here, however, is that as with white women the central focus of black women's lives was home and family.

Because the overwhelming majority of plainswomen were domestically oriented people trying to function in a demanding environment that placed severe limitations upon them as domestic practitioners, a significant question is, How did they manage to carry on? Did they do so by hanging on in bitterness and despair, as so many of the customary myths regarding women would have us believe, or did they somehow transcend adversity? Did they blame their misfortunes on opportunistic men who initiated the migration to the Plains, or did they take the responsibility for their lives into their own hands? These are questions that have fascinated historians of plainswomen for decades, yet many of the answers are available in the women's own writings.

Some women did indeed persevere in a spirit of hostility and disillusionment. Woman after woman described the crushing work loads that she bore, the births and illnesses that gradually eroded her health, and the recurring depression that she felt. Again and again, women chronicled their battles with loneliness, homesickness, and fear. One claimed that the Wyoming wind made her feel crazy and that the winters, when she was confined on a ranch with no other women, seemed unbearable.[98]

Others lamented the absence of other white women in their area or that their husbands were frequently absent because of business matters. Still others wrote to their families and begged them to move westward; the women professed that they could be happy if only their families would do so. And a number of women fled these and other rigors of Plains living by returning to their former homes or by migrating to a more hospitable frontier.

It would be a mistake, however, to take these lamentations at face value without examining the rest of the evidence. A woman did not often remain the only non-Indian female in an area for more than a few months, nor was she deprived of the company of neighbors, friends, and family members for very long. Neighbors moved in, friendships were formed, and family members often did move west. In addition, the women who were the most plaintive in their complaints were often the same ones who later maintained that they now liked their new homes and that they wouldn't have had it any other way. As a case in point, the Wyoming woman, who didn't think that she could endure either the wind or the isolation later maintained, "Those years on the Plains were hard years but I grew to like the West and now I would not like to live any other place." Another woman, who said that she hated Wyoming for many years because it was "death on women," later claimed that she had come to love Wyoming and her life there.[99]

Also, significant numbers of other women, who were perhaps pluckier, healthier, or more fortunate in some way, took the hardships in stride. They supported or even suggested the idea of migrating, liked the Plains from the beginning, and continued to respond to life there with equanimity and even joy. They reveled in the beauty of the region, rhapsodizing over "flowers up to your neck" and calling it a "paradise in the Wilderness." They asserted that isolation didn't bother them and that they had too much to do to be lonely. They basked in the freedoms and opportunities now available to them. They savored the opportunities that were offered to their children and the "better times" for themselves that either lay just ahead or had already arrived. They survived by looking on the bright side whenever possible. One outstanding example of this buoyant optimism was Flora Moorman Heston, a Kansas settler of the 1880s, who faced the usual annoyances of weather, poverty, hard work, and longing for the family that she had left behind. Yet she wrote to her family, "We have the best prospect of prosperity we ever had and believe it was right for us to come here. . . . I have a great deal more leisure time than I used to have it dont take near the work to keep up one room that it does a big house."[100]

Some women did indict men for their plight. In some cases, women seemed to be using men as scapegoats for their own unhappiness, but in others, they had good cause. Many plainsmen were abusive, alcoholic, lazy, financially inept or irresponsible, hesitant to recognize women's labor or give women a voice in family affairs, and just plain unsympathetic to women's cares. Sad and frightening accounts of men who verbally and physically abused women disclose a dark side to female-male relationships on the Plains frontier. Family structure was, after all, patriarchal, with its attendant implications of the male's right to dominate a female, control her, and coerce her. Women's diaries and memoirs show that many men acted upon these prerogatives. Newspaper accounts also reflect the existence of wife abuse. In 1885 the *Laramie* (Wyo.) *Sentinel* noted that a "worthless whelp named Smith was arrested and jailed this week for assaulting, beating and threatening to murder" his wife.[101] They also lend credence to the suggestion, put forth as early as 1862 by the United

States commissioner of agriculture in his annual report, that the insanity that was supposedly so prevalent on the Plains had more to do with men's treatment of women than it did with landscape, finances, or infant mortality.[102]

On the other hand, numerous women were delighted with fathers, brothers, and husbands who worked hard, participated in community affairs, helped with home and children, were loving and kind, and were generally support-ive. One woman related her husband's eighty-mile round trip on horseback to get her a rocking chair after the birth of their first child. Another was inspired by her husband's "cheerful spirit" and was pained more by his hard work than by her own "tired feelings." Another not only thought that her husband was a "patient and loving" father but also paid him the compliment of seeing "feminine qualities of thoughtfulness and sympathy" in him. And the North Dakota woman whose plaintive cry "There is nothing to make a shadow" is so often quoted was sustained through her travails by her husband.[103]

The answer to how plainswomen dealt with harsh frontier conditions does not seem to lie so much in women's personal feelings toward themselves, their situations, and their men; rather it derives from three characteristics of plainswomen themselves: their ability to create a rich social life from limited resources, the tremendous reward they derived from their roles as cultural conservators, and their willingness and ability to bond to each other.

Most plainswomen created or sought interesting social lives. Even during the first hard years, they sang and played the guitars, pianos, and small parlor organs that they had insisted upon bringing with them; they spent hours chatting with other women and exchanging household lore; they kept jour-nals that they cherished; they wrote letters home to friends and families; they read whatever was available, including the newspaper on the cabin walls; and they organized taffy pulls, oyster suppers, and quilting bees, which re-minded them of their former homes. As more settlers came into an area, women organized or participated in dinners and picnics; such holiday celebra-tions as Thanksgiving, Christmas, and the Fourth of July; box suppers and other "socials" at churches; spirited weddings and charivaris; spelling bees and other events in the local schoolhouse; and dances that included quadrilles, schottisches, polkas, square dances, and reels, danced to the music of fiddles, guitars, mouth harps, and pianos. Gradually, theaters appeared, offering per-formances of songs, puppet shows, readings, folk-dancing, and vaudeville acts; and carnivals, circuses, and the Chatauqua began to tour. The arrival of the mail provided another social event by bringing news of the larger world through letters and postcards and by furnishing such reading materials as magazines, journals, ethnic and other newspapers, and books.[104]

Moreover, the social implications of the railroads cannot be overlooked. Railroad companies actively encouraged settlers to come into an area, spon-sored fairs and local celebrations, and provided a tie, however ephemeral, with other regions. One Wyoming woman in 1907 claimed that just the existence of the railroad alleviated her discouragement, for with "no trees and few buildings" to hamper her view, she could see passing trains clearly, thus keeping herself "in touch with the outside pretty well."[105]

Besides finding occasional relief from the demands of Plains living through various entertainments and other amusements, many women also enjoyed conserving the culture of their families and former homes. They also tried to derive the most satisfaction possible from acting as cultural conservators and as civilizing forces by protecting a family; holding a home together; preserving traditional values, folkways, and mores; and passing on family and ethnic traditions. That women saw themselves as cultural forces is illustrated by their writings in which they often referred to such efforts. Their feelings are perhaps best summed up by one poetic plainswoman who wrote, "Without her gentle touch, this land / Would still be wilderness."[106]

Plainswomen acted as cultural conservators through the preservation and use of family treasures. They insisted that their children learn the proper use of a butter knife and other pieces of tableware, insisted upon covering their tables with cloths made of fabric rather than oilcloth, served holiday eggnog to cow hands in silver goblets, and proudly displayed their china dishes whenever the opportunity arose. One army wife felt at home, even in a tent, once she had unpacked her linen and silver; and a Nebraska woman who lived in a dugout and had only codfish, coffee, sorghum, and dried raspberries to serve for Thanksgiving dinner still got out her best silver and tablecloth. Similarly, a Montana woman adorned her Christmas dinner of scalloped oysters with her grandmother's silver candlesticks, white doilies, and every piece of silver she owned.[107]

Women also tried to establish culture on the Plains through the use of rituals, particularly the celebration of the Christmas holidays. Women's early attempts to celebrate Christmas properly with the paucity of resources available on the Plains frontier were often pathetic and touching. They scrimped, saved, and worked with scraps of cloth and other materials to produce something that resembled a decoration to go under a small tree devoid of all but the sparest of decorations. They also raided their limited stocks of food to produce as festive a dinner as they could possibly manage. As time went on, it became easier for women to recreate the warmth and family spirit of holidays as they had been celebrated "back home." Special foods, more elaborate trees, hymn singing, presents, and visitors—all contributed to the feeling that home truly did exist on the Plains. Also important were public Christmas trees in schools, churches, and town halls. Decorated with nuts, popcorn balls, strings of cranberries, wax candles, homemade decorations and candy wrapped in mosquito netting, these trees stood over presents brought by family members and friends for each other, as well as presents for poor children who might otherwise not receive any.[108]

A particular form of culture was brought to the Plains by ethnic women who wanted to preserve their rich heritages. They subscribed to a variety of newspapers and magazines in their own languages, continued to wear traditional clothing, and practiced holiday rituals from their homelands. One Norwegian woman in Nebraska explained that she and her husband spoke Norwegian in their home, sent their children to parochial school, and saw the children confirmed in Norwegian. She also cooked Norwegian food, especially at Christmas time, when the entire family assembled and enjoyed such special dishes as lutefisk.[109]

Social life and the conservation of culture were extremely important to women, but perhaps more important yet as a survival technique was their ability to bond with other women. One woman claimed that she did not fear migrating to Montana, because she would make new friends wherever she went.[110] There were certainly numerous opportunities for women to form friendships with other women, since isolation was a rapidly passing condition in most areas. One investigator has shown that Plains farmsteads often adjoined each other and that villages and towns existed at fairly regular intervals.[111] Another writer emphasized that farms were frequently less than half a mile apart and that four families often settled together, each taking a quarter section as a homestead and building their homes on adjacent corners, so as to be close to each other.[112] Furthermore, settlers streamed into many areas. In 1886 a South Dakota woman wrote to a friend, "It does beet all how fast this country is getting up. . . . Im looking round and see two new houses been put up since yesterday."[113]

Most women seemed to regard the need for female companionship as a given fact of life. An early North Dakota settler who was one of three women in the area, simply stated, "Naturally I was very lonely for women friends."[114] The importance of the company of other women was so great that few allowed age, ethnic background, color, or race to interfere when female friendships hung in the balance. Leola Lehman, a settler in Oklahoma Territory in the early 1900s, emphasized that one of her close friends was a native woman, whom she thought to be "one of the best women" she had ever known.[115] Others wrote about transcending language barriers in order to communicate with women of a different race or culture.

Women's friendships were typically established with calls. Lehman had been approached by the native woman, who became her friend when Lehman was hanging out her wash. "I came to see you," the Indian woman explained. "I thought you might be lonesome."[116] Other women visited wherever they happened to be; in homes, in stores, in hotels, in military forts, at social events, and on railroads and steamboats. In her diary during the late 1870s, Fanny McGillycuddy of South Dakota frequently logged calls and visits with other army women at Fort Robinson.[117] And a North Dakota settler of the 1880s recalled that on their way to Grand Forks, she and her brother knew they would be able to investigate the steamboat on which they traveled "just as soon as mother found a lady pasenger to visit with." She added: "The opportunity soon came. . . . Mrs. McClernan and mother were soon conversing in a very friendly way. There was no formal introduction necessary and they had many things in common to talk over. The need for companionship was felt as soon as one got a glimpse of the prairie."[118]

The arrival of a new bride in a town or rural area precipitated a good deal of social interaction among the women. The *Bozeman* (Mont.) *Chronicle* quoted an 1869 bride as remarking, "In all there were just fourteen women in the town in 1869, but they all vied with each other to help us and make us welcome." One of these women was even kind enough to give this seventeen-year-old novice some much-needed cooking lessons.[119]

Quilting bees and sewing circles were other ways in which plainswomen established and developed friendships. Although women customarily offered each other encouragement and technical knowledge, these functions served as support groups and informational networks of a somewhat more formal nature. Quilts that the women worked on at home were also important, because a quilting project gave them a pleasurable, leisure-time task to share with relatives and friends. Women not only shared scraps of material from one another's dresses and baby's clothes but also a means of creative self-expression and moments of comradeship.[120]

Perhaps the most frequent and truly bonding experience that women shared, again without much concern for age, ethnicity, color, or race, was by giving aid in times of childbirth, illness, and death. The *Nebraska Farmer* quoted an 1871 settler as saying that "neighbors acted as doctors, nurses and housekeepers, without a thought of reward," experiences that cemented them into "unbreakable friends."[121] Drawing upon their knowledge of common remedies and herbal medicines, women ushered in new lives, cared for those who were threatened by injury or illness, and presided over the ends of lives as well. A Jewish woman in North Dakota described the process surrounding childbirth during the 1880s: "When a baby was born, the children in the family were sent to the neighbors to stay for the time, so that the mother could have rest and quiet the first few days, the only rest many of these women ever knew. The rest of us would take home the washing, bake the bread, make the butter, etc."[122] A Nebraska woman explained not only that neighbor women shared the tasks of caring for a mother and her new baby but also that in times of illness they would "take turns watching the patient, giving medicine, and bringing dainties."[123]

Women often recorded their strong feelings regarding the need to have the help of other women at the time of birth, illness, and death.[124] One of the most dramatic expressions of such sentiments was that of Nannie Alderson, a Montana ranch wife of the 1880s, when she herself was sick. Urged to call a doctor from Miles City, she replied: "I don't want a doctor. I want a woman!"

Pressed again to seek a doctor's help, she sent for a neighborhood woman instead. She emphasized that "I simply kept quiet and let her wait on me, and I recovered without any complications whatever."[125]

That women turned to other women in their attempts to establish homes and families in the harsh Plains environment is understandable, as men's pursuits, activities, and attitudes diverged widely from those of women. While the center of women's lives was home and hearth, that of men lay outside the domestic realm. Just as women's and men's "centers" differed, so did their lives themselves.

Although numerous examples exist to support this point, one does so particularly well. When packing for the trip to the Plains, Faye Cashatt Lewis's father strongly urged his wife to sell her Haviland china. To him, it was little more than a nuisance and a frippery, useless in their struggle to succeed as settlers. Yet his wife clung to the china with despair and heartbreak in her face. Uncomprehending, he finally allowed the china to be packed. But as a woman, Faye easily understood her mother's position. She explained that the dishes were more even than beauty; they were "a tangible link" to the refinements of civilized living that would be difficult to re-create in the "rugged frontier condition" that so attracted her father.[126]

For women, the Plains frontier did not offer great opportunities and numerous activities. Rather than changing women's established routines and concerns, it simply made women's pursuits and lives more difficult.

5
Employment and Income Production on the Prairie

Because the central focus of the lives of prairie women was the domestic realm, it has been easy to overlook the huge numbers of women who engaged in paid employment or income-producing enterprises. The tendency to disregard women's money-earning activities was so prevalent during the nineteenth century that census takers frequently simply dismissed female settlers under the category "Not Gainfully Employed." Town and county business directories were also often male oriented in the types of enterprises that they listed.[1] Further investigation, however, indicates that in addition to their domestic endeavors, significant numbers of women were indeed gainfully employed.

Women's employment did differ markedly from that of men. Although the rich soil and abundant rainfall, along with the rapid settlement that resulted from such abundant resources, created a huge demand for willing workers of both genders, the jobs that each held were actually determined by gender. While men were free to experiment as farmers, entrepreneurs, professionals, and laborers, women were limited to areas believed appropriate for females. Occasionally a woman would defy the line, but more often women followed convention. In addition, men could devote their full time and energies to their jobs. Most women, on the other hand, engaged in employment only secondarily and as a supplement to their domestic functions.

A variety of sources offers tantalizing views of the existence and potential extent of women's employment activities on the prairie. As early as 1836, for example, the territorial census of Iowa listed a large number of women as heads of household or as living in groups of three or four females. Although women were not asked about their occupations during those years, it seems apparent that some of them must have been contributing to their own support.[2] By the 1850s, some census takers had begun to ask women about their occupations. In Bloomington, Illinois, the census listed women as laborers, teachers, and milliners. In addition, it included other potentially self-supporting women: female heads of household, constituting 10 percent of all families; five women boarders at the National Hotel, with no occupations listed; and an Esther Hanes, fifty-one years of age, who owned property worth $2,000 and who had living with her three unrelated women between the ages of seventeen and twenty-five, one of whom had a one-year-old child.[3] Later in the decade, an announcement in the *Weekly Pantagraph* (Bloomington, Ill.) confirmed the importance of female laborers in this frontier town's economy. It asserted that of the nearly eighty young women whom the Women's Protective Emigration Society had brought to Bloomington, all had found employment within days of their arrival.[4] The variety of jobs that such women took was suggested by the Iowa State Gazetteer of 1865, which listed twenty-five female milliners, one female stocking manufacturer, one female vintner, and numerous female music teachers, restaurant operators, and dealers in millinery and dry goods.[5]

In 1884, physician Jennie McCowen attempted to study working women in one prairie region. She claimed that Iowa women worked "in almost every department of human activity" and pointed out that the state's 1880 census listed over eighty thousand employed women, the majority of whom worked in such customary female areas as groceries, dry-goods stores, millinery shops, medicine, education, religion, science, and art. As she looked back over the history of Iowa, McCowen found numerous cases of employed and income-producing women.[6]

The validity of McCowen's observations is supported by many other source materials, particularly those produced by prairie women themselves. In combination with census returns and newspapers, women's writings reveal that women worked in such areas as education, business, medicine, religion, domestic service, the professions, and agriculture. Thousands more created their own "jobs" in their homes, through economic pursuits that produced much-needed cash for them, their children, and the family farm or other business venture. While the enterprises of prairie women sometimes deviated sharply from what was thought "acceptable" for nineteenth-century females, far more were an extension in some way of women's domestic functions and focus.

Teaching, in particular, was considered a natural concomitant of women's domestic duties because of the inherent qualities that women supposedly possessed in the areas of child care and nurturing. Advocates of women as teachers stressed women's innately high character; their capacity for affection, which would make students anxious to respond to them; and maternal instincts that would allow a greater rapport with students than would be proper for the "other sex," as men were often called. On their part, women who were committed to exercising their moral responsibilities, farm girls who were interested in escaping the drudgery of farm work, single women who wanted to earn money and fill time before marriage, and women who needed to support themselves and family members—all welcomed the opportunity to become teachers. Such jobs became increasingly available as men discovered that they could earn better pay and have steadier employment on farms and in factories, stores, and offices. As men left teaching, they created a void that women were willing to fill, so that in some prairie regions, women teachers accounted for 55 to 60 percent of the employed teachers. Commentators noted that women teachers gradually "began to crowd out the ancient men teachers" and were not hesitant to "elbow" them out completely wherever possible.[7]

Unfortunately, the United States census did not differentiate between male and female teachers until 1870. By this time, there were large numbers of female schoolteachers in all the prairie states. Illinois and Iowa both had more than 5,000 female teachers in 1870, with 5,728 and 5,663 respectively. Male teachers in these states numbered 3,141 for Illinois and 1,540 for Iowa. By 1880, Illinois had 10,768 female teachers and Iowa had 10,157. The number of male teachers in Illinois was 6,148, in Iowa, 4,380. Even Minnesota, with its smaller population, had 1,907 female teachers in 1870 and 3,538 female teachers in 1880.[8] Town manuscript census records show that black female teachers also existed on the prairie. In 1850, Bloomington, Illinois, had a "twenty-year old black school teacher born in Kentucky." Some years later, in 1878, there is evidence of at least one black female teacher in the Exoduster town of Nicodemus, Kansas.[9]

At first, female teachers simply organized schools in their own homes. These were subscription schools, meaning that students paid a fee to attend them.[10] In the first such school in Rochester, Minnesota, in 1856, the pupils even had to bring their own seats from home, while the teacher sat in her personal rocking chair.[11] In other cases, women were hired to conduct a school in a family cabin or in an out-building, a church, or a similar structure.[12] Gradually, teachers found themselves holding forth in log or frame schoolhouses, usually one or two rooms with benches for seats, a pot-bellied stove for heat, and very little other equipment.[13]

Teachers included not only women who had already been living on the prairie but also eastern women who had come to the West specifically to teach school. Reformer Catharine Beecher particularly believed that it was women's mission to migrate westward as teachers of children, immigrants, and the unschooled lower classes. She conducted many fund-raising and speaking tours in prairie areas, promoting the idea of women as teachers; while there, she founded seminaries, such as the Dubuque (Iowa) Female Institute, to train women who were already living in the West. Out of Beecher's preaching on behalf of women teachers came the Board of National Popular Education, a nonsectarian organization founded in 1847, which sent teachers west after brief training in Hartford, Connecticut.[14]

Neither eastern nor western female teachers received adequate compensation for their endeavors. They drew low wages, which were always less than those paid to male teachers. A Chicago schoolmistress of the 1830s received $24.00 per term for instructing nearly fifty students of varying levels of abilities.[15] One 1836 account listed teachers' wages as $1.50 per week for women and $12.00 per month for men, plus room and board provided by student's families, while another from that same year recorded a salary of $3.00 per week, from which the teacher supplied her own board. Some years later, Iowa teacher Ellen Strang mentioned a young woman who in 1863 was to receive $26.00 per month plus her board. Later in the decade, another source maintained that the average weekly compensation for Iowa teachers was $4.40 for women and $6.28 for men.[2]

Although these meager wages were usually supplemented by room and board, many teachers discovered that the arrangements for board were not always desirable ones. Alice Money Lawrence of Iowa described her living place as dirty and its mistress as a poor cook. Breakfast consisted of bread and an egg fried in lard, which Alice surreptitiously gave to the youngest boy of the family. To escape her boarding place, she spent as much time as possible at the schoolhouse, engaged in reading, class preparations, and writing letters to her sister. Another Iowa teacher, Agnes Briggs, had a similar experience. Although she did not mind boarding with the "front-room family" in a two-family two-room cabin, she did object to some of the family's customs and chose to live at home and walk the five miles to school each day. Pleasant situations, like those of Arozina Perkins, who claimed that she had plenty of space and good food, seemed to be the exception rather than the rule.[17]

In the schoolroom, teachers also faced limited resources. Although blackboards were common, other equipment, such as maps and globes, was not. Teachers often produced their own ink and quill pens, and one even made a globe out of a blown-out egg. Textbooks were whatever the students' families happened to own. When students presented their textbooks to a teacher on the first day of school, she usually saw a conglomeration that might include Webster's blue-back speller, Smith and Smiley's arithmetic, the English reader, McGuffey's readers, and an assortment of dictionaries, almanacs, and gazetteers. Only a few teachers were fortunate enough to have students like the young woman who explained that her mother raised turkeys and did sewing for others in order to buy her a "complete set of schoolbooks."[18]

Discipline was another challenge to women teachers. Often smaller in size and approximately the same age as the "big boys" who attended in greater numbers during winter terms, women teachers frequently lamented the need to discipline their students. In 1857, Mary Ellis wrote home, "What shall I do with the big boys this winter. . . . They never had a woman teacher and such a thing is scarcely thought of in the winter here." In 1869, during her first assignment as a teacher, Alice Money Lawrence wrote to her sister, "I had to keep all my scholars but one in at recess today, and I had to whip one boy—the first punishment of that kind that has been necessary." On another occasion, she caught an impudent boy off guard, pushed him into the aisle, and spanked him with his own geography book.[19]

Despite their many problems, teachers instructed their students in an amazing range of subjects. Some teachers found it necessary to begin by teaching the English language to their non-American-born students. Other subjects that were taught to primary students included reading, writing, spelling, elocution, arithmetic, geography, and history. High-school level students might be introduced to world history, literature, rhetoric, and algebra if the teacher herself possessed the necessary knowledge.[20] One young Illinois woman was certified in 1873 to teach this array of courses: orthography, reading in English, penmanship, arithmetic, geography, English grammar, history of the United States, botany, philosophy, zoology, physiology, and hygiene.[21]

Teachers in ladies seminaries and academies offered high-school-level instruction in an even greater number of subjects. As early as 1838 a Missouri woman remarked that a friend of hers was running a popular school in which thirty girls pursued "all the branches of education which are taught in Eastern Fem-Sem's [female seminaries]."[22] A year later, the Select School for Young Ladies in Burlington, Iowa, promised to teach orthography, reading, writing, and sewing for a fee of $1.50 per month or all "higher branches" of learning for only $2.00 per month.[23] During the 1850s and 1860s, instructors at the girls' schools that were proliferating on the prairie vied with each other by claiming to have expertise in college-preparatory subjects, teaching methods, Greek, Latin, business, and such female accomplishments as needlework and pianoforte.[24]

Numerous women used their positions as springboards to becoming administrators. Sarah Raymond Fitzwilliam accepted the challenge of being principal of the Bloomington, Illinois, high school during the 1860s and then city superintendent of schools, a position that she held until 1892. In 1877 she wrote a widely used manual of instruction for Illinois teachers.[25]

Yet other female teachers became instructors at the college level. In 1858, for example, Druscilla Stoddard accepted the headship of the Woman's Department at Iowa Central College in Pella. Other cases were Margaret Evans Huntington, who taught German, Latin, Greek, and American literature at Carleton College, and Matilda Jane Wilkin, who taught English, German, history, Latin, and Anglo-Saxon at the University of Minnesota, both during the 1870s.[26]

One particularly important prairie woman who became a college teacher was Mary B. Welch, who first came to Iowa State College (later Iowa State University) in 1869 as the wife of its new president, Adonijah S. Welch. In his presidential address, Welch made it clear that the college would soon offer training in practical skills necessary to women: "The most alarming feature of educating our girls is the almost total disregard of these branches, known as the useful and practical, that will prepare them for the proper discharge of the best and noblest duties of rational and intelligent women."[27] Under his leadership, every student at Iowa State contributed two and a half hours of labor per day to the school. Women students worked in squads in the dining room, the kitchen, the laundry, and the bakery on a rotating basis, which was designed to train them in all tasks. In 1872, classes in domestic science, taught by Mary Welch, were added to this regimen. Her course, Domestic Economy, began in a basement experimental kitchen and quickly attracted many women students to the school. Two years later, Welch became head of the new Department of Domestic Economy. During her ensuing years at Iowa State College, Mary Welch gained fame as as home economist, the initiator of a new curriculum titled General Science for Ladies, and the author of *Mrs. Welch's Cookbook* (1884).[28]

Another significant woman who taught at the college level was Arabella Babb Mansfield. Actually, Mansfield became a licensed attorney before she turned to college teaching. At the time of her exam in 1869, one of her examiners complimented her highly: "Your committee takes unusual pleasure in recommending the admission of Mrs. Mansfield, not only because she is the first lady who has applied for this authority in this state, but because in her examination she has given the very best rebuke possible to the imputation that ladies cannot qualify for the practice of the law."[29] But Mansfield never practiced law; instead, she joined the faculty of Iowa Wesleyan for some years as professor of English and in 1881 moved with her husband to DePauw University in Indiana, where she was professor of history and served in several other capacities. When she died in 1911 at the age of sixty-five, she was overlooked as the nation's first licensed woman lawyer; but later had a building at DePauw named in her honor.[30]

Besides teaching, another career that was thought acceptable for nineteenth-century prairie women was writing. Women worked as correspondents for newspapers, as authors of sketches, stories, and essays for newspapers and journals, and as novelists. A writer who achieved a modicum of fame was Alice French, who is better known by her pen name of Octave Thanet. Born in 1850 in Massachusetts, French migrated with her parents to Davenport, Iowa, in 1857. Here she built a reputation as one of the best authors of fiction in the West with such works as *Knitters in the Sun, Otto the Knight, Stories of a Western Town,* and *Expiation.*[31]

Other women worked as editors. By the late nineteenth century there were twenty-five editors and newspaper owners in Missouri alone.[32] Undoubtedly, the most famous woman editor who was living on the prairie during the nineteenth century was Jane Grey Swisshelm of Minnesota. Arriving in St. Cloud in 1857, Swisshelm soon brought notoriety through her activities as editor of the *St. Cloud Visiter,* as a political activist, and as an outspoken feminist.

In 1858 a gang of men who were opposed to her support of abolitionism and women's rights broke into her office, destroyed her press, and threw her type into the river. When she resumed publication of her newspaper later in 1858, she made it clear that she viewed the attack as a criticism of her as a professional woman. She asserted that she would continue to "stand publicly as the advocate of the oppressed of our own sex, as a representative of woman's right, under God, to choose her own sphere of action."[33]

While Jane Swisshelm was an outspoken and aggressive career woman who frequently deviated from the idea that women's employment should be related to domestic endeavors in some way, a few other prairie women moved even farther away from the norm by impersonating men in order to join the armed forces. One of these was Elizabeth C. Smith of Missouri, who dressed like a man, took the name Bill Newcom, and in 1847 volunteered for service in the Mexican War. She served as a private in a regiment of Missouri infantry volunteers for eight months before her true identity was discovered and she was discharged. She later married and applied to the United States Congress for back pay for her military service. During the ensuing congressional hearings, witnesses attested that she had performed all of her duties thoroughly and well as long as she had been allowed to do so. After much debate, members of Congress declared that because the law providing for soldier's pay made no distinction with regard to gender and because Newcom's services were as useful to the country as if she had indeed been a man, she would receive all the wages she was due, plus 160 acres of government land in the West.[34]

Another instance of a prairie woman who joined the armed forces disguised as a man occurred during the Civil War. In this case, nineteen-year-old Jennie Hodgers, an Irish immigrant to Illinois, donned male attire, assumed the name Albert Cashier, and enlisted in the Union Army in 1862. As Private Cashier, Jennie traveled with the Illinois Ninety-fifth Volunteer Infantry Regiment's Company G for nearly ten thousand miles, fought in some of the most important battles of the war, and was mustered out in 1865. Unlike Bill Newcom, Jennie Hodgers's real identity was not revealed, nor did she resume life as a female and marry. Cashier eventually received a military pension. The discovery that she was a woman was not made until 1911, as the result of an automobile accident; and the revelation remained a closely guarded secret until after her death in 1915.[35]

Unlike these male impersonators, the majority of prairie women who pursued jobs, careers, and business ventures stayed within the realm of what was considered acceptable for nineteenth-century females. Rather than flouting societal norms, they tended to work in areas that were in some way associated with women's customary domestic labor. Gender expectations determined women's duties within the home as well as in the larger world of work.

An outstanding example of a "proper" woman's economic activity was anything associated with needlework. In prairie towns, dressmakers, seamstresses, mantua (cloak) makers, and milliners abounded. Clothing production was time-consuming and difficult because of the lack of effective technology, so women turned to professionals for help whenever possible. The need for skilled assistance grew in importance as the nineteenth century progressed, because women's fashions became more complex. The "Cotton Revolution" of the early nineteenth century provided readily available and relatively inexpensive fabrics, which in turn led to a huge increase in the amount of material used in an outfit. Also, Victorian ideas of fashion contributed to the idea that multitudinous decorations were necessary on gowns, cloaks, and hats.[36]

On the prairie frontier, the days of rough homespun, animal-skin clothing, bare feet, and sunbonnets rapidly gave way to tastes for this finer and more complex apparel, at least on special occasions. Evidently, prairie women were determined not to become dowdy or outmoded by eastern standards. Because they did not come to the frontier to live in a "primitive" fashion, but rather to transplant civilization as they knew it, female settlers on the prairie adopted such fashionable fads as hoopskirts, bustles, whalebone corsets, and heavily adorned dresses and bonnets. In addition, remaining in fashion, at least to a degree, was extremely important to women who were living in a country that had stripped away so many of their other luxuries and vanities.[37]

Increasingly, prairie women sought help from other women who possessed the necessary skills and knowledge to produce their clothing. As a result, large numbers of skilled needlewomen plied their trades early in the settlement period of prairie regions. In 1860, Indiana had a total of 3,619 women who worked as mantua makers, milliners, seamstresses, or tailoresses. In that same year, in Iowa, 1,459 women were working at these trades. The number of female clothing workers on the prairie grew rapidly. By 1880, 9,425 Indiana women worked as milliners, dressmakers, seamstresses, or tailoresses, as did 7,664 Iowa women. Illinois possessed huge numbers of female garment workers, with nearly 23,000 reported in the 1880 census.[38] Anecdotal evidence suggests that black women also entered, and sometimes excelled in, the needle trades. In frontier St. Paul, for example, a mother and her daughters were highly esteemed by their customers in the years after the Civil War.[39]

Seamstresses and dressmakers worked in a variety of establishments. On the simplest level, women "did sewing" in their home for other women. Some women combined homework with part-time employment in shops, usually located in towns or cities. Others worked full time for established firms or undertook their own business ventures. These seamstresses and dressmakers often learned their trade from their mothers and sisters, through apprenticeships, or on their own. Typically, they worked for several years before marriage, intermittently after marriage, and, less commonly, full time for most of their lives.[40] Business notices in newspapers and business directories reflected the large number of dressmakers that existed on the prairie, as well as the elaborate services that they provided. In Burlington, Iowa, in 1856, numerous listings for seamstresses and dressmakers appeared. A few years later, a Bloomington, Illinois, newspaper ran a business announcement notifying the public that the "Misses Naylor" produced neat and lovely work as well as teaching "Weston's method of cutting and fitting dresses" to interested women.[41]

Many accessories completed a stylish woman's outfit. These included gloves, mitts, reticules (small handbags), shawls, mantuas, cloaks, and high-button shoes. The ensemble was topped off by an elaborate bonnet or cap, adorned with laces, ribbons, artificial flowers, and other fashionable furbelows. By the mid 1860s the most popular bonnet decoration was a real stuffed bird.[42]

Bonnets and caps of complex design emanated from the shops of ubiquitous prairie milliners. Their advertisements appeared in newspapers soon after the initial settlement of a region. One such advertisement in the *Illinois Statesman* (Bloomington) in 1860 claimed to offer the "most fashionable and extensive Millinery" ever seen in Bloomington. An advertising postcard, issued some years later in that same city, maintained that the products of the Millinery Parlor were of the finest styles known, because the head milliner had studied in Chicago.[43] Milliners marketed their goods in several ways. They might sell their products through general merchandise stores, work in shops owned by others, or own millinery businesses themselves. Millinery shops were often located above other business establishments, in one side of a store, in hotels, or in their own buildings. Some were one-person shops, but most involved a number of employees. "Assistants," as they were called, might work seasonally, perhaps combining teaching with millinery between school terms.[44]

Besides supplying prairie women with the latest in stylish bonnets and caps, milliners provided another crucial service to their customers. They kept women, who were always afraid of becoming barbarized by the frontier, in contact with the civilized East through such fashion magazines as *Godey's Lady's Book,* the latest patterns and designs, and firsthand information culled on their buying trips to larger cities. In addition, informal gatherings in millinery shops offered companionship and support to women who were hungry for contacts with other women. Thus, milliners not only served prairie women in a number of ways, but they also held a respected position in the community as a result.[45]

Although they may seem unusual, these female entrepreneurs did not stand alone among prairie women. Women actually engaged in numerous business ventures. They ran post offices, trading posts, stage stops, hotels, taverns, and inns. They also supplied goods and services through their own dry-goods stores, grocery shops, and photography studios. Like dressmakers and milliners, however, these female business owners usually discovered that hours were long and problems were rife. Most prairie hotels, for example, were rough and inconvenient structures, demanding energy and ingenuity on the part of the women who ran them. Women stored kitchen and other equipment in odd corners, set up their work areas in hallways and on the tops of barrels and boxes, and created acceptable meals from limited resources. Women also supervised personnel, purchased supplies, collected money, settled debts, and pored over accounts. Their days frequently began at six or seven a.m. and ended late at night. Yet, like milliners and other female businesspeople, they often gained a certain sense of satisfaction from running their own shows and achieved a modicum of standing in the community as well.[46]

These female business owners were like milliners in yet another way, because they worked in areas that were associated with women's customary domestic responsibilities. Like the majority of employed women on the prairie, they engaged in pursuits that were closely associated with family-oriented goods and services. They also demonstrated their "feminine" ability to provide aid and care by bringing people mail from loved ones; feeding, housing, and clothing them; and taking their own and their children's "likenesses."

Another area that was particularly suited to women's assumed talent in tending people was medical care. Thousands of prairie women acted as midwives, nurses, apothecaries, and doctors in times of birth, illness, and injury. United States census statistics on female medical workers provide ample evidence that prairie women in the later 1800s worked in a number of medical careers. The 1860 statistics for Missouri indicate that 39 women were midwives. In that same year, Illinois had 168 nurses, Indiana had 115 nurses, and Iowa reported 29 nurses. By 1880, women were serving as surgeons and even dentists. The 1880 United States census listed, for Illinois, 477 nurses, 107 midwives, 68 female physicians and surgeons, and 6 female dentists; for Missouri, 307 nurses, 113 midwives, 68 female physicians and surgeons, and 4 female dentists; and for Minnesota, 121 nurses, 20 midwives, 28 female physicians and surgeons, and 2 female dentists.[47]

Despite the image of the prairies that promoters attempted to project as being a health-giving locale, medical problems were abundant. Childbirth often led to complications. Then, children and adults alike were vulnerable to the common ailments, such as ague and cholera. In 1838 a western traveler called ague the "scourge of the West." Ranging from flu in some people to actual malaria in others, ague caused shakes, weakness, upset stomach, fever, and chills. Even more dreaded was cholera, a disease that swept the prairie in epidemic proportions as early as the plague of 1832. And of course, farm, hunting, and other accidents were frequent in a day of primitive equipment and no safety precautions. Yet there were few trained doctors and no pharmacies to provide assistance with medical problems occurring between birth and death.[48]

Women who assisted others in childbirth were known as midwives, from the English term *mid-wif,* or *with-women.* While midwives had increasingly been displaced by male physicians in America in general, because of the introduction of forceps (which midwives did not know about), formal medical school training that excluded women, and licensing examinations that women who had been denied training could not pass, midwives continued to practice in less-settled regions. Usually holding a respected position in the community, a midwife attended local women in childbirth. Her primary function consisted of helping the mother to deliver a baby as naturally as possible. A midwife might use herbal teas, wine, or liquor to reduce the discomfort, but she usually avoided mechanical devices and drugs. She might be joined in her endeavors by sisters, mothers, aunts, friends, and neighbors of the mother-to-be. Among them, these women laid out the linen, prepared basins and towels, walked the expectant mother about to relieve her distress, and held her as she delivered her baby in a propped-up position or through a seatless chair called a birthing stool. Midwives often participated in virtually every birth in their area; one Minnesota midwife claimed to have seen fourteen hundred babies into the world. Midwives were like other employed women in several respects. They charged for their labor, although payment might be in kind rather than in cash. They also advertised their services in newspapers and business directories. And they adhered to a set of professional standards that in some regions involved examinations and licensing.[49]

Large numbers of women also served as nurses to those who were injured or ill. Many of these were "neighborhood nurses," who attended those in need for wages that ranged from a simple thank you to a cash payment. Others worked fairly regularly for wages, as did Mary Barncard of Minnesota, who worked as a nurse for Dr. William W. Mayo, father of the renowned Mayo brothers of Rochester. Very few early nurses boasted any formal training, because nursing was not yet professionalized. Rather, it was considered as a task to be conducted within the home by women. In 1860, Florence Nightingale's manual, *Notes on Nursing,* which addressed itself to women, opened with the assertion that "every woman is a nurse."[50]

Gradually, however, nursing was separated from women's domestic responsibilities and became paid work that required specialized training. This trend was given a huge boost by the Civil War. Desperately needed nurses were trained in the field, because few nursing schools existed. Huge numbers of prairie women worked as nurses during the war. Perhaps the best known of these was Mary Ann Bickerdyke, a Quaker from Illinois. Known as "Mother" Bickerdyke, this woman gained a reputation as a tireless worker and a fearless administrator in the nineteen battlefield hospitals in which she served between 1861 and 1865. A co-worker of Bickerdyke's who said that Bickerdyke feared nothing, including male hospital administrators, also exclaimed, "Lord, how she works!"[51]

Although for their work, Civil War nurses received only miserably low pay, verbal thanks from President Abraham Lincoln, and a pension of $12 per month, which Congress granted in 1892, they not only established the validity of the concept of women as nurses but also demonstrated the need for formal training. Within a decade after the war, several nursing schools opened their doors. Advocates of improved nursing services also worked for increased professionalization, licensing, and nursing associations. Thus, prairie nurses of the later pioneer period were more likely to have had some type of training than were those of earlier years.[52]

Numerous medicines came from the hands of female apothecaries. As accomplished herbalists, these women picked, dried, brewed, and mixed herbs into medicinal teas, tonics, bitters, or poultices, which they gave, bartered, or sold to those who needed them. Female apothecaries were guided by family knowledge that had been passed on to them and by special recipes for medicine that were included in cookbooks and "doctor" books of the time. They utilized many efficacious herbs that are now unknown by medical practitioners. These included teas made from Culver's root, dandelion, mint, and ginger; tonics made from the butterfly weed, sweet flag root, sassafras bark, and boneset; and ointments of pennyroyal, prairie balm, horse mint, and smartweed. To the natural herbal remedies were added potent medicines prepared from quinine, morphine, and, especially, whisky.[53]

A number of prairie women also became physicians. In Iowa were Dr. Margaret V. Clark of Humboldt and Waterloo and Dr. Rebecca Hanna of Red Oak. In early Minnesota, female doctors were Mary Gould Hood, who graduated from the Women's Medical College of Pennsylvania in 1874; Mary Lizzie Swain, who graduated from Boston Medical School in 1877; and Ethel Hurd, who received her medical degree from the Homeopathic Medical School of the University of Minnesota sometime during the 1880s. Perhaps the best known of all female physicians on the prairie was Dr. Martha G. Ripley, who practiced in Minnesota during the 1880s. As a homeopath, obstetrician, and social reformer, she worked on behalf of unwed mothers and established a maternity hospital. In addition, she was professor of children's diseases in the Homeopath's Medical College and was a well-known lecturer.[54]

Besides ministering to people's bodies, many women also chose occupations in which they cared for people's spirits. Women religious, such as the nuns at St. Joseph's in Minneapolis, were one example of a religiously oriented vocation. Both women religious and lay women also entered the foreign-mission field or became missionaries to the American Indians. The latter was a gradual development, because the boards that controlled western missions were composed of eastern men who did not believe that women could handle the demanding and dangerous tasks involved in being a missionary to native peoples. Eventually these boards hired women to wash, cook, clean, and assist the teachers in prairie missions. Thus, between 1820 and 1850, women increasingly joined missions in the trans-Mississippi West. Here they expanded their responsibilities to include teaching, preaching, and other mission work.[55]

A few prairie women even became ordained preachers, despite the restrictions that most denominations placed upon allowing women to enter the ministry. The 1870 United States census lists two female "clergymen" for Illinois, two for Indiana, three for Iowa, one for Minnesota, and two for Missouri. By 1880 these numbers had increased to twelve in Illinois, five in Indiana, ten in Iowa, two in Minnesota, and four in Missouri. Examples are Mary Safford and Marian Murdock, both of whom graduated from the Unitarian Theological Seminary in Meadville, Pennsylvania, and held pastorates in Humboldt, Iowa.[56]

Other occupations that attracted women demanded no formal training but were also associated in some way with women's domestic aptitudes. One of these that employed huge numbers of women was domestic service. Despite women's frequent complaints that hired help was difficult or even impossible to find on the prairie, records relating to employed women demonstrate that thousands of them labored as nursemaids, cooks, and general house servants for some period of their lives.[57] Unfortunately, male and female domestic servants were counted together by national census takers until 1870. The reports from that year, however, show large numbers of women working as domestic servants; by 1880 the numbers were even greater. In Indiana, for example, 21,342 women were working as domestics in 1870; by 1880 the number had grown to 26,538. Illinois was the prairie state with the largest number of female domestic servants—42,046 women worked as domestics in 1870, and 51,106 did so in 1880.[58]

Women, frequently young women, became nursemaids and governesses to children who were often not much younger than they. Their duties ranged from basic childcare to rudimentary instruction in reading, writing, elocution, and arithmetic. Wages were often meager but were supplemented by room, board, and such other extras as clothing or the use of a horse. An Illinois woman was especially fortunate in finding a pleasant position as a nursemaid and governess after her graduation from a female academy in 1869. She cared for three young girls on a cattle ranch and also instructed them in basic school subjects because their mother mistrusted the country schools. The nursemaid went home to Jacksonville every few weeks; and in between, she enjoyed the kindness of the family and the use of a pony named Ben. Not all nursemaids were this fortunate, however, and others complained about cramped quarters, unruly children, and poor pay.[59]

Women also worked as cooks. During the 1830s, Sarah Welch Nossaman of Iowa was paid the grand sum of seventy-five cents a week to cook in an open fireplace for forty men who were building a mill. She was pleased with her pay, however; not only was it the highest ever paid in that locale, but it also allowed her to buy the first ready-made clothes that she had ever owned. Other cooks worked in family situations, as did Kate, who was employed by the Fuller family of St. Paul in 1860. According to a daughter of the family,

Kate could prepare a tasty meal of oyster soup, roast turkey, and plum pudding when she felt "disposed to astonish the natives."[60]

Other evidence suggests that many cooks were black women. The Cooper County, Missouri, census of 1851 listed a number of free blacks, among whom were Dido Wood, aged forty-eight, and Fanny, aged fifty, both of whom were cooks by occupation. A woman referred to as "Black Ann" not only received the kudos of passengers on the Mississippi steamers on which she was a cook, but she also earned enough money to buy her own freedom and that of her children. And in Sioux City, Iowa, Pearl Street was named after a pioneer black woman who arrived on a steamboat during the early 1860s and gained a local reputation as a cook. It is believed that Pearl regularly competed with yet-another black female cook called Aunty Wooden, who was locally renowned for her opossum dinners.[61]

Women also worked as maids and general servants. On the prairie, hired girls were particularly in demand during the spring and summer as domestic assistants to farm wives who were harried by such seasonal chores as canning and cooking for threshers. Because their numbers were smaller than the demand, some families brought help with them from the East when they migrated to the prairie. More than one mother sent servants, white or black, with newly married daughters to the West as wedding presents. Most women, however, hired maids and servants once they had established their new homes on the prairies.[62]

Employers registered a wide range of responses to their female help. Female employers often complained that white servants were "uppity," requiring many dispensations and privileges.[63] Various ethnic groups received their share of criticism: Irish servants were disparaged as drinkers, and Scandinavian help in Minnesota was seen as inept and untidy. Servants of all backgrounds annoyed their employers by taking large amounts of time off, usually due to illness or family problems. It not infrequently turned out that they had actually been securing more amenable positions for themselves.[64] Black servants, on the other hand, were described as loyal, willing, and usually competent. Although black women constituted a much smaller proportion of domestic laborers than did immigrant women, they seemed to have gained a better reputation among employers. Anna Ramsey of St. Paul wrote to her daughter that Martha, Anna's maid, performed many duties, from housecleaning to packing the family's clothes for trips. Ramsey regretted the onset of Martha's old age, which necessitated her retirement, and continued to refer to her as "beloved" Martha.[65]

Female cooks and domestics also worked for larger establishments, such as restaurants and hotels. Members of the Yoacham family felt that they could not have run the log hotel that they constructed in Westport, Missouri, during the 1830s without the assistance of black maids and cooks. White hotel maids also performed critical services, which included scrubbing floors, making beds, washing and ironing clothes, washing dishes, cooking meals, and baking bread, cookies, and cakes. Women's contributions to such businesses thus tended to be crucial but very low paid on the prairie frontier.[66]

Another occupation that women practiced, particularly in prairie towns and cities, was prostitution. Here, again, women provided a "domestic" service of sorts. Known as soiled doves, ladies of the night, and a host of other appellations, prostitutes offered their sexual favors anywhere there were large numbers of men, especially itinerant or unattached ones. The river towns along the Mississippi and Missouri rivers, the rough and rapidly growing boom towns, the rail and shipping centers, and the bustling state capitals—all provided prime markets for the wares marketed by prostitutes. Predictably, the thriving frontier city of Chicago attracted many prostitutes. Female settlers in Chicago at mid century complained that prostitutes roamed the streets, operating just as openly as the thieves, gamblers, and confidence men. Even after frontier days, prostitution continued to be such a flagrant ill in the city that in 1899 the newspaper *Skaninaven* made an unprecedented attempt at social control by listing the names of Norwegian women who had been arrested during a police raid on one of the twenty brothels owned by the infamous madam Sadie Richards.[67]

Typically, prostitutes could easily be located through hotels and inns. In fact, men often expected a frontier hotel to provide such services as a matter of course. One entrepreneur, when writing to a land speculator who was planning to open a hotel in Pontiac, Illinois, recommended to him not only an experienced hotel manager but also a "fine lot of beautiful ladies" who would be an "ornament" to the new establishment.[68] "Fancy ladies" were also to be found in taverns, tap rooms, dance halls, and, of course, bordellos. Red-light districts and tenderloin zones contained brothels that helped to support towns through fines and taxes but greatly distressed both the respectable citizenry and business owners who wished to attract more stable and permanent population to their towns.

As towns grew in size and importance, there was usually an accompanying movement to reduce or repress prostitution within their boundaries. Because prostitution usually had its supporters as well as its opponents, municipal antiprostitution ordinances often amounted to little more than a series of fines levied on brothel owners, employees, and patrons. For instance, the town of Bloomington, Illinois, passed a series of restrictive ordinances beginning in the mid-nineteenth century. One of Bloomington's early antiprostitution measures simply established prostitution as a misdemeanor and levied a fine of $100 upon anyone who maintained, was an inmate of, or contributed to the support of a "disorderly house, or house of ill-fame, or place for practice of fornication." Some twenty years later, the proceedings of the Bloomington City Council indicated that instead of disappearing, prostitution still existed, as did the arrests and the fines. In 1884, twenty-two employees and eight owners of houses of ill fame and disorderly houses were arrested and fined.[69] Frequently, such fines were imposed in a regular way that amounted to little more than having brothel owners and prostitutes pay a fee to the local government in return for relatively unhampered operation. This system had the advantage of bringing in badly needed revenue to governmental coffers, pleasing those who wanted prostitution to continue, and offering assurance to antiprostitution factions that some action was being taken against prostitution.

Although a large number of the occupations discussed here were town-based by nature, this was not a feature of all women's employment. Numerous women also engaged in farm labor. Because a higher proportion of agrarian occupations existed on the prairie than in more settled regions, it is likely that more people, including women, worked at farm-related jobs. Certainly, some farm writers of the nineteenth century recognized and advocated the need for young women to be educated in the agricultural pursuits that would be an integral part of their lives.[70]

Census figures reflect some of the many women who were employed in farm work, particularly those who received wages for their labor or who owned farms. As with other occupations, the United States census did not begin to enumerate female farmers and female agricultural laborers separately from their male counterparts until 1870. Though the numbers for this year and for the following census in 1880 are not huge, the figures show that women definitely did farm in the prairie states. Illinois, for example, reported 775 female farmers and 244 female agricultural laborers in 1870. Minnesota, by comparison, had fewer female farmers in 1870—only 90 were reported; but it had more female agricultural workers—403. By 1880, Illinois had a total of 1,739 female farmers, while Iowa and Indiana had 955 and 982, respectively.[71]

Thousands of other female farm workers and owners were less visible for a number of reasons. Many of them held farm employment for only a short period of their lives. Alice Money Lawrence shepherded one hundred sheep for the summer of 1865 in order to earn tuition money for a term at Albion Seminary.[72] Others were wives who ran farms owned by their husbands. These women were seen as farm wives rather than farm owners. Yet, an Iowa woman whose husband held several political positions during the early 1860s actually ran their farm on her own. Similarly, a Norwegian woman settler in Minnesota during the 1860s, lived on the farm alone with her two small children, fully operating it, while her husband practiced his trade as a bricklayer and plasterer in nearby towns.[73] Still other women farmed alongside their husbands. Another Norwegian settler in Minnesota, Bertha Sonsteby, began to do heavy farm labor at the age of eight and simply continued the practice after her marriage. She helped to build the house, planted trees, and did her share of the outside work, as well as all of the inside chores. In later life she claimed that "there isn't any kind of work which I have not done."[74] And widows who took over or bought farms after the deaths of their spouses tended to be seen as widows, rather than as farmers. This oversight occurred even though many widow-farmers owned considerable land and conducted all of their own business affairs.[75]

The Homestead Act of 1862, which offered 160 acres of government land to any "citizen or intending citizen" who was the head of a family and was over twenty-one years of age, after he or she had lived on it for five years, increased the numbers of prairie women who farmed their own land. The Homestead Act was especially attractive to widowed, deserted, or divorced women who had children to rear. However, because much prairie land had already been claimed by the mid 1860s, the Homestead Act did not have as large an impact on female land ownership as it would have for later generations of women settlers farther west.

Although farm labor and farm ownership did not fit a strict interpretation of women's domestic sphere, both involved skills and abilities that were believed to be peculiarly female. Women farm workers and owners "helped" other family members, particularly men. These women cared for and nursed plants and animals. They produced such household goods as fruits, vegetables, eggs, butter, and cheese. They supervised and trained children, who worked alongside them in the field and the barn. And they held home and family together by contributing their labor to the continued existence of their family's farmsteads.

Other women, who more rigidly interpreted the nineteenth-century prescription to remain within their domestic sphere and thus did literally stay within their homes and yards, were still cash workers. Not only did they produce the numerous foodstuffs and other goods needed for their families' survival but they also generated much-needed cash income. Like their female counterparts who worked for pay, these women were also gainfully employed, even though no wages or paycheck ever passed through their hands.

The "butter and egg" money that women earned is perhaps the most widely known form of home income production. Historian Gilbert Fite has pointed out that butter was a primary cash product in agrarian regions, its income often keeping farms financially afloat during the rocky years.[76] Women themselves were well aware of their economic importance to fledgling farm operations. May Lacey Crowder of Iowa remarked: "Frequently enough while the men were learning to farm the women and children actually supported the families. They raised chickens and eggs for the table, raised the vegetables and fruit, and made butter to sell in exchange for things not produced at home. The women were not unaware of this fact and were quite capable of scoring a point on occasion when masculine attitudes became too bumptious."[77]

Women sold not only butter and eggs but all types of surplus produce. Margaret Murray explained that her "mother sold butter Eggs & Beeswax

& anything we could spare off the farm in the summer and fall we gathered Blackberries, wild grapes & anything we raised on the farm that would bring money or exchange for groceries." When Murray's aunt and uncle worked together constructing a brick-drying kiln, her aunt realized that she could use the kiln to dry fruit as well. She soon earned one dollar selling kiln-dried peaches.[78] Bigger profits were to be had as farms and locales became more settled. An Illinois woman of the 1870s told about milking her first cows by hand, thus producing only enough milk and related products for the family's consumption. Then, she got a cream separator, and refrigerated railroad cars reached a nearby town. She began to make butter, which she packed in 25-, 40-, or 60-pound-size wooden tubs and shipped to commission houses in Chicago, thereby making a tidy profit for herself.[79]

Textile products were other items produced and sold by numerous prairie women. During the 1840s in Iowa, young Kitturah Belknap discovered that she could add a few coins to the savings box that was to finance the family's new home by making a few extra pieces of linen for sale while she was doing her own spinning and weaving. Other women spun woolen thread, wove cloth, knitted socks, pieced quilts, fashioned carpets on looms, and braided rugs for sale to neighbors or local merchants.[80]

Fowl and animals were also raised by women who intended to sell them or their produce. Chickens and their eggs were an all-time favorite, but cows and hogs were popular as well. May Lacey Crowder's mother even combined cow raising, which sustained her lucrative trade in butter, with raising hogs, which were fed on the surplus milk. This tactic was so successful that within a few years, hog raising constituted the family's principal industry.[81]

Taking in boarders was yet another method that women devised in order to bring in the cash that often saved their menfolk from "going under," as Emery Bartlett of Grinnell, Iowa, said.[82] Although taking boarders into already-crowded quarters created considerably more work for women, it did generate income. Iowan Matilda Peitzke Paul cared for herself, her husband, two baby girls, and a hired man; yet she agreed to board the local teacher for two dollars a week. Paul said that the rent from the boarder "helped out a little."[83] When a branch of the Rock Island Railroad cut through the Newtons' Iowa farm, they boarded some of the laborers. With the Newtons and their five children, this created a large and demanding household of eleven people for which Mary Ann Newton had to care.[84] Paradoxically, some women were so successful with boarders that they, like a Missouri widow and her daughter, eventually had to hire help to assist them with the additional work.[85]

Apparently, the prairie frontier offered female settlers the chance to engage in a number of jobs, occupations, professions, and cash-producing activities. Prairie life did not, however, redefine in any basic way the concept of women's work. Men's employment included a huge variety of jobs, ranging from

farmer to explorer to minister. In addition, men's jobs were often characterized by a great deal of mobility, both from one type of job to another and
from one place to another.[86] But women's employment, from midwifery to
millinery, continued to be thought of primarily in terms of what it was
"proper" for women to do, rather than allowing them to respond to the needs
and to exploit the opportunities of the new land.

6
Employment and Income Production on the Plains

Plainswomen, much like prairie women, often added jobs, professions, or income-producing activities to their already-considerable domestic responsibilities. Although the economic pursuits of plainswomen varied slightly from those of prairie women in nature and extent, they shared two very important characteristics. Plainswomen's employments were determined primarily by gender expectations—that is, what it was thought acceptable for women to work at—and they differed noticeably from the occupations of plainsmen.[1]

On the Great Plains, men pursued a great number of jobs, while most women found their opportunities more limited. Farming, ranching, mining, railroading, business, and the professions were all open to males but seldom, or only in a restricted way, to females. For example, gold deposits in the Dakota Territory lured men to become miners, while the women who accompanied or joined them were miner's wives and daughters, teachers, milliners, and prostitutes. The Plains offered men the chance to ranch and to herd, while women usually ran the ranch home, perhaps sewing, writing, or teaching for income on the side. Even shopkeeping, a necessary enterprise in a land of settlement and development, held out vast promise to men at the same time that women generally worked as clerks, seamstresses, milliners, and boardinghouse keepers.

Census figures indicate that the number of paid working women on the Plains was relatively low compared to that of working men. In 1870, for example, 160 women and 5,727 men composed the labor force in the Dakotas. In that same year, the Kansas labor force had 6,509 women and 117,344 men; Montana's, 171 women and 13,877 men; Nebraska's, 1,894 women and 41,943 men; and Wyoming's, 300 women and 6,345 men. The figures increased for both women and men who were employed during the decades between 1870 and 1910, with gains in ratios of women to men in a few cases. By 1910 there were 19,363 employed females to 28,714 employed males in South Dakota;

29,045 females to 188,372 males in North Dakota; 80,694 females to 540,639 males in Kansas; 159,896 females to 188,851 males in Montana; 37,811 females to 63,303 males in Nebraska; and 6,013 females to 68,593 males in Wyoming.[2]

As on the prairie and, indeed, as in older, more settled areas, many of these employed women worked as teachers. Because teaching was widely seen as an extension of women's childcare skills and because it involved lower wages than most men were willing or able to accept, female teachers outnumbered male teachers in all of the Plains areas. In 1870 there were 15 female teachers as opposed to 5 male ones in the Dakota Territory; 12,273 females to 2,763 males in Kansas; 2,217 females to 449 males in Montana; 10,442 females to 1,564 males in Nebraska; and 843 females to 152 males in Wyoming. By 1910 the female:male teacher ratios had changed to 4,638:857 in North Dakota; 12,273:2,763 in Kansas; 2,217:449 in Montana; 10,442:1,564 in Nebraska; and 843:152 in Wyoming.[3]

Teaching in a Plains school demanded much from these women, including a willingness to accept low pay, poor conditions, seasonal employment during winter or summer terms, and responsibility for schoolroom maintenance.[4] As one young Kansas teacher of the 1880s described her situation, she held a three-months' contract to teach seventeen students, ranging in age from six to thirteen, during the summer months, when they assuredly would have preferred to be out of doors. Her school was a small frame building without benches, seats, a blackboard, or a teacher's desk. On her first day of school she noted: "I am now sitting on the floor with my paper on 'the Teacher's chair,' which is as high as my chin (almost). For seats we have two boards placed on rocks." A few days later, still awaiting the arrival of schoolroom furniture, she contemplated teaching as a career: "I think I like it. I know I would like it better if things were different." Some of the furniture arrived, but then cleaning the schoolhouse soon proved to be an onerous chore. After one particularly exhausting cleaning session, she commented that "it was very hard work, the floor was quite dirty." On the last day of the term she rejoiced: "It is all over and done with. And I am just a little glad, and considerable tired."[5]

When Laura Brown Zook began her teaching career in Custer County, Montana, in 1886, she confronted a number of similar problems. A trustee of the school board, who was a local rancher, loaned her a horse, told her that her wages would be $65 a month and that her board would cost her $12 a month. "Was I ever thrilled," she later exclaimed, "seventeen years old and earning so much!" Then she added, "I earned it all right." Homemade benches, a blackboard, and a teacher's desk were the sole contents of the schoolroom, which she took great pride in keeping exceptionally clean. She finished her four-months' term despite rumors of Indian troubles, warnings from local military officers to stay home, and a terribly hard winter.[6]

Another teacher's account from 1904 showed that conditions had improved little in frontier schoolrooms over the years. She held a five-months' contract that paid $35 dollars a month, plus board with a student's family. Her school was located a quarter of a mile from her boarding place, and she had "to climb mountains" to reach it. She found that she had to be a strict disciplinarian; the teacher who preceded her had left after a day and a half because she could not control the children.[7]

Also in 1904, Martha Stoecker began to teach school in a room that was furnished with "a fine, big hard coal stove, old rickety table, a chair, two planks and four boxes." Although the planks were placed on the boxes to make seats for the pupils, they were so uncomfortable that Stoecker let her students sit on the floor and put their books and slates on the planks, which were used as desks. She burned scrap lumber from building projects until the school board finally supplied some coal. When proper furniture finally arrived, Stoecker "bought some material for sash curtains, put up pictures and we looked quite cozy." During one particularly dangerous blizzard, she tied her teacher's apron of black sateen over one boy's head, tied towels, dust rags, and scarves over the other children's heads, and with hands joined, led them through the storm to the hotel. For such labors, she received $40 per month.[8]

That discipline was a problem that Plains teachers faced consistently, one that did not subside throughout the decades, was reinforced by the 1884/85 diary of an eighteen-year-old Kansas teacher, Clara Conron. After only a few weeks in the classroom, Conron wrote: "I like teaching sometimes and then again I don't. I think it is rather trying to ones nerves and mine are rather 'touchy' I am afraid." A few days later, after "whopping" one of the older male students, she plaintively added, "O my, I think school teaching is very trying." Conron's diary entries were representative of many young, inexperienced female teachers who were confronted by less-than-ideal schoolroom conditions and a number of "big boys" among their students. In the words of another young woman, it was "necessary to use a good deal of firmness" to control her students. After successfully managing a number of disciplinary incidents, including introducing her own unique plan for "preventing whispering and laughing," she was asked whether a woman could govern a schoolroom as well as a man, a query to which she simply and confidently responded yes.[9]

The stories of several other Kansas teachers reveal many additional difficulties involved in educational situations. One who began teaching in 1890 at the age of sixteen was paid $20 per month to instruct ten students. She rented a pony for 25 cents per day, which she rode the nearly twenty-mile round trip to her school. The schoolhouse was a 14-foot-square sod hut, with half windows, a dirt floor, and no plastering on its walls. Because her students brought their own books according to whatever the family might own, she had to teach "many classes." When another young Kansas teacher of the 1890s learned that she was financially unable to pursue the college training that she longed for, she began to teach at the age of seventeen. She had a seven-months' contract, paying $30 per month to instruct eighteen pupils. "I had to study as hard as any of my pupils to keep ahead of them," she later wrote, "and it was considered quite a disgrace for a teacher not to be able to solve all the problems in arithmetic." She added: "The schools were not graded so very well and the equipment was very poor. We had no libraries as the schools have now."[10]

Some teachers devoted their full energies to teaching, while others combined teaching with some other type of economic pursuits. Anna Webber, for example, taught full time during the 1880s and early 1890s in various townships in Nebraska and at the Kansas Industrial School for Girls in Beloit, while Sarah Jane Price of Nebraska saved enough money from her small teacher's salary to buy a farm, which she worked while continuing to teach. Other female teachers were homesteaders, and one even became a cook on a trail drive to North Dakota during the summer of 1885.[11]

Other women teachers sought to improve their economic status by taking the position of county superintendent of schools. Although this was a demanding job that required regular travel to inspect county schools and their teachers, it was frequently held by women who were either appointed or elected to it. In Park County, Montana, women consistently held the post of superintendent from the founding of the county in 1887 until well into the twentieth century. In another Montana county, Mary Johnstone served first as principal and then as county superintendent during the early 1880s. Accompanied by her sister, she traveled from school to school in a light buggy, drawn by one horse, over dangerous roads, boarding with ranch families along the way.[12]

In some cases, marriage terminated these women's careers; in others it did not. Johnstone, like the majority of women teachers, ended her career as a county superintendent when she married, a practice that was required by many school districts. Other women, however, kept on teaching and serving as principals and county superintendents after they had wed. One of these was Adelia Spohr of Bozeman, Montana, who married but continued to teach and was soon elected to the post of county superintendent, which she held for several terms.[13]

A few women managed it all: teaching, homesteading, serving as a county superintendent, and marriage. One of these was Grace Reed Porter of South Dakota. She left her job as head of the Latin Department of Boone, Iowa, high school in 1906, when she became interested in land opportunities in South Dakota. Along with several other teachers and some family members who filed on adjoining claims, Reed entered her homestead claim. She then took a job teaching a school one and a half miles from her claim, to which she rode a borrowed pony. Her school included pupils of all eight primary grades, one who wanted first-year high-school studies, and several who could

not speak English. In 1908, Reed took on the duties of deputy superintendent for the county. Every week she traveled on inspection tours during the
week and rode twenty miles to her claim to work it on weekends. In 1908
she successfully ran for county superintendent of schools on the Progressive
ticket. After hiring two women homesteaders to run her office, Reed set out
on her inspection trips by horseback. She explained: "I ate and slept in road
houses and in private homes. One night one of the teachers and I slept in
a bin filled with fresh oats." In 1909, this energetic woman introduced teacher-
training institutes while writing bonds for new schoolhouses and helping to
find markets for those bonds. After she married a horse rancher in 1910, she
continued to serve as county superintendent until 1913. She then lectured
at teachers' institutes and in 1914 became the principal of the Fort Pierre
high school, where she taught history, coached girls' basketball, and ad-
ministered the school until 1918.[14]

Although the employment of women as teachers in "white" frontier schools
on the Plains has received some attention from historians, much less notice
has been paid to the many female teachers who chose to work with Indian
students. One example is Thisba Hutson Morgan, a physician's daughter who
was born in Montour, Iowa, and was reared in northwestern Nebraska. She
taught Oglala Sioux children at the United States Government Boarding
School on the Pine Ridge Agency, South Dakota, between 1890 and 1895.
Rather than boarding around with students' families, as teachers in white
schools did, Hutson lived in one of Pine Ridge's two three-story dormitories,
which contained the students' and teachers' rooms, classrooms, the dining
room, the kitchen and bakery, the laundry, and sewing rooms. Hutson's room,
which opened onto her classroom, was furnished with a regulation iron bed,
dresser, table, chairs, and a few personal possessions of her own. Kerosene
lamps illuminated the rooms, while Franklin stoves provided the heat for
the one hundred female and one hundred male students and their teachers.

Hutson had different contacts with and obligations to her students than
did most other teachers on the frontier. Her first task regarding new students
was to cut their hair, bathe them, dress them in white-style clothing, and
force them to wear "awful brogans," furnished by the government. Once the
students were in the classroom, Hutson, who spoke no Indian dialects, found
it necessary to devise her own sign language, to reach children who could
speak no English.[15] Hutson's daily experiences differed from those of other
teachers in additional ways. As she proceeded to teach her students English
and the other subjects that were dictated by governmental policy, Hutson often
found visitors in her classroom, ranging from Chief Spotted Horse to a steady
stream of inspectors who were sent by the Indian Office in Washington, D.C.
In the course of her five years at Pine Ridge, Hutson also witnessed many
tragedies, including the killing of Sitting Bull and the Battle of Wounded
Knee, both in late 1890.[16]

That the jobs of teachers of Indian students differed in many ways from those of their colleagues who were employed in white schools is further illustrated by the case of Elaine Goodale Eastman, a teacher on the Great Sioux Reservation in Dakota Territory between 1886 and 1891, when she married a Sioux physician, Charles A. Eastman. According to her, she rejected service in the white classroom in favor of Indian students because she felt a "call" to help the "newly transplanted, leaderless, bewildered little community." Goodale's copious writings concerning Indian problems, in combination with her memoirs, which were written in the late 1930s, show a woman and a teacher who accepted the superiority of white culture yet also came to see Indians as complex and creative individuals. She was often torn by her own ambivalence over the stated governmental policy of rejecting and destroying "everything characteristically native without regard to intrinsic values." She herself wore moccasins, a practice for which she was taken to task by a colleague. On another occasion, she was rebuked by a reservation official for traveling for several days and nights with an Indian family. When "solicitous white friends" urged her never to travel with Indians unarmed, she judged them to be "poor psychologists and poorer realists." To her, complete trust in her native companions was her "sole and sufficient guarantee of safety."[17]

Like so many other female teachers on the frontier, Goodale eventually moved up to the position of superintendent. By 1890 she was serving as governmental supervisor of all the Indian Schools in South Dakota, a position that required a good deal of traveling to perform her visits of inspection. During the summer of 1890, Goodale visited the Pine Ridge school and came into contact with Thisba Hutson. The two young teachers immediately found that they had much in common, and Goodale invited Hutson to accompany her on an inspection tour into an area that Hutson described as "a region rarely frequented by white people." Camping throughout the Dakota Bad Lands, they survived the ravages of a prairie fire and a blinding rainstorm in order to visit and evaluate isolated teachers in one-room day schools established to serve outlying native groups. After her marriage to Eastman, Goodale turned her attention to the duties of wife and mother. Yet, while raising her six children, she did collaborate with her Sioux husband on nine books about native life, aided him in his career as a physician, lobbyist, and lecturer on behalf of Indian peoples, and, by herself, wrote plays and four children's books about Sioux life.[18]

Teachers of another type who worked with American Indians were those who served as missionaries to Plains Indian groups. Their goal was to teach natives the tenets of Christianity, the "three R's," and elements of white culture and value systems. One of these was Mary Clementine Collins, who served as a Congregational missionary to the Sioux people in the Dakotas between 1875 and 1910. Collins was first stationed at the Oahe mission, two miles upstream from Yankton, the territorial capital. Here she worked to educate Sioux Indians, who, according to her, were living in terrible poverty and despair. In 1885, Collins's career took a slightly different direction when she relocated to the outstation of Standing Rock, near Grand River, a small mission that eventually became one of the most successful of those established by the Congregational church. She later commented that Standing Rock was where her "real labor for the people began." Here, Collins not only served as a teacher to the Sioux people but also became known as a medicine woman among them because of her knowledge of a number of simple remedies and treatments. She participated in reform movements that were designed to modify United States governmental policies toward Indian groups.[19]

Yet another group of missionaries, teachers, and nurses to Plains Indians were members of the many religious orders who dedicated their careers to serving native peoples. Because of the fine work of historian Susan C. Peterson, the contributions of these women religious have been brought to light during recent years. Peterson has documented the arrival of the first small band of the Presentation Sisters in Dakota Territory in 1880, their gradual emergence as effective parochial-school teachers and hospital builders, and their fortitude as frontier settlers and laborers.[20] She has similarly reconstructed the work and energy of the Sisters of St. Francis among the South Dakota Indian missions between 1885 and 1910 and that of the Grey Nuns at Fort Totten Indian Reservation in Dakota Territory between 1874 and 1900. Peterson has shown that in their career activities, women religious, like lay teachers, often found themselves limited to prevailing stereotypes of "proper women's work."[21]

Another "suitable" employment for women was domestic service, particularly as servants and nursemaids.[22] This job had widespread appeal because it required no special training beyond that received at home or from the employer and was considered to be a suitable economic pursuit for most women (but not those of the upper class), because it was an extension of their domestic sphere. By 1870, 4,002 women were working as domestic servants in Kansas, while 1,285 were doing so in Nebraska. By 1910 these figures had reached 11,771 in Kansas and 10,760 in Nebraska.[23]

Domestic service attracted a wide variety of women. Orphans and young girls from poorer families frequently became helpers in a family home in return for room, board, and a small wage. When Etta Parkerson learned in 1874 that she could no longer continue her education at Kansas State Agricultural College, she became her uncle's housekeeper for room, board, and one dollar per week. Barely twenty-one years old and with a serious deformity of her back, Etta ran her storekeeper uncle's Manhattan household and cared for his hired helper, who boarded with them. On one Saturday, Etta "baked light bread, made brown bread, cooked meat and potatoes for dinner, cooked applesauce, and rice, swept, made beds, washed dishes, got the meals, scrubbed the floor, and spent the evening in stirring cream." Another Saturday she was up until 1 o'clock in the morning doing her chores. At one point, Etta grumbled, "I wonder if I shall always be obliged to drudge."[24]

One variant of domestic service was employment as a cook, waitress, or chambermaid in restaurants, hotels, or on large farms and ranches.[25] Some women alternated housekeeping in a private home with work for one of these types of employers. One Dakota woman worked in a private home during the winter and cooked for farm crews during the summer. In 1880 she secured a job as cook for a crew of thirty men on a "bonanza" farm, where she received a good salary and had a male helper to carry fuel and water, cut meat, and wash dishes. Her duties included planning and producing the meals, baking all the pies and bread, and helping on Mondays with washing the clothes of all the farm helpers. Similarly, in 1910 a Wyoming woman cooked for fifty people in a long tent with a dirt floor. With her sixteen-year-old female helper, she "cooked in big black iron kettles" and baked breakfast rolls in "big black pans." Their table dishes were simply "gray enameled pie plates."[26]

Domestic service also attracted black women. Many white employers viewed serving as cook, washerwoman, nursemaid, or maid as logical and appropriate derivations of the roles that black women had fulfilled as slaves. Limited in the area of employment by both gender and race, black women were often forced to take domestic service jobs despite their ambitions to enter other types of employment. From these menial positions, however, black women sometimes became keepers and owners of hotels and boardinghouses.[27]

While a great number of women worked in jobs such as teaching and domestic service, which seemed to be a direct extension of their domestic duties, others engaged in business pursuits that were also commonly domestic in orientation. These included the running of boardinghouses and hotels. Sarah Millard Schultz ran a boardinghouse and managed the Park County (Montana) Poor Farms after her divorce in the 1880s; and Percie Matheson Knowles, also of Montana, ran a boardinghouse that she converted into a health resort after her husband's death in 1910.[28] In yet another Montana town, a black woman known as Aunt Tish converted a former brothel into a fine dining room and boardinghouse, thus establishing a business reputation that she refused to tarnish by even speaking to the other black woman in town, a madam known as Mammy Smith.[29]

Women also commonly served as postmasters, a job that was often done in their homes and was frequently combined with or parlayed into some other business. Sarah A. Robertson of Montana served as a postmaster and hotelkeeper and was also known to sing, dance, and pick the banjo for the amusement of her customers.[30] Martha Waln, a Wyoming woman who left her husband because of his alcoholism, both served as postmaster and ran a small shop in her home. She gave up her shop to become a traveling peddler, then joined the Watkins Medicine Company as a traveling salesperson, later returned to her home base of Ten Sleep to establish a small retail store, and finally bought a small ranch. Still other women worked as salesclerks or ran their own shops, usually selling household and medical items.[31]

Other popular business ventures for women were those associated with the needle trades. Women worked as milliners, dress and mantua makers, and seamstresses. In Kansas in 1870 there were 439 milliners and 256 seamstresses, while in Nebraska there were 115 milliners and 57 seamstresses.[32] Such enterprises were attractive to women because they offered employment that was judged appropriate for women, paid better wages than some of the alternatives, provided relatively steady work, and made it possible for women to own their own businesses. In addition, such employments offered opportunities to earn extra money by supplying a wide line of goods, including collars, cuffs, gloves, ribbons, needles and thread, children's wear, and such hair pieces as artificial braids, switches, and curls. Moreover, seamstresses and milliners often derived satisfaction from providing psychological services to plainswomen who found solace in their workrooms and shops, where they chatted with other women and tried to remain in touch with the "civilized" East by means of catalogues, pattern books, and models.[33]

The services of seamstresses and milliners were in wide demand on the Plains, especially in towns. Although one might reasonably think that women were too busy settling and improving the Plains to follow current fashions, few women lost their interest in eastern modes of dress. Many of them assiduously studied *Godey's Lady's Book*, fashion magazines, and catalogs. They also turned to other women for help in remaining stylish. As early as 1864 a southern lady who was new to the rough mining town of Virginia City, Montana, found her fashionable bonnet carried off by the local milliner, who wanted to copy its style.[34] Plainswomen typically rejected sunbonnet and calico whenever possible, a characteristic that was illustrated some years later when a young woman in Lincoln, Nebraska, sent her sister a letter filled with elaborate descriptions of the latest bonnets, ribbons, gloves, frizzes, and artificial curls, along with detailed advice on how to wear them properly. According to a South Dakota woman, during the 1880s and 1890s, plainswomen were also intensely interested in "ruffles, buttons, bows and beads . . . leg-of-mutton sleeves lined with crinoline . . . the 'hobble' skirt and 'tube' dress," as well as French plumes for hats, white kid gloves, and confining corsets.[35]

Evidently, this ongoing interest in sartorial matters created a demand for milliners and seamstresses even during the early years of settlement. In fact, on buying trips to Omaha, Chicago, and other cities, Plains milliners often recruited workers, and milliners who migrated found their skills easily marketable. When Mary Macrae came to Wyoming in 1887, she found her talents as a seamstress much in demand by a Laramie dress shop that was already employing two other women. She related that "in those days it took much more time and money to have a new dress; the entire dress was lined and interlined; it would usually take two or three days at the least to finish a dress." She added that the material cost from $1 to $5 a yard and that she earned $1.25 a day for her labor.[36]

Besides business ventures, some women entered a variety of professions other than public-school teaching. They did so in far lesser numbers than in those job areas already discussed because of the social and legal barriers to women's entering most professions and because of the difficulties that women encountered in obtaining the necessary specialized training. Because most professions were seen as being removed from the domestic sphere, there was widespread prejudice against women's entering them. Still, several women became successful and well-known photographers in the decades after the Civil War.[37] Some became skilled typesetters, printers, and telegraphers.[38] Others became writers and newspaper reporters. At least one of this last group, Alice Nelson Page, owned and published her own newspaper in Grand Forks, North Dakota.[39] Still others began to practice law, notably Ella L. Knowles, who became the first female attorney in Montana in 1889, and Grace McDonald Phillips, who was the first woman to practice law in Wyoming, although she was the second one to be admitted to the bar in that state.[40] Sarah E. Gardinier practiced dentistry and dental surgery in Wyoming during the early 1890s.[41] In 1900, Annette B. Gray came from her training at the Moody Bible Institute in Chicago to the pastorate of the South Congregational Church in Cheyenne, Wyoming.[42] And in 1902, Agnes Mathilde Wergeland, a Norwegian woman with a Ph.D. from the University of Zurich, became professor of history and Spanish, and soon a poet and writer as well, at the University of Wyoming.[43]

Medical care, because it was so often given by women to their families and friends, was much easier to visualize as a possible profession for women than were those mentioned above. As a result, women commonly practiced medicine as nurses, midwives, and doctors. When the widowed nurse Jean Todd of Edinburgh, Scotland, arrived in South Dakota in 1887, she not only practiced nursing but also served as midwife and mortician. Another widow and nurse, the Englishwoman Ellen Robinson, owned and operated a hospital in Wilsall, Montana, during the early 1900s.[44] A number of black women also practiced nursing.[45] Some of these women turned to nursing without any training, seeing it as a logical extension of women's family duties, while others were fortunate enough to receive formal training.[46]

Women physicians, however, often had medical training. German-born Friede Feige learned medicine in her homeland and practiced it in Dakota Territory during the 1880s, while her minister husband homesteaded. She also raised eight children, two of whom became physicians. Abbie Ann Jarvis, who was already a wife and the mother of four children, acquired her medical training at the Women's Medical College in Chicago, graduating fourth in a class of twenty-four in 1898. She was thought to be both the first licensed woman doctor and the first licensed woman pharmacist in South Dakota.[47]

Another group of employed females who followed a profession of sorts—
one that is closely related to one of women's common domestic activities,
sex—was the numerous prostitutes who worked in the towns scattered across
the Plains. They were known by many euphemisms, including *nymphs du
prairie*, Mary Magdalenes, soiled doves, calico queens, sporting ladies, girls
of the night, fancies, and painted cats.[48] In some areas the presence of prostitutes was further obscured by census takers who listed them under such
occupational labels as cook, dancer, housekeeper, or not employed. Yet, in
other places, census-data takers not only counted prostitutes but also recorded such details as their race or national origin.[49]

Recently, scholars have used census data, police records, newspapers, and
other sources to demonstrate that numerous women, usually unmarried
and between fourteen and twenty-three years of age, worked as prostitutes.
The majority of prostitutes and madams were white, but a number of black
women worked at these jobs as well.[50] The prostitutes often arrived in
cattle towns in early spring, with the opening of the cattle-shipping season,
and departed in September, when the season ended. In the cattle towns of
Abilene, Wichita, and Dodge City, Kansas, among others, the young male
population rose dramatically during the summer months, with males out-
numbering females by two or three to one, a situation that the prostitutes
exploited.[51] Court and other official records indicate that while prostitution
was illegal in these towns, the laws were loosely enforced, and prostitutes
were "taxed" through a series of regular fines, which provided badly needed
funds to town governments and allowed the prostitutes to operate without
much interference. As the century progressed, however, so did restrictive
measures.[52]

Prostitutes and "brothel districts," or "tenderloins," also developed in other
types of towns. Newspapers, court dockets, plat maps, city directories, and
other local records show that in the "respectable" railroad town of Grand
Island, Nebraska, the first brothel, built in the mid 1880s by a husband-
wife team, was only the beginning of the growth of the town's "burnt
district." As in the cattle towns, Grand Island's prostitutes operated freely
for a number of years during the nineteenth century but far less openly after
the turn of the twentieth century.[53]

The mining towns at the far-western edge of the Plains had their brothel
districts as well. In fact, in Helena, Montana, between 1865 and 1886, prostitution was the largest single source of paid employment for women. Some
prostitutes only worked Helena during the summer months, when the mines
were open. Even in their busiest season, prostitutes were regularly fined
but not run out of business.[54] Nor were such infamous "hurdy-gurdy" halls,
or dancing "saloons," as "Chicago Joe" (Josephine) Welch's Red Light Saloon
seriously threatened during the boom years.[55] After the Northern Pacific
Railroad had reached Helena in 1883, bringing in families and business-

people, the legislation and reform campaigns that began to attempt to control prostitution had driven most prostitutes underground by the beginning of the new century.[56] In nearby Butte, a similar antivice campaign led the city attorney's office to shut down the town's tenderloin district in 1917.[57]

Still another area that provided jobs for plainswomen, and in a sense a surprising one, given the heavy labor that was often involved, was agriculture. Of course, many plainswomen had engaged in farm work in their European homes; thus, both women and men were accustomed to the idea of women's working the land. In addition, labor was scarce on the Plains, so it was frequently necessary for plainswomen to work outdoors. Certainly the Homestead Act of 1862 and the Kinkaid Act of 1904 encouraged women to take up land. It might also be hypothesized that caring for soil, crops, and animals was simply another part of women's domestic duties; if she could aid family members inside the home she could also do so outside it.

Census figures indicate that a significant number of women did work at farm jobs. Using the Plains state of Kansas as one example, the census of 1870 showed that 299 of the women who were listed in the agricultural category were farmers, while ten were laborers and one was a dairywoman.[58] In Nebraska, as another example, 29 women farmed, while 2 were farm laborers; but no dairywomen were listed.[59] By the end of the first decade of the twentieth century, these figures had jumped to 6,505 women engaged in agriculture in Kansas, including 3,936 farmers, 3,439 laborers and "forewomen," and no listing at all for dairywomen. Similarly, in Nebraska, of the 5,279 women who worked in agriculture, 2,718 were farmers, with the rest being laborers and forewomen.[60]

Of course, these figures for female agriculturalists excluded married women who "held down" the family farm by living on it and often actually farming it while their husbands worked elsewhere for the money to develop these farms. Since land was both so difficult to conquer and so crucial to family survival, as well as to eventual success, there was even more pressure upon plainswomen than was usual on other agrarian frontiers to aid in demonstrating that people could endure and maybe even prosper on a Plains farmstead. Laura Ingalls Wilder wrote that she, like so many plainswomen, felt a great need to prove that "farming was as good as any other business," a desire that led her and many other women to live alone or with their children on isolated farms for months on end.[61]

The census also tended to overlook female ranchers and trail hands, although anecdotal evidence demonstrates the existence of both single and married women who engaged in these occupations. There are documented cases of women in Kansas, Montana, Wyoming, and Texas who ran ranches and drove their own cattle to distant markets or worked as partners with their husbands as helpers who undertook a variety of tasks, ranging from cooking to wrangling cattle.[62]

Another group of women whom the census takers would not have counted as farm laborers or farmers consisted of the great numbers of women who participated in farm work along with their menfolk. In a representative case, the Wells family of Wyoming, an unmarried man was aided by his unmarried sister and widowed mother in building his homestead into a ranch. Lucy Wells recalled that her mother drove the wagon through the fields, while she and her brother Charles threw rocks in it to be hauled away. Lucy later wrote: "I always worked outside, just like a man. I could handle the horses, milk cows, mow and rake in the fields—in fact, I have done everything there is to be done on a ranch except plow."[63]

Other women agriculturalists who were often left out of census data were former wives who continued to run family farms and ranches after divorce or the death of a spouse. In these cases, women had to support themselves and usually children as well, supplying yet another reason why women's agricultural labor might be considered acceptable. One North Dakota widow initially rented her farm after her husband's death, but she found town life so distasteful that she and her children soon ousted the renters and resumed farming with the help of a hired man. A Montana woman ran the family dairy operation quite successfully for several years after her husband's death. And a Kansas widow continued the family farm operation, so that at the time of her own death in 1894, her schedule of property included not only numerous household goods but also farm equipment and such valuable stock as several horses, cows, and a bull.[64]

Yet another sizeable group of female farmers were "girl homesteaders," as they were commonly known. These women were sometimes included in census tabulations, but other times were not. They did, however, appear regularly in land records. One investigator, who sampled the land-office data in Colorado and Wyoming, discovered that 11.9 and 18.2 percent of the homestead entrants were women. In addition, the data showed that 42.4 percent of the women "proved up" their final claim, whereas only 37 percent of the men did so.[65]

Despite their numbers, women homesteaders have received only occasional notice from historians of the Plains. Everett Dick was one of the few who discussed the phenomenon, maintaining that a "noteworthy proportion of the first settlers were single or unattached women." In an essay on homesteading, Dick included the case of a woman claimant who was almost crushed in the mass of applicants who pressed into the Beatrice, Nebraska, claim office. Another historian of the Plains, Mary W. M. Hargreaves, has cited a source estimating that as many as one-third of the homesteads in Dakota Territory were held by women in 1877.[66]

Women homesteaders have also received occasional mention in the writings of novelists. Mari Sandoz, as a case in point, recalled the many women homesteaders who poured into her area of Nebraska during the early

1900s. According to her, they were classified as either "Boston school-teachers," who were known for their genteel ways and graying hair, or "Chicago widows," who were somewhat more colorful and gay. Sandoz added that "in the largely male population of our homestead region more of the Chicago widows got married than the Boston school ma'am type." Whether they married or not, Sandoz's description indicates that women homesteaders were a common sight in Nebraska during her girlhood.[67]

These women were not thought to be oddities in other states either. It was widely accepted that they used the opportunity to gain land that was offered first by the Homestead Act of 1862 and later by the Kinkaid Act of 1904 as a chance to look for husbands, to seek investments, to earn money for additional education, to find a way to support their children after being widowed or divorced, to add to a husband's farm or ranch through their homestead claims, or to homestead as part of a family or companionate group. Furthermore, women homesteaders were the products of a slowly liberalizing attitude toward women during the last two decades of the nineteenth century and the opening decades of the twentieth century, which freed them from much criticism from their peers.

Homesteading appealed to many types of women who were in need of employment. Enid Bern, a member of a North Dakota homestead family, remarked upon the number of young single women who were seized by "Homestead Fever."[68] While the majority of women homesteaders were, just as Bern noted, young women who had never been married, the opportunity to claim free land also attracted a number of widowed women with children or widows of fifty or sixty years of age who had only themselves to support. One widow with two children became a Kansas homesteader during the early 1880s after learning that a number of her friends were starting off to Kansas to take up timber claims. She recalled: "I jumped up, saying, 'I am going to Kansas.' In a few minutes I left the door with my collar in my mouth and putting on my cuffs, and I was soon on the train to join the western party." Her venture turned out quite well: she entered a timber claim and also took a homestead of one hundred and sixty acres, receiving four years' credit on it for her husband's war service. Cora D. Babcock was another widow who took up a South Dakota claim after her husband's death in 1884.[69] Divorced and deserted women also became homesteaders. One recently divorced woman who had a four-year-old daughter boarded a train for Montana, where she chose a 360-acre homestead, which had a 14-by-16-foot shack with two windows, a door, and a shingled roof. Another case was that of Kate E. May, a divorced Oklahoma woman who joined a land run to obtain a homestead to support herself and her four-month-old child. Other "single parents," as they would today be called, also courageously decided to take up homesteads on their own in order to support themselves and their families.[70]

The decision to homestead was not purely an economic one for many women who were also lured by what Bern termed the "enchantment" of the land or what homesteader Edith Ammons Kohl saw as the "wild adventure" of homesteading.[71] Abbie Bright maintained that her "desire to cross the Mississippi and a love of traveling" caused her to seek a piece of homestead land.[72] Another woman remarked that letters from homesteading cousins in Wyoming gave her the urge to go "apioneering."[73] In 1904, Martha Stoecker, without articulating her reasons, reacted positively to a letter of invitation from her brother to join a party of homesteaders; but after more reflection, she felt that it would be "a thrill" to own her own land. She also recognized the venture as an opportunity to see Dakota, "that awfully barren state we'd heard so much about in the song 'Dakota Land,'" a dubious inducement, because the song ended with the lines, "We do not live, we only stay / We are too poor to get away."[74]

Once established on their claims, many women found that beautiful scenery and an aura of adventure were frequently offset by the hard work involved in the undertaking. Yet most women demonstrated an admirable measure of pluck and daring in their jobs as homesteaders. They took on tasks and mastered skills that had not been part of their repertoires before coming to the Plains. One young teacher-homesteader in her mid twenties learned to use a rifle effectively. On one occasion she killed a "pesky gopher" with her rifle, and on another "shot 5 little birds to make broth of." The Erickson sisters not only learned to use rifles, but they added carpentry and wallpaper-hanging to their list of skills. And a Montana woman picked rock from her land and dug her own cellar.[75]

When confronted by tasks that they could not handle, women homesteaders turned to men for help. Fathers, brothers, friends, and hired hands filled the breach when necessary. Susan Carter planted her own corn and beans, but she had to hire a well digger to create her water supply while her future husband broke sod for her. Similarly, Abbie Bright planted her corn, hoed her beans and peas, and worked on her claim shack; but she paid to have her dugout constructed, and she relied upon her brother Philip for help with much of the heavy work of the claim.[76] With no male friend or relative to depend upon, Bess Corey hired men to break sod, put up fencing, construct her frame shack, and build a dam. A Montana woman similarly hired neighboring homesteaders to break her land, remove the rocks, and seed forty acres in flax.[77]

The claim shacks were not usually very attractive dwellings for women who had been accustomed to well-established homes and domestic work places. The first cabin that homesteader Abbie Bright shared with her brother in Kansas in 1880 was 12-feet square, with a fireplace made of sticks daubed with mud. According to Bright, the roof was "split limbs covered with dirt," which had a "growth of sunflowers and grass on it." When she moved to her own claim in 1871, Bright lived in a 12-by-14-foot dugout in the side of a hill:

> A fire place, and chimney were dug out and built up at one end, plastered with mud and it answered well. . . . My bed in the corner has one leg. . . . Then comes my hay filled tick, and my bed is a couch of comfort . . . in the corner at the foot of the bed are boxes and various things including the tub, which is often pushed under the bed. Boxes are nailed to the wall, in which the table funature [sic] is kept, also some groceries. Chairs are pieces of logs.[78]

Homesteading near Mitchell, South Dakota, in 1880, Cora Babcock described her first home as a "little sod shanty." By 1881 she had replaced it with a "little framed house," which measured 9 by 12 feet and had a shingled roof, a half-window, and one door. A Montana homesteader of 1886 recalled that her shack was 12 feet square and had a cellar, where she kept her fuel "to keep it from blowing away." The house was furnished with a bed, a trunk, a bookcase, a wardrobe, a cookstove, and cupboards made of "goods-boxes."[79]

Homestead shacks had changed little by the first decades of the twentieth century. One Montana woman who homesteaded in 1910 moved a 14-by-20-foot frame shack to her claim. Her furniture consisted of a bed, a table, a few chairs, and a "small fourhole coal cookstove." Her table was homemade, and her cupboard was simply several shelves nailed in the corner, with white muslin curtains across the front. A Wyoming woman of the same period described her 12-by-14-foot shack as a "tiny adobe," with one door and one window, and furnished with a homemade bedframe; a table with two loose boards, so that it could be used as an ironing board; a small cookstove; a washstand; cupboards made of crates; and an old trunk, placed outside to serve as a refrigerator. Snow, which drifted in through the open laths, covered the interior with a fine dusting of flakes, a predicament that was solved with the common remedy of covering the shack with tar paper.[80]

A variety of other problems faced women homesteaders. Some feared and detested the ever-present snakes, particularly rattlesnakes.[81] One Nebraska woman in 1909 remembered with distaste "gumbo mud," scarce water, and torrential spring rains.[82] A North Dakota woman who homesteaded in 1907 disliked the scorching sun and her many non-English-speaking Russian neighbors.[83] Another homesteader in South Dakota during these years complained about high prices, the drying effect that the wind and hard water had on her face, and the lack of flowers and trees.[84] Others despaired over the ever-present dust and dirt, which no amount of house cleaning could remove.[85]

The difficulties of homesteading overwhelmed some women, who eventually deserted their claims and returned to their former homes. One such woman explained that she was fond of life on the Plains but that she was

not able to make a living from her land. With her old job awaiting her in
Chicago, she reluctantly proved up her claim as a future investment and
left South Dakota. Assessing her homesteading years, she wrote: "From a
business standpoint the whole venture was a losing game, since I did not
realize enough from my holding to cover what I had spent. But I have always
considered it a good investment. . . . I had a rested mind and a broadened
outlook. I always say—and mean it—that I would not give up my pioneering experience for a fortune."[86] Others simply felt that life on the Plains
was too different from their former homes and lives. In 1911, Anna Erickson
wrote to her parents that she and her sister had decided that they didn't
want to live permanently in North Dakota: "it's too much of a change." She
added that although they liked the state, they longed for all the amenities
of their Iowa home.[87]

Despite the problems, many women found much to enjoy and cherish in
the homesteading experience. They regularly emphasized how much they
liked Plains living, noted the opportunities that it offered, and decided to
remain on the Plains for the rest of their lives.[88] Many women found the
comradeship involved in homesteading to be very satisfying. Myrtle Yoeman,
a 1905 homesteader in South Dakota, was pleased that her grandmother's,
her father's, and her aunt's claims all lay within a few miles of her own.
In addition, she wrote to a friend that "we have very good neighbors here."
Mary Culbertson and Helen Howell, friends who homesteaded together in
Wyoming in 1905, were delighted that they had settled on adjoining claims
and had built one house, which straddled both pieces of land and in which
they both lived, each sleeping on her own side of the property line.[89]

Edith Eudora Ammons Kohl particularly recognized the influence of what
might be termed collegiality in successful homesteading. Around the turn
of the twentieth century, she and her sister Ida Mary Ammons took up an
"improved" claim, boasting a 10-by-12-foot tar-paper shack, that was located near Pierre. Initially disillusioned and homesick, they quickly decided to head "back East." But this resolution was rescinded when they met
a large number of "girl homesteaders" already in the area. Encouraged to
stay, the sisters supported their claim by teaching school and by publishing
a newspaper, then moved on to a more promising claim where they established a post office, a newspaper, and a store.[90]

Throughout her account of her homesteading years, Kohl emphasized that
she and Ida Mary gradually came to see many advantages in homesteading
for women. They soon realized that although women homesteaders worked
hard, they also led satisfying lives, took delight in the countryside, and frequently lost their desire to return to their former homes. Although the
demands of the Plains environment were great, Kohl believed that a woman
"had more independence here than in any other part of the world." When
she was told, "The range is no place for clingin' vines, 'cause their hain't

nothin' to cling to," she felt it was a challenge that she was learning to meet. For her, the hardships of wresting a living from the Plains "were more than compensated for by its unshackled freedom. . . . The opportunities for a full and active life were infinitely greater here. . . . There was a pleasant flow of possession in knowing that the land beneath our feet was ours."[91]

That women derived much satisfaction from their employment as homesteaders has been supported by a recent in-depth study of women homesteaders on Colorado's northeastern homestead frontier, which revealed that there were expanded opportunities for responsibility and power for women within the family and community, greater equity between women and men, new friendships and mutual reliance between women and men, a quickly improving standard of living, and great possibilities for future economic gains—all benefits that far outweighed the drawbacks of homesteading for most Colorado women who tried it. These findings were substantiated by another study, which noted the high percentage of women who participated in the Oklahoma land runs of the 1890s and early 1900s. Despite the incredible tension and even violence associated with these land runs, women entrants were numerous. Hundreds of women's names appeared in the lists of claimants who registered in the land offices after such contests. The authors of the study thus concluded that women were instrumental in the development of Oklahoma's homestead frontier.[92]

By the beginning of World War I, homesteading on the Great Plains had become so popular among large numbers of women that farm and other journals regularly carried articles encouraging women to homestead and giving them instructions about how to do so effectively. One such essay, written by a woman homesteader in South Dakota, offered advice concerning legal procedures and the costs of claiming, the clothing and equipment needed, and the use of a rifle. Interestingly, other articles debated the feasibility and "social righteousness" of women who took up farming on their own. One of these concluded that "farming is one of the industries that has longest been open to women" and added that it was the "perfect occupation for women who have a taste for country life. . . . The sources of information about methods in farming are everywhere open to her."[93]

Of course, it must be remembered that employed plainswomen also, unless they were fortunate enough to have paid help, labored within their homes as well. Even single employed women, who frequently faced fewer domestic demands because of the absence of a spouse and children, had to contribute to their own household or to the ones in which they lived. The diary of Sarah Jane Price, an unmarried woman teacher in Nebraska, indicates that in addition to teaching, she also farmed her own place and performed all the necessary home production and maintenance tasks as well. Similarly, the diary of Abbie Bright reveals that she wrote articles for the *Wichita* (Kans.) *Tribune*, worked her claim, and spent innumerable hours baking bread; cook-

Women often assumed duties outside the home as well as inside. Mrs. Bertie Lord, with a coyote that she shot on the West Fork River in Montana around 1900. Courtesy of the Montana Historical Society, Helena.

(Right) From dropping seed into axe-cut slashes in the earth to using more advanced technology, women engaged in planting. Nancy Hendrickson planting corn in Morton County, North Dakota, around 1918. Courtesy of the State Archives and Historical Research Library, Bismarck, North Dakota. (Below) Despite their "delicate" nature, frontierswomen often engaged in field work. Spring plowing on the Stasney farm a few miles south of Mandan, North Dakota, 23 April 1906. Courtesy of the State Archives and Historical Research Library, Bismarck, North Dakota.

(Top) Ella Martfeld, "girl homesteader" in Wyoming, outside her shack around 1910. Courtesy of the Museum Division of the Wyoming State Archives, Museum, and Historical Department, Cheyenne. (Bottom) Numerous single, divorced, and widowed women homesteaded on their own or with their children. Four "girl homesteaders" outside a tar-paper claim shack, circa 1907/8. Courtesy of the South Dakota State Historical Society, Pierre.

(Top) Some women engaged in heavy labor, as these working with a sawmill crew near Pekin, North Dakota, did around 1897–1900. Courtesy of Jim Erickson Photography, Devil's Lake, North Dakota. (Bottom) Employment as store clerks attracted numerous women. Dry-goods store, Lakota, North Dakota, undated. Courtesy of the State Archives and Historical Research Library, Bismarck, North Dakota.

Providing diversion for men created employment for scores of frontierswomen. Josephine Hensley, a dance-hall and hurdy-gurdy-hall proprietor known as "Chicago Joe," around 1880. Courtesy of the Montana Historical Society, Helena.

Era Bell Thompson, who homesteaded with her family in North Dakota in 1914, became a leading woman journalist and author. Painting by Skaug, 1977, in the Rough Rider Hall of Fame in the State Capitol, Bismarck, North Dakota. Courtesy of the State Historical Society of North Dakota, Bismarck.

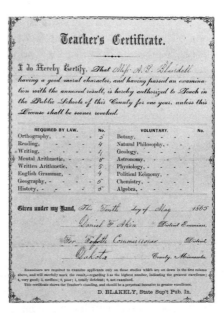

(Right) Thousands of frontierswomen supported themselves or helped to support their families by becoming teachers. Teacher's certificate issued to Anne Grace Blaisdell on 10 May 1865 in Dakota County, Minnesota. Courtesy of the Minnesota Historical Society, St. Paul. (Below) Many women became missionaries and teachers on American Indian reservations. A Miss Ganson, with Flathead Indian children in Montana, August 1910. Courtesy of the Montana Historical Society, Helena.

ing; washing, ironing, and starching clothes; sewing; and cleaning the shack, which included sweeping the floor with turkey wings because she had no broom. And the letters of Bess Corey relate in detail her teaching activities, farm and other work on the claim, and such domestic chores as baking bread and preserving sand cherries and other fruits.[94]

In their domestic roles within the home, plainswomen who were not otherwise employed frequently earned cash income, or wages of sorts, which they contributed to the family coffers. These "wages" resulted from the sale of goods produced by women, which ranged from textiles to butter and eggs. One example of such domestic enterprise was Anne Davies of Kansas, who, during the 1880s, carried on a brisk trade in butter and eggs while her husband traveled to various construction jobs and her father did the outdoor work of the family farm. Davis received 20 to 28 cents per pound for her butter and 14 to 18 cents a dozen for her eggs, figures that seem small even for the 1880s until one discovers that Davis sold as much as 8 to 10 pounds of butter at a time and as many as 21 dozen eggs per sale. On one occasion, she purchased 300 pounds of flour with the money that she had earned by selling only 7 pounds of butter and 6 dozen eggs. In addition to her dairy enterprise, Davis conducted most of the family's business, cared for her children, and filled out her days with washing, ironing, churning, baking, canning, sewing, and milking the cows.[95]

Other women sold a large number of goods and services. Some baked bread, pies, and cakes for local customers, raised chickens for market, or sold the produce of their gardens. Others wove rugs for sale, sewed and knitted garments and socks, or washed, ironed, and mended for pay. Many took in boarders: female or male teachers, male laborers, freighters, travelers, ministers, and cowboys. Some "worked out" as domestics to bring in much needed cash.[96] And some even became part-time authors and journalists, usually emphasizing family and domestic matters in their writings.[97]

Women often added considerable amounts of cash to the family income, often to the surprise of the men of the family, who frequently considered female activities incidental. After Lucy Wells and her mother had developed a number of ways to make money, they paid $500 in cash for a piece of land to add to the family ranch, which was owned by Lucy's brother, Charles. Lucy related a common male attitude when she recalled that Charles "had never paid any attention to my business and Mother's . . . and was amazed at our thrift."[98]

Of course, many women often combined work outside the home before marriage with income production in the home afterward. One Norwegian-born woman repaid her passage to America by working in hotels for $1.50 a week, by plowing with a walking plow pulled by oxen for $1.00 a day, and by hauling hay. After her marriage, she produced butter and eggs for sale, earned a heifer calf by caring for her brother-in-law's cow, and then added to what became her successful livestock venture by trading her husband's watch, unbeknownst to him, for a second heifer. With her help, the couple soon expanded their South Dakota farm and built a spacious, comfortable home on it.[99]

Apparently, the customary image of plainswomen that portrays them as only domestic creatures laboring diligently, and without pay, alongside their men in family enterprises is far from being a full picture. Rather, many plainswomen engaged in an unexpected number of jobs, professions, and income-producing businesses, both outside and inside their homes. Moreover, plainswomen held income-producing employment for much of their lives. Many worked not only when young and single for a few years before marrying, but they often chose lifetime employment with or without marrying. Even those who stayed primarily within their homes often found many means of earning income to enhance their family's financial position.

In the majority of cases, women's jobs and economic pursuits were shaped and limited by the prevailing ideas about acceptable female activities. Life as settlers on the Great Plains involved an untold number of employment possibilities for men, but it expanded women's economic horizons little. As in other regions of the United States, women's jobs continued to be defined largely by gender. While plainsmen developed the resources of the Plains as farmers, ranchers, miners, soldiers, explorers, and entrepreneurs, women commonly focused their lives on family first and only secondarily on employment.[100]

7
Community Participation on the Prairie

During the early 1830s a nationwide reform movement began to develop in the United States. As reformism grew, it drew numerous women into activities and causes that reshaped their lives and values. Consequently, although the widespread belief in the sanctity of the domestic sphere remained intact, the boundaries of that sphere expanded greatly, to encompass the larger community outside the home. Soon, women were accepted as moral housekeepers within their homes and social housekeepers in their communities. Although this trend first emerged in eastern cities, it soon appeared on the midwestern prairie as well, where women freely drew upon eastern thinkers and innovations as models.

This is not meant to suggest that prairie men did not also participate in community-improvement activities. Men did, of course, serve on school and church boards, promote such reform movements as temperance and the abolition of slavery, and hold political office. But men did not have to fight for their right to do these things. Education was primarily for males, as was politics. And early temperance and abolitionist organizations were male as well. Women had to argue for the right to be educated, to participate in politics, and to become involved in the community, using their imputed morality and "caretaker" role as rationales. Once their rights were recognized, women often found themselves segregated in a "female" school, a women's temperance society, or a women's political group. When integrated with men, women almost always had less say, less power, and less influence than did the men.

Women's push to reform and improve American life and institutions had many early proponents in the East. The editor and writer Sarah Josepha Hale was one of the first women to urge other women to expand the domestic realm by the pursuit of reading and writing of morally improving literature, of education beyond the female accomplishments, of charity work, of the creation of

148

voluntary associations, and of temperance reform. As the new editor of *Godey's Lady's Book* in 1837, Hale explained that under her leadership the mission of the magazine would be to "carry onward and upward the spirit of moral and intellectual excellence in our own sex, till their influence shall bless as well as beautify civil society."[1] At the same time, the very popular novelist E. D. E. N. Southworth gave her readers strong and capable heroines as models, while Elizabeth Fries Lummis Ellet championed the cause of historical women who nurtured democracy in early America, helped fight the Revolution, and contributed to the settlement of the frontier. The best known of the advocates of women's moral guardianship was Harriet Beecher Stowe. From a family of reformers and deeply involved in social reform herself, Stowe's early essays and stories discussed such issues as temperance and improved education for women.

Although these writers exhorted women to expand their duties and responsibilities, they were also very careful not to deprecate the customary view of women's place in the family. These advocates of women's involvement in a community supported a view of women that emphasized their moral guardianship of a home and family first and community second. According to these writers, women were highly moral and virtuous people who had a deep responsibility to family members, friends, neighbors, and those in need. Therefore, reform inside and outside the home was the duty of women, who, because they were superior beings, had to serve as moral caretakers of family members and had to increasingly act as guardians against the evils that existed in society as well.[2]

Women who lived on the prairie frontier soon became aware of these emerging ideas regarding women's roles and responsibilities as moral guardians. They were exposed to these beliefs especially through reading newspapers, books, and journals. Even during the early stages of settlement in any region, many prairie women managed to find time to read. And many women who had little formal education filled their homes with books, which they read in spare moments.[3] These women considered reading an important and enjoyable undertaking in a land that denied them so many other aspects of "civilization." As early as 1836, Julia Barnard of Missouri wrote to her aunt that her family had brought "a good stock of books" with them, which they took turns reading aloud.[4] Some years later, an Illinois settler explained that on Sundays, neighbors would come to hear newspapers, journals, and literature of the day read.[5] Other women wrote about family reading and study sessions, buying books from itinerant peddlers, having "plenty to read," and reading more than women who lived in eastern cities.[6]

Ladies' books, including *Godey's,* were popular on the prairie. Frontier newspapers regularly advertised the various ladies' books and magazines. In 1859 a Saline County, Missouri, woman wrote to her sister that she and her companions were just finishing reading a recent issue of the *Ladies'*

Repository.[7] Women who could not afford their own individual subscription to one or more of these women's journals joined with other women to form subscription clubs, each member putting in twenty-five or fifty cents toward the purchase of a three-dollar annual subscription for the group. In 1849, *Godey's* announced that it had "received a club of four subscribers" from the "rather remote settlement" of St. Paul, Minnesota.[8] When the journal arrived, members shared it, then passed it on to friends, neighbors, and relatives, who also read the articles and stories and studied the fashion plates in it. Those women who could not read listened attentively as family members and friends read to them or distilled the thoughts that they had gleaned through reading.

Besides reading ladies' journals, prairie women also read the works of E.D.E.N. Southworth, Elizabeth Ellet, and Harriet Beecher Stowe, which were readily available. For instance, Southworth's novel *The Hidden Hand* was serialized in the *Burlington* (Iowa) *Daily Hawk-Eye* in 1859.[9] Advertisements in other prairie newspapers promoted not only the works of Southworth, Ellet, and Stowe but also books by such authors as Lydia H. Sigourney, Caroline Lee Hentz, Eliza Leslie, and Catharine M. Sedgwick, all widely read and much loved in their own time. Called domestic novels because of their homey themes, these books often went through multiple and even world-wide editions. Repeating the message that women were moral caretakers of home and society, they reached the eyes and ears of significant numbers of women.[10]

Prairie women read widely in a range of other types of materials. Almanacs, gazetteers, household-hint books, and etiquette books were often mentioned by women in their diaries and letters.[11] Such newspapers as the *National Intelligencer,* such periodicals as *Harpers' Magazine,* non-American-language publications, such young peoples' magazines as the *Youth's Companion,* and such farm journals as the *Garden Arbor* often came to settlers' homes on a subscription basis.[12] Women also read books, including travel accounts, works on philosophy and religion, morally improving literature such as *Pilgrim's Progress,* current novels, and works on agriculture.[13]

Reading was done not just at home but in special groups and organizations as well. Women formed literary societies and reading groups, in both urban and rural settings. Joining together in one another's homes or in a church or school building, they read and discussed a wide array of books, from the classical to the contemporary. In 1880 the Philomathian Society of Bloomington, Illinois, studied "lessons" in works by nineteenth-century British authors, including Sir Walter Scott and Lord George Gordon Byron.[14] These organizations also sponsored public programs and lectures, which informed others about literary works and topics as well as encouraging them to read more by themselves.[15]

As they read, especially in lady's magazines and domestic novels, women found that they were being encouraged to enhance their supposedly inborn moral powers through continuing their educations. A number of these women had already realized how important education was to them. They longed for more education, and some were already studying on their own when schools did not exist or were denied to them for other reasons.[16] The discovery that improved education was becoming a moral imperative for women gave an easily acceptable rationale for improved female education, as it was beginning to be called.[17]

At the same time, developments in women's education in the East during the early and middle parts of the nineteenth century provided a vigorous model and an impetus for prairie settlers who were interested in better education for women. Catharine Beecher was particularly active in attempting to reform female education. During the 1820s, Beecher, with her sister Mary, ran the Hartford Female Seminary in Connecticut. During the 1830s she established the Western Female Institute in Cincinnati, where she collaborated with William H. McGuffey on his famous readers. Beginning in the 1840s, Beecher publicly lectured and wrote on the cause of improved female education. She crusaded for teachers to be sent West and for normal schools to train teachers to be established on the frontier. She also traveled to Indiana, Illinois, Missouri, and Iowa, promoting women's education and laying the groundwork for women's schools, notably the Dubuque Female Seminary in Iowa.[18]

During this period, Mary Lyon of Massachusetts took the revolutionary step of raising funds for and organizing the first woman's college in the United States—Mt. Holyoke College—which enrolled its first student in 1837. Over the years it provided a model for other women's schools. In the opening address of the Iowa Female Collegiate Institute in Iowa City in 1853, Dr. Charles O. Waters pointed to Mt. Holyoke: "Mt. Holyoke Female Seminary has already done much to bless the world by making American mothers worthy of the name." He added that the Collegiate Institute would similarly prepare women "to accomplish the grand and lofty mission of their sex," which would deeply alter the moral tone of the entire Republic.[19]

Along with revised concepts of women's education came innovative notions regarding women's health and physical training. Catharine Beecher was one of the first to argue that women's responsibilities as wives and mothers required a robust physical condition, stamina, and endurance.[20] These new ideas concerning women's education quickly gained support in prairie locales. As early as 1827 the *Missouri Intelligencer* (Fayette) maintained not only that education would help women become better mothers but also that because women's influence reached into every part of society, a moral and happy society would result from giving women a large degree of "mental improvement."[21] Other writers, too, espoused the then-current view that education would enhance the moral abilities of women, thus improving their effectiveness as caretakers both at home and in the community.[22]

As a consequence of these changing views regarding women's education, literally hundreds of women's high schools, academies, and seminaries that offered secondary education to women sprang up all over the prairie. These schools were private institutions, which relied upon tuition fees as their primary source of income. There were no formal qualifications for teachers, nor was there any licensing process. As a result, curriculums diverged greatly in the subjects that were offered and in the quality of the instruction.[23]

The manner in which these schools advertised their offerings bespoke a confidence that seemed not to be consonant with their limited resources and experience. Numerous seminaries and academies claimed to teach such subjects as orthography, reading, writing, English, mathematics, science, geography, history, philosophy, business, French, Spanish, German, Latin, and Greek. The female accomplishments were usually taught as well, including music, pianoforte, drawing, painting, fancywork, and embroidery. Some schools asserted that they specialized in college-preparatory work; and others, in teacher training. The type and number of courses that a student selected determined the amount of tuition paid, with prices ranging around $5 for a ten-week term in basic subjects, an additional $2 to $5 for advanced subjects, and $2 to $10 more for music and the ornamental arts.[24]

Although their claims may have been grandiose, ladies' academies and seminaries produced achievements in their students that met with approbation from many observers. In 1843 a Missourian who attended the graduation exercise of the Columbia Female Seminary deemed the pupils' performances an exhibition of "rare merit." During the ensuing years, a number of others who reported upon the closing exercises of women's schools were pleased that women had received training to become "vigorous and effective thinkers and speakers."[25]

Although some new conceptions of women's education evidently were developing, many women's schools dedicated themselves to preparing women for a life of quiet domesticity, rather than for participation in the larger community beyond the home. When the Dubuque Academy opened in Iowa in 1838, its founder promised women a solid education in basic subjects, as well as proficiency in ornamental needlework and pianoforte in the school's "female department." Although some changes were taking place, many people still agreed with the French commentator Jean Jacques Rousseau: "The whole education of women ought to be relative to men. To please them, to be useful to them, to make themselves loved and honored by them, and to make life sweet and agreeable to them—these are the duties of women at all times, and what should be taught them from their infancy."[26]

That other prairie schools continued to emphasize the domestic arts and to neglect traditional academic areas was indicated by the harsh critiques of several close observers of women's education. During the 1830s the English writer Harriet Martineau was especially incensed by the weak and domestically oriented curriculum of a young ladies' school that she visited. She particularly disliked the public exhibitions of the students' proficiency or, in her view, their lack thereof. She scathingly wrote, "The poor ignorant little girls take degrees . . . their heads must be so stuffed with vain glory that there can be little room for anything else."[27] Martineau complained that the only possible life course open to women educated in these ways was marriage. The Swedish writer Fredrika Bremer was even more vitriolic than Martineau concerning the low grade of women's education in the West. Visiting St. Louis in 1850, Bremer reported disgustedly that women were physically weak because of their "effeminate education" and that they lived a constricted "harem life" in which they were the pampered sultanas and men were their subjects.[28]

What was at issue in these high schools, seminaries, and academies was not whether women would work or pursue careers after graduation, for such ideas were yet in their infancy, but whether women would confine their activities within the walls of their homes or would move into community affairs alongside men. The traditional view that women would remain in the home held strong sway. School after school operated "female departments," segregated women's and men's classes, and built separate buildings for women students and for men students. Numerous other schools limited themselves to instructing only women students. Although coeducation seemed to come easily to small rural schools that had limited numbers of fairly young students, it was a greater problem when students who were approaching adulthood and were preparing themselves for adult duties based on gender were involved. The implications of the suggestion that women might actively participate in community matters were as yet unclear. If women were to take an active role in community activities, did that mandate their receiving educations like men's in the same classrooms as men, which some educators argued.[29]

Segregation by sex was also an issue at the college level. When Iowa College moved from Davenport to Grinnell in 1858, both female and male students at first used the same building because of lack of space. But separate facilities were soon provided at a "safe" distance from each other. During the Civil War, the withdrawal of men students for military service decreased the need for and the feasibility of gender segregation at Iowa College, as well as at other schools. After the war, however, many institutions quickly resumed the practice. In 1866, Iowa College widely advertised its Ladies' Department and its Ladies' Boardinghouse.[30] The segregation of students by gender in prairie high schools and colleges was not unique to the region, but it was at least partially a result of having schools model themselves after eastern institutions, where ladies' departments, seminaries, and colleges were very popular. In 1865, Vassar College, in Poughkeepsie, New York, opened its doors to a class of 353 women. In 1875, Smith College, in Northampton, Massachusetts, and Wellesley College, in Wellesley, Massachusetts, both exclusively for women, opened.

Coeducation developed haltingly in prairie colleges. When the State University of Iowa opened in 1856, it was coeducational only in its Normal, or teacher-training, Department. When members of the Board of Trustees attempted to bar women from the normal school in 1858 as part of a retrenchment program, they encountered great resistance and quickly dropped the plan. Women began to receive degrees from the Normal Department in 1857 and bachelors' degrees from the university in 1863. Having accepted support from the Morrill Act of 1862, which provided grants of land for agricultural colleges, the school also had to accept the mandate that its program be coeducational. The presence of female students often created confusion, because the school tried to treat them equally by integrating them into a male-oriented curriculum. One result of Iowa State's attempt at absolute fairness was uniformed women, who toted rifles and performed drills in mandatory military-science programs. At the same time, the school tried to speak to the special needs of its women students, and under the leadership of Mary B. Welch it instituted one of the first domestic-science—or, in modern parlance, home-economics—programs in the United States.[31]

Clearly, the question of how women would use the knowledge that they had acquired or the degrees that they had been awarded by prairie colleges and universities was a thorny one. Like secondary schools, these advanced institutions of learning did not usually advocate jobs or careers for women. The common conception remained that the majority of women would become wives and mothers. What a woman was to do with the segment of her education that did not have direct domestic applications was not clear. That the pursuit of most careers would subvert the ideals of home and family seemed apparent. The resulting dilemma was not easily resolved.

However, there was one career that seemed to blend with women's other responsibilities: teaching school. Teaching did not demand the commitment of every work day year around, because schools were only in session during winter and summer terms; the profession could be entered and left easily, because contracts were issued for one term at a time; and it now had the added attraction of allowing a woman to carry her inbred morality to young people during the formative stages of their lives. Consequently, young women who were anxious for further education flocked to normal colleges and normal departments of colleges and universities for teacher training. When the Normal School opened at Cedar Falls, Iowa, in 1876, the number of women who enrolled far exceeded the number of men. And a Missouri woman who attended the Normal School in Kirksville during the 1850s with a female friend soon discovered that the majority of the students were women, and even a few of the instructors were females. Not unexpectedly, the first woman graduates of colleges and universities were certified by the normal departments. As a case in point, Lulie Gillette of Hannibal, Missouri, claimed the distinction of being the first woman to graduate from the University of

Missouri, doing so in 1870; she graduated in normal studies at the end of the first year that the university admitted women.[32]

Only gradually did women gain admission to all branches of colleges and universities on an equal footing with men. In 1872, the University of Missouri awarded a bachelor of science degree to Anna S. Ware and, in 1874, a bachelor of arts to Julia Ripley, both of Columbia. When Gillette received her degree from the University of Missouri in 1870 there were 201 men and 42 women in her class. By 1872, these figures had jumped to 384 men and 48 women, and in 1874, to 460 men and 93 women. Although the gap between women and men did not close, the absolute numbers of women enrolled did increase.[33]

During these years, women's colleges engaged in their own kinds of struggles. Affected by theories of the day that claimed that higher education would in all likelihood debilitate women mentally and physically, women's colleges attempted to educate women without destroying health and femininity in the process. Instead, the colleges attempted to combine academics, physical education and hygiene, and domestic science and training. Among these schools, some were dedicated to perpetuating customary domestic ideals, others began to question them, and still others began to break with them.

Quite commonly, women's colleges adhered to traditional ideas of preparing women for endeavors that were primarily domestic. These schools stressed their ability to teach women students the ornamental arts while regulating their lives, just as their parents would do. Jewelry and ornate dresses were often confiscated, candy was seized as "contraband," personal funds could be spent only on books, church attendance was compulsory, and fathers and brothers were the only men who were allowed to communicate with female students. In 1859 the rules for boarding pupils at the Howard Female College in Fayette, Missouri, even decreed that students would "not be allowed to correspond with young gentlemen, to speak to them on the streets, to receive presents from them, or to receive or return salutations of any kind from the windows of the boardinghouse or schoolrooms." Any student who ventured into town could do so only in the company of "the Governess or other suitable person."[34]

These so-called women's colleges seem to have been little more than finishing schools that offered some advanced course work. Apparently, the terms *seminary* and *college* were often used loosely and interchangeably, so that it is difficult to determine if the school actually offered secondary or higher education. An excellent example of the confusion in terms was Rockford Female Seminary, later Rockford College, in Illinois. Originally formed in 1844 by a group of ministers, Rockford Female Seminary was supposed to provide proper education to "young ladies" who had been deprived of it by frontier living. In 1851 the school finally became a seminary, according to the original design. It now offered a full preparatory and collegiate course of study, the latter being divided into four departments: Mental and Moral Philosophy, Mathematics and Natural Science, History and English Literature, and Ancient Languages. By 1861 the school boasted a college-preparatory course of two years, a normal course of three years, and a collegiate course of three years, "corresponding with that of the best Female Seminaries at the East." Thus, it actually combined secondary education in its preparatory course, an intermediate type of education in its normal course, and college training in its collegiate course.[35]

Rockford Female Seminary is also an example of a woman's school that experimented with stretching the definitions of domesticity. In addition to curriculum development, the seminary's policy makers were concerned about the messages that were being imparted to female students regarding their futures. The primary objective was to "form noble, Christian women, with cultivated minds, pure hearts, refined manners, and an enlarged view of Christian benevolence and personal usefulness."[36] Read carefully, it can be seen that this statement provided for a harmonious blending of traditional views of women with the newer concept that they should also act as the moral guardians of society in general. Consequently, the school's leaders demonstrated little interest in the female accomplishments and a good deal of pride in the teachers, missionaries, churchworkers, and reformers that their school produced.

The belief that women should indeed be active conservators of culture and reformers of social ills was imparted not only to college-educated prairie women. When many women read newspapers, journals, and novels; attended public lectures; listened to sermons; and spoke with other women who did all of these things, they increasingly got a sense of moral guardianship and the acceptability of their own participation in activities outside of their homes. Taking their moral responsibilities very seriously, thousands of women accordingly began to enter a variety of reform movements, ranging from temperance to charity work.

One of the earliest crusades that attracted reform-minded women was that of temperance. Beginning in the late 1820s, thousands of women, both in the East and in the West, began to join the American Temperance Society, which was formed in Boston in 1826. They either became members of men's temperance units, where they soon found their participation circumscribed because of their gender, or they formed their own groups, in which they could vote, hold office, and set policy. During these early years, women engaged largely in moral suasion to bring about temperance among drinkers, an approach that certainly suited all that they had been told about their own moral powers.[37]

One of the first prairie locales in which women developed a strong interest in temperance reform was Bloomington, Illinois. Here, women joined the first temperance society from its inception in 1832. During its early years, members of the Bloomington society tried to persuade drinkers and non-drinkers alike to sign a "teetotal" pledge, committing them to total abstinence from alcohol. Some years later, the Woman's Temperance League was also established in Bloomington. Its programs included public speakers, pamphlets, and the organization of total-abstinence societies in Sunday Schools, churches, schools, and elsewhere.[38]

As an outgrowth of their temperance work, many women began to see alcoholism as a male problem. They learned of the oppression and abuse many wives and daughters suffered at the hands of drunken husbands and fathers. They also recognized that because women and children were economically dependent upon men, alcoholic husbands could easily destroy an entire family.[39] At the same time, these women reformers felt thwarted because the exercise of their moral powers did not seem potent enough to solve the difficulty. They began to realize that the achievement of temperance would require help from the political realm, an area in which power was denied to women. Consequently, when the temperance movement in general rejected moral suasion as ineffective during the 1840s and turned to seeking the legal prohibition of alcohol instead, women felt totally powerless to act on behalf of the very cause that they now saw as their own.[40]

Women temperance reformers reacted to their exclusion from political action first by clinging to moral suasion as a tactic and then by developing new methods of their own. In unprecedented numbers they joined the Daughters of Temperance, which was organized in 1843. Its members held temperance meetings, petitioned legislatures for legislation on prohibition, resorted to pressure techniques that included confrontation and extralegal force, and formed bands that prayed and sang hymns outside, or sometimes inside, saloons. During the early 1850s, they actually entered saloons and destroyed stocks of liquor.

For their aggressive methods, these respectable wives, mothers, daughters, and sisters often received approval from families, friends, and male temperance workers, who saw the women as protecting their homes and children in the only ways open to them. A typical broadside, which was distributed by an early temperance union of Iowa women, clearly reflected a prevalent interpretation of women's roles in temperance reform. Printed in Muscatine, Iowa, in 1850 for the Bloomington Union No. 1 of the Daughters of Temperance, it pictured a woman with her foot implanted firmly on a serpent, while one of her hands was pouring the contents of a jug of wine on the ground and the other hand was holding a staff topped by a liberty cap.[41]

This early wave of temperance reform peaked around 1855, when thirteen states included prohibitory laws in their statutes; it then receded during the Civil War period, when abolitionism, warfare, and postwar reconstruction consumed people's attention. During the 1870s, temperance

reform reappeared with renewed vigor with the establishment of the Prohibition party and the Woman's Christian Temperance Union (WCTU), an
organization that grew out of the Women's Crusade of 1873/74. The WCTU
was founded in Cleveland, Ohio, in 1874, with Iowan Annie Turner Wittenmyer as its first president. During the next few years, thousands of loosely
organized women's temperance bands, unions, and societies all over the
prairie aligned themselves with the WCTU, so that WCTU locals could soon
be found in many towns and in every county.[42]

During these renewed phases of the temperance movement, prairie women
translated their desire to solve the evil of alcoholism into a variety of actions. Founded in 1884, a Columbia, Missouri, unit of the WCTU, which took
as its objective the "suppression of temperance," asked its members to ab-
stain from alcohol themselves and to "discourage the use of and traffic in"
alcohol in any way possible. The members of this group sponsored prayer
sessions, talks, lectures, temperance parades, and other public programs.
In Minnesota, a Swedish chapter of the WCTU, which formed in 1885, took
a similar pledge and also promoted Bible reading, prayer, hymn singing, and
temperance talks.[43]

Local and state WCTU groups also devised numerous other programs in
the hopes of solving problems that either caused or were related to alcoholism
in some way. In Minnesota, where the state WCTU first organized in 1877,
the groups' records show that the organization secured a curfew ordinance,
originated a plan for hiring a police matron and paid part of her salary,
started a free kindergarten, established an industrial school for girls, encouraged the teaching of cooking in the public schools, started a Gospel Mission, convinced the state legislature to raise the age of consent from seven
years of age to eighteen, encouraged the use of nonalcoholic medicines and
unfermented wine in religious ceremonies, and held Mothers' Meetings. In
addition, it supported a full-time lobbyist in the state legislature and also
lobbied individuals through pamphlets, tracts, free temperance books, and
speakers. Other groups experimented with petition campaigns for local and
state legislation on prohibition, the forceful closing of dram shops, and the
establishment of temperance colonies.[44]

Abolitionism was another reform cause that attracted the energies of
thousands of women. Here, too, the cause emerged first in the East but
quickly had supporters on the prairie.[45] Migrants of abolitionist persuasion
helped to carry the cause westward. During the 1830s, 1840s, and 1850s,
for example, antislavery settlers chose to move to Iowa because of the pockets
of abolitionist thought and because of the number of underground-railroad
stations that existed there. To the settlers' dismay, they soon learned that
the poisonous controversy knew no boundaries and shadowed them wherever
they went. Joanna Harris Haines recalled the "rumpus" that she had created
as a young girl by singing an antislavery song on the boat en route to Iowa

in 1852. She also vividly remembered the pain, alienation, and "sense of loneliness" that her family suffered once in Lee County as a result of their firmly rooted abolitionist ideas. The family soon moved to the more hospitable atmosphere of Grinnell, an abolitionist center, where her home became a "station" on the underground railroad.[46]

Free blacks also promoted abolitionism in prairie regions. The Pyles family, who were freed by their owner, a woman, who relocated them in Keokuk, Iowa, raised money to buy other family members out of slavery. Charlotta Pyles launched a speaking tour in the East to raise funds, and in the mid 1850s, she converted her home into a station on the underground railroad. Joining with white abolitionists, she helped many slaves on their way to Canada.[47]

Although abolitionism clearly involved both women and men, women tended to see it as a peculiarly female reform. They not only believed that their moral responsibilities made it imperative for them to attempt to end slavery, but they also felt a growing sense of identification with black women. In 1837 the abolitionist Angelina Grimké pointed out to a women's antislavery convention that black slave women were in a sense "sisters." Indeed, abolitionist women believed that if one woman was sexually degraded, then all women suffered, and if one mother was devalued, then the institution of motherhood lost stature. Abolitionist women also saw a relationship between themselves and black slave women because of the restrictions on white women's lives and their frequent treatment as chattel. Antislavery women came to hope that if they played an instrumental part in ending slavery, a measure of liberation would be extended to them, as well as a logical and just reward for their efforts.

Prairie women who participated in abolitionism soon found that their ability to wield their moral powers on behalf of their black "sisters" was limited by their lack of political rights. When prairie women first formed abolitionist societies during the 1830s and 1840s, they engaged in fund raising and in morally toned exhortation. Sensing the limitations of these approaches, they soon moved to more aggressive tactics, which included organizing petition campaigns, holding conventions, and speaking on the public platform. But like their counterparts in temperance reform, they gradually realized that it was difficult to exert one's moral powers and responsibilities in the absence of a degree of political influence.[48]

While temperance and abolitionism were compelling reforms for many prairie women, thousands more worked on behalf of the bereaved, the displaced, the disabled, and the destitute. Because many people now agreed that women were the "natural" caretakers of society and the solvers of its ills, prairie women increasingly involved themselves in what today would be called community-action projects.[49] In Decatur, Illinois, in 1855, for example, a group of women organized a masquerade ball at the fashionable Revere House, which raised $120 for the relief of several indigent widows with small children. And when Luther College was founded in Iowa in 1861, a minister's wife, Diderikke Brandt, took on the formidable task of organizing groups of women who attempted to provide a homelike atmosphere for the students.[50]

Most of women's benevolent efforts, however, were associated in some way with a church or a religious sect. Women particularly dominated the Sunday Schools that were beginning to appear in many churches during the early decades of the nineteenth century. As a consequence of the growing belief that the virtue thought to be inherent in females qualified them, rather than men, to instruct children in religious values and through their devoted and selfless commitment to their Sunday-School work, women created a new and respected view of themselves.[51]

Women also formed and participated in a variety of benevolent organizations associated with churches, including sewing societies, charity associations, and missionary-aid groups. Sewing societies usually made articles to be sold at auction, the revenue going to provide improvements for the church or to give aid to some needy person. Charity associations, usually called Ladies Aid societies, pursued a wider array of activities, from holding charity fairs to visiting ill people. Missionary-aid groups raised money and gathered supplies to be sent to religious missionaries both at home and abroad.[52]

The numerous women's voluntary associations that sprang up all over the prairie during the pre–Civil War decades not only dispensed charity; they also drew women out of their homes, trained them in business skills, and turned women's morality into a major social force. During the 1840s and 1850s, a number of female critics lamented that the dirty work of society was left to women and complained that because men were unwilling to do the necessary cleanup work, they were willing to let women assume it as part of their proper sphere. But other women insightfully noted that women's entry into community action transformed them from "household utensils" into respected, energetic living beings.

These women's voluntary associations received a tremendous boost during the Civil War. When the war began in 1861, women all over the prairie quickly realized that soldiers would need more clothing, blankets, food, and other goods than the federal government or individual state governments could mobilize on such short notice. Groups of women began to band together in Ladies Aid societies, sanitary commissions, and benevolent associations within the first few months of the war. Here, they stitched clothing, rolled bandages, prepared and preserved foodstuffs, and packed boxes of supplies to be shipped to military camps and hospitals. These women also sponsored charity fairs and bazaars, where they sold homemade foods, clothing, quilts, and craft items to raise money for the purchase of provisions that they could not produce themselves.[53]

These Ladies Aid societies, or Sanitary Commissions as they were also called, often organized around a particular person, theme, or ethnic identification. In Cedar Rapids, Iowa, Mary Ely, a "conductor" on the underground railroad, converted her home into an aid station. She drew in relatives, friends, and neighbors as members of an energetic group for which she served as president throughout the war. In Metamora, Illinois, young women whose boyfriends and fiancés had volunteered their services to the war effort joined together in an aid association named the Girls of 1861. And in Mankato, Minnesota, a number of German women established the German Sewing Society, where they labored to sew clothing for soldiers entirely by hand.[54]

Because these generous women were usually not very experienced in organizational or business techniques on such a large scale, they soon ran into major problems in coordinating efforts between relief groups and in distributing their products to soldiers. When Ann E. Harlan of Iowa went into the field with sanitary goods, she was appalled at the waste of the materials sent by "patriotic ladies all over the land."[55] Common problems were clothing left lying on the ground after one use because no one was available to wash it, wagonloads of goods rotting on roadsides because of misrouting or the inability to penetrate the lines of troops and munitions, and an excess of goods in one hospital while another lacked supplies.

As more and more women went to the front themselves as nurses, sanitary workers, or to visit wounded husbands, alarming reports flowed back from them concerning the paucity and misappropriation of materials. They told about soldiers and wounded men who were desperately in need of such basic items as sheets, blankets, socks, slippers, handkerchiefs, combs, writing paper, envelopes, fruit, vegetables, and bread. A Missouri woman noted that many of the men with whom she worked at Benton Barracks also requested magazines, books, and Bibles.[56]

Women themselves attempted to solve the supply problem by serving as forwarding agents and state sanitary agents. The best known of these from a prairie state was Annie Turner Wittenmyer of Iowa. At the outbreak of the war she joined with other Keokuk women to roll bandages, sew clothing, and package foodstuffs for the troops. Realizing that more organization was needed, these women formed the Soldiers' Aid Society of Keokuk, with Wittenmyer as executive secretary. In this position, she traveled to the front to send back firsthand reports of conditions and needs. Wittenmyer's field reports helped sanitary workers more efficiently to decide what kinds of supplies should be sent and where, and soon women all over the state were asking Wittenmyer to take charge of the resources produced by their aid groups.[57]

Wittenmyer also became a strong proponent of diet kitchens because of an experience in 1862. In making rounds of field hospitals, Wittenmyer came upon her youngest brother, who was refusing a breakfast tray that held "a tin cup full of black, strong coffee, beside it . . . a leaden looking tin platter, on which was a piece of fried fat bacon, swimming in its own grease, and a slice of bread."[58] Thus, she conceived the idea of kitchens that would serve balanced and healthful meals to men who were desperately in need of proper nutrition. In September 1862, Wittenmyer was recognized for her work by being appointed as one of the official sanitary agents for the state of Iowa. Gen. Ulysses S. Grant later said of her, "No soldier on the firing line gave more heroic service than she rendered."[59]

In 1863, Wittenmyer took on yet another cause, the founding of a home for soldiers' orphans. Although Wittenmyer was successful in founding several homes to meet the pressing need of caring for soldiers' orphans, she found her other work pushed aside because of her increasing need to raise support money for these institutions. The diary of her aide, Mary E. Shelton, is filled with accounts of the hundreds of letters that Wittenmyer laboriously wrote by hand, the innumerable speeches that she gave, and the many politicians that she lobbied. At one point, Shelton noted, "Mrs. Wittenmyer addressed the General Assembly and succeeded charmingly" in convincing them of pressing necessity for orphans' homes.[60]

Wittenmyer's achievements were important in themselves, but the role model that she provided to other women had great significance as well. She played an instrumental role in urging other women to participate in relief and reform work on a more massive scale than had ever been known before. After the war she continued to be an active reformer by helping to organize the Woman's Home Missionary Society in 1871, by becoming the first president of the WCTU in 1874, and by serving as president of the Woman's Relief Corps, the women's auxiliary of the Grand Army of the Republic, beginning in 1889. In so doing, she led women to turn their moral guardianship and volunteerism into a demonstration of female capabilities, training for future undertakings, and sometimes even paid employment. As prominent as Wittenmyer was, however, it must be remembered that she was only one of thousands of prairie women who devoted their time and energies to benevolent activities during the Civil War years.[61]

Wittenmyer's home state of Iowa contained examples of many other war workers who were more representative of the mass of women than she was. One of these was Marjorie Ann Rogers. When her physician husband became an assistant surgeon with the Thirtieth Iowa Infantry in 1862, Rogers rented out the family farm and moved herself and their four children into town, where she soon became engrossed in sanitary activities, supplying bandages, bedding, and food to the front. But she was dismayed to learn from her husband's letters that the parcels that the women so laboriously prepared were often waylaid by other war traffic and never reached the soldiers for whom they were intended. When Governor Samuel J. Kirkwood assembled a convention in Des Moines to design a more efficient way of routing goods, Rogers was a delegate.[62] Rogers was pleased that after the Des Moines meeting, the organization of the war effort improved. She was often moved by the many women who offered small contributions that they could ill afford. She later recalled that "it was touching beyond my power to describe the stories of these women, these mothers, wives, and daughters—their endurance, their hardships, sickness, poverty and deaths, in many families doing the work of the absent father or husband on the farm, saving from his poor salary to pay off a mortgage perhaps or a debt that would soon eat up their home."[63]

Rogers's war work did not end with the declaration of peace at Appomattox Courthouse, Virginia, in April 1865. "Mother" Rogers, as she was now known as a result of her extensive relief activities, continued to dispense sanitary goods to orphans and widows, attempted to aid fugitive blacks as well, and actively backed the Orphans' Home in Davenport. During the postwar years she also engaged in philanthropic endeavors on behalf of needy women, children, and the aged. Widely known and much loved as a philanthropist and reformer, she died within a year of the publication in 1894 of the memoirs of her war experiences.

The number of prairie women who, like Rogers, became deeply involved in war relief was so great and their impact was so widely felt that newspapers that had ignored women's activism at the beginning of the war carried regular announcements and reports of the meetings of Ladies Aid societies at its midpoint. When Burlington, Iowa, women staged a successful benefit concert in 1863, the local newspaper reported it in full, commenting that "the ladies . . . not only deserve the gratitude of the soldiers but the thanks of the community."[64]

At the conclusion of the war in 1865, there was a general expectation that these patriotic women would retreat into their homes. This was not to be the case. While many women did return to their homes, relinquishing much of their responsibility and the recognition that it had brought to them, thousands of others did not. Like Wittenmyer and Rogers, they held a firm conviction about the validity and worth of their public-housekeeping role both for themselves and for society. Thus, thousands of women continued to engage in the voluntary associations that proliferated all over the prairie during the postwar years.

The majority of these clubs involved white middle- and upper-class women and were frequently based in prairie towns. They tended to be of two basic types during the postwar years: those that had a religious affiliation and secular groups whose primary objects were the enhancement of learning and cultural improvement. An early and representative religiously oriented group was the Woman's Christian Association of Minneapolis, which was founded in 1866. This Christian Aid Society, as its members called it, dedicated itself to "provide homes for the destitute . . . to provide food, clothing, religious, and literary instruction for the needy irrespective of class or color." This organization, which claimed to be the oldest philanthropic association in Minnesota, extended its services to free blacks and to prison inmates, both being groups that were often slighted by other aid and rehabilitation efforts of the time.[65] Other similar societies that were founded during the next few years had as goals the furnishing of their churches, aiding orphans and poor families, and generally dispensing charity to those in need. These societies raised the necessary funds for their work by holding suppers, fairs, and charity bazaars and by selling the articles that they sewed at home and during their meetings. Still other associations devoted themselves to the furtherance and support of church mission boards around the world.[66]

Clubs that were interested in education and culture also grew rapidly in size and number on the prairie after the Civil War. A historian of these societies in Bloomington, Illinois, portrayed the emergence of the women's-club movement in that town as "a veritable avalanche of literary clubs, giving Bloomington the reputation of being the 'clubbiest' town in the state." The earliest formally organized group was the History and Art Club, founded in 1879. Within the next decade at least a half a dozen more associations came into existence in Bloomington, including the Longfellow Club, Ariel, Four O'Clock, and Ein Dutzend. Others that emerged here and in other prairie towns were the Sketch Club, Travel Club, Ilders, Philomathian Society, Margaret Fuller Club, Clio, Friday Evening History Club, Schubert Club, Musical Society, As You Like It, Castalian, and a host of literary, musical, and library societies. These organizations usually met once a week to pursue a prescribed course of study and discussion. Their activities also included the sponsoring of public programs and lectures, the staging of concerts and musicales, the establishing of libraries and orchestras, and the supplying of books and other resources to nonmembers.[67]

Not all such clubs involved white women; black women were also highly involved in community activities. Like white women, large numbers of black women became Sunday School teachers. One young black woman in St. Paul remembered her Sunday School teacher as a "lovely" woman who knew the "Bible from cover to cover" and gave her a "love of the Savior and his teachings."[68] Also, such early black churches as the Pilgrim Baptist Church of St. Paul, organized in 1866, soon sponsored black women's-aid associations, charity groups, and missionary societies.[69] Black women participated in cultural societies as well. Here, they worked to bring music, books, and education to their families and neighbors.[70]

Another group of women who banded together in charity and cultural groups was Jewish women. Often, early Jewish synagogues included one or more women's-aid societies. Such Jewish women's groups as the Hebrew Ladies' Benevolent Society, Ladies' Sewing Society, Hebrew Ladies' Aid

Society, Sisters of Peace, and Bichor Cholum provided relief for needy Jewish families, helped orphans and widows, established medical-aid facilities, sponsored suppers and charity fairs, and sewed clothing and other items for sale or as gifts to the needy. One commentator upon Jewish women's associations listed a number of specific objectives: to feed the hungry and give drink to the thirsty, to clothe the naked, to visit the sick, to bury the dead and comfort the mourners, to educate the fatherless, and to shelter the homeless.[71]

Rural women participated in the club movement, too, for it reached into the countryside as well, even to areas still in an early frontier stage. Virtually every rural church had its own Ladies Aid society, sewing circle, or other charity auxiliary. Rural women also joined forces to establish a library in the nearest small town, as did the Floral Club of Austin, Minnesota, or met in each other's homes to discuss works of literature or issues of the day.[72] Farmer's Wives Societies were particularly popular in rural areas. Here, according to one historian of these groups, women joined forces "as a means of creating a friendly social feeling among the families in the country, an opportunity for discussing informally those things pertaining to the duties of a farmer's wife, and a relief from the routine and monotony of such a life." She added that even though rural women were scattered over the prairie and were thus denied the privileges enjoyed by urban women, they "possessed all the social qualities, talent, and culture" of town dwellers. Meeting every week or two, farm women's societies studied various topics, discussed books, sewed items to be contributed to charitable causes, and shared such skills as candle dipping, quilt piecing, and food processing.[73]

The numerous women's societies that emerged on the prairie during the postwar years offered many benefits to their members. First was the opportunity to exercise women's much-touted moral guardianship of their communities in particular and society in general. In addition, these organizations served as support groups for women who came together to give each other encouragement, sympathy, and aid with specific problems. The societies further offered a sense of identification and an opportunity for communication to minority women, particularly black and Jewish women. At the same time, the societies created an opportunity for different kinds of women—young, old, single, widowed, divorced, and married—to get to know each other and understand each other's viewpoints, problems, and perspectives. Women's associations also brought together women of different social-class backgrounds, so that women of all standings worked together, helped each other, and, again, came to know one another. In many cases, membership in a women's group also led to the politicization of prairie women. Chafing against the lack of political and other power as they tried to effect community improvement and reform, many women began to discuss emerging issues of women's rights. And now that action-oriented organiza-

tions were considered acceptable for women, a number of the women who
were becoming interested in political issues and women's rights joined or
formed groups dedicated to improvement in these areas.[74]

By the mid 1850s, women's rights was a topic of discussion in most prairie
towns and regions. A great deal of the sentiment was negative, as was the
case with the commentator who declared women's rights conventions to be
"a novel riot" composed of "dames indignant and of mad reformers." Others
capitalized on the issue, as did the advertiser who used the leader "A
Woman's Rights Meeting" to draw attention to a sale of women's clothing
and shoes. But others took the matter quite seriously. In 1854 the traveling lecturer Frances Dana Gage attracted huge audiences and widespread
support on a midwestern lecture tour on behalf of woman suffrage. A few
years later the Iowa State Teachers Association passed a resolution in favor
of woman suffrage. And by the end of the 1850s, lyceum and other discussion programs regularly focused upon the question of equal rights for
women.[75]

By the 1860s and 1870s, the discussion of women's rights gained great
momentum in prairie locales. For instance, when John Stuart Mill made
an impassioned address to the British House of Commons in 1866, arguing
that the members should extend the right to vote to English women, it was
reported with respect and great attention to detail. In that same year, the
Iowa General Assembly considered a woman-suffrage bill as a result of a
petition submitted to them by twenty-six women. During the next few years,
both women and men turned out in large numbers to hear fiery lectures
delivered by the noted speaker Anna Elizabeth Dickinson. And when the
nationally known suffragist Susan B. Anthony distributed copies of *The
Revolution* to supporters in prairie states and then toured the area, her ideas
met with attention and respect in many quarters.[76]

As support for women's rights, particularly equal suffrage, grew, so did
the opposition become more visible and vocal. For many, the cause of women's
rights was still no more than a nonsensical fashion of the day. Jokes, car-
toons, and satirical essays often took as their butt the question of woman
suffrage. Some antisuffrage factions had more specific complaints. Liquor
interests feared the impact that women's interest in temperance reform might
have on their businesses if women could vote for liquor controls and perhaps
even prohibition. Conservative immigrant groups also registered their dismay
at the changes that a woman-suffrage provision would bring in their traditional ideas concerning the proper roles of women and men. In 1870, Governor
Horace Austin of Minnesota remarked that because three-fifths of the population of his state were not American-born, they were "hostile to the measure
to a man." The sting of Austin's observation was slightly offset by the great
numbers of non-American-born women who supported woman suffrage and
who pushed their vote-wielding men to do so as well.[77]

But the debate over women's rights was larger than these specific factions. Historian Ruth Gallaher has wisely speculated that the "division of opinion was . . . between the progressives and conservatives of both sexes." As the debate intensified, these two sides rapidly multiplied their arguments for and against women's right to vote. The prosuffragists argued that equal suffrage was socially just; would be of potentially great benefit to women, whose effectiveness in reform and professional endeavors depended upon their having a voice in government; would be useful to the nation, because women would be able to vote on social issues in which they were highly involved; would be effective in abolishing the moral double standard that was being advocated by the great political leaders of the times; would be able to socialize one-half of the human race; and would be capable of converting women into men's equals. These weighty arguments were countered by the antisuffragists, who maintained that woman suffrage would not work because women were naturally inferior, too emotional, and lacked the strength to wield authority; should stay within the domestic sphere; were represented by men who would reform any existing wrongs against women; were already taking jobs from men; would become men's rivals and thus ruin the institutions of marriage and the family; would be degraded by entering polling places; would vote only as their husbands and other males told them to; should be silent according to scriptural command; would dominate men and make them inferior; and did not want the vote anyway.[78]

Jane Grey Swisshelm was one of the most widely known of these prairie suffrage leaders. As a result of her editorship of the progressive and controversial *St. Cloud Visiter* and her energetic lectures for abolition and women's rights, her views on women received much attention. Arguing for improved education for females, reform in taxation laws that assessed women but gave them no voice in the disbursement of those monies, and woman suffrage, Swisshelm saw herself as a spokesperson for all Minnesota women. After the Civil War she also served as a western correspondent for the suffrage paper *Woman's Journal.* In 1870, one of her letters to that journal explained that the Minnesota woman spent her first years in the new country engaged in extensive domestic labor, assisted by only the very basic "implements of her trade." She maintained that despite the demands upon their time and energies, many of these women cared about their right to vote. When Governor Austin vetoed a woman-suffrage bill that year, she caustically wrote, "Must women go down on their knees to ask for that which is unjustly held from them?"[79]

Another leading figure was Amelia Jenks Bloomer of Iowa. Before coming to Council Bluffs, Bloomer had lived in Seneca Falls, New York, where in 1848 she had begun to edit a temperance journal named *The Lily,* the first newspaper in the United States to print arguments for women's rights.[80] In 1851, Bloomer and *The Lily* were catapulted into the national limelight because of Bloomer's adoption of a reform dress that was a combination of skirt and trousers. She wore the bloomer outfit when she and her husband moved to Ohio in 1853 and then to the Missouri River town of Council Bluffs in 1855. On their way to Iowa the Bloomers traveled in a stagecoach with several other passengers, among whom was the famous Kit Carson. Bloomer observed that she saw nothing remarkable about him, except for his clothing; given the opportunity, Carson might have said the same of her, since bloomers were generally thought to be a very strange sight.[81]

Because Bloomer arrived in Council Bluffs without *The Lily,* which she had recently sold, she put her energies into the reform of the ragged frontier town that was her new home. She lectured on temperance and on woman suffrage, thus becoming the only woman in Iowa to speak publicly on women's rights before the Civil War. During the war, Bloomer formed the Council Bluffs Soldiers' Aid Society. When the hostilities ended, she resumed her women's-rights work and in 1870 helped to found the Iowa Woman's Suffrage Association. She served as the group's second president and continued to organize, write, and speak for suffrage until her death in 1894.[82]

Literally thousands of prairie women contributed their time and energy to the woman-suffrage movement. Mary Newbury Adams of Dubuque, Iowa, was representative of these lesser-known figures. As the wife of an attorney and the mother of five children, Adams had her hands full yet managed to study on her own and to participate in community affairs. When her oldest child was about ten years old, Adams launched a speaking career and organized a woman's study club. In 1869 she was hired by the *Dubuque* (Iowa) *Times* to cover a woman-suffrage meeting at Galena, Illinois, featuring Elizabeth Cady Stanton and Susan B. Anthony. Adams later helped to found the Northern Iowa Suffrage Association of Dubuque while continuing to speak on behalf of women and organize women's clubs.[83]

By the 1870s the Patrons of Husbandry, or Grange, units that were spreading over the prairie encouraged even more women to move from social to political action. Drawing women in on an equal basis with male members because of the efforts of Carrie A. Hall, the Grange provided a forum not only for agriculture-related issues but also for wider questions that directly affected farm women. Prairie Granges educated women in domestic skills, farm concerns, and women's issues. They also taught women how to lobby and think. It is not surprising, then, that female Grange members soon supported having reforms that particularly interested them added to the Grange agenda. Temperance was one of these; woman suffrage was another. By the latter decades of the nineteenth century, female Grange members saw equal suffrage as their right. As one phrased it, "We demand equal suffrage without regard to sex or condition, so that the intelligent women of America may have the power to protect themselves, their homes, and their families."[84]

Despite the countless hours of effort that suffrage reformers devoted to

(Above) Thousands of women, like these St. Paul clubwomen, circa 1885, attempted to civilize and reform frontier towns. Courtesy of the Minnesota Historical Society, St. Paul. (Left) One of the best-known reformers and clubwomen on the frontier was Annie Turner Wittenmyer, state sanitary agent for Iowa during the Civil War and the first president of the Women's Christian Temperance Union. Courtesy of the Iowa State Historical Department, Des Moines.

THE ORIGINAL ACT GRANTING TO THE WOMEN OF THE WYOMING TERRITORY THE RIGHT OF SUFFRAGE AND TO HOLD OFFICE.

(Top left) As women liberalized their domestic sphere on the frontier, many began to pursue higher education and increased physical activity. Physical-education class in the Armory, University of North Dakota, Grand Forks, 1904. Courtesy of the State Archives and Historical Research Library, Bismarck, North Dakota. (Bottom left) Rather than being intimidated by the frontier environment, women increasingly moved into it, as did these female hunters along the Red River in Dakota Territory during the 1870s. Courtesy of the State Archives and Historical Research Library, Bismarck, North Dakota. (Above) In 1869, Wyoming Territory passed the first woman-suffrage provision in the nation. Courtesy of the Museum Division of the Wyoming State Archives, Museum, and Historical Department, Cheyenne.

the cause, woman suffrage did not come to the prairie until the approval of the Nineteenth Amendment in 1920. The one anomaly was Illinois, which in 1913 granted women the limited rights of suffrage in presidential and municipal elections. The states of Indiana, Iowa, Minnesota, and Missouri considered the woman-suffrage issue on many occasions and even sent referenda to the voters on other occasions, but did not achieve passage of the measure before 1920.[85]

Evidently, although modifications in the roles and the responsibilities of prairie women during the nineteenth century were extensive, they were not deep-seated enough to underwrite such a major revision of policy as the extension of suffrage to women. To Amelia Murdock Wing of Iowa it seemed that change in women's status was widely resisted: "Now, in those days a woman who had very decided opinions of her own was frequently sneeringly called by some men 'a strong-minded woman'!"[86]

A considerable number of male settlers did consider that the political realm was exclusively theirs. Fearing everything from the diminishment of their own power to the corruption of women through contact with the "ballot box," they often actively resisted women's growing interest in politics. For their part, men were frequently willing to participate in campaigns and elections, hold local office for little or no pay, and serve as justices of the peace and sheriffs.[87]

At the same time, however, men often felt grateful for women's attempts to "tame" the prairies and civilize its inhabitants. While men's own involvement in financially supporting themselves and perhaps a family as well limited the amount of time they could invest in community action, they were quite often willing to believe that women's housekeeping duties could expand to encompass the community as well as the family. Clearly, many women accepted this idea but had difficulty in accepting the limitations that accompanied it.

8
Community Participation on the Plains

Sunbonnets, children, chickens—these are some of the props associated with women of the Great Plains in the mind's eye, when the customary image is drawn upon for information. Isolation, despair, passivity—these tend to be some of the assumed characteristics of plainswomen's lives. Yet the reality of plainswomen's activities frequently belies the fiction. Not only did they serve as wage earners and income producers, in addition to their innumerable and highly significant domestic functions; they often participated in affairs of the larger community outside of the home as well.

In a sense, plainswomen's community activities were an extension of their domestic roles. Women, who produced families and held them together in times of stress, kept homes orderly, perpetuated traditions, conserved values, and innovated creative solutions to difficulties of everyday living within the domestic realm, also felt the responsibility to perform these tasks in the public arena. Thus, many became social, or municipal, housekeepers. Women, especially those of the middle and upper classes, entered community affairs with a strong commitment to protect their families in the face of increasing social problems, to maintain a well-regulated society, to preserve certain forms and customs, and to devise inventive ways of coping with community troubles.

This trend toward public involvement was not unique to plainswomen. Throughout the early decades of the nation's history, both in the older settled regions of the country and on the prairie frontier, women had engaged in such activities as dispensing charity to the disabled and the poor, cleaning up parks and other aspects of the environment, and fighting for the cause of the black slave. On the Plains, the frontier setting and the demanding environment offered women many opportunities to "housekeep," some of which were similar to those tackled by earlier reformers, but some slightly different. The tremendous mobility of people also created an unusually high demand for the re-creation of known forms and institutions.

173

In fact, the rough Plains environment impelled men, along with women, to attempt to civilize and reform it. From helping to build a church to putting a checkered tablecloth on a bachelor's table, men contributed to making the Plains a sociable and hospitable place in which to live. But men's community work differed from women's in a number of ways, the most crucial being that men could vote and hold public office in order to implement community action. At the same time, men were also absorbed in the economic development of the Plains, a particularly demanding task, because of the region's relatively arid, treeless, and sometimes even barren land. Thus, men often left community work to their politically powerless womenfolk. Numerous women, although their own work loads were also incredibly heavy, willingly assumed a great part of the burden of refining the new society that was gradually emerging on the Plains.

Such community involvement and activism sound like a very tall order for plainswomen, but many of them were readers, thinkers, and doers, in addition to being domestic practitioners and wage workers. Because they seized opportunities to broaden their horizons, enhance their awarenesses, and educate themselves in a variety of ways, many plainswomen were well equipped to handle activities outside of the confines of their homes and work places. These women were not only informed on current issues; they also held a strong set of values, which guided them in coping with those issues.

Although the stereotype of plainswomen seldom represents them sitting with books before them, thousands of them expanded their minds and horizons by reading. From the printed page, women derived many of their ideas and much of their information as well as finding much-needed companionship, entertainment, solace, and advice.[1] One Kansas woman described the scene in her grandmother's home after dinner: "When the reading lamp was lit in the dining-room, the various members of the family, hired help and all, would gather together there to read." Another woman claimed that the arrival of her grandmother's library in the "book-hungry land" of Dakota Territory drew many visitors to her home. Other women spoke of longing for more books than were available to them, of feeling settled in a cabin only when their books were unpacked, and of borrowing precious books from neighbors. Faye Cashatt Lewis of South Dakota touchingly expressed women's thirst for books when she wrote: "Finishing the last book we borrowed from the Smiths, and having it too stormy for several days to walk the mile and a half to return it and get more, was a frequent and painful experience. Seeing the end of my book approaching was like eating the last bite of food on my plate, still hungry, and no more food in sight."[2]

Women also relied upon reading materials to educate themselves and others. Scores of non-English-speaking women learned to read English from books and newspapers. One Norwegian woman, who was working as a domestic, learned not only to read but also to enjoy reading from books that she borrowed from the daughters of the family. Other women used books to supplement the sketchy educations that their children received in local schoolhouses. Anne Bingham of Kansas noted that during the 1870s, on a regular basis, she used her limited supply of books to instruct her daughter, in spite of the many interruptions and demands on her time. "Many times I went about with a book in one hand and a broom in the other," she explained.[3]

The appeal of reading was not limited to any social class, income level, or racial group. The account book of a young domestic worker indicated that she regularly spent a relatively large proportion of her very meager income on books. Farm women's ledgers, which carefully noted every expense in detail, also listed sums for books, amounts that sometimes exceeded what was spent on necessities. That these women often had to scrimp for book money is suggested by the Montana woman who hoarded in a sugar bowl some of the money that she earned by washing and ironing clothes for men in a nearby logging camp so that when the traveling book agent, also a woman, drove into the yard, she would be able to purchase books from her. Black plainswomen, too, struggled to buy books from the wages they earned as farmers or in such jobs as being a domestic or a nursemaid.[4]

Reading was so important to plainswomen that they often formed literary clubs to pursue the activity with other women. Located in villages and towns, these clubs soon dotted the Plains. Although their members were typically urban, white, and middle or upper class, these clubs did attract other members, particularly from farms and far-flung ranches. Often called literary societies, these clubs held meetings, or "literaries," every week or two. Sometimes also referred to as study clubs, they often invited speakers to address their meetings. One such group was the Round Table Club of Crete, Nebraska, which was founded in 1884. During their first year, the members of the Round Table Club concentrated upon the study of ancient Egypt and then turned their attention to the religious beliefs of Assyria. A historian of the group later asserted: "We were ambitious in the line of study. We wanted to get at the beginning of things." A later group was the Shakespeare Club of Cheyenne, which formed in 1899 with this stated goal: "We, the members of this club, realizing that our highest advancement comes through study and that association is an incentive to our own best effort, do establish this club for that purpose." Their first project was the intensive study of *The Taming of the Shrew.*[5]

Literary-club members often carried their love of reading and study one step further by establishing local libraries, to serve those who were already literate and educated and to reach out to those who wished to be. Clubwomen served on library boards, volunteered their services as librarians, and sponsored charity functions to raise funds to build a library building and to fill it with books or to augment the holdings of an existing library. One Wyoming clubwoman chronicled the beginning of the Powell Public Library in the corner of her living room: "Since we had no money to buy books, we asked people to contribute anything they thought was suitable. . . . In no time at all we had our shelves filled. Books were used more and more. . . . We organized a Club and rented the front of a store building next door to my home. Members took turns at keeping the library open and soon started money-making projects with a library building of our own as our aim. . . . How brave and ambitious our little Club was!"[6]

Whether living in a town or a more isolated area, women showed good taste in their choices of reading material. An army wife at Fort Randall in Dakota Territory during the late 1860s favored Charles Dickens and Victor Hugo. Other women mentioned reading novels, social commentary, political philosophy, and the numerous magazines, journals, and English- and non-English-language newspapers that arrived in the mail.[7] Women also relied upon recipe books, household manuals, etiquette books, moral guidebooks, didactic novels, and articles in newspapers for ideas, opinions, values, and advice. Although prescriptive literature has often been dismissed by critics, who argue that women themselves spurned its lofty and impractical suggestions, sales figures suggest otherwise. Many such works enjoyed wide sales, frequently went through seven or eight editions, and were sometimes reprinted into languages other than English. Women's diaries and letters indicate that they carried household and other manuals with them to the Plains, ordered them through the mail, received them as gifts, or borrowed them from neighbors. They also subscribed to a large number of journals, which offered guidance on current issues; these ranged from *Harper's Bazaar* and *Godey's Lady's Book* to *Youth's Companion* and *Good Form.*[8]

These materials stretched plainswomen's minds in some ways while limiting them in others. Household-hint books included all the customary discussions of cooking, cleaning, and childcare, but increasingly toward the turn of the twentieth century, they added ways of earning money and other "worldly" concerns. They combined chapters on dress, weddings, and children's pastimes with others titled "Earning a Living," "The Medical Profession for Women," "Good Manners in Business Relations," and "Woman's Higher Education." A 1903 manual even included the section "Limitation of Offspring." Women were reminded that marriage was their greatest privilege, that their "mission" in life was to become mothers, and that they should please men by following such rules as: "Don't hurt a man's pride. . . . Don't be too positive in your statements. . . . Don't become emotional. . . . Don't rub it in when he fails. . . . Don't try to outrival him. . . . Don't belittle or correct him. . . . Don't nag, no matter what happens. . . . Never be unsympathetic."[9]

These injunctions suggest that an overriding principle in women's behavior was deference to men. As they moved into the public world, women did tend to manifest that deference in a number of ways. Taking to heart the advice not to "outrival" men and fearing their own propensity toward emotionality or making a positive statement, plainswomen, just as prairie women had done, formed organizations exclusively for women. They also limited themselves to "women's concerns," or they justified their entry into such a "male" concern as politics by imputing a domestic dimension to it. At the same time, in increasing numbers, they were subtly and slowly challenging most established male bastions.

One of the most important of these was formal education. Plainswomen sought to widen their perspectives, or to help other women do so, through formal education. Often struggling to rise above their own meager educational backgrounds, they worked as teachers, principals, and county superintendents; served as members of school boards; assisted with industrial and other vocational-training schools for girls; and advanced the cause of night schools and other schools for immigrants. Thousands of women flocked to teachers' institutes, district training meetings, and the emerging normal schools to improve their teaching skills. And thousands more attended college, often receiving an undergraduate or graduate degree.[10]

Women's efforts to improve their educations often demanded real sacrifices from them and their families, who were hard-pressed to supply the necessary tuition money. During the 1890s, for example, a Norwegian woman in South Dakota organized a trio of vocalists, who traveled about the countryside giving concerts, cultivating onions, and husking corn for an early canning plant. She used her share of the proceeds to finance her musical education. A Kansas woman taught in a sod schoolhouse and took up a homestead claim so that she might pursue a college education. Another, who entered the University of Wyoming in 1897, worked as a student assistant for a female professor for the grand sum of ten cents an hour.[11]

Plainswomen who were anxious to improve themselves through higher education were often encouraged to do so by colleges and universities, which gradually began to admit them as students. In 1866 the newly founded University of Kansas became the first state university in the nation to invite women to enter on equal terms with men. This action was pushed by Mary Tenney Gray, who led a group of women in lobbying the Kansas Constitutional Convention to grant women equal educational opportunities.[12] In 1871 the University of Nebraska opened its doors to women and men. By the end of the decade, it had initiated a very early and complete physical-education program for women, one that offered women the opportunity to engage in gymnastics, drill teams, basketball, folk dancing, tennis, and classes in hygiene and physiology. Despite Victorian notions of female modesty, the 1898/99 catalogue declared: "Every woman should have a knowledge of the wonderful mechanism of the human body and know how to take proper care of it. She needs also definite, systematic physical training." That women were eager to seize such opportunities was demonstrated by Louise Pound, a champion tennis player from Lincoln, who earned a Ph.D. from the University of

Heidelberg and taught literature at the University of Nebraska, where she also introduced girl's basketball and pioneered in the playing of women's golf.[13]

As plainswomen of the latter decades of the nineteenth century broadened their horizons through reading, writing, studying, and teaching, they also accelerated their efforts and increased their participation in the area of community reform. Both a concomitant and a result of reading and education, women's heightened involvement in reform causes continued to extend female activities and influence. In particular, female reformers attacked the growing evils associated with alcoholism.

Told repeatedly that it was their duty to protect the home, plainswomen quickly moved into combat against alcohol as being one of the biggest threats to home and family. Some learned from firsthand experience about the destruction that liquor could wreak within their families. A young wife in Topeka during the 1890s endured her husband's ill temper, verbal abuse, loss of work time, expensive "cures" in Chicago, and finally his death as a result of alcohol. In a different type of situation, Nellie Rogney, a homesteader in Montana during the second decade of the twentieth century, watched in despair as her husband began to distill and sell "moon." His illegal business eventually led to his arrest and death and her commitment to a sanitarium.[14]

Local meetings of the Women's Christian Temperance Union, which was founded in 1874, with Annie Turner Wittenmyer as its first president, attracted huge numbers of plainswomen. By 1890 the WCTU had become the largest women's organization in existence in America up to that time. Under the aggressive leadership of Frances Willard, who served as its president between 1879 and 1898, the WCTU reached out to women of all racial, ethnic, social-class, and regional identities. In 1883, Willard organized a Montana state temperance union in Butte and local unions in Missoula, Helena, and Butte. She also courted influential women across the Plains. One of these was the Reverend Alice Barnes, who toured as an evangelist for the WCTU, held the offices of state treasurer, editor, and president of the Montana WCTU, and was dubbed "Saint Courageous" by Butte women. These influential women in turn fought not only alcohol but other frontier ills as well, including dance halls, hurdy-gurdy establishments, and houses of prostitution. The efforts of these women were widely applauded. As the *Abilene* (Kans.) *Chronicle* put it in 1871, "Personal virtue and purity are necessary to the real happiness and growth of a community."[15]

Of the many women who played active roles in the WCTU, a plainswoman achieved the greatest fame and notoriety. Perhaps because her first husband died from delirium tremens, Carry Nation of Kansas felt called upon by God to fight "Demon Rum." She invaded saloons with hatchet in hand and proceeded to destroy mirrors, glasses, bottles, and furniture. Abetted by "bands" of women, she destroyed numerous taverns in Topeka during the early 1900s, often spending time in jail as a result. Because Kansas was technically "dry" at the time, Nation thought her violence against illegal saloons was justified. She also founded a Topeka temperance paper called the *Smashers Mail,* wrote several books, lectured extensively, and organized a home for the wives of alcoholics.[16]

In most regions of the Plains, female advocates of temperance chose less violent techniques than those of Nation in their work for the "cause." Perhaps discouraged by the formal complaints against them by saloon owners or by the red paint that was thrown upon their clothes when they arrived at a saloon, temperance workers used a wide variety of more acceptable approaches. A Kansas woman of the 1890s remembered the great variety and popularity of temperance songs. Another described meetings, songs, recitations, and books. Of one particularly memorable meeting she wrote: "I carried a little white banner . . . which said, 'Tremble King Alcohol, I shall grow up.' Each member wore a bow of white ribbon. They sang songs and talked about the curse of drunkeness."[17]

The records of temperance organizations on the Plains list many other techniques. The Bismarck WCTU, founded in 1882, utilized temperance lectures, reading rooms, annual state conventions, and a lobbyist to the state legislature to get their point across.[18] The Grand Forks Scandinavian WCTU circulated petitions, sent out literature, put reading materials in jails, sponsored essay contests in schools, organized an enforcement league, and sent Christmas baskets to the afflicted. And the Bottineau, North Dakota, WCTU added "Food-vs-Beer" demonstrations and celebrations of "Frances E. Willard Anniversaries" to the growing arsenal of methods.[19]

It is important to note that these WCTU groups typically represented alcoholism as a male problem, seldom mentioning that women became addicted as well. They talked at great length about the injury done to men's health by alcohol, the disastrous effects of drunkenness on men's families, and the benefits that would accrue to society if men could be prohibited from drinking.[20] A founder of the Nebraska WCTU in the mid 1870s claimed: "I was sure . . . that God had called the women into this work, and that the command was to go forward. . . . In all ages since the creation, woman at critical times has come to the front and with her quick discernment and her great moral courage has so changed the on sweeping tide of sentiment for revenge and cruelty, that the Moral and the Spiritual have taken the throne and the nation has been saved."[21]

The church was another arena that offered women a chance to influence men while utilizing women's special moral powers. Plainswomen who were involved in church work often found that one of the benefits of religious activism was the opportunity to motivate men who were in need of salvation. Women's husbands, sons, and brothers often followed women into the church at the adamant insistence of those women. Many men remained dubious, it seems. After joining the local Baptist church in 1891, Alice Richards of Wyoming attended both Sunday School and the newly organized Baptist Young People's Society. "I tried to get the boys in my neighborhood to go to church," she asserted, "and sometimes one would go with me—at my insistence—but not regularly."[22]

In addition to aiding their less moral menfolk, plainswomen who engaged in church work gained many other rewards. As founders of churches, as Sunday School teachers, and as active workers on behalf of missions at home and in the field, women found companionship, fulfillment, and a sense of purpose. But it was the thousands of Ladies Aid societies that were particularly attractive to plainswomen. Emma Brandt, a Norwegian pastor's wife in Dakota Territory during the 1880s, gave a detailed account of her Kvindeforening, or Ladies Aid society: "We met in the various homes and each member paid ten cents each time, whether present or not. We had strict rules about serving; refreshments had to be simple and not burdensome to anyone. Our membership soon increased, and a sum was laid aside each year toward the future church." She added that a Pigeforening, or Young Ladies Aid Society, was also organized. Mothers were so anxious to have their daughters accepted for membership that Brandt accepted some as young as six years of age. The girls embroidered bits of handiwork, which were later sold to raise funds for the new church. Other aid societies sponsored dinners, box suppers, "socials," bazaars, and fund-raising functions to help their church, local poor people, or some other worthy cause.[23]

It was not just religious organizations that attracted plainswomen; they also invested their energies in a whole panoply of secular voluntary associations. This trend paralleled the national women's-club movement, which started with the founding of the New England Women's Club in Boston and of Sorosis in New York, both in 1868, and eventually resulted in the formation of a national association called the General Federation of Women's Clubs in 1890.[24] The club movement quickly spread to the Plains. By the 1880s there were so many clubs available to plainswomen that one Wyoming woman called the period "the golden age of women's clubs."[25] Women frequently belonged to fifteen to twenty clubs at a time. One leading Oklahoma clubwoman founded or headed over forty organizations during her lifetime.[26] These clubs included hospital and veterans' auxiliaries, cemetery associations, sewing groups, Epworth Leagues, Dickens clubs, Order of the Eastern Star chapters, housekeeper's societies, current-events clubs, Women's Relief Corps chapters, musical groups, Society of the Daughters of the American Revolution chapters, tourist clubs, Rebekah Lodge chapters, world peace groups, Red Cross units, physical-culture organizations, and literary and study clubs, most of which were under the umbrella of the National Federation of Women's Clubs.

Virtually all of these women's organizations on the Plains shared the general goal of self-improvement for their members and their communities. As one active clubwoman noted, "These clubs were mostly purposeful . . . aiming to preserve the values of life . . . and an aim for better communities, nation and world."[27] They worked on behalf of child welfare, improved schools, improved libraries, poor relief, women matrons for women prisoners, vocational and industrial training for girls, domestic-science courses in the schools, college scholarships for women, municipal rest lounges for farm women, and other causes too numerous to list.[28] Some women's voluntary associations helped to support homes for orphans and for unemployed and alcoholic women. The associations donated freely to the Florence Crittenden Homes for Unwed Mothers; they helped WCTU groups and antisaloon leagues, and they occasionally went farther afield than their own region by aiding such agencies as Near East Relief.[29]

Although these women's voluntary associations were primarily urban and white, they did attract women from farms and ranches who drove their farm wagons or carriages into towns for meetings. In addition, separate clubs were organized for or by rural women. These groups included homemakers' extension clubs, which offered members training in such domestic skills as canning and bread making, as well as social opportunities with other farm women.[30]

Black plainswomen usually formed their own organizations. Black women's clubs resembled white groups in that they held raffles, bazaars, and bake sales to raise money for deserving causes. But they had the special goal of helping black people by providing health-care programs and other social services to them. The Searchlight Club of Cheyenne, founded in 1904, was such a group. One of its members explained that it was the only club for black women in Cheyenne, but that a black woman could join a white woman's club if this was not barred by prejudice on one side or the other.[31]

Many aspects of life on the Plains drew the attention and the reform efforts of both white and black women who were committed to promoting the same state of order and progress in the world outside their homes as they tried to maintain within them. Leaving little unexamined, social housekeepers of the latter part of the nineteenth century and the opening years of the twentieth century found an almost unending number of causes that could profit from their energies. Plainswomen of every social class, age, region, and ethnic or racial group fought an unbelievably wide spectrum of ills. Although their early campaigns tended to focus upon issues that were closely related to home and family—the availability of books being one such issue and the threat of alcohol another—reform-minded women soon broadened their perspective to include causes that were farther from home, including American Indians, the environment, farm and economic problems, and their own political participation.

The cause of the American Indian first began to receive attention during the late nineteenth century. As a result of being exposed to the Plains Indians and having observed the many injustices suffered by them, plainswomen were often both sympathetic to the plight of the Indian and anxious to help remedy the situation. In addition, numerous plainswomen believed it was their moral responsibility to help these "unfortunate" natives, whom they viewed as being uncivilized and immoral savages.[32] They thus called for a more humane and understanding view of Indians. A Kansas settler of the 1880s, for example, agreed that while Indians might have many faults, whites were not free from character flaws either. She felt that it was unfair for whites to denounce what she referred to as the Indians' state of degradation. "Are our souls refined and free from all impurity?" she asked.[33]

A number of plainswomen sharply criticized settlers' actions toward Indians. Miriam Colt decried the common practice of cheating Indians in trade: "Is it right, I ask. Three dollars for a buffalo robe, worth twelve at home." Army wife Frances Roe, who had called the Indians "dirty, and nauseous-smelling savages" early in her time on the Plains, came to believe that there was blatant injustice involved in the mass killing of buffalo, which deprived the Plains Indians of their primary source of support. She wrote scathingly, "If the Indians should attempt to protect their rights it would be called an uprising at once, so they have to lie around on sand hills and watch their beloved buffalo gradually disappear, and all the time they know only too well that with them will go the skins that give them tepees and clothing, and the meat that furnishes almost all of their sustenance." Another army wife was even more adamant concerning the unfairness of seizing the precious resources that were so crucial to native populations. While at Fort Laramie during the 1860s, Frances Carrington observed that "at the time of my arrival it had become apparent to any sensible observer that the Indians of that country would fight to the death for home and native land, with spirit akin to that of the American soldier of our early history, and who could say that their spirit was not commendable and to be respected."[34]

Other plainswomen criticized the government's land policies and the reservation system. They pointed out that the loss of their lands condemned native peoples to lives of poverty and virtual homelessness.[35] Despite the death of her first husband in the Fetterman "massacre," Frances Carrington expressed sympathy for Indians who had been forced to surrender the hunting grounds upon which their existence depended. Margaret Carrington, the wife of the commander of Fort Kearney during the conflict, supported Frances in her interpretation of the events. Even Elizabeth Custer could understand the Indians' side of the story. She described the Battle of Washita with such sympathy for the Indians that a friend wrote in response: "It confused my sense of justice. Doubtless the white men were right, but were the Indians entirely wrong? After all, these broad prairies had belonged to them."[36]

Many women tried to fill the gap themselves. Pitying the needy Indians, plainswomen, from their own resources, gave food, clothing, and medical care to Indians. A woman who lived a few miles south of the Kansas Indian reservation during the 1860s dispensed what charity she could, given her own meager supplies. On one occasion she turned away a hungry Indian because of her dwindling larder, but he coughed so hard that she later asserted, "If I could have called him back, I would have given him bread." Army wife Ada Vogdes, who initially felt great enmity toward native peoples, also came to pity their destitute condition. When twenty Indians entered Fort Laramie in search of food, she recorded a compassionate response in her journal: "I did pity these poor things paddling around in the cold and snow."[37]

Still other plainswomen indicted the military for its treatment of the Plains Indians. According to Margaret Carrington, military men were reprehensible in their bargaining with Indians, a situation that led her to be very enthusiastic about an 1866 policy at Fort Kearney that barred soldiers from trading with Indians. Caroline Winne of Nebraska rebuked Gen. Philip H. Sheridan for being "drunk all the time in Chicago in his fine house," and she blamed Gen. William T. Sherman for having made uninformed and ruinous decisions about Indians while existing "on his general's pay in Washington, never having fought an Indian & knowing nothing at all about them." According to her, the Custer debacle was caused "uselessly by his own folly and disobedience of orders."[38]

Numerous plainswomen translated their feelings regarding American Indians into a variety of actions to help native peoples. Women served as teachers and missionaries to American Indians. They wrote to their own friends and families, asking them to spread the "truth" about the abusive and irresponsible treatment of the Plains Indians. Some plainswomen formed firm friendships with Indian women, married Indian men, and hired native women, men, and children as cooks, clothes washers, dishwashers, and nursemaids. And one South Dakota woman even went to Washington, D.C., in 1891 as a representative of a club in Pierre to remonstrate with governmental officials against allowing Indians to be exhibited around the world in Buffalo Bill's and other Wild West shows.[39]

Appreciation for and conservation of the physical environment was another reform cause that attracted the attention of many women, both as individuals and in organized groups. As early as the 1870s, national attention was drawn to the environment by the pioneering work of Ellen Swallow Richards, the holder of a doctoral degree in chemistry from Massachusetts Institute of Technology, who was instrumental in establishing the fields of home economics and environmental science in America. Numerous other women drew attention to the cause of the environment. In 1878, the Englishwoman Isabella Bird's *A Lady's Life in the Rocky Mountains* caught the attention of the American public with its vivid portrayal of the western wilderness. During this same period, Martha Maxwell of Denver became one of the first women naturalists in the country. Maxwell, a skilled hunter and marksperson who collected her own specimens, contributed much to taxonomy and to exhibit techniques, especially through her Rocky Mountain Museum. Anna Botsford Comstock, an entomologist at Cornell University, founded the Department of Nature Study and in 1911 wrote the classic *Handbook of Nature Study.* And in 1890, Fay Fuller, wearing bloomers and sturdy boy's shoes, became the first woman to climb Mount Rainier.[40]

This blossoming attentiveness to the physical environment was manifested by the many women who initiated or participated in expeditions into Plains wilderness areas. Some of these were elaborate, as the one into the Black Hills under Gen. George A. Custer in 1874, which included a woman, Annie D. Tallent. Claiming to have been the first white woman in the Black Hills, Tallent later published two books extolling the glories of the area.[41] Other women traveled through Yellowstone Park in covered wagons and carriages. Here they camped out in tents and spent their time fishing, hunting, and studying the flora and fauna. Others sallied forth with families or women friends into canyons, valleys, and deserts in their own regions of the Plains. These women all reflected the newly emerging attitude that the outdoors was a place in which to gain knowledge, health, and recreation, rather than a hostile force to be conquered.[42]

Some plainswomen undertook the study of the environment in a systematic way. In 1885 a twenty-six-year-old schoolteacher joined a summer cattle drive to North Dakota as a cook, so that she might enhance her knowledge of wilderness regions. Her diary of the trip indicates that she spent most of her spare time in studying the landscape about her and in collecting specimens of soil, sand, and rocks. Similarly, in 1892, a number of Montana women contributed flower specimens from their private collections to a prize-winning botanical exhibit that was prepared for the Columbian Exposition. Other women formed travel clubs to promote their understanding of their regions, while women's clubs increasingly focused on ecological topics, opposed the wearing of real stuffed birds on fashionable hats, and supported the lobbying of their state and national legislators for additional parks and other conservation areas.[43]

As improved cameras became available, other women ventured forth into the hinterland to photograph wildlife and landscapes. These female photographers of the landscape exhibited a high degree of physical stamina, because during the wet-plate era of photography, it was necessary to carry heavy equipment and a darkroom tent into the field. It is to the credit of these early landscape photographers that their fine work frequently brought prime prices, sometimes was used in classroom instruction, and appeared as illustrations in natural-science books and articles.[44]

Rather than allowing themselves to be overwhelmed by vast spaces, these women attempted to shape and control the world about them. Although the topic of women and the landscape is just beginning to be explored by scholars, studies show that women's reactions to space and wilderness were not all negative, as has been believed. Plainswomen did not confine themselves to their homes; they moved freely into yards, barns, fields, and forests for work and play. Because their long skirts were unsuitable, they donned split skirts, bloomers, or even pants.[45] Instead of being intimidated by such features as rattlesnakes, they carried weapons and, with pride, counted the number of rattles after a kill. Nor were these women driven to insanity by the winds, storms, and other aspects of nature. They often characterized the outdoors as being full of beauty and romance. They used such words as *awe, grandeur,* and *magnificence* in their descriptions of their physical settings.[46]

In yet another area—the farm problem of the 1880s and 1890s—numerous plainswomen worked for reform, in this case through political action. Although women were not expected to enter the political arena, thousands did so. Fearing the demise of the farms that sustained their homes and families, they joined Populist organizations in large numbers during the closing decades of the nineteenth century and the opening one of the twentieth.

Many plainswomen pursued reform through an important farm group, the Farmers' Alliance. Some of these women soon emerged as leaders of that organization. One of these was Luna E. Kellie of Nebraska, who later explained that when the first Farmers' Alliance unit was organized in her neighborhood in the late 1870s, it was not supposed to be political in orientation. But in her view, it was inevitable that farmers, by coming together to discuss their situation, would "eventually find they had to resort to politics to get any needed reform." She claimed that she did not foresee her own eventual involvement: "Politics was the furthest thing from my mind then." But by the time her family had grown to eleven children, Kellie was serving as an editor, secretary, bookkeeper, and speaker for the Alliance. She also wrote several Populist songs and edited the Populist newspaper *Prairie Home* in her dining room. Annie La Porte Diggs of Kansas was a later Farmers' Alliance activist. Diggs was a magnetic speaker who was known for her religious liberalism, Populist ideas, and writings, particularly *A Life of Sockless Jerry Simpson, the Socrates of the Plains* (c. 1908).[47]

As the Populist movement gathered momentum, thousands of other plainswomen spoke and worked on behalf of its programs. Farm women mounted wagons and platforms to address crowds, which they had not considered doing before. They also joined Populist glee clubs, prepared banners, and marched in processions. Observing the situation early in the 1890s, the political humorist Joseph Billings wrote, "Wimmin is everywhere."[48] The goals that these "wimmin" supported included the direct election of senators, a graduated income tax, the regulation of monopolies and utilities, and governmental control of currency. Many of these ideas eventually became public policy.

The best known of the Populist women reformers was from a Plains state: Mary Elizabeth Lease, a mother of four who studied law and was admitted to the Kansas bar in 1885, distinguished herself as a compelling and charismatic orator who gave over 160 speeches in support of the Populist cause in 1890 alone. Known as the Pythoness of the Plains and as Queen Mary, she became famous for her reported admonition to Kansas farmers to "raise less corn and more hell." She became a media figure, and when one newspaper misunderstood her name to be Mary Ellen, they dubbed her "Mary Yellin'" instead. When the Populist party took over Kansas government in 1893, she was appointed the director of the state board of charities, an appointment that was in line with her other activities, which had long included work with civic clubs and the Irish National League. In the following year, her book *The Problem of Civilization Solved* appeared. In 1896, she opposed the Populist merger with the Democratic party, became a Progressive Republican, and worked on behalf of woman suffrage.[49]

Some plainswomen embraced political action to such a degree that they even ran for office on the Populist ticket. One of these was Ella Knowles, a Montana lawyer who sought the office of state attorney general in 1892, after having successfully lobbied in 1889 for the passage of a state law that allowed women to practice law in Montana. Although she gained five thousand more votes than any other candiate on the Populist ticket, she lost the election in the outlying precincts, where she was relatively unknown. After her Republican opponent had gained office, she was appointed to a four-year term as assistant attorney general. During the mid 1890s she also served as a delegate to county, state, and national Populist conventions and as a member of the Populist National Committee.[50]

At the height of its popularity during the 1890s, the Populist cause inspired many women to hold high hopes for the future. They flocked to political meetings and enthusiastically supported demonstrations. They even extended their concern to issues that were not directly related to the farm problem. In 1894, many of them took an active role in Coxey's March on Washington, which appealed to the Congress of the United States to aid the unemployed by creating temporary public-works jobs. Coxey's March gained a large following on the Plains, where men joined "regiments" as marchers and women served as home guards, auxiliaries, and suppliers of food and other resources. Although "Coxey's Army" achieved little actual relief for the unemployed, the large number of women who worked on its behalf indicated the strong political activism of women on the Great Plains.[51]

That many plainswomen entered the political sphere during the latter decades of the nineteenth century is not as revolutionary as it may at first sound. Women had long held elected positions on local, county, and state school boards. One particularly appropriate case was that of Olive Pickering Rankin, the mother of Jeanette Rankin, the first woman to serve in the United States Congress. Olive Rankin was the only woman on the school board in Missoula, Montana, for many years.[52] Also, women occasionally held municipal offices. Perhaps the most notable of these was Meodra Salter, who in 1887 was elected mayor of Argonia, Kansas, allegedly the first woman in the world to hold such an office. And women often served as county superintendent of schools, an elected position. One example is Grace Reed Porter of South Dakota, who in 1908 campaigned successfully for the office of county superintendent on the Progressive ticket. After an energetic campaign that involved a good deal of traveling and public speaking, Porter carried every precinct in the county except the one in which her opponent lived.[53]

Women who chose political action often did so because they believed it was the only way to protect their homes and families on a particular issue. Luna Kellie first became aware of the possibilities of political power for women when a number of men who did not have school-age children tried to cut down the length of the school term in order to reduce local taxes. To achieve their ends, these men enlisted the votes of their grown sons and a temporary hired man. Kellie realized that she and her female friends who had small children had little recourse because they themselves lacked the right to vote. "Right then I saw for the first time that a woman might be interested in politics and want a vote," she later explained. "I had been taught it was unwomanly to concern oneself with politics and that only the worst class of women would ever vote if they had a chance etc etc but now I saw where a decent mother might wish very much to vote on local affairs at least." Sharing her concern, both Kellie's father and her husband promoted a movement that resulted in women's being allowed to vote in local school elections. Not satisfied with that, Kellie's husband urged her on to further political involvement by arguing that women should also have a voice in establishing a "clean community" by voting in general elections.[54]

Although thousands of plainswomen began to believe, like Kellie, that the vote was a logical and necessary tool in women's fight to maintain order and morality in both home and society, many more opposed the idea. While in 1888, one Kansas woman placed on her daughter's head a cap that had presidential candidate Belva Lockwood's name on it, other women insisted that voting should continue to be the province of men. Antisuffragists declared that women's duties should center on their homes and families and that only men should make political decisions. These women spoke out publicly against suffrage and often formed antisuffrage associations to combat the prosuffrage groups.[55]

Despite the opposition, some strong voices urged on those plainswomen who believed in their right to vote. Soon after the founding of the National Woman Suffrage Association in 1869, Elizabeth Cady Stanton and Susan

B. Anthony began to travel through the western states, speaking on behalf of woman suffrage. In 1871 the pair took their initial westward trip traveling on the new transcontinental railroad. They were particularly interested in learning about conditions in Wyoming Territory, the first place in the nation to grant women the right to vote. They stopped first in Cheyenne, where they were met by Amalia B. Post, a Wyoming suffragist who was also a justice of the peace. Post told them that Wyoming's two thousand women enjoyed their political rights and practiced them responsibly. Stanton later described Wyoming as a "blessed land, where for the first time in the history of the world, the true idea of a just government is realized, where woman is the political equal of man."[56]

Wyoming's women won the right to vote in 1869, partly because of the growth of the belief that women needed the ballot to become more effective reformers and moral caretakers of the rough frontier society in which they lived. It was an idea that had particular impact in a territory composed largely of cattle ranches, towns, and long drives; cowboys, prostitutes, and other highly migratory workers; ubiquitous saloons; unregulated vigilance committees; and other ills. In the raw Wyoming Territory, people who were concerned with ensuring the future growth of the area as well as those who were anxious to expand the rights of women soon saw the possibilities of the "law and order" position. According to these women and men, women needed access to the ballot box if they were to be truly effective social housekeepers. In turn, the right of suffrage would attract women to Wyoming. As these women settlers established law and order, Wyoming Territory would grow and prosper.

Although Esther Hobart Morris is commonly given credit as being the prime mover in the achievement of suffrage in Wyoming, other authorities dispute the importance of her role. As the person who reportedly pushed legislator William H. Bright to introduce the suffrage bill in the Wyoming Territorial Legislature, Morris was later heralded as the Mother of Woman Suffrage. Evidently, she did pledge her support to his candidacy for the first territorial legislature if he would promise to initiate a suffrage bill, if he was elected.[57] Bright, the husband of an ardent suffragist, followed through on his pledge. In late November 1869 he offered a simple resolution to the council, or upper house, over which he presided: "That every woman of the age of eighteen years, residing in this Territory, may, at any election to be holden under the laws thereof, cast her vote." The bill would also give women the right to hold political office. The proposal drew opposition from several legislators and occasioned some satire in the Laramie press.[58] However, after amending the proposal to read twenty-one years of age instead of eighteen, the totally Democratic legislature adopted the Woman's Rights Bill in early December. Governor John A. Campbell, Wyoming's Republican executive, signed the suffrage bill into law on 10 December 1869.[59]

The first woman to go to the Wyoming polls in Laramie on 6 September 1870 was Eliza Swain, who was later described as a "gentle white-haired old lady who . . . wore a little shawl over her shoulders, and who had put on a clean white apron."[60] As the first woman in the world known to have cast a legal vote in a general election, Swain established a tradition that many other women were delighted to follow. In recalling the election some years later, the *Laramie Republican-Boomerang* noted that ninety-three women went to the polls on that fall day in Laramie; sixty-four voted the Republican ticket, and twenty-nine supported the Democratic one. The newspaper also reported that shortly after the election, the editor of the *Laramie Sentinel* received a letter from a Minnesota woman, relating her desire to bring her daughters to Wyoming. This pro-Wyoming sentiment on her part stemmed from her "conviction that in Wyoming, woman is respected and given some chance for her life." Over the years, many women made similar statements, which revealed the great pride they derived from their status as voters.[61]

Meanwhile, in 1872, certain members of the second territorial legislature who questioned the impact of woman suffrage decided to attempt to end it after it had been in force for only two years. The attempt to repeal woman suffrage was spearheaded by Ben Sheeks, an attorney from South Pass City, who had been the most vehement opponent of the original resolution in 1869. All of the Democrats in the legislature voted for repeal, supposedly because so many women supported their Republican opponents, while all of the legislature's Republicans cast their ballots against repeal.[62]

In addition to exercising the right of franchise, some Wyoming women also seized the opportunity to serve in positions that had formerly been closed to them. In March 1870 the first female jurors sat in a Laramie courtroom. The first woman called to jury service was Eliza Stewart Boyd, who was also one of the first teachers in Laramie. The judge's opening remark to the jury was his pledge of protection of the women members from "the sneers, jeers, and insults" of their detractors. The judge, however, could not shield them from the attentions of the numerous reporters who poured into Laramie to observe this unprecedented phenomenon. Despite the unpleasant situation created by the media, other women jurors and a woman bailiff were soon appointed.[63]

Other women held political office. During the fall of 1870, Esther Morris, at fifty-seven years of age, became the first woman to hold the position of justice of the peace. Morris presided in her hometown of South Pass City, where she heard her first case on 20 October 1870. Newspapers both at home and in other states termed her commanding, venerable, and just.[64] Years later, Mary Godot Bellamy, a teacher and dedicated clubwoman, became the first woman to be elected to the Wyoming Legislature. Taking her seat in 1910, Bellamy began her work for laws to protect women and children, to grant more liberal probate provisions for married women, and to increase the support for the state university.[65] In 1924 the voters of Wyoming once again elected a woman to high political office by choosing Nellie Tayloe Ross as the first female to be governor of any state.[66]

As interest in woman suffrage grew among Plains' settlers, so did the number of groups advocating it. From the mid 1870s on, the Grange advocated equality between women and men, women's participation in political life, and woman suffrage. After educator and temperance reformer Frances Willard became president of the Women's Christian Temperance Union in 1879, that organization also added woman suffrage to its multifaceted program of reform. According to Willard, "a government organized and conducted by one half of the human unit, a government of the minority, by the minority, for the minority, must always bear unequally on the whole." On the Plains, WCTU groups sponsored prosuffrage programs, held suffrage rallies, distributed suffrage literature, and sent lobbyists to state legislatures. One such lobbyist from North Dakota soon grew disgusted with her state legislators. In 1882 she bitterly wrote, "The one thing that has served as a pleasing recreation to our Solons, helped to smooth the furrows from their noble brows, & given new zest to life . . . is the periodical coquetting with the women suffrage bill." Still, she admitted that although "the standing committee on woman suffrage used to be considered a standing joke," it was gradually being taken more seriously.[67]

Despite the efforts of these groups and of the proponents of woman suffrage in individual states, the achievement of woman suffrage came haltingly on the Plains. In Kansas, for example, in 1861 the first constitution not only guaranteed women an equal share in the control of their children and property, but the state legislature also gave them the right to vote in school elections. In 1887, this provision was widened to include city and bond elections. The Kansas suffrage movement was aided in large part by Clarinda I. H. Nichols, a member of the first constitutional convention in 1859 and an energetic speaker and writer on behalf of women's rights until her death in 1885. Yet it was not until 1912 that the endeavors of Nichols and other suffragists resulted in a state constitutional amendment that provided for universal suffrage in Kansas.[68]

In Nebraska the process by which woman suffrage became a serious issue was indeed slow. Here, the suffrage fight began as early as 1855, when reformer Amelia Bloomer addressed the territorial legislature in Omaha on the topic of woman suffrage. In 1867, Nebraska became the second state to grant suffrage to its female citizens in school elections, yet women's access to all elections was not easily achieved. In 1871 the Nebraska Constitutional Convention discussed and rejected woman suffrage. In that year a broadside titled "The Great Platte Circus" reflected the attitude of many

Nebraskans by satirizing women's-rights reformers as being little more than circus performers with wide public appeal.[69]

A long suffrage campaign followed in Nebraska. It involved the appearances of Stanton, Anthony, the British suffragist Emmeline Goulden Pankhurst, and the nationally known suffragist Anna Howard Shaw. A strong state suffrage association was also organized. In a 1910 letter, one of the officers of this Nebraska Woman Suffrage Association speculated that a recent woman-suffrage provision had failed as a result of the opposition of the "liquor interests," who feared the possibility that women would vote in prohibition. With the strength of the liquor interests in mind, the suffrage association increased its pressure through rallies, open meetings, state conventions, literature, and petition campaigns. Yet, strong opposition kept woman suffrage from becoming a reality in Nebraska until 1919, when Nebraska became the fourteenth state to ratify the national suffrage amendment.[70]

A similar process occurred in Colorado, where woman suffrage was first discussed by the territorial legislators in 1868 and 1869. Despite Governor Edward M. McCook's 1870 recommendation that woman suffrage be adopted and despite an energetic petition campaign by its proponents, the measure failed to pass. When it was again considered in 1867, the woman-suffrage issue was largely side-stepped, although Colorado women were granted the right to vote in school elections. Even though Susan B. Anthony spoke on behalf of the issue all over Colorado in 1877, a woman-suffrage referendum failed. Public debate over the woman-suffrage issue rose and fell periodically until 1893, when the people of Colorado approved a woman-suffrage amendment, with a margin of some six thousand votes.[71]

Victory came much later in Dakota Territory, even though many women exhibited an interest in voting during the 1870s. They participated in local and national suffrage associations and rallies and supported the appearances of such suffrage campaigners as Matilda Joslyn Gage, Susan B. Anthony, and Elizabeth Cady Stanton in Yankton and other towns. In 1885 a woman-suffrage amendment passed the territorial legislature, only to be killed by Governor Gilbert A. Pierce, who feared that it would delay the granting of statehood for South Dakota. When statehood was realized in 1889, the Constitution of South Dakota allowed male voters to delete the word *male* from its suffrage clause if they so wished, thus giving women the right to vote, but the voters rejected the idea. Subsequent woman-suffrage provisions also failed. Many more years of suffrage efforts followed, based on the work of such individuals as Jane Rooker Breeden and Mary Shields Pyle and such organizations as the WCTU, the South Dakota Federation of Women's Clubs, and the Women's Relief Corps. Suffrage leaders increased the intensity of petition campaigns, and in 1905 a petition measuring thirty-six yards in length was carried up the aisle of the house chamber. Yet, in spite of all the energy expended, South Dakota women did not receive the vote until 1918, only two years before the ratification of the Nineteenth Amendment to the United States Constitution.[72]

In Montana the suffrage campaign began relatively late. The first state suffrage association was formed in 1895, at the instigation of the Helena Suffrage Club. Carrie Chapman Catt, president of the National American Woman Suffrage Association, was present to address and instruct the group in their work. In the following year, the Populist attorney Ella Knowles secured a woman-suffrage plank in the Populist state platform, and in 1897 she invaded the halls of the state legislature with a petition bearing the names of three thousand Montanans who favored suffrage. The suffrage resolution that was introduced in the house failed by only five votes. During the opening decade of the twentieth century, Catt returned to Montana on a lecture tour, and suffragists repeatedly appealed to the state legislature. In 1911, Glendive women were successful in having a suffrage bill introduced. When this bill also met with defeat, another was introduced in 1913, largely through the efforts of Jeanette Rankin, who had recently entered the suffrage fray. At the same time, the Montana WCTU launched a strenuous campaign of its own, which brought much attention to the suffrage issue, although it also alarmed the state's liquor interests. Finally, in 1914, Montana became the eleventh state in the nation to grant its women the right of elective franchise. Three years later, it sent Jeanette Rankin to the House of Representatives of the Congress of the United States.[73]

At the time of the ratification of the Nineteenth Amendment, seventeen states, all of them in the West except for New York, were already allowing women to vote. On the Plains, only North Dakota, Oklahoma, and Texas had failed to adopt woman suffrage before the federal government mandated it in 1920. Although these states had not been immune from the woman-suffrage debates that often raged about them, they had not been able to enact such provisions as had their neighbors.[74]

The remaining question concerns the types of rewards that plainswomen derived from their tremendous range of community activities, whether they were in a library, a church, or a polling place. It is virtually a truism that people join a voluntary association because it answers a basic social need and that the ideologies and goals espoused by such a group allow individuals to sustain or enhance their own self-images.[75] These principles certainly apply to plainswomen who obtained satisfactions on many levels from their community involvement. It is quite apparent that they gained the companionship not only of other women but usually of like-minded women as well. They achieved much-needed reforms in frontier societies. And they also learned skills that would serve them in other capacities. By acting as leaders, secretaries, bookkeepers, editors, and organizers of voluntary associations, numerous plainswomen inadvertently prepared themselves for a variety of other undertakings. At the same time, they increased their personal pride in their own achievements.

Probing a little deeper, it might be argued that these reform-oriented women also resisted cultural values that restricted them to a domestic sphere. By moving into community action, these social housekeepers expanded their own world and forced society in general to recognize their social worth. As civilizing forces, community-minded women could gain a heightened sense of self-esteem as well as a certain measure of superiority over a group of people—in other words, men—who enjoyed privileges denied to women. The broadening of women's lives and roles was, according to its numerous proponents, not supposed to threaten men. Because its underlying rationale was that women needed whatever was at issue—such as some freedom from domestic duties or even the vote—in order to carry out their moral obligations in the larger community, it was hoped that they would not be seen as the potential usurpers of men's roles.[76]

Indeed, women did not replace men as community workers and reformers. Men continued to engage in a wide range of projects that centered on social problems, culture, religion, education, and politics. Numerous men opposed the consumption of alcohol and the existence of saloons. Some men supported cultural activities by forming bands or by helping to establish public lending libraries. Others helped to build church and school buildings, sang in church choirs, and served as members of school boards. Other men joined political organizations and held office.[77]

Although women's entry into the public sphere did not push men out, neither did women and men typically integrate their efforts. Rather, frequently working through women's clubs, societies, and auxiliaries, women established their own community roles and duties. As women increasingly entered this growing area of activity and influence, so did they expand women's traditional domestic sphere by becoming housekeepers of the community as well as of the home.

Whatever the region or era, frontierswomen's lives exhibited many similar and enduring characteristics. Pioneer Woman statue in Ponca City's State Park, Ponca City, Oklahoma. Courtesy of Bob Westmoreland.

9
The Female Frontier
on the Prairie and on the Plains

This comparative view of the lives of women settlers on the prairie and on the Plains illustrates a number of significant similarities, despite the differences between the regions. Because these women focused their attention upon domestic production, childbirth, childcare, family relationships, and other tasks defined as female, they were affected only secondarily by the resources of an area. These female settlers pursued a comparable list of duties and interests in every frontier setting. They managed or helped to manage their families and households; they also acted as the conservators of family, religious, racial, and ethnic traditions. When they held paid employment or produced income in some way, gender, rather than region, was the determining factor, so that women were typically limited to such "female" occupations as teacher, milliner, shop clerk, and domestic servant. Even when women moved into the larger community as civic innovators and reformers, they did so in a gender-defined way—as "social housekepers," rather than as integral parts of the male world of power and politics.

The roles of female settlers were also shaped only marginally by the occupations and economic pursuits of their fathers, brothers, and husbands. Women helped with farm and ranch work, ran taverns and inns, clerked in family stores and other businesses, and kept a parsonage or the office of an Indian agent going. But in virtually every case, women's focus continued to be domestic. More often the helper than the boss, these women cared for animals, aided in planting and harvesting, cooked meals for threshers or customers, cleaned business places and offices, arranged goods, and dealt with clients. This, of course, was all in addition to continuing their own domestic responsibilities and the production of the necessary household supplies and foodstuffs.

In addition, the lives of prairie women and of plainswomen retained a similarity, despite the passage of time. Because the new technology appeared more slowly in the home than it did in the field or the business place, women's work showed a wearying sameness, whether it was in the early or the late nineteenth century. Although hand-dipped candles were replaced by kerosene lamps, the work involved was still tedious, and it largely belonged to women and whatever help they might be able to enlist. Sewing did become easier when the treadle-powered sewing machine appeared, but the production of family clothing remained a laborious female responsibility. When labor-saving equipment did make its way into the home, support technology was slow to accompany it, so that generations of women carried buckets of water from a well or a pump, whether they were washing "on the board" or in a new-style washing machine.

This is not to argue that region, men's occupations, or era had no effect at all on women's lives. Region did create some differences in women's work. Plainswomen, for example, faced greater difficulties in obtaining water for washing and other tasks than did women living on the prairie. A man's occupation also set certain limitations on a woman's life. A ranchwoman might live in a fairly isolated setting, while a judge's wife had to cope with the crowding and associated problems of urban living. Era contributed further differentiation. A woman of 1900 might have an indoor pump available to her, while a woman of 1820 hauled water from an outdoor well. The key point, however, is that women, whether living on the prairie or the Plains, whether associated with a farmer, miner, or professional, whether early in the nineteenth century or early in the twentieth, carried almost total responsibility for the maintenance of home and family. The orientation and the direction of women's lives were forged far more by gender than by region, male pursuits, or era.

Even such factors as social class, ethnicity, race, religion, education, and marital status did not alter the gender expectations of prairie women and plainswomen in any substantial way. The wealthy woman might pursue her domestic tasks with the help of slaves or servants, but it was her duty to see that the tasks were done. Non-American-born women and black women usually faced more difficult adjustments to frontier living than did the average American-born white woman, but the former confronted the same challenges in fulfilling their domestic roles. A woman of a particular religious or educational background might approach her domestic functions in a slightly different manner than did other women, but she accepted them as hers. And a single woman might be somewhat freer from domestic chores than a married woman, but she was still expected, as a matter of course, to contribute to the care of whatever family or household she lived in.

Women who resisted the dictates of this female world usually encountered pervasive social controls, which enforced the traditional rules. Women who emulated men—for example, "Mountain Charley" and Elizabeth "Bill Newcom" Smith—were seen as odd and deviant. Other women who rejected the norm in lesser ways—by riding astride, seeking more education than was usual for women at the time, or even requesting the right to vote—often received their share of criticism and scorn as well. Widespread and general resistance to alterations in women's sphere perhaps explains why women who forged into new areas tended to bolster their actions with domestically oriented rationalizations and arguments. Suffrage, for example, was said to be necessary to women's responsibilities as community caretakers and moral guardians. Apparently, even women who expanded their horizons did so with traditional female values as their guides.

That women's lives on the prairie and on the Plains were more alike than they were disparate and that men's were more disparate than alike can be reinforced by a brief review of a number of women's and men's stories that are recorded in diaries, daybooks, journals, letters, memoirs, reminiscences, and oral-history interviews. Women's words demonstrate that their experiences exhibited a remarkable similarity as a result of being shaped by the prevailing concepts of the female gender and associated ideas of "women's work." Men's words, on the other hand, show an equally remarkable differentiation among their lives, roles, and contributions to prairie and Plains society.

Beginning with farm and ranch women, it is apparent that women's lives centered on home and family, while men not only farmed or ranched but also pursued such additional occupations as carpenter, railroad worker, mail carrier, or harness maker. In these jobs, men exercised a wide variety of skills, traveled away from the farm or ranch, and were often absent for extended periods of time. Their wives, daughters, and sisters, however, were tied to the farm or ranch home and the specific duties that this entailed. Although these women did often help their brothers, fathers, or husbands with their jobs, the women themselves concentrated upon their domestic cares. A case in point was Mary Huntress Carruthers of Montana, who married a carpenter-farmer in 1893, when she was nineteen years old. From that time on, Carruthers devoted her energies to rearing a family of adopted children, sewing for extra cash, and helping with the family farm and dairy. It was not until her husband died that she added total control of the dairy to her myriad other tasks. She soon remarried and resumed the position of wife and mother without the additional burden of being dairy manager.[1] In the case of Lillie Goodrich of Wyoming, who chose to handle most of the farm work in her family beginning in the 1880s, the domestic responsibility still dominated her thinking. She hired her sister to do the housework, rather than automatically assigning it to her husband, as he would have done with her had he gone into the fields. She also dutifully shaved her house-husband spouse every morning before she went out to the fields, and she carried her babies with her in a cracker box, which she attached to her plow.[2]

The centrality of the domestic side for farm and ranch women can be seen in situations involving professional women. Beginning in the 1870s, nurses

Jean Todd and Muriel B. Scott followed their professions as sidelines to home and family, while physician Abbie Ann Jarvis carried on an active practice in addition to fulfilling all of her domestic responsibilities as a farm wife and mother.[3] Although Evelyn Cameron was a skilled and talented photographer of the late nineteenth century, she practiced her profession only when she could take time from her family and ranch responsibilities.[4] Around the turn of the twentieth century, Grace Reed Porter put her farm home and family first, developing her distinguished career as an educator and clubwoman on the side.[5]

Women who were attached to professional men, on the other hand, handled all the domestic responsibilities, besides helping out in many ways. Thus, unlike professional women, these men were free to pursue their talents and often had the assistance of an unpaid helper as well. The reminiscences of a doctor's wife revealed that after her marriage in 1875, she cooked, cleaned, and cared for herself, her husband, and their children, while also cooking and caring for his patients, cleaning his office, laundering his soiled towels and bandages, and keeping his accounts.[6] Throughout the nineteenth century, minister's wives similarly maintained their homes and families while attending religious meetings, running church auxiliaries, handling the church's financial accounts, and tending to parishioners. One such wife, who was also a minister herself, ranked domestic matters first, her husband's religious duties second, and her own career as a minister a weak third.[7]

Numerous other women followed their men to widely disparate locations, yet their lives were still very much like other women's lives once they had arrived, because they all revolved around the domestic scene. For instance, during the 1830s, Caroline Phelps established crude homes and raised her children in the fur trader's back country. During the early 1850s, "Mother" Baldwin created a home and bore the first child in a mining camp and then in an Indian trading post. And during the 1870s and 1880s, Mary Ronan and Coraline Boesl kept house and raised their children on Indian reservations. Aside from packing furs or weighing ore, their stories were largely interchangeable.[8]

Women who followed their men to towns on the prairie and on the Plains also found their lives shaped more by gender than by location. Attached to men who were judges, attorneys, postmasters, business entrepreneurs, and druggists, these women were just as consumed by home and family as were their counterparts on a ranch or in a mining camp. A Grand Forks, North Dakota, woman who married an attorney recalled that she sat "on the sidelines and watched" as he established himself professionally during the 1880s.[9] In another case, the letters of Mary Wright Edgerton, the wife of the first governor of Montana Territory during the early 1860s, reflected little of the mining town of Bannack in which she lived. Instead, they overflowed with concerns about children, clothing, cooking, and the lack of hired help.

Neither region nor her husband's profession seemed to have any discernible impact upon her life style.[10]

The point that gender was the prime determinant of women's roles and responsibilities on the prairie and on the Plains can be seen even more dramatically in the writings of women who lived in several areas, whose husbands changed occupations, and who lived through several historical eras, yet whose focus was unwaveringly domestic. One such woman married a sheepman in 1897. A few years after their marriage he pursued a number of odd jobs and finally signed on with the Chicago, Milwaukee, and St. Paul Railroad. During these years, she bore her first child on a sheep ranch in Montana, her second child in a log cabin there, then moved to the town of Malta, served as the cook on another sheep ranch, and lived in a frame house and then over a restaurant in Aberdeen, South Dakota, while her husband was gone for weeks at a time with the railroad. She followed him to Washington State, and when he was killed in a boiler explosion, she returned to Aberdeen as a widow with children to raise. Here, she "made beds" in a local hotel and eventually lived out her later years "helping out" in the home of a married son.[11] Another case was that of Susan Carter, who started her adult life as a single homesteader and teacher in 1886, later lived in Lead, South Dakota, and Morrill, Nebraska, as a wife and mother, and finally relocated as a widow to Torrington, Wyoming, where she cooked in a restaurant.[12] Throughout the nineteenth century, numerous other women moved from railroad town to farm to mining town; were married, widowed, and remarried; and saw seventy or eighty years of history pass before their eyes, yet never wavered from home and family as the primary force in their lives.[13]

Unmarried, divorced, deserted, and widowed women were also not able to escape this powerful domestic and gender orientation. If they lived with their birth families, they were expected to contribute fully to the care of the younger children and to the maintenance of the household. Although they often attended school or held paid employment outside the home, domestic duties filled their hours at home and sometimes demanded that they take a day off from the schoolroom or the work place.[14] Many unmarried women chose to become unpaid household help for a single or married brother.[15] Others lived with friends, perhaps in a homestead shack or what one young woman called a teacherage.[16] Here, unmarried women cared for themselves, their homes, and their jobs, in contrast to many single men, who actively sought wives, hired help, sisters, or cousins, or at least packages from home, to alleviate the need to tackle their own domestic needs.[17]

An examination of men's writings discloses a very different life progression for male settlers on the prairie and the Plains, as compared with females. While earning a living might be pinpointed as the primary factor that influenced men's lives, the range of occupations, locales, and experiences that accompanied men's "bread-winning" function were much more diversified than those associated with women's domestic roles. The key word in describing men's diaries, letters, memoirs, reminiscences, and oral-history interviews is, in fact, variety. Male settlers on the prairie and the Plains recorded daily details of farm and business transactions, but they also wrote about experiments with crops, new machinery, political involvements, business enterprises, professional advancement, mining and lumber camps, ranch work, trail drives, stagecoaching, railroading, musical and literary performances, military adventures, and travel.[18]

Despite their great interest in occupational and other endeavors in the world outside their homes, men also sometimes noted their concern for, and their ties to, home and family. In his diary in 1838, Edmund F. Ely of Minnesota confided his joy over the birth of a daughter: "A.M. my dear Catharine gave birth to a second daughter—both doing well . . . The Lord give us grace."[19] Other men expressed their loneliness when separated from their wives. In 1865, Dr. Noah M. Glatfelter wrote to his wife, Mary: "I wish you were here. I hope you are well & pass your time pleasantly. . . . I am very anxious to hear from you."[20] A few years later, politician David Davis told his wife, Sarah: "The separation Dearest is hard to bear—A few friends & my family are all I want."[21] Yet although they had their domestic side, men's activities ranged farther afield than women's were ever allowed to do.

This is not to suggest that men's lives were more significant than women's, only that they were different and more varied. Region, occupation, and era created many dissimilarities between men's roles, responsibilities, and contributions at the same time that they exerted a far-lesser impact upon women. The dissimilarities were evident in contemporary expectations of women's and men's lives. When people described what they thought to be the achievements of women, they usually did so in terms of wifehood and motherhood, domesticity, home, and family. Yet when people recounted what they saw as significant in the lives of men, they emphasized public achievements and minimized their private lives. The same people who believed that the domestic realm was adequate, indeed fulfilling, for women felt that men's lives should move far beyond the confines of their homes. Parents who protectively held their daughters close to them also beamed with pride as their sons journeyed to the ranches, farms, mines, and lumber camps of the Far West.

Because of this pervasive domestic orientation and associated ties to household and children, it was the women who stayed at home waiting, while the men of the family made and lost fortunes as Argonauts, scouted the West for better farm or business sites, worked on far-flung ranches or in lumber camps, or spent several months or years establishing new homes for their families. Women also stayed at home while their fathers, brothers, and husbands participated in the many scientific or military expeditions that pushed into virtually every frontier area at one time or another. Instead of being able to venture forth on their own, most women waited for the return of the wanderers or to be summoned to join them. What is perhaps most significant for the purposes of this discussion is that although "women-in-waiting" frequently became pseudo men who ran family farms and businesses, their letters and diaries did not begin to sound like men's. Far from abandoning their domestic concentration, most of the women who held things together in the absence of men were anxious to relinquish most of the cares that it brought to them.[22]

Additional insight into the dissimilarities between female and male settlers can be gained from comparing the diaries of wives and husbands. Catharine Bissell Ely and Edmund F. Ely of Minnesota both kept diaries between 1835 and 1839. Presumably, the experiences that they shared as settlers were somewhat alike, yet their records of the events of those years are very different. For instance, Catharine's copious notations regarding her two daughters' first steps, teeth, and words and other little achievements made Edmund's diary entries concerning the births of these children seem absolutely brusque by comparison. Moreover, Catharine's diary brimmed over with household affairs, while Edmund's was filled with his travels and his work as a preacher. Her accounts emphasized the activities of family members and books that she had read, while his focused upon the people whom he met and the wilderness adventures that he survived. The daily jottings of wife and husband made it apparent that although they shared a marriage, a home, a family, and a life in frontier Minnesota, they did so not only as two different people but also as two people with disparate gender roles and expectations.[23]

Clearly, the lives of male settlers on the prairie and the Plains exhibited much heterogeneity, while those of females were marked by a high degree of homogeneity. Women's shared responsibilities, life styles, and sensibilities constituted a female frontier, that is, a comparable set of orientations and responses that in most ways transcended the region of the frontier in which they settled, the occupations of the men of their families, and the historical period in which they lived. Unlike the concepts of the cattle or the mining frontier, which are male defined, the concept of the female frontier speaks to the experiences of the frontierswoman rather than the frontiersman. By so doing, it provides a perspective, a methodological tool, by which the history of women's westering can eventually become as complete as that of men's.

Appendixes

Numbers of Women and Men (All Races) in the
Prairie States during the Early Period of Settlement

	1830	1840	1850	1860	1870
Illinois					
Women	73,829	218,904	403,149	809,169	1,223,354
Men	82,872	257,279	448,321	902,750	1,316,537
Indiana					
Women	165,291	329,361	476,523	650,999	822,643
Men	177,742	356,505	511,893	699,139	857,994
Iowa					
Women	NA	18,757	91,168	320,382	568,103
Men	NA	24,355	101,052	354,466	625,917
Minnesota					
Women	NA	NA	2,361	77,824	204,407
Men	NA	NA	3,716	91,930	235,299
Missouri					
Women	54,069	180,607	324,212	502,233	824,948
Men	62,036	203,095	537,832	564,828	896,347

NA=figures not available

Sources: Abstract of the Returns of the Fifth Census (Washington, D.C.: Printed by Duff Green, 1832), pp. 48–51; *Sixth Census or Enumeration of the Inhabitants of the United States, 1840* (Washington, D.C.: Blair & Rives, 1841), pp. 396, 374, 368, 418; *The Seventh Census of the United States, 1850* (Washington, D.C.: Robert C. Armstrong, 1853), pp. 702, 756, 943, 993, 655; *Preliminary Report on the Eighth Census, 1860* (Washington, D.C.: Government Printing Office, 1862), p. 134; and *Ninth Census*, vol. 1: *The Statistics of the Population of the United States* (Washington, D.C.: Government Printing Office, 1872), p. 606. All statistics were compiled by my research assistant, Rebecca L. Wheeler.

APPENDIX 2
Numbers of Women and Men (All Races) in the
Plains States during the Early Period of Settlement

	1870	1880	1890	1900	1910
Kansas					
Women	162,175	459,429	674,984	701,779	805,037
Men	202,224	536,667	752,112	768,716	885,912
Montana					
Women	3,824	10,982	44,277	93,487	149,181
Men	16,771	28,177	87,882	149,842	226,872
Nebraska					
Women	52,568	203,161	486,086	501,708	564,432
Men	70,425	249,241	572,824	564,592	627,782
North Dakota					
Women	5,303	52,881	81,129	141,653	259,502
Men	8,878	82,296	101,590	177,493	317,554
Oklahoma					
Women	NA	NA	27,101	183,972	775,577
Men			34,733	214,359	881,578
South Dakota					
Women	NA	NA	148,558	185,406	266,776
Men			180,250	216,164	317,112
Wyoming					
Women	1,899	6,637	21,362	34,387	54,295
Men	7,219	14,152	39,343	58,184	91,670

NA=figures not available

Sources: Ninth Census, vol 1: *Population and Social Statistics* (Washington, D.C.: Government Printing Office, 1872), p. 606; *Compendium of the Tenth Census,* rev. ed., pt. 1 (Washington, D.C.: Government Printing Office, 1885), p. 2; *Abstract of the Eleventh Census,* 2d ed. (Washington, D.C.: Government Printing Office, 1896), p. 38; *Abstract of the Twelfth Census of the United States,* 1900, 3d ed. (Washington, D.C.: Government Printing Office, 1904), p. 39; and *Thirteenth Census of the United States, Taken in the Year 1910,* vol. 1: *Population: General Report and Analysis* (Washington, D.C.: Government Printing Office, 1913), p. 258. See also David J. Wishart, "Age and Sex Composition of the Population on the Nebraska Frontier, 1860–1880," *Nebraska History* 54, 1 (Mar. 1973): 106–19. This and other tables do not include Texas and Colorado, because only portions of those states were part of the Great Plains and statistics for those portions alone are not available.

APPENDIX 3
Ages of Women in the Prairie States during the Early Period of Settlement

	1830	1840	1850	1860	1870
Illinois					
Under 20	46,728	132,262	234,384	446,003	648,466
20 to 39	19,311	61,508	116,637	249,418	373,135
40 to 59	5,797	19,226	42,714	91,301	158,354
60 and over	1,177	4,032	9,109	22,314	43,339
Indiana					
Under 20	103,977	199,996	280,460	368,187	441,387
20 to 39	42,405	87,884	131,743	186,641	241,683
40 to 59	13,836	30,726	51,099	75,222	106,630
60 and over	3,296	7,319	13,077	20,987	32,935
Iowa					
Under 20		11,292	54,257	182,819	310,724
20 to 39	NA	5,654	26,151	94,463	166,092
40 to 59		1,473	9,011	35,205	72,160
60 and over		245	1,716	7,895	19,117
Minnesota					
Under 20			1,322	42,644	112,694
20 to 39	NA	NA	826	26,706	58,928
40 to 59			185	7,896	26,311
60 and over			28	1,692	6,474
Missouri					
Under 20	34,191	93,552	191,709	320,012	453,637
20 to 39	13,912	41,219	93,427	167,521	250,731
40 to 59	4,217	12,839	32,062	58,570	96,917
60 and over	1,064	2,808	6,954	13,491	23,660

NA=figures not available
Figures for 1830 and 1840 are for whites only; others include all races.

Sources: Abstract of Returns of the Fifth Census (Washington, D.C.: Duff Green, 1832), pp. 49–51; *Sixth Census or Enumeration of the Inhabitants of the United States, 1840* (Washington, D.C.: Blair & Rives, 1841), pp. 396, 368, 374, 416–17; *The Seventh Census of the United States, 1850* (Washington, D.C.: Robert Armstrong, 1853), pp. 694–701, 748–55, 644–54, 938–42, 988–92; *Population of the United States in 1860* (Washington, D.C.: Government Printing Office, 1864), pp. 84–85, 110–11, 136–37, 252–53, 284–85; and *Ninth Census,* vol. 2: *The Vital Statistics of the United States* (Washington, D.C.: Government Printing Office, 1872), pp. 565, 568, 570, 574.

APPENDIX 4

Ages of Women in the Plains States during the Early Period of Settlement

	1870	1880	1890	1900	1910
Kansas					
Under 20	88,865	247,793	342,393	330,203	349,067
20 to 39	52,344	139,963	201,068	212,997	258,175
40 to 59	17,437	58,342	101,603	115,378	108,258
60 and over	3,526	13,311	29,484	42,195	59,582
Montana					
Under 20	1,825	5,608	20,062	43,184	64,461
20 to 39	1,564	3,944	17,771	34,728	55,298
40 to 59	351	1,241	5,238	12,414	23,596
60 and over	34	189	982	2,997	5,541
Nebraska					
Under 20	28,239	109,618	250,119	246,006	253,624
20 to 39	17,652	63,522	154,911	153,641	182,421
40 to 59	5,551	24,206	63,227	76,582	91,958
60 and over	1,117	5,815	17,471	24,977	35,925
North Dakota					
Under 20	2,820	27,647	41,722	75,625	131,399
20 to 39	1,781	17,790	27,173	42,299	84,766
40 to 59	574	6,008	9,184	18,281	33,531
60 and over	128	1,436	2,927	5,277	9,396
Oklahoma					
Under 20			14,285	97,431	402,531
20 to 39	NA	NA	8,612	54,461	242,466
40 to 59			3,555	25,012	100,367
60 and over			605	6,513	29,235
South Dakota					
Under 20			76,824	95,394	126,835
20 to 39	NA	NA	46,397	53,088	86,068
40 to 59			19,366	27,574	40,172
60 and over			3,609	9,166	13,381
Wyoming					
Under 20	786	3,246	10,453	17,029	24,293
20 to 39	947	2,565	7,914	11,713	20,351
40 to 59	151	631	2,516	4,578	7,755
60 and over	15	108	454	970	1,830

NA=figures not available

Sources: *Ninth Census*, vol. 2: *The Vital Statistics of the United States* (Washington, D.C.: Government Printing Office, 1872), pp. 565, 568, 570, 574; *Report on the Mortality and Vital Statistics of the United States at the Tenth Census*, pt. 2 (Washington, D.C.: Government Printing Office, 1886), pp. 679, 682, 685, 689; *Report of the Population of the United States at the Eleventh Census, 1890*, pt. 2 (Washington, D.C.: Government Printing Office, 1897), pp. 54–57, 70–71, 74–75, 84–85, 102–3; *Twelfth Census of the United States, Taken in the Year 1900: Population*, pt. 2 (Washington, D.C.: Government Printing Office, 1902), pp. 40–41, 60–63, 76–77, 80–81, 90–91, 108–9; and *Thirteenth Census of the United States, Taken in the Year 1910*, vol. 1: *Population: General Report and Analysis* (Washington, D.C.: Government Printing Office, 1913), pp. 375, 385–86, 393, 395, 400, 409.

APPENDIX 5
Settlers in the Prairie States by Race, 1830–1870

	1830	1840	1850	1860	1870
Illinois					
White	155,061	472,254	846,034	1,704,323	2,511,096
Black	1,640	3,929	5,436	7,628	28,762
Indiana					
White	339,499	678,698	977,154	1,339,000	1,655,837
Black	3,634	7,168	11,262	11,428	24,560
Iowa					
White	NA	42,924	191,881	673,844	1,188,207
Black		188	333	1,069	5,762
Minnesota					
White	NA	NA	6,038	171,864	438,257
Black			39	259	759
Missouri					
White	114,789	323,888	592,004	1,063,509	1,603,146
Black	1,316	59,814	90,040	118,503	118,071

NA=figures not available

Sources: Abstract of the Returns of the Fifth Census (Washington, D.C.: Duff Green, 1832), pp. 48–51; *Sixth Census or Enumeration of the Inhabitants of the United States, 1840* (Washington, D.C.: Blair & Rives, 1841), pp. 396, 368, 374; *Compendium of the Seventh Census by J. D. B. DeBow* (Washington, D.C.: A. O. P. Nicholson, 1854), pp. 48, 66, 82; *Preliminary Report on the Eighth Census, 1860* (Washington, D.C.: Government Printing Office, 1862), p. 131; and *Ninth Census,* vol. 1: *The Statistics of the Population of the United States* (Washington, D.C.: Government Printing Office, 1872), pp. 4–5.

APPENDIX 6
Settlers in the Plains States by Race, 1870–1910

	1870	1880	1890	1900	1910
Kansas					
White	346,377	952,155	1,376,553	1,416,319	1,634,352
Black	17,108	43,107	49,710	52,003	54,030
Other	0	19	97	43	173
Montana					
White	18,306	35,385	127,291	226,283	360,580
Black	183	346	1,490	1,523	1,834
Other	1,949	1,765	2,538	4,180	2,894
Nebraska					
White	122,117	449,764	1,046,888	1,056,526	1,180,293
Black	789	2,385	8,913	6,269	7,689
Other	0	18	216	183	730
North Dakota					
White	12,887	133,147	182,123	511,712	569,855
Black	94	401	373	286	617
Other	0	238	29	180	98
Oklahoma					
White	NA	NA	58,826	367,524	1,444,531
Black	NA	NA	2,973	18,831	137,612
Other	NA	NA	25	31	187
South Dakota					
White	NA	NA	327,290	380,714	563,771
Black	NA	NA	541	465	817
Other	NA	NA	195	166	163
Wyoming					
White	8,726	19,437	59,275	89,051	140,318
Black	183	298	922	940	2,235
Other	143	914	465	854	1,926

NA=figures not available
Other indicates Chinese and Japanese but not Indians.

Sources: Ninth Census, vol. 1: *The Statistics of the Population of the United States* (Washington, D.C.: Government Printing Office, 1872), pp. 606, 608; *Compendium of the Tenth Census,* rev. ed., pt. 1 (Washington, D.C.: Government Printing Office, 1885), p. 3; *Abstract of the Eleventh Census,* 2d ed. (Washington, D.C.: Government Printing Office, 1896), p. 40; *Abstract of the Twelfth Census of the United States, 1900,* 3d ed. (Washington, D.C.: Government Printing Office, 1904), p. 41; and *Thirteenth Census of the United States, Taken in the Year 1910,* vol. 1: *Population: General Report and Analysis* (Washington, D.C.: Government Printing Office, 1913), p. 141.

APPENDIX 7
Blacks in the Prairie States by Sex
during the Early Period of Settlement

	1830	1840	1850	1860	1870
Illinois					
Female	816	1,885	2,659	3,819	10,179
Male	824	2,044	2,777	3,809	11,240
Indiana					
Female	1,777	3,436	5,547	5,637	8,426
Male	1,857	3,732	5,715	5,791	9,122
Iowa					
Female	NA	89	168	503	2,167
Male	NA	99	165	566	2,502
Minnesota					
Female	NA	NA	18	133	196
Male	NA	NA	21	126	318
Missouri					
Female	685	29,625	45,195	59,446	50,533
	(400)	(28,742)			
Male	631	30,189	44,845	59,057	49,879
	(347)	(29,498)			

NA=figures not available
Figures in parentheses are numbers of slaves.

Sources: Abstract of the Returns of the Fifth Census (Washington, D.C.: Duff Green, 1832), pp. 50–51; *Sixth Census or Enumeration of the Inhabitants of the United States, 1840* (Washington, D.C.: Blair & Rives, 1841), pp. 418, 396, 374, 368; *The Seventh Census of the United States, 1850* (Washington, D.C.: Robert C. Armstrong, 1853), p. 615; *Preliminary Report of the Eighth Census, 1860* (Washington, D.C.: Government Printing Office, 1862), p. 134; and *Ninth Census,* vol. 1: *The Statistics of the Population of the United States* (Washington, D.C.: Government Printing Office, 1872), p. 608.

APPENDIX 8
Blacks in the Plains States by Sex
during the Early Period of Settlement

	1870	1880	1890	1900	1910
Kansas					
Female	8,452	20,955	24,462	25,461	26,066
Male	8,566	22,152	25,248	26,542	27,964
Montana					
Female	51	155	437	611	776
Male	132	191	1,053	912	1,058
Nebraska					
Female	338	1,089	3,670	3,368	3,430
Male	451	1,296	5,243	2,901	4,259
North Dakota					
Female	49	176	154	113	236
Male	45	225	219	173	381
Oklahoma					
Female	NA	NA	1,360	9,322	65,675
Male	NA	NA	1,613	9,509	71,937
South Dakota					
Female	NA	NA	178	193	349
Male	NA	NA	363	272	468
Wyoming					
Female	45	138	270	309	691
Male	138	160	652	631	1,544

NA=figures not available

Sources: Ninth Census, vol. 1: *The Statistics of the Population of the United States* (Washington, D.C.: Government Printing Office, 1872), p. 608; *Compendium of the Tenth Census,* rev. ed., pt. 1 (Washington, D.C.: Government Printing Office, 1885), p. 556; *Abstract of the Eleventh Census,* 2d ed. (Washington, D.C.: Government Printing Office, 1896), p. 47; *Abstract of the Twelfth Census of the United States, 1900,* 3d ed. (Washington, D.C.: Government Printing Office, 1904), p. 43; and *Thirteenth Census of the United States, Taken in the Year 1910,* vol. 1: *Population: General Report and Analysis* (Washington, D.C.: Government Printing Office, 1913), p. 141.

Notes

Short forms used in the notes:

ISHD-HS	Iowa State Historical Department, Historical Society, Iowa City
ISHD-MA	Iowa State Historical Department, Museum and Archives, Des Moines
ISHL	Illinois State Historical Library, Springfield
KSHS	Kansas State Historical Society, Topeka
MAMBP	Montana American Mothers Bicentennial Project, 1975/76, in Montana Historical Society, Helena
MHS	Minnesota Historical Society, St. Paul
MLCHS	McLean County Historical Society, Bloomington, Illinois
MSULSC	Montana State University Library Special Collections, Bozeman
MTHS	Montana Historical Society, Helena
NSHS	Nebraska State Historical Society, Lincoln
PDC	Pioneer Daughters Collection, in South Dakota State Historical Resource Center, Pierre
SDSHRC	South Dakota State Historical Resource Center, Pierre
SHSND	State Historical Society of North Dakota, Bismarck
UMWHMC and SHSMM	University of Missouri Western History Manuscript Collection and State Historical Society of Missouri Manuscripts, Joint Collection, Columbia
UWAHC	University of Wyoming American Heritage Center, Laramie
WHCUO	Western History Collection, University of Oklahoma, Norman
WSAMHD	Wyoming State Archives, Museum, and Historical Department, Cheyenne

Chapter 1. The Female Frontier:
Definitions, Interpretations, and Images

1. Frederick Jackson Turner, *The Frontier in American History* (New York: Holt, Rinehart & Winston, 1962), p. 4; and George F. Parker, *The American Pioneer and His Story* (Iowa City: State Historical Society of Iowa, 1922), p. 3.

2. Emerson Hough, *The Passing of the Frontier* (New Haven, Conn.: Yale University Press, 1921), p. 93.

3. Everett Dick, *The Sod-House Frontier, 1854–1890* (New York: D. Appleton-Century, 1937), pp. 144–245; see also ibid., pp. 232–43; idem, "Sunbonnet and Calico, the Homesteader's Consort," *Nebraska History* 47, 1 (Mar. 1966): 3–13; and Walter Prescott Webb, *The Great Plains* (New York: Grosset & Dunlap, 1931), p. 505.

4. Dee Brown, *The Gentle Tamers: Women of the Old Wild West* (New York: Bantam Books, 1974), p. 269; Lillian Schlissel, *Women's Diaries of the Westward Journey* (New York: Schocken Books, 1982), pp. 53–66; Page Smith, *Daughters of the Promised Land: Women in American History* (Boston: Little, Brown, 1970), p. 4; Christine Stansell, "Women on the Great Plains, 1865–1900," *Women's Studies* 4, 1 (1976): 87–98; Susan Armitage, "Reluctant Pioneers," in *Women and Western American Literature,* ed. Helen Winter Stauffer and Susan J. Roswski (Troy, N.Y.: Whitston, 1982), pp. 40–50. For historiographical discussions of this phenomenon see Sandra L. Myres, "Women in the West," in *Historians and the American West,* ed. Michael P. Malone (Lincoln: University of Nebraska Press, 1983), pp. 369–86; Glenda Riley, "Women on the Great Plains: Recent Developments in Research," *Great Plains Quarterly* 5, 2 (Spring 1985): 81–92; idem, "Frontier Women," in *American Frontier and Western Issues: A Historiographical Review,* ed. Roger L. Nichols (Westport, Conn.: Greenwood, 1986), pp. 179–98; Paula A. Treckel, "An Historiographical Essay: Women on the American Frontier," *Old Northwest* 1, 4 (Dec. 1975): 391–403; Ruth Tressman, "Home on the Range," *New Mexico Historical Review* 26, 1 (Jan. 1951): 1–17; and June O. Underwood, "Western Women and True Womanhood: Culture and Symbol in History and Literature," *Great Plains Quarterly* 5, 2 (Spring 1985): 93–106. For examples of mythical descriptions of western women by popular historians see John Frost, *Pioneer Mothers of the West; or, Daring and Heroic Deeds of American Women* (Boston: Lee & Shepard, 1875); William W. Fowler, *Woman on the American Frontier* (1879; reprint, New York: Source Books Press, 1970); Helena H. Smith, "Pioneers in Petticoats," *American Heritage* 10, 2 (Feb. 1959): 101–3; and Beverly Utley, "They Made the West Worth Winning," *American History Illustrated* 2, 8 (1967): 27–33.

5. One of the most extreme cases of a woman's emulating men was frontier scout and wagon master Mountain Charley, a woman who masqueraded as a man for thirteen years (see E. J. Guerin, *Mountain Charley; or, The Adventures of Mr. E. J. Guerin who was Thirteen Years in Male Attire* [1861; reprint, Norman: University of Oklahoma Press, 1968]). Another unusual example was Elizabeth C. Smith of Missouri, who took the name Bill Newcom, donned male attire, and fought in the Mexican War for ten months before her true identity was revealed (see Elizabeth C. Smith, Mexican War Service, 1848, MLCHS).

6. For additional discussion of the transregional and transhistorical nature of women's lives see Julie Roy Jeffrey, *Frontier Women: The Trans-Mississippi West, 1840–1880* (New York: Hill & Wang, 1979), pp. 9–13, 22–24, 72–73, 177–78; Glenda Riley, "Farm Women's Roles in the Agricultural Development of South Dakota," *South Dakota History* 13, 1 and 2 (Spring/Summer 1983): 55–62; idem, "The 'Female Frontier' in Early Illinois," *Mid-America* 67, 2 (Apr.–July 1985): 69–81; June Sochen, "Frontier Women: A Model for All Women," *South Dakota History* 7, 4 (Winter 1976): 35–56. For theories of behavior/environment interactions see Roger G. Barker, "The Influence of Frontier Environments on Behavior," in *The American West: New Perspectives, New Dimensions,* ed. Jerome O. Steffen (Norman: University of Oklahoma Press, 1979), pp. 61–93.

7. Ray Allen Billington, *Westward Expansion: A History of the American Frontier* (New York: Macmillan, 1949); see also Jack D. Forbes, "Frontiers in American History," *Journal of the West* 1, 1 (July 1962): 63–73. Two examples of this approach that predated Billington's were Merrill G. Burlingame, *The Montana Frontier* (Helena: State Publishing Co., 1942), and Edward E. Dale, *The Range Cattle Industry* (Norman: Univer-

sity of Oklahoma Press, 1930). That other disciplines also suffer from a male bias is demonstrated in Rae Carlson, "Understanding Women: Implications for Personality Theory and Research," *Journal of Social Issues* 28, 2 (1972): 17–32.

8. See, e.g., Robert G. Dunbar, "The Significance of the Colorado Agricultural Frontier," *Agricultural History* 34, 3 (July 1960): 119–25; Robert Dykstra, "The Last Days of 'Texan' Abilene: A Study in Community Conflict on the Farmers Frontier," *Agricultural History* 34, 3 (July 1960): 107–19; Gilbert C. Fite, "The American West of Farmers and Stockmen," in *Historians and the American West*, pp. 209–33; Henry E. Fritz, ed., "The Cattlemen's Frontier in the Trans-Mississippi West; An Annotated Bibliography," *Arizona and the West* 14, 1 (Spring 1972): 45–70, and 14, 2 (Summer 1972): 169–90; Sidney Glazer, "The Lumber Frontier," *American Heritage* 2 (Summer 1951): 46–49; Sandra L. Myres, "The Ranching Frontier: Spanish Backgrounds of the Plains Cattle Industry," in *Essays on the American West*, ed. Harold M. Hollingsworth and Sandra L. Myres (Austin: University of Texas Press for the University of Texas at Arlington, 1969); Duane A. Smith, *Rocky Mountain Mining Camps: The Urban Frontier* (Bloomington: Indiana University Press, 1967); and David C. Smith, "The Logging Frontier," *Journal of Forest History* 18, 4 (Oct. 1974): 96–106.

9. Gilbert C. Fite, *The Farmers' Frontier, 1865–1900* (New York: Holt, Rinehart & Winston, 1966); and Rodman Wilson Paul, *Mining Frontiers of the Far West, 1848–1880* (New York: Holt, Rinehart & Winston, 1963).

10. Richard C. Wade, *The Urban Frontier: Pioneer Life in Early Pittsburgh, Cincinnati, Lexington, Louisville and St. Louis* (Chicago: University of Chicago Press, 1964); see also Lawrence H. Larsen, *The Urban West at the End of the Frontier* (Lawrence: Regents Press of Kansas, 1978).

11. Oscar O. Winther, *The Transportation Frontier: The Trans-Mississippi West, 1865–1890* (New York: Holt, Rinehart & Winston, 1964).

12. John Francis Bacon, *The Spanish Borderlands Frontier, 1513–1821* (New York: Holt, Rinehart & Winston, 1970); Ray Allen Billington, *America's Frontier Heritage* (New York: Holt, Rinehart & Winston, 1966); Douglas Edward Leach, *The Northern Colonial Frontier, 1607–1763* (New York: Holt, Rinehart & Winston, 1966); Paul, *Mining Frontiers of the Far West;* W. Stitt Robinson, *The Southern Colonial Frontier, 1607–1763* (Albuquerque: University of New Mexico Press, 1979); and Jack M. Sosin, *The Revolutionary Frontier, 1763–1783* (New York: Holt, Rinehart & Winston, 1967).

13. Frederick Jackson Turner, "The Significance of Section in American History," in *The Selected Essays of Frederick Jackson Turner* (Englewood Cliffs, N.J.: Prentice-Hall, 1961), pp. 115–18, and "Sections and Nations," ibid., pp. 150–53.

14. Bernard De Voto, *The Course of Empire* (Boston: Houghton Mifflin, 1962), pp. 403–4.

15. Henry Nash Smith, *Virgin Land: The American West as Symbol and Myth* (Cambridge, Mass.: Harvard University Press, 1950), pp. 125–32; and Richard Slotkin, *The Fatal Environment: The Myth of the Frontier in the Age of Industrialization, 1800–1890* (New York: Atheneum, 1985), pp. 33–47; see also idem, *Regeneration through Violence: The Mythology of the American Frontier, 1600–1860* (Middletown, Conn.: Wesleyan University Press, 1973).

16. Dorothy Anne Dondore, *The Prairie and the Making of Middle America: Four Centuries of Description* (Cedar Rapids, Iowa: Torch Press, 1926), pp. 288–89, 305–25.

17. Donald Jackson, "Zebulon Pike and Nebraska," *Nebraska History* 47, 4 (Dec. 1966): 361–62.

18. Richard N. Ellis, ed., "General Pope's Report on the West, 1866," *Kansas Historical Quarterly* 35, 4 (Winter 1969): 349–50; see also Edward O. Parry, ed., "Observations on the Prairies: 1867," *Montana, the Magazine of Western History* 9, 4 (Autumn 1959): 22–35.

19. Louis Bernard Schmidt, "The Agricultural Revolution in the Prairies and the Great Plains of the United States," *Agricultural History* 8, 4 (Oct. 1934): 169–95; Smith, *Virgin Land*, pp. 181–83; William F. G. Shanks, "The Great American Desert," *Lippincott's Monthly Magazine* 49 (May 1892): 735–42; Webb, *Great Plains*, pp. 3–9, 510–15. For other discussions of images of the Great Plains see W. Eugene Hollon, *The Great American Desert: Then and Now* (New York: Oxford University Press, 1966); G. Malcolm Lewis, "The Cognition and Communication of Former Ideas about the Great Plains," in *The Great Plains: Environment and Culture,* ed. Brian W. Blouet and Frederick C. Luebke (Lincoln: University of Nebraska Press, 1979), pp. 27–41; Frederick C. Luebke, "Introduction," ibid., pp. ix–xxviii. An interesting analysis of Henry Nash Smith and the problem of regional images is found in Laurence R. Veysey, "Myth and Reality in Approaching American Regionalism," *American Quarterly* 12, 1 (Spring 1960): 31–43; see also John L. Allen, "The Garden-Desert Continuum: Competing Views of the Great Plains in the Nineteeth Century," *Great Plains Quarterly* 5, 4 (Fall 1985): 207–20.

20. Wendell W. Norris, "The Transient Frontier Weekly as a Stimulus to Homesteading," *Journalism Quarterly* 30, 1 (Winter 1953): 44–48.

21. David M. Emmons, *Garden in the Grasslands: Boomer Literature of the Central Great Plains* (Lincoln: University of Nebraska Press, 1971), pp. 47–77. For an example of the promotional efforts by a governor see William Gilpin, "The Pacific Railway," in *The American Frontier: A Social and Literary Record,* ed. C. Merton Babcock (New York: Holt, Rinehart & Winston, 1965), pp. 231–37.

22. Emmons, *Garden in the Grasslands,* pp. 25–46.

23. *Iowa News* (Dubuque), 5 Aug. 1837.

24. *Eddyville* (Iowa) *Free Press,* 16 Apr. 1855.

25. Robert P. Porter, *The West: From the Census of 1880* (Chicago: Rand McNally, 1882), pp. 333, 372, 396–408.

26. Mary Baillie and George Baillie, Recollections in the Form of a Duet, 1939, WSAMHD.

27. *Prairie versus Bush: Iowa as an Emigration Field* (Davenport: Iowa Land Office, 1859); and Iowa Board of Immigration, *Immigration to Iowa: Report of the Secretary of the Board of Immigration, April 4, 1871* (n.p., n.d.).

28. Jerzy Jedlicki, "Images of America," *Polish Perspective* 18, 11 (Nov. 1975): 26–38; see also D. L. A. Ashliman, "The American West in Twentieth Century Germany," *Journal of Popular Culture* 2, 1 (Summer 1968): 81–92; Preston A. Barba, *Balduin Mollhausen: The German Cooper,* vol. 17 in *America Germanica* (Philadelphia: University of Pennsylvania Press, 1914), pp. 9–36; Ray Allen Billington, "Cowboys, Indians and the Land of Promise: The World Image of the American Frontier," opening address, Fourteenth International Congress of Historical Sciences, San Francisco, Calif., 22–29 Aug. 1975, Bancroft Library, Berkeley, Calif.; idem, *Land of Savagery, Land of Promise: The European Image of the American Frontier in the Nineteenth Century* (New York: W. W. Norton, 1980); and Hugh Honour, *The European Vision of America* (Cleveland, Ohio: Cleveland Museum of Art, n.d.).

29. For analyses of images and myths of frontierswomen see Susan Armitage, "Women and Men in Western History: A Stereotypical Vision," *Western Historical Quarterly* 16, 4 (Oct. 1985): 380–95; Susan H. Armitage, "Women's Literature and the American Frontier: A New Perspective on the Frontier Myth," in *Women, Women Writers, and the West,* ed. L. L. Lee and Merrill Lewis (Troy, N.Y.: Whitston, 1979), pp. 5–14; Linda K. Downey, "Woman on the Trail: Hough's North of 36," *Western American Literature* 14 (Fall 1979): 215–20; Anne Falke, "The Art of Convention: Images of Women in the Modern Western Novels of Henry Wilson Allen," *North Dakota Quarterly* 42, 2 (Spring 1974): 17–27; Claire R. Farrer, "Women and Folklore: Images

and Genres," *Journal of American Folklore* 88, 347 (Jan.–Mar. 1975): v–xv; Dorys Crow Grover, "The Pioneer Women in Fact and Fiction," *Heritage of Kansas* 10 (Spring 1977): 35–44; Elizabeth Jameson, "Women as Workers, Women as Civilizers: True Womanhood in the American West," *Frontiers* 7, 3 (1984): 1–8; Barbara Howard Meldrum, "Images of Women in Western American Literature," *Midwest Quarterly* 17, 3 (Apr. 1976): 252–67; idem, "Women in Western American Fiction: Images, or Real Women?" in *Women in Western American Literature*, pp. 55–69; Beverly J. Stoeltje, " 'A Helpmate for Man Indeed': The Image of the Frontier Woman," *Journal of American Folklore* 88, 347 (Jan.–Mar. 1975): 25–41; Glenda Riley, "Images of the Frontierswoman: Iowa as a Case Study," *Western Historical Quarterly* 8, 2 (Apr. 1977): 189–202; idem, "Women in the West," *Journal of American Culture* 3, 2 (Summer 1980): 311–29.

30. Mary Hartwell Catherwood, "The Career of a Prairie Farmer," *Lippincott's Magazine* 25 (June 1880): 706–13.

31. E. W. Howe, "Provincial Peculiarities of Western Life," *Forum*, 14 (Sept. 1892): 97; and Charles Moreau Harger, "The Prairie Woman: Yesterday and To-Day," *Outlook* 70, 17 (26 Apr. 1902): 1008–12.

32. R. Wallace, "Frontier's Fabulous Women," *Life*, 11 May 1959, pp. 66–76; see also Joan Swallow Reiter, *The Women* (Alexandria, Va.: Time-Life Books, 1978).

33. Edward L. Wheeler, *Deadwood Dick's Eagles: or, The Pards of the Flood Bar* (Cleveland, Ohio: Arthur Westbrook, 1899), pp. 8, 10; An Old Scout, *Young Wild West Surrounded by Sioux: or, Arietta and the Aeronaut* (New York: Frank Tousey, 1917), pp. 10–11, 18; and Jack Shadoian, "Yuh Got Pecos! Doggone, Belle, Yuh're as Good as Two Men," *Journal of Popular Culture* 12, 4 (Spring 1979): 721–36. For other examples see Edward S. Ellis, *Hurricane Gulch: or, A Tale of the Aosta and Bufferville Trail* (New York: Beadle, 1892); Wheeler, *Deadwood Dick's Eagles;* Chickering Carter, ed., *Kid Curry's Last Stand: or, Nick Carter in Dangerous Surroundings* (New York: Street & Smith, 1907); An Old Scout, *The White Boy Chief: or, The Terror of the North Platte* (New York: Frank Tousey, 1908); and F. A. Briggs, *Buffalo Bill's Witchcraft: or, Pawnee Bill and the Snake Aztecs* (New York: Street & Smith, 1911).

34. Sandra L. Myres, *Westering Women and the Frontier Experience, 1800–1915* (Albuquerque: University of New Mexico Press, 1982), p. 2.

35. W. Gilmore Sims, *Yemassee* (1853; New York: W. J. Widdleton, 1878), pp. 85–89, 204–5, 298–301, 311–13; and James Fenimore Cooper, *The Prairie* (1827; New York: Dodd, Mead, 1954), pp. 116, 148–54, 166–68; see also Richard Drinnon, *Facing West: The Metaphysics of Indian-Hating and Empire Building* (Minneapolis: University of Minnesota Press, 1980), pp. 131–40; and Smith, *Virgin Land*, pp. 211–49.

36. Willa Cather, *My Antonia* (Boston: Houghton Mifflin, 1946); and Vardis Fisher, *The Mothers: An American Saga of Courage* (New York: Vanguard, 1943). For discussions of these and other writers who presented capable women see Annette Atkins, "Women on the Farming Frontier: The View from Fiction," *Midwest Review* 3 (Spring 1980): 1–10; Ruth Ann Alexander, "South Dakota Women Writers and the Blooming of the Pioneer Heroine, 1922–1939," *South Dakota History* 14, 4 (Winter 1984): 281–307; Samuel Irving Bellman, "Where the West Begins: Constance Rourke's Images of Her Own Frontierland," in *Women and Western American Literature*, pp. 267–82; Mildred R. Bennett, "Willa Cather and the Prairie," *Nebraska History* 56, 2 (Summer 1975): 230–35; and Sue Mathews, "Pioneer Women in the Works of Two Montana Authors: Interviews with Dorothy M. Johnson and A. B. Guthrie, Jr.," in *Women and Western American Literature*, pp. 124–31.

37. Ole Rölvaag, *Giants in the Earth* (New York: Harper & Row, 1929); Hamlin Garland, *Main Travelled Roads* (1891; New York: Harper & Brothers, 1899); idem, *Son of the Middle Border* (New York: Macmillan, 1922); and idem, *A Pioneer Mother*

(Chicago: Bookfellows, 1922); see also Dick Harrison, "Rolvaag, Grove and Pioneering on the American and Canadian Plains," *Great Plains Quarterly* 1, 4 (Fall 1981): 252–62; Francis W. Kaye, "Hamlin Garland and Frederick Philip Grove: Self-Conscious Chroniclers of the Pioneers," *Canadian Review of American Studies* 10 (Spring 1979): 32–39; idem, "Hamlin Garland's Feminism," in *Women and Western American Literature*, pp. 135–61; Richard W. Etulain, "Western Fiction and History: A Reconsideration," in *American West*, pp. 152–74; Jeannie Lewis McKnight and Clark College, "American Dream, Nightmare Underside: Diaries, Letters, and Fiction of Women on the American Frontier," in *Women, Women Writers and the West*, pp. 25–43; and Diane Dufva Quantic, "The Ambivalence of Rural Life in Prairie Literature," *Kansas Quarterly* 12, 2 (Spring 1980): 109–19. For analyses of themes in fiction and poetry involving women see Lewis Atherton, "The Farm Novel and Agricultural History: A Review," *Agricultural History* 40, 2 (Apr. 1966): 131–40; Frances B. Cogan, "Weak Fathers and Other Beasts: An Examination of the American Male in Domestic Novels, 1850–1870," *American Studies* 25, 2 (Fall 1984): 5–20; Caren J. Deming, "Miscegenation in Popular Western History and Fiction," in *Women and Western American Literature*, pp. 90–99; Carol Fairbanks, "Lives of Girls and Women on the Canadian and American Prairies," *International Journal of Women's Studies* 2, 5 (Sept./Oct. 1979): 452–72; Melody Graulich, "Violence against Women in Literature of the Western Family," *Frontiers* 7, 3 (1984): 14–20; Madelon E. Heatherington, "Romance without Women: The Sterile Fiction of the American West," *Georgia Review* 33 (Fall 1979): 643–56; Francis W. Kaye, "The 49th Parallel and 98th Meridian: Some Lines for Thought," *Mosaic* 14, 2 (Spring 1981): 165–75; Annette Kolodny, *The Land before Her: Fantasy and Experience of the American Frontiers, 1630–1860* (Chapel Hill: University of North Carolina Press, 1984); Robert Kroetsch, "Fear of Women in Prairie Fiction: Erotics of Space," *Canadian Forum* 58 (Oct./Nov. 1978): 22–27; Margaret Solomon, "A Study of Feminism as a Motif in 'A Journey to Pike's Peak and New Mexico,' by Julia Archibald Homes," in *Women and Western American Literature*, pp. 28–39; Robert H. Solomon, "The Prairie Mermaid: Love-Tests of Pioneer Women," *Great Plains Quarterly* 4, 3 (Summer 1984): 143–51; Robert Thacker, " 'Twisting toward Insanity': Landscape and Female Entrapment in Plains Fiction," *North Dakota Quarterly* 52, 3 (Summer 1984): 181–94; and June O. Underwood, "The Civilizers: Women's Organizations and Western American Literature," in *Women and Western American Literature*, pp. 3–16; Underwood, "Western Women and True Womanhood," pp. 93–106; and Robert H. Walker, "The Poets Interpret the Western Frontier," *Mississippi Valley Historical Review* 47, 4 (Mar. 1961): 619–35.

38. Abbie Gardner-Sharp, *The Spirit Lake Massacre and the Captivity of Miss Abbie Gardner* (Des Moines: Iowa Printing Co., 1885); Mary Butler Renville, *A Thrilling Narrative of Indian Captivity* (Minneapolis, Minn.: Atlas Company's Book and Job Printing Office, 1863); and Emeline L. Fuller, *Left by the Indians: Story of My Life* (Mount Vernon, Iowa: Hawk-Eye Steam Print, 1892); see also Roy Harvey Pearce, "The Significances of the Captivity Narrative," *American Literature* 19, 1 (Mar. 1947): 1–20; James A. Levernier, "Indian Captivity Narratives: Their Function and Forms" (Ph.D. diss., University of Pennsylvania, 1975); and Richard Van Der Beets, "The Indian Captivity Narrative as Ritual," *American Literature* 43, 4 (Jan. 1972): 548–62.

39. Ann Uhry Abrams, "Frozen Goddess: The Image of Woman in Turn-of-the-Century American Art," in *Women's Places: Female Identity and Vocation in American History*, ed. Mary Kelley (Boston: G. K. Hall, 1979), pp. 93–108; see also Carlann Gee Bush, "The Way We Weren't: Images of Women and Men in Cowboy Art," *Frontiers* 7, 3 (1984): 73–78. For other discussions of western art see Stephen C. Behrendt, "Originality and Influence in George Caleb Bingham's Art," *Great Plains Quarterly*

5, 1 (Winter 1985): 24–38; Rene N. Coen, "David's *Sabine Women* in the Wild West," *Great Plains Quarterly* 2, 2 (Spring 1982): 67–76; Robert V. Hine, *The American West: An Interpretive History* (Boston: Little, Brown, 1973), pp. 283–99; Kirsten H. Powell, "Cowboy Knights and Prairie Madonnas: American Illustration of the Plains and Pre-Raphaelite Art," *Great Plains Quarterly* 5, 1 (Winter 1985): 39–52; and Roger B. Stein, "Packaging the Great Plains: The Role of the Visual Arts," *Great Plains Quarterly* 5, 1 (Winter 1985): 5–23. For analyses of women's roles in western films see Cheryl J. Foote, "Changing Images of Women in the Western Film," *Journal of the West* 22, 4 (Oct. 1983): 64–71; Andrew Jefchak, "Prostitutes and Schoolmarms: An Essay of Women in Western Films," *Heritage of the Great Plains* 16, 3 (Summer 1983): 19–26; and Howard Movshovitz, "The Still Point: Women in the Westerns of John Ford," *Frontiers* 7, 3 (1984): 68–72.

40. For examples of early dissidents see Mary W. M. Hargreaves, "Homesteading and Homemaking on the Plains: A Review," *Agricultural History* 47, 2 (Apr. 1973): 156–63; idem, "Women in the Agricultural Settlement of the Northern Plains," *Agricultural History* 50, 1 (Jan. 1976): 179–89; Dorothy K. Gray, *Women of the West* (Millbrook, Calif.: Les Femmes, 1976); and Nancy Wilson Ross, *Westward the Women* (New York: Alfred A. Knopf, 1944). For reviews and analyses of recent scholarship see Joan M. Miller and Darlis A. Miller, "The Gentle Tamers Revisited: New Approaches to the History of Women in the American West," *Pacific Historical Review* 49, 2 (May 1980): 173–214; Myres, "Women in the West," pp. 369–86; Paula Petrick, "The Gentle Tamers in Transition: Women in the Trans-Mississippi West," *Feminist Studies* 11, 3 (Fall 1985): 677–94; Riley, "Women on the Great Plains," pp. 81–92; and Glenda Riley, "Frontier Women," pp. 179–98.

41. Glenda Riley, *Frontierswomen: The Iowa Experience* (Ames: Iowa State University Press, 1981), p. xv; idem, "Farm Women's Roles," pp. 55–62; and idem, " 'Female Frontier' in Early Illinois," pp. 69–81.

42. Frederick C. Luebke, "Regionalism and the Great Plains: Problems of Concept and Method," *Western Historical Quarterly* 15, 1 (Jan. 1984): 19–38.

43. For other definitions of prairie and plains see Carol Fairbanks and Sara Brooks Sundberg, *Farm Women on the Prairie Frontier: A Sourcebook for Canada and the United States* (Metuchen, N.J.: Scarecrow Press, 1983), pp. 3–36; Michael J. O'Brien et al., *Grassland, Forest, and Historical Settlement: An Analysis of Dynamics in Northeast Missouri* (Lincoln: University of Nebraska Press, 1984), pp. 58–134; David J. Wishart, "The Changing Position of the Frontier of Settlement on the Eastern Margins of the Central and Northern Great Plains, 1854–1890," *Professional Geographer* 21, 3 (May 1969): 153–57; and Webb, *Great Plains*, pp. 1–8.

My special thanks go to botanist Marshall Sundberg, who created customized maps for my use in this study.

*Chapter 2. A Profile of Frontierswomen
on the Prairies and on the Plains*

1. Everett Dick, "Sunbonnet and Calico, the Homesteader's Consort," *Nebraska History* 47, 1 (Mar. 1966): 3–13, and *The Sod-House Frontier, 1854–1890* (New York: D. Appleton-Century, 1937), p. 235. The helpmeet image is discussed by Sara Brooks Sundberg in "A Study of Farmwomen on the Minnesota Prairie Frontier: 1850–1900" (Master's thesis, University of Wisconsin-Eau-Claire, 1984), pp. 1–11, 24–25; see also Carol Fairbanks and Sara Brooks Sundberg, *Farm Women on the Prairie Frontier: A*

Sourcebook for Canada and the United States (Metuchen, N.J.: Scarecrow Press, 1983), pp. 71–86. For embodiments of the helpmeet see Bess Streeter Aldrich, *A Lantern in Her Hand* (New York: D. Appleton-Century-Crofts, 1928), and "The Story behind *A Lantern in Her Hand*," *Nebraska History* 56, 2 (1975): 237–41; Meridel le Sueur, *North Star Country* (New York: Buell, Sloan & Pearce, 1945), pp. 115–24; Neola J. Y. Schleuning, "Meridel le Sueur: Toward a New Regionalism," *Books at Iowa* 33 (Nov. 1980): 22–41; Eliza W. Farnham, *Life in Prairie Land* (New York: Harper & Brothers, 1846); Mary Hartwell Catherwood, "The Monument of the First Mrs. Smith," *Kokomo* (Ind.) *Weekly Dispatch,* 7 Nov. 1878; see also Frank Luther Mott, *The Literature of Pioneer Life in Iowa* (Iowa City: State Historical Society of Iowa, 1923); and Glenda Riley, "European Views of White Women in the American West," *Journal of the West* 21, 2 (Apr. 1982): 71–81.

2. Emerson Hough, *The Passing of the Frontier* (New Haven, Conn.: Yale University Press, 1921), p. 93; Page Smith, *Daughters of the Promised Land: Women in American History* (Boston: Little, Brown, 1970), p. 223; Helena H. Smith, "Pioneers in Petticoats," *American Heritage* 10, 2 (Feb. 1959): 36, 103; Dee Brown, *The Gentle Tamers: Women of the Old Wild West* (New York: Bantam Books, 1974), p. 269; Hamlin Garland, *A Pioneer Mother* (Chicago: Bookfellows, 1922); a note dated 1891, enclosed in an 1893 edition of *Main Travelled Roads,* by Hamlin Garland, in UMWHMC and SHSMM; Hamlin Garland, *Iowa, O Iowa* (Iowa City: Clio Press, 1935), p. 45; see also Ole Rölvaag, *Giants in the Earth* (New York: Harper & Row, 1929), for the presentation of a woman who suffered to the point of madness, yet persevered. For discussions of these and similar images in history and literature see Anne Falke, "The Art of Convention: Images of Women in the Modern Western Novels of Henry Wilson Allen," *North Dakota Quarterly* 42, 2 (Spring 1974): 17–27; Dorys Crow Grover, "The Pioneer Women in Fact and Fiction," *Heritage of Kansas* 10 (Spring 1977): 35–44; Barbara Howard Meldrum, "Images of Women in Western American Literature," *Midwest Quarterly* 17, 3 (Apr. 1976): 252–67; Glenda Riley, "Images of the Frontierswoman: Iowa as a Case Study," *Western Historical Quarterly* 8, 2 (Apr. 1977): 189–202; and Beverly J. Stoeltje, " 'A Helpmate for Man Indeed': The Image of the Frontier Woman," *Journal of American Folklore* 88, 347 (Jan.–Mar. 1975): 25–41.

3. Reprinted in *Iowa News* (Dubuque), 14 June 1837.

4. Quoted in "When Men Were Hard to Get," *Palimpsest* 50, 11 (Nov. 1969): 629.

5. *Davenport* (Iowa) *Courier,* 1855, reprinted in *Annals of Iowa* 36 (Oct. 1944): 89 and Nathan H. Parker, *Iowa As It Is in 1856* (Chicago: Keen & Lee, 1856), p. 52.

6. See Appendixes 1 and 2 for census data; see also James E. Davis, *Frontier America, 1800–1840: A Comparative Demographic Analysis of the Settlement Process* (Glendale, Calif.: Arthur H. Clark, 1977), pp. 111–17.

7. Harold E. Briggs, "The Great Dakota Boom, 1879 to 1886," *North Dakota History* 4, 2 (1929): 78–108; Roy L. Roberts, "Population Changes in the Great Plains," *Rural Sociology* 7, 1 (Mar. 1942): 40–48; and *Thirteenth Census,* vol. 1, pp. 253–54. For Kansas see James C. Malin, "The Turnover of Farm Population in Kansas," *Kansas Historical Quarterly* 4, 4 (Nov. 1935): 330–43; Walter M. Kollmorgen and George F. Jenks, "A Geographic Study of Population and Settlement Changes in Sherman County, Kansas," Kansas Academy of Science *Transactions* 54 (Dec. 1951): 458; and John L. Madden, "An Emerging Agricultural Economy: Kansas, 1860–1880," *Kansas Historical Quarterly* 39, 1 (Spring 1973): 101, 111. For Nebraska see Everett Dick, "The Great Nebraska Drought of 1894: The Exodus," *Arizona and the West* 15, 4 (Winter 1973): 333–34; Gilbert C. Fite, "The Great Plains: Promises, Problems, and Prospects," in *The Great Plains: Environment and Culture,* ed. Brian W. Blouet and Frederick C. Luebke (Lincoln: University of Nebraska Press, 1979), pp. 187–90; and Charles G. Rob-

bins, *A Physicist Looks at the 1860 and 1870 Hall County Census* (Grand Island, Nebr.: Prairie Pioneer Press, 1983), pp. 184–85.

8. John B. Newhall, *Glimpse of Iowa in 1846* (Iowa City: State Historical Society, 1957), p. 62.

9. *Wapello* (Iowa) *Intelligencer,* 17 Apr. 1855.

10. Edeen Martin, "Frontier Marriage and the Status Quo," *Westport Historical Quarterly* 10 (Mar. 1975): 100.

11. *Eleventh Census,* p. 57; *Abstract of the Twelfth Census,* pp. 82–83; and *Thirteenth Census,* vol. 1, p. 547.

12. John C. Hudson, "The Study of Western Frontier Populations," in *The American West: New Perspectives, New Dimensions,* ed. Jerome O. Steffen (Norman: University of Oklahoma Press, 1979), p. 49.

13. Eleanor E. Gordon, *A Little Bit of a Long Story for the Children* (Humboldt, Iowa: n.p., 1934), pp. 10–12; see also Milo Custer, Recollections of Mrs. Charlotte A. Scott, 1915, MLCHS; and William G. B. Carson, "Anne Ewing Lane," *Missouri Historical Society Bulletin* 21, 2 (Jan. 1965): 87–99.

14. Gertie May Cowles Valentine, PDC, SDSHRC; and Lottie Holmberg (interviewer), Early Experiences of Miss Lucy Wells in Wyoming, 1936, WSAMHD.

15. Nellie N. Barsness, Highlights in Careers of Women Physicians in Pioneer Minnesota, 1947, MHS.

16. Susan C. Peterson, "Doing 'Women's Work': The Grey Nuns at Fort Totten Indian Reservation, 1874–1900," *North Dakota History* 52, 2 (Spring 1985): 18–25, and "From Paradise to Prairie: The Presentation Sisters in Dakota, 1880–1896," *South Dakota History* 10, 3 (Summer 1980): 210–13. For a discussion of the Sisters of St. Francis in South Dakota see idem, "Challenging the Stereotypes: The Adaptation of the Sisters of St. Francis to South Dakota Indian Missions, 1885–1910," *Upper Midwest History* 4 (1984): 1–10.

17. Thisba Hutson Morgan, Reminiscences of My Days in the Land of the Ogallala Sioux, 1968, SDSHRC; and Kay Graber, ed., *Sister to the Sioux: The Memoirs of Elaine Goodale Eastman* (Lincoln: University of Nebraska Press, 1978), pp. xi–xii.

18. Richard Lowitt, "George W. Norris and the Kinkaid Act of 1904: A Footnote," *Nebraska History* 57, 3 (1976): 398–404; Sheryll Patterson-Black, "From Pack Trains to Publishing: Women's Work in the Frontier West," in *Western Women in History and Literature,* ed. Sheryll Patterson-Black and Gene Patterson-Black (Crawford, Nebr.: Cottonwood Press, 1978), pp. 1–14; idem, "Women Homesteaders on the Great Plains Frontier," ibid., pp. 15–31; idem, "Women Homesteaders on the Great Plains Frontier," *Frontiers* 1, 2 (Spring 1976): 67–88.

19. Myrtle Yoeman, letter to Grace H. Carpenter, 24 June 1905, SDSHRC; Paul Corey, "Bachelor Bess: My Sister," *South Dakota Historical Collections* 37 (1974): 4–5, 101; and Edith Eudora Ammons Kohl, *Land of the Burnt Thigh* (New York: Funk & Wagnalls, 1938), pp. 84, 290; see also Enid Bern, ed., "They Had a Wonderful Time: The Homesteading Letters of Anna and Ethel Erickson," *North Dakota History* 45, 4 (Fall 1978): 4–31. Neither of the Erickson sisters ever married.

20. Elinore Pruitt Stewart, *Letters of a Woman Homesteader* (Lincoln: University of Nebraska Press, 1961), and *Letters on an Elk Hunt* (Lincoln: University of Nebraska Press, 1979); Adelaide Jewett Skinner, poetry, undated, probably c. 1880–85, NSHS; Mrs. William Bangs, My Homesteading Days, undated, MHS; and Joseph W. Snell, ed., "Roughing It on Her Kansas Claim: The Diary of Abbie Bright, 1870–1871," pt. 1, *Kansas Historical Quarterly* 37, 3 (Autumn 1971): 233–68, and pt. 2, ibid., 37, 4 (Winter 1971): 394–428. Other examples of women who married male homesteaders or other neighbors are Jennie Williams Duret (sketch, Polk County Women, 1977,

MSULSC); Grace Fitzgerald West (biography, Montana American Mothers Bi-Centennial Project, 1975–76, MTHS); and Martha Stoecker Norby (First Trip to South Dakota, 1961, manuscript privately held by Gretchen Norby Jacobson of Cedar Falls, Iowa).

21. *Missouri Intelligencer* (Franklin), 19 June 1824 and 12 May 1926.

22. Caroline Phelps, diary, 1833, ISHD-HS; and James E. Armstrong, *Life of a Woman Pioneer* (Chicago: John F. Higgins Printing, 1931), pp. 9, 25–39.

23. Martha Waln, The Life of Martha Waln, Pioneer of Tensleep, Wyo., 1939, WSAMHD; and Walker D. Wyman, ed., *Frontier Woman: The Life of a Woman Homesteader on the Dakota Frontier* (River Falls: University of Wisconsin/River Falls Press, 1972), pp. 90–91, 113.

24. *Laws Passed by the Fourth General Assembly of the State of Illinois, 1824–25* (Vandalia, Ill.: Robert Blackwell, 1825), pp. 120, 169.

25. Ruth A. Gallaher, *Legal and Political Status of Women in Iowa, 1838–1918* (Iowa City, Iowa: State Historical Society, 1918), pp. 21, 66–69.

26. Albert D. Richardson, *Beyond the Mississippi* (Hartford, Conn.: American, 1867; reprinted, Johnson Reprint, 1968), p. 148; and Gallaher, *Legal and Political Status of Women*, pp. 39, 17, 21, 84.

27. Nelson Manfred Blake, *The Road to Reno* (New York: Macmillan, 1962), pp. 80–81.

28. United States, Bureau of the Census, *Marriage and Divorce, 1867–1906,* vol. 1 (Washington, D.C.: Government Printing Office, 1907), pp. 16–19, 73–75.

29. Matilda Peitzke Paul, Recollections, 1938, ISHD-HS; Sarah Randleman Barnes, Papers, 1909, and Ursula Terry, letter to Dear Father, 5 Apr. 1843—both UMWHMC and SHSMM; Daisy Barncard Schmidt, History of the Jacob Zed Barncard Family, 1960, MHS; and Edith S. Burris, Patsy the Pioneer, n.d., UMWHMC and SHSMM.

30. G. F. Naumann, "Search for Three Sisters," *Concordia Historical Institute Quarterly* 39, 1 (1966): 20–32; and Agnes Powell Davis, letters, 1876–95, UMWHMC and SHSMM; and William R. Gentry, Jr., Ann Hawkins Gentry, 1960, UMWHMC and SHSMM; see also Rebecca Z. Carse, Our Trip Out West in 1842 and a Sketch of Our Lives in Illinois in That Early Day, 1920, ISHL; and Henry S. Wood, A Woman of the Frontier, n.d., MHS.

31. Cora D. Babcock, Reminiscences, 1880–85, SDSHRC; and Mrs. W. M. Lindsay and Isabella Diehl, Biographies, Pioneer Daughters Collection, SDSHRC.

32. Linda Peavy and Ursula Smith, "Women in Waiting in the Westward Movement," *Montana, the Magazine of Western History* 35, 2 (Spring 1985): 2–17; and Lillian Schlissel, "Frontier Families: Crisis in Ideology," in *The American Self: Myth, Ideology and Popular Culture,* ed. Sam B. Girgus (Albuquerque: University of New Mexico Press, 1981), pp. 159–60. An example of the separation of spouses because of the husband's spending several years in California working in the gold fields and at other jobs is found in the Willis Family Papers, 1843–1908, UMWHMC and SHSMM. A case in which a Kansas woman refused to resume life with her gold-seeking husband upon his return is found in Mary E. H. Kelly, Sand in Their Craws, n.d., privately held by Joseph Fallon, Dublin, Ireland.

33. Davis, *Frontier America,* pp. 103–10; Allan G. Bogue, *From Prairie to Corn Belt: Farming on the Illinois and Iowa Prairies in the Nineteenth Century* (Chicago: Quadrangle Books, 1968), pp. 23–24; Hudson, "Study of Western Frontier Populations," p. 43.

34. See Appendixes 3 and 4 for more complete data.

35. W. Kirkland, "The West, the Paradise of the Poor," *United States Magazine and Democratic Review* 15 (Aug. 1844): 182–90; and Jane M. Johns, *Personal Recollections of Early Decatur* (Decatur, Ill.: Daughters of the American Revolution, 1912), p. 39.

36. Carson, "Anne Ewing Lane," pp. 87–99; Dorothy St. Arnold, reminiscences, c. 1926, MHS; and Sarah Randleman Barnes, Papers, 1909, UMWHMC and SHSMM.

37. Abbie Mott Benedict, "My Early Days in Iowa," *Annals of Iowa* 17, 5 (July 1930): 323–55; and Anna Howell Clarkson, "A Beautiful Life: A Biographical Sketch," *Annals of Iowa* 11, 2/3 (July–Oct. 1913): 188–99.

38. Kathie Ryckman Anderson, "Era Bell Thompson: A North Dakota Daughter," *North Dakota History* 49, 4 (Fall 1982): 12.

39. Mathilda E. Engstad, The White Kid Glove Era, n.d., SHSND; Susan Leaphart, ed., "Montana Episodes: Frieda and Belle Fligelman: A Frontier-City Girlhood in the 1890s," *Montana, the Magazine of Western History* 32, 3 (Summer 1982): 85–92; Alice Richards McCreary, Various Happenings in the Life of Alice Richards McCreary, n.d., WSAMHD; Homer E. Socolofsky, ed., "The Private Journals of Florence Crawford and Arthur Capper, 1891–92," *Kansas Historical Quarterly* 30, 1 and 2 (Spring and Summer 1964): 15–61, 163–208; Sarah Wood Ward, PDC, SDSHRC; see also Scott G. McNall and Sally Allen McNall, *Plains Families: Exploring Sociology through Social History* (New York: St. Martin's Press, 1983), pp. 246–77.

40. James P. Allen, "Ethnicity," in *This Remarkable Continent: An Atlas of United States and Canadian Society and Culture*, ed. John F. Rooney, Wilbur Zelinsky, and Dean R. Louder (College Station: Texas A & M University Press, 1982), pp. 157–58; see Appendixes 4 and 5 for census data on the racial origins of women.

41. See Appendixes 4 and 5 for census data on the gender of blacks on the prairies and on the Plains.

42. Cooper County, Mo., United States Census, 1850, vol. 1, UMWHMC and SHSMM; manuscript census (unpaginated) and McLean County, United States Census, 1850, MLCHS.

43. Mattie Lykins-Bingham, "Recollections of Old Times," *Westport Historical Quarterly* 7, 2 (1971): 18; Anna Ramsey letters to My Darling Children, 31 Mar. 1876; to My Dear Daughter, 17 June 1875 and 8 Dec. 1875, MHS; and Howard County, Mo., Registry for Free Negroes, 1836–61, UMWHMC and SHSMM.

44. Davis, *Frontier America*, pp. 121–33; and Kenneth Wiggins Porter, *The Negro on the American Frontier* (New York: Arno Press, 1971), pp. 1–4, 360–61.

45. Sherman Savage, *Blacks in the West* (Westport, Conn.: Greenwood Press, 1976), p. 69; Jean I. Castles, "The West: Crucible of the Negro," *Montana, the Magazine of Western History* 19, 1 (Winter 1969): 83; and Richard B. Morris, ed., *Encyclopedia of American History* (New York: Harper & Row, 1961), p. 159.

46. Eliza Dyer Price, Recollections of My Father, Samuel Dyer, 1905; Delia Richerson McDaniel, diary, 1841; James A. Ward, autobiography, n.d.; and Adrienne Christopher, The Story of Daniel Yoacham, Westport Pioneer Innkeeper, n.d.—all in UMWHMC and SHSMM.

47. For examples of prairie women's attitudes toward slavery see Lizzie Marshall, letter to Dear Sis, 10 July 1859, in Joseph Marshall Family Papers, 1852–1909, UMWHMC and SHSMM; Harriet Sanborn, Life Story of Harriet Sanborn, n.d., MHS; Nettie Sanford, *Early Sketches of Polk County* (Newton, Iowa; Chas. A. Clark, 1874), p. 134; and anonymous, "Seventy Years in Iowa," *Annals of Iowa* 27, 2 (Oct. 1945): 100, 114–18; see also Christian S. Bykrit, "A Derailment on the Railway Invisible," *Annals of Iowa* 14 (Oct. 1923): 95–100; and Jacob Van Eck, "Underground Railroad in Iowa," *Palimpsest* 2, 5 (May 1921): 129–43.

48. *Burlington* (Iowa) *Tri-Weekly Telegraph*, 27 Aug. 1850.

49. Ruth A. Gallaher, "Slavery in Iowa," *Palimpsest* 28, 5 (May 1947): 158–60.

50. William T. Katz, *The Black West* (New York: Doubleday, 1971), pp. 54, 283–84;

Missouri Intelligencer (Fayette), 23 Jan. 1829; Emancipation Contract of Susan, 29 Dec. 1853, UMWHMC and SHSMM.

51. David V. Taylor, "The Blacks," in *They Chose Minnesota: A Survey of the State's Ethnic Groups*, ed. June Drenning Holmquist (St. Paul: Minnesota Historical Society Press, 1981), pp. 73–75.

52. Eva Neal, Papers, 1881–1963, and Mattie V. Rhoads, Papers, 1872–1968, MHS; and Patricia C. Harpole, ed., "The Black Community in Territorial St. Anthony: A Memoir," *Minnesota History* 49, 2 (Summer 1984): 42–55.

53. Harold M. Rose, "The All-Negro Town: Its Evolution and Function," *Geographical Review* 55, 3 (July 1965): 362–81; and anonymous, Pilgrim Baptist Church: A Brief Resume of History, c. 1977, MHS.

54. Sandra L. Myres, *Westering Women and the Frontier Experience, 1800–1915* (Albuquerque: University of New Mexico Press, 1982), pp. 5, 86; George R. Lamplugh, "The Image of the Negro in Popular Magazine Fiction, 1875–1900," *Journal of Negro History* 57, 2 (Apr. 1972): 177–89; Minnie Miller Brown, "Black Women in American Agriculture," *Agricultural History* 50, 1 (Jan. 1976): 204–8; and Diary of Eliza Ann Bartlett, 1854–64, Grinnell College Library, Grinnell, Iowa. For purposes of comparison, descriptions of black women and their families in eastern urban areas can be found in James O. Horton, "Freedom's Yoke: Gender Conventions among Antebellum Free Blacks," *Feminist Studies* 12, 1 (Spring 1986): 51–76; Diann H. Painter, "The Black Woman in American Society," *Current History* 70, 416 (May 1976): 224–27, 234; and Lee Rainwater, "Crucible of Identity: The Negro Lower-Class Family," *Daedalus* 95, 1 (Winter 1966): 172–216.

55. Ava Day, two letters to the Nebraska Historical Society, 28 Mar. and 23 May 1964, NSHS; and "A Colored Man's Experience on a Nebraska Homestead," *Omaha World Herald*, 11 Feb. 1899; see also Sarah L. Bernson and Robert J. Eggers, "Black People in South Dakota History," *South Dakota History* 7, 3 (Summer 1977): 245–53; and Brown, "Black Women in American Agriculture," pp. 202–12. For a discussion of images of black settlers on the Plains in novels and films see Chester J. Fontenot, Jr., "Oscar Micheaux, Black Novelist and Film Maker," in *Vision and Refuge: Essays on the Literature of the Great Plains*, ed. Virginia Faulkner and Frederick C. Luebke (Lincoln: University of Nebraska Press, 1982), pp. 109–25.

56. Roy Garvin, "Benjamin, or 'Pap,' Singleton and His Followers," *Journal of Negro History* 33 (Jan. 1948): 7–8; Glen Schwendemann, "Wyandotte and the First 'Exodusters' of 1879," *Kansas Historical Quarterly* 26 (Autumn 1960): 233–49; and idem, "The 'Exodusters' on the Missouri," *Kansas Historical Quarterly* 29 (Spring 1963): 25–40; Nell Irvin Painter, *Exodusters: Black Migration to Kansas after Reconstruction* (New York: Alfred A. Knopf, 1977; reprint, Lawrence: University Press of Kansas, 1986), pp. 108–17; see also Robert G. Athearn, *In Search of Canaan: Black Migration to Kansas, 1879–80* (Lawrence: Regents Press of Kansas, 1978), and "Washwomen, Maumas, Exodusters, Jubileers," in *We Are Your Sisters: Black Women in the Nineteenth Century*, ed. Dorothy Sterling (New York: Norton, 1984), pp. 355–94.

57. Anne E. Bingham, "Sixteen Years on a Kansas Farm, 1870–1886," Kansas State Historical Society *Collections* 15 (1919/20): 520–21.

58. George H. Wayne, "Negro Migration and Colonization in Colorado, 1870–1930," *Journal of the West* 15, 1 (Jan. 1976): 102–20; Mozell C. Hill, "The All-Negro Communities of Oklahoma: The Natural History of a Social Movement," *Journal of Negro History* 31, 3 (July 1946): 254–68; and Arvarh E. Strickland, "Toward the Promised Land: The Exodus to Kansas and Afterward," *Missouri Historical Review* 69, 4 (July 1975): 405–12.

59. William C. Sherman, *Prairie Mosaic: An Ethnic Atlas of Rural North Dakota* (Fargo: North Dakota Institute for Regional Studies, 1983), p. 14.

60. Quoted in Glen Schwendemann, "Nicodemus: Negro Haven on the Solomon," *Kansas Historical Quarterly* 34 (Spring 1968): 14, 26.

61. Day, letters, NSHS.

62. Anderson, "Era Bell Thompson," pp. 11–12.

63. Sudie Rhone, interview, 8 Nov. 1979, UWAHC.

64. Bogue, *From Prairie to Corn Belt,* pp. 14–16, 22; Frank Herriott, "Whence Came the Pioneers of Iowa?" *Annals of Iowa* 7 (Apr. and July 1906): 372–73; Joel H. Silbey, "Proslavery Sentiment in Iowa, 1838–61," *Iowa Journal of History* 55, 4 (Oct. 1957): 289–91; Morton M. Rosenberg, *Iowa on the Eve of the Civil War: A Decade of Frontier Politics* (Norman: University of Oklahoma Press, 1972), p. 14; Ray Allen Billington, *Westward Expansion: A History of the American Frontier,* 3d ed. (New York: Macmillan, 1967), p. 5; and John Mack Faragher, *Women and Men on the Overland Trail* (New Haven, Conn.: Yale University Press, 1979), p. 18.

65. Margaret E. Archer Murray, "Memoir of the William Archer Family," *Annals of Iowa* 39, 5 (Summer 1968): 357–71; Sarah Welch Nossaman, "Pioneering at Bonaparte and Near Pella," *Annals of Iowa* 13, 6 (Oct. 1922): 441–46; May Lacey Crowder, "Pioneer Life in Palo Alto County," *Iowa Journal of History and Politics* 46, 2 (Apr. 1948): 156–61; Dyer, Recollections of My Father, and Susan D. Vanarsdale, diary, 1847, UMWHMC and SHSMM; Neal, Papers, and Rhoads, Papers, MHS; and Harpole, ed., "Black Community in Territorial St. Anthony," p. 43.

66. Fannie Forbes Russel, My First Year in Montana, 1864–65, 1920, MHS; see also Nannie T. Alderson and Helen Huntington Smith, *A Bride Goes West* (Lincoln: University of Nebraska Press, 1942; reprint, 1969), pp. 1–48.

67. A compilation of foreign-born groups in Iowa in 1860 appeared in Rufus Blanchard, *Hand-book of Iowa* (Chicago: Rufus Blanchard, 1869), p. 76. For these settlers' roles in prairie development see Theodore Saloutos, "The Immigrant Contribution to American Agriculture," *Agricultural History* 50, 1 (Jan. 1976): 46, 67.

68. Frederick C. Luebke, "Ethnic Group Settlement on the Great Plains," *Western Historical Quarterly* 8, 4 (Oct. 1977): 405–11. For suggestions on how to approach the study of rural Plains immigrants see Kathleen Neils Conzen, "Historical Approaches to the Study of Rural Ethnic Communities," in *Ethnicity on the Great Plains,* ed. Frederick C. Luebke (Lincoln: University of Nebraska Press, 1980), pp. 1–18. For a discussion of assimilation patterns see Bradley H. Baltensperger, "Agricultural Change among Nebraska Immigrants, 1880–1900," and J. Allen Williams, Jr., David R. Johnson, and Miguel A. Carranza, "Ethnic Assimilation and Pluralism in Nebraska," in *Ethnicity on the Great Plains,* pp. 170–89, 210–29.

69. One exception, designed for Canadians against whom nativist sentiment was not as strong as against Europeans, was *Prairie versus Bush: Iowa as an Emigration Field* (Davenport: Iowa Land Office, 1859); see also A. R. Fulton, "An Invitation to Immigrants," *Palimpsest* 18, 7 (July 1937): 226; Iowa Board of Immigration, *Immigration to Iowa: Report of the Secretary of the Board of Immigration, April 4, 1871* (n.p., n.d.); Kathryn S. H. Moody, Territorial Days in Minnesota, 1960, MHS; and William J. Petersen, "Immigrants from Near and Far," *Palimpsest* 49, 7 (July 1968): 299–304.

70. *Iowa: The Home for Immigrants* (Des Moines: Iowa Board of Immigration, 1870), pp. 63–65.

71. Moody, Territorial Days in Minnesota, MHS; see also George T. Flom, "The Growth of the Scandinavian Factor in the Population of Iowa," *Iowa Journal of History* 4, 2 (Apr. 1906): 267–85; Julian E. McFarland, *A History of the Pioneer Era on Iowa*

Prairies (Lake Mills, Iowa: Graphic, 1969), pp. 140–41; and George F. Robeson, "The Early Iowans," *Palimpsest* 4, 9 (Sept. 1923): 296–97.

72. H. Arnold Barton, *Letters from the Promised Land: Swedes in America, 1840–1914* (Minneapolis: University of Minnesota Free Press, for the Swedish Pioneer Historical Society, 1975) p. 3; and George M. Stephenson, "Scandinavians," in *The Aliens: A History of Ethnic Minorities in America,* ed. Leonard Dinnerstein and Frederic C. Jaher (New York: Appleton-Century Crofts, 1970), p. 108.

73. Ardith K. Melloh, "New Sweden, Iowa," *Palimpsest* 59, 1 (Jan./Feb. 1978): 2–19; C. J. A. Ericson, "Memories of A Swedish Immigrant of 1852," *Annals of Iowa* 8, 1 (Apr. 1907): 1–12; and John G. Rice, "The Swedes," in *They Chose Minnesota,* pp. 248–52. For descriptions of life in these Swedish colonies see Barton, *Letters from the Promised Land.*

74. Laurence M. Larson, *The Changing West* (Northfield, Minn.: Norwegian-American Historical Association, 1937), p. 16; George Flom, *History of Norwegian Immigrants in the United States* (Iowa City, Iowa: privately printed, 1909), p. 190; and Carlton C. Qualey and Jon A. Gjerde, "The Norwegians," in *They Chose Minnesota,* pp. 220–22; see also Arlow W. Anderson, *The Norwegian-Americans* (Boston, Mass.: Twayne, 1975); Theodore C. Blegen, *Norwegian Migration to America: The American Transition* (Northfield, Minn.: Norwegian-American Historical Association, 1931); and John Gjerde, *From Peasants to Farmers: The Migration from Balestrand, Norway, to the Upper Middle West* (Cambridge, Eng.: Cambridge University Press, 1985); Lawrence M. Nelson, *From Fjord to Prairie: Norwegian-Americans in the Midwest, 1825–1975* (Chicago: Norwegian Immigration Anniversary Commission, 1976); and Carlton C. Qualey, *Norwegian Settlement in the United States* (Northfield, Minn.: Norwegian-American Historical Association, 1938).

75. David T. Nelson, ed., *The Diary of Elisabeth Koren, 1853–1855* (Northfield, Minn.: Norwegian-American Historical Association, 1955), pp. 159, 370; see also Diderikke Brandt, letters, n.d., Luther College Library, Decorah, Iowa; Pauline Farseth and Theodore C. Blegen, eds., *Frontier Mother: The Letters of Gro Svendsen* (Northfield, Minn.: Norwegian-American Historical Association, 1950); Peer Stromme, *Halvor: A Story of Pioneer Youth* (Decorah, Iowa: Luther College Press, 1960); "A Young Minister's Wife, Elisabeth Koren," in *The Promise of America: A History of the Norwegian American People,* ed. Odd S. Lovoll (Minneapolis: University of Minnesota Press, 1984), pp. 6–7; Bessie L. Lyon, "Gunda's Coffee Pot," *Palimpsest* 13, 10 (Oct. 1932): 416–25; N. Tjernagel, ed., "Immigrants' Trying Experiences," *Annals of Iowa* 31, 1 (July 1951): 64–71; Geraldine Schwarz, "Family Cohesion in a Norwegian-American Settlement," in *Conversations with the Recent Past,* ed. Luis Torres (Decorah: Northeast Iowa Oral History Project, 1975), pp. 1–5; and B. L. Wick, "Pioneers of the Norway Community," *Annals of Iowa* 29, 5 (July 1948): 366–78; Melvin N. Tatley, Johanna Tatley Who Settled Near Hawley, Minnesota, Minnesota American Mothers Committee, Inc., Biographies, 1975, MHS; see also Arnold Gladager, Memoir of My Mother, Mrs. M. Gladager, 1927, Alma Amalie Gutterson, The Youth of Alma Amalie Gutterson, n.d., and Emily Veblen Olsen, Memoirs, 1941–all at MHS; Theodore C. Blegen, "Immigrant Women and the American Frontier," *Norwegian-American Studies* 5 (1930): 14–29; and Frank C. Nelsen, "The Norwegian-American's Image of America," *Illinois Quarterly* 36, 4 (Apr. 1974): 5–23.

76. Louise Bohach, "Settlement of St. Ansgar, A Miniature Melting Pot," *Iowa Journal of History* 46, 3 (July 1948): 296–315; George T. Flom, "The Danish Contingent in the Population of Early Iowa," *Iowa Journal of History* 4, 2 (Apr. 1906): 220–44; and Ann Regan, "The Danes," in *They Chose Minnesota,* pp. 277–81; see also Thomas P. Christensen, *A History of the Danes in Iowa* (Solvang, Calif.: Dansk folkesamfund,

1952); and Kristian Hvidt, *Danes Go West* (Rebild, Denmark: Rebild National Park Society, 1976).

77. John B. Newhall, *The British Emigrant's Handbook* (London: T. Sutter, 1844), pp. v–x; Jacob Van der Zee, *The British in Iowa* (Iowa City, Iowa: State Historical Society, 1922), pp. 28–32; Curtis Harnack, *Gentlemen on the Prairie* (Ames: Iowa State University Press, 1985), pp. 40–56; Ruth A. Gallaher, "The English Community in Iowa," *Palimpsest* 2, 3 (Mar. 1921): 80–94; E. Grahame Paul, Reminiscences, 1880, MHS; Sarah P. Rubinstein, "The British," in *They Chose Minnesota*, pp. 111–15; and Grant Foreman, "English Emigrants in Iowa," *Iowa Journal of History* 44, 4 (Oct. 1946): 385–420.

78. Charlotte Erickson, *Invisible Immigrants: The Adaptation of English and Scottish Immigrants in Nineteenth-Century America* (Coral Gables, Fla.: University of Miami Press, 1972), pp. 14–15, 24; and Wilbur S. Shepperson, *Emigration and Disenchantment: Portraits of Englishmen Repatriated from the United States* (Norman: University of Oklahoma Press, 1965), pp. 24–27, 113–14; Rebecca Burlend and Edward Burlend, *A True Picture of Immigration* (New York: Citadel Press, 1968), p. 141; Lucy Rutledge Cooke, *Covered Wagon Days: Crossing the Plains in 1852* (Modesto, Calif.: privately published, 1923), pp. 73–81; Henry L. Norton, "The Travels of the Marstons," *Journal of the Illinois State Historical Society* 58, 3 (Autumn 1965): 292; Claude E. Simmons, George Davies—Wright County Pioneer, 1946, MHS; and Brian P. Birch, "Possessed of a Restless Spirit: A Young Girl's Memories of the Southern Iowa Frontier," *Palimpsest* 66, 5 (Sept./Oct. 1985): 174–84.

79. Janette Murray, "Women of North Tama," *Iowa Journal of History and Politics* 41, 3 (July 1943): 295, 309; see also Janette Murray and Janette Murray Fiske, *Hurrah for Bonnie Iowa* (Lake Mills, Iowa: Graphic, 1963); Marguerite Conroy, My Life—Helen Ross Hall, n.d., MLCHS; see also Ann Regan, "The Irish," in *They Chose Minnesota*, pp. 130–39; and Dwight G. McCarty, *Stories of Pioneer Life on the Iowa Prairie* (Emmetsburg, Iowa: Emmetsburg Publishing, 1974), pp. 20–21. For accounts of the Welsh see Agnes Powell Davis, letters, 1876–95, UMWHMC and SHSMM; Florence M. Edwards, Richard Edwards, 1908, MLCHS; and James W. Whitaker, ed., "Welsh Settlements in Iowa," *Palimpsest* 59, 1 (Jan./Feb. 1978): 24–31.

80. Hildegard Binder Johnson, "The Germans," in *They Chose Minnesota*, and "German Forty-Eighters in Davenport," *Iowa Journal of History* 44, 1 (Jan. 1946): 3–6; Thomas P. Christensen, "A German Forty-Eighter in Iowa," *Annals of Iowa* 26, 4 (Apr. 1945): 245–53; Carson, "Anne Ewing Lane," p. 95; and anonymous, "Some Letters of James Mathews and Carolyn Mathews Stone," *Iowa Journal of History* 45, 3 (July 1947): 311–20.

81. Louise Sophia Gellhorn Boylan, My Life Story, 1867–1883, ISHD-HS; and Moody, Territorial Days, MHS. Two other especially good accounts by German women in Minnesota are Agnes Mary Kolshorn, My Parents Henry Kolshorn and Mary Teitge, 1983, and St. Arnold, reminiscences, MHS. For Illinois see Tildy Keist Heitman, reminiscences, c. 1840s–1860s, ISHL. For sources of other German accounts of life in Illinois see Raymond Jurgen Spahn, "German Accounts of Early Nineteenth-Century Life in Illinois," *Papers on Language and Literature* 14 (Fall 1978): 473–88.

82. See, e.g., Louis M. deGryse, "The Low Countries: Belgians, Netherlanders, and Luxembourgers," in *They Chose Minnesota*, pp. 185–89; Gerald F. DeJong, *The Dutch in America, 1609–1974* (Boston, Mass.: Twayne, 1975), pp. 150–71; Henry S. Lucas, *Netherlanders in America: Dutch Immigration to the United States and Canada* (Ann Arbor: University of Michigan Press, 1955), pp. 151–249, 322–51; idem, "The Beginnings of Dutch Immigration to Iowa, 1845–1847," *Iowa Journal of History and Politics* 22 (Oct. 1924): 483–531; Lenora Scholte, "A Stranger in a Strange Land: Romance

in Pella History," *Iowa Journal of History* 37, 2 (Apr. 1939): 115–203; Gertrude Vandergon, Reminiscences, 1940–41, MHS; Jacob Van der Zee, *Hollanders of Iowa* (Iowa City, Iowa: State Historical Society, 1912), pp. 67–126, and "Diary of a Journey from the Netherlands to Pella, Iowa in 1849," *Iowa Journal of History and Politics* 10, 3 (July 1912): 363–82; and Maria C. DeLange Van Kerkove, letters, 1848–1859, ISHD-HS. For Czech settlers see Martha E. Griffiths, "Czechs in Cedar Rapids," pts. 1 and 2, *Iowa Journal of History* 42, 2 and 3 (Apr. and July 1944): 114–61 and 266–315; Pauline S. Merrill, "Pioneer Iowa Bohemians," *Annals of Iowa* 26, 4 (Apr. 1945): 261–274; anonymous, "The Hungarians in Iowa," *Annals of Iowa* 3, 30 (July 1950): 465–67; James D. Allen, "Iowa's 'Little Switzerland,' " *Annals of Iowa* 3, 30 (July 1950): 378–84; and Mary Ellen McElligott, ed. " 'A Monotony Full of Sadness': The Diary of Nadine Turchin, May, 1863–April, 1864," *Journal of the Illinois State Historical Society* 70, 1 (Feb. 1977): 27–89.

83. Robert C. Ostergren, "European Settlement and Ethnicity Patterns on the Agricultural Frontiers of South Dakota," *South Dakota History* 13, 1 and 2 (Spring/Summer 1983): 49–82; see also Timothy J. Kloberdanz, "Plainsmen of Three Continents: Volga German Adaptation to Steppe, Prairie, and Pampa," in *Ethnicity on the Great Plains*, pp. 54–72. For Germans from Russia see Pauline Neher Diede, *Homesteading on the Knife River Prairies* (Bismarck, N.Dak.: Germans from Russia Heritage Society, 1983); Adam Giesinger, "Causes of German Immigration from South Russia to North Dakota," paper read at the Germans from Russia Immigration Centennial Conference, Bismarck, N.Dak., 29 Sept. 1984; Gordon L. Iseminger, "Christina Hillius: Learning to Read at 62," paper presented at the Northern Great Plains History Conference, Bismarck, N.Dak., 28 Sept. 1984; Allen, "Ethnicity," p. 165; Norman E. Saul, "The Migration of the Russian-Germans to Kansas," *Kansas Historical Quarterly* 40, 1 (Spring 1974): 38–62; and William C. Sherman, "German-Russian House Forms in North Dakota: Distribution, Changing Patterns, and Survival," paper read at the Germans from Russia Immigration Centennial Conference, Bismarck, N.Dak., 29 Sept. 1984.

84. Diede, *Homesteading*, pp. 14–25, 31–40, 44–51, 55–64.

85. Agness Kratochvil, Huntley Project Homesteading, 1968, MSULSC.

86. Ellen Agnes Feeney Hughes, biography, Pioneer Women Collection, SDSHRC.

87. Ibid.

88. Mary Alice Canon, biography, PDC, SDSHRC; see also Paul M. Edwards, "Great Britain in Dakota Territory," *South Dakota History* 3, 2 (Spring 1973): 169–86; Erickson, *Invisible Immigrants*, pp. 14–15; Shepperson, *Emigration and Disenchantment*, p. 46; Oscar O. Winther, "The English and Kansas, 1865–1890," in *The Frontier Challenge: Responses to the Trans-Mississippi West*, ed. John G. Clark (Lawrence: University Press of Kansas, 1971), pp. 236–68.

89. Isabella Diehl and Robertina MacDonald, PDC, SDSHRC; and Nelly Sinclair Maclay, MAMBP, MTHS.

90. Myra Waterman, PDC, SDSHRC; and Mrs. W. M. Lindsay, My Pioneer Years in North Dakota, 1933, SHSND.

91. Mrs. R. O. Brandt, "Social Aspects of Prairie Pioneering: The Reminiscences of a Pioneer Pastor's Wife," *Norwegian-American Studies* 7 (1933): 1–46; and Hannah Birkley, Mrs. Iver O. Birkley, 1957, NSHS.

92. Lorna B. Herseth, ed., "A Pioneer's Letter," *South Dakota History* 6, 3 (Summer 1976): 309; see also Theodore C. Blegen, *Norwegian Migration to the United States*, vol. 1 (Northfield, Minn.: Norwegian-American Historical Association, 1931), pp. 506–11.

93. Tone Sauer Bamble, Gusta Anderson Chapin, Sigri Watnaas-Gronseth, Ger-

trude B. Gunderson, Lena Aaker Johnson, Anna Warren Peart, Inez Thompson Peterson, Ingeborg Aaker Simons, PDC, SDSHRC; and Barbara Levorsen, "Early Years in Dakota," *Norwegian-American Studies* 21 (1962): 158–97. For a discussion of Scandinavian life and culture on the Great Plains as shown by literature see Dorothy Burton Skardal, "Life on the Great Plains in Scandinavian-American Literature," in *Vision and Refuge,* pp. 71–91.

94. Lena Aaker Johnson, Ingeborg Aaker Simons, and Gusta Anderson Chapin, PDC, SDSHRC.

95. Ibid.

96. Emily Lindstrom, Reminiscences, n.d., SHSND; Mary Louise Thomson, PDC, SDSHRC; Kathrine Newman Webster, "Memories of a Pioneer," 1971, in *Old Timer's Tales,* vol. 2, pt. 1, NSHS; Barton, *Letters from the Promised Land,* for letters by both women and men, pp. 14–15, 28–33, 85–87, 98–101, 113, 118–21, 136–38, 221–22, 290–91; see also Robert G. Ostregen, "Prairie Bound: Migration Patterns to a Swedish Settlement on the Dakota Frontier," in *Ethnicity on the Great Plains,* pp. 73–91.

97. Bertha Josephson Anderson, autobiography, c. 1940, MTHS; see also Howard Palmer, "Escape from the Great Plains: The Icelanders in North Dakota and Alberta," *Great Plains Quarterly* 3, 4 (Fall 1983): 219–33.

98. Bertha Josephson Anderson, autobiography, c. 1940, MTHS.

99. W. H. Elznic, biography, PDC, SDSHRC; see also Kate Bouzck (whose family settled with the Elznics) and Meri Shindler Reha, ibid.; see also Bruce M. Garver, "Czech-American Freethinkers on the Great Plains, 1871–1914," in *Ethnicity on the Great Plains,* pp. 147–69.

100. Marilee Richards, ed., "Life Anew for Czech Immigrants: The Letters of Marie and Vavrin Stritecky, 1913–34," *South Dakota History* 11, 4 (Fall–Winter 1981): 253–77.

101. Gerald DeJong, "The Coming of the Dutch to the Dakotas," *South Dakota History* 5 (Winter 1974): 20–51, and *The Dutch in America,* pp. 138–237; and Lucas, *Netherlanders in America,* pp. 351–60, 376–89.

102. Consuelo Rocha, interview, 19 Sept. 1979, UWAHC. For a discussion of a literary image of the Plains as a refuge for Mexicans see Tomas Rivera, "The Great Plains as Refuge in Chicano Literature," in *Vision and Refuge,* pp. 126–40.

103. Elizabeth H. Coale, Friends, 1898, MLCHS; Lida L. Greene, ed., "Diary of a Young Girl" (on Quakers), *Annals of Iowa* 36, 6 (Fall 1962): 437–59; J. F. Swartzendruber, "An Amish Migration," *Palimpsest* 17, 10 (Oct. 1936): 342–57; Benedict, "My Early Days in Iowa," pp. 323–55; Jacob Van der Zee, "The Mormon Trails in Iowa," *Iowa Journal of History* 12, 1 (Jan. 1914): 3–16; Cardinal Goodwin, "The American Occupation of Iowa, 1833 to 1860," *Iowa Journal of History and Politics* 17, 1 (Jan. 1919): 83–102; Myres, *Westering Women,* pp. 88–95; Glenda Riley, *Women and Indians on the Frontier, 1825–1915* (Albuquerque: University of New Mexico Press, 1984), pp. 228–40; and Jan Shipps, *Mormonism: The Story of a New Religious Tradition* (Urbana: University of Illinois Press, 1985), pp. 155–61.

104. James R. Shortridge, "Religion," in *This Remarkable Continent,* pp. 183–203. For a discussion of the significant role played by railroads in bringing religious groups to the Plains see John R. Unruh, Jr., "The Burlington and Missouri River Railroad Brings the Mennonites to Nebraska, 1873–1878," pts. 1 and 2, *Nebraska History* 45, 1 and 2 (Mar. and June 1964): 3–30, 177–206. A good recent study of the Amish on the Plains is John A. Hostetler, "The Old Order Amish on the Great Plains: A Study in Cultural Vulnerability," in *Ethnicity on the Great Plains,* pp. 92–108.

105. Ingeborg Aaker Simons, biography, PDC, SDSHRC.

106. Simon Glazer, *Jews of Iowa* (Des Moines, Iowa: Koch Brothers, 1904), pp. 158, 162; and Mount Zion Hebrew Congregation, Papers, 1857–1956, MHS. Florence Shuman Sher, reminiscences, 1976, MHS; see also "The Jews in America," in James Stuart Olson, *The Ethnic Dimension in American History* (New York: St. Martin's Press, 1979), pp. 269–85; and Harold I. Sharfman, *Jews on the Frontier* (Chicago: Henry Regnery, 1977).

107. Lois Fields Schwartz, "Early Jewish Agricultural Colonies in North Dakota," *North Dakota History* 32, 4 (Oct. 1965): 217, 222–32; Lipman Goldman Feld, "New Light on the Lost Jewish Colony of Beersheba, Kansas, 1882–1886," *American Jewish Historical Quarterly* 60, 2 (Dec. 1970): 159, 165–67; Julia Niebuhr Eulenberg, "Back to the Land: Jewish Homesteaders in North Dakota," paper read at the Northern Great Plains History Conference, Bismarck, N.Dak., on 29 Sept. 1984; James A. Rudin, "Beersheba, Kansas: 'God's Pure Air on Government Land,'" *Kansas Historical Quarterly* 34, 3 (Autumn 1968): 282–98; Elbert L. Sapinsley, "Jewish Agricultural Colonies in the West: The Kansas Example," *Western States Jewish Historical Quarterly* 3, 3 (Apr. 1971): 157–69; and Sherman, *Prairie Mosaic*, pp. 53–54.

108. Sherman, *Prairie Mosaic*, pp. 19–20, 53–54, 70, 112.

109. Susan Leaphart, ed., "Frieda and Belle Fligelman: A Frontier-City Girlhood in the 1890s," *Montana, the Magazine of Western History* 32, 3 (Summer 1982): 85–92; Frank J. Adler, *Roots in a Moving Stream: The Centennial History of Congregation B'Nai Jehudah of Kansas City, 1870–1970* (Kansas City, Mo.: Temple, Congregation B'Nai Jehudah, 1972), pp. 3–36, 87–88, 96–98, 115–18; and Joseph P. Schultz, ed., *Mid-America's Promise: A Profile of Kansas City Jewry* (Kansas City, Mo.: Jewish Community Foundation of Kansas City, 1982), pp. 44–45, 82–98, 106, 204–5, 210–36, 309–24. For an account of several Jewish women in southwestern cities see Harriet Rochlin and Fred Rochlin, "Jews on the Western Frontier: An Overview," *Arizona Highways* 61, 9 (Sept. 1985): 2–11.

110. Robbins, *A Physicist Looks*, pp. 60–109. All data analysis was done by my research assistant, Rebecca L. Wheeler.

111. Ibid., pp. 148, 60–109. See C. O. Stout, Huntley Project Homesteading, 1968, MSULSC, for a description of the many states represented by Bingham's neighbors and their children; and Bingham, "Sixteen Years on a Kansas Farm," p. 511; and Anna Rudser Serumgard, Pioneer Homes in the Lake Region, n.d., SHSND, for comments on different ethnic groups in their areas.

112. Harriet Bonebright-Closz, *Reminiscences of Newcastle, Iowa, 1848* (Des Moines: Historical Department of Iowa, 1921), p. 39.

Chapter 3. Home and Hearth on the Prairie

1. See Kathryn Kish Sklar, *Catharine Beecher: A Study in American Domesticity* (New York: Norton, 1976), for a discussion of the ideology of domesticity. For men, no parallel literature or ideology exists concerning their family roles.

2. Katherine Horack, "In Quest of a Prairie Home," *Palimpsest* 5, 7 (July 1924): 255. For other similar descriptions see Kathryn S. H. Moody, Territorial Days in Minnesota, 1960, MHS; and Agnes Mary Kolshorn, My Parents Henry Kolshorn and Mary Teitge, 1983, ibid.

3. Matilda Peitzke Paul, recollections, 1938, and Caroline Phelps, diary, 1832—both in ISHD-HS; see also Abbie Mott Benedict, "My Early Days in Iowa," *Annals of Iowa* 17, 5 (July 1930): 339; and Sarah Welch Nossaman, "Pioneering at Bonaparte and Near Pella," *Annals of Iowa* 13, 6 (Oct. 1922): 451.

4. Eliza W. Farnham, *Life in Prairie Land,* (New York: Harper & Brothers, 1846), p. 85.

5. Margaret E. Archer Murray, "Memoir of the William Archer Family," *Annals of Iowa* 39, 5 (Summer 1968): 363; see also Janette Stevenson Murray, "Women of North Tama," *Iowa Journal of History and Politics* 41, 3 (July 1943): 187–88; and Benedict, "My Early Days in Iowa," p. 359.

6. Pauline Farseth and Theodore C. Blegen, eds., *Frontier Mother: The Letters of Gro Svendsen* (Northfield, Minn.: Norwegian-American Historical Association, 1950), p. 40.

7. Julia K. S. Hibbard, reminiscences, 1856–68, MHS; see also Benedict, "My Early Days in Iowa," p. 343; Horack, "In Quest of a Prairie Home," p. 257; Emery S. Bartlett, letter to My Dear Children and Grandchildren, Dec. 1911, ISHD-MA.

8. Melvin N. Tatley, Biography of Johanna Tatley, 1975, MHS; see also Brian P. Birch, "Possessed of a Restless Spirit: A Young Girl's Memories of the Southern Iowa Frontier," *Palimpsest* 66, 5 (Sept./Oct. 1985): 180; and Annette Atkins, *Harvest of Grief: Grasshopper Plagues and Public Assistance in Minnesota, 1873–78* (St. Paul: Minnesota Historical Society Press, 1984).

9. Paul, Recollections, ISHD-HS.

10. Helena Carlson Vigen, reminiscences, 21 June 1921, MHS; see also Nossaman, "Pioneering at Bonaparte and Near Pella," p. 449; Harriet Bonebright-Closz, *Reminiscences of Newcastle, Iowa, 1848* (Des Moines: Historical Department of Iowa, 1921), p. 45.

11. Farseth and Blegen, *Frontier Mother,* p. 40; Nossaman, "Pioneering at Bonaparte and Near Pella," p. 448; Paul, recollections, ISHD-HS; and Matie L. Baily, "Prairie Homesteading," *Palimpsest* 23, 7 (July 1942): 232.

12. Nossaman, "Pioneering at Bonaparte and Near Pella," p. 448; Murray, "Memoir of the William Archer Family," pp. 358–59; Mary S. Ellis, letter to Dear Mother and Sister, 25 Sept. 1856, John Kenyon Papers, ISHD-HS; and Harriet Sanborn, Life Story, n.d., MHS.

13. Anonymous, "Frontier Fear of the Indians," *Annals of Iowa* 3, 29 (Apr. 1948): 315–22; Glenda Riley, "The Specter of a Savage: Rumors and Alarmism on the Overland Trail," *Western Historical Quarterly* 15, 4 (Oct. 1984): 427–44; Roy Harvey Pearce, "The Significances of the Captivity Narrative," *American Literature* 19, 1 (Mar. 1947): 9; Richard Van Der Beets, "The Indian Captivity Narrative as Ritual," *American Literature* 43, 4 (Jan. 1972): 553. For interpretations of women's perceptions of American Indians see Ronald J. Quinn, "The Modest Seduction: The Experience of Pioneer Women on the Trans-Mississippi Frontier" (Ph.D. diss., University of California at Riverside, 1977); Dawn Gherman, "From Parlor to Tepee: The White Squaw on the American Frontier" (Ph.D. diss., University of Massachusetts, 1975); and Glenda Riley, *Frontierswomen: The Iowa Experience* (Ames: Iowa State University Press, 1981), pp. 177–81, and *Women and Indians on the Frontier, 1825–1915* (Albuquerque: University of New Mexico Press, 1984).

14. Examples of precautions are found in Bessie L. Lyon, "Grandmother's Story," *Palimpsest* 5, 1 (Jan. 1924): 8; idem, "Prospecting for a New Home," ibid., 6, 7 (July 1925): 226; idem, "Hungry Indians," ibid., 9, 10 (Oct. 1928): 369; and Louise Sophia Gellhorn Boylan, My Life Story, 1867–83, ISHD-HS. Accounts of Indian scares are found in Doris Faulkner, ed., "Letters from Algona, 1856–65," *Palimpsest* 61, 6 (Nov./Dec. 1980): 186–89; Harriet M. Hill Townshend, memoir, n.d., privately held by Frank Kerulis, Waterloo, Iowa; and Riley, *Women and Indians,* pp. 83–119. For forts that were built but seldom attacked see Ruth S. Beitz, "They Guarded Iowa's Last Frontier," *Iowan* 9, 3 (Feb./Mar. 1961): 10–15, 46.

15. O. J. Pruitt, "Tales of the Cherokees in Iowa," *Annals of Iowa* 3, 30 (July 1950): 359–67.

16. Moody, Territorial Days, MHS.

17. Arnold Fladager, Memoir of My Mother, Mrs. M. Fladager, 1927, MHS; Paul and Mary Ann Ferrin Davidson, "An Autobiography and a Reminiscence," *Annals of Iowa* 37, 4 (Spring 1964): 256–67.

18. Edith S. Burris, Patsy the Pioneer, n.d., UMWHMC and SHSMM.

19. Cecil Eby, *That Disgraceful Affair: The Black Hawk War* (New York: Norton, 1973).

20. Hubert E. Moeller, "Iowa's Other Indian Massacre," *Iowan* 2, 4 (Apr./May 1954): 40; Abbie Gardner-Sharp, *The Spirit Lake Massacre and the Captivity of Miss Abbie Gardner* (Des Moines: Iowa Printing, 1885); and Curtis Harnack, "Prelude to Massacre," *Iowan* 4, 3 (Feb./Mar. 1956): 36–69; see also Rodney Fox, "Stark Reminder of an Indian Raid," *Iowan* 9, 1 (Oct./Nov. 1960): 20–21, 53; John E. Briggs, "Indian Affairs," *Palimpsest* 21, 9 (Sept. 1940): 261–77, and "Indian Affairs in 1845," *Palimpsest* 26, 8 (Aug. 1945): 225–38; and Leland Sage, *A History of Iowa* (Ames: Iowa State University Press, 1974), pp. 48–51, 107–8.

21. Rebecca Sumner McAlmond, diary, 1862; Sanborn, Life Story; and Marion Louisa Sloan, reminiscences 1926, 1936, 1937—all in MHS; and Theodore C. Blegen, ed., "Immigrant Women and the American Frontier," *Norwegian-American Studies* 5 (1930): 26–29.

22. Fladager, Memoir of My Mother; Moody, Territorial Days; and Hattie A. R. Eaton, Reminiscences, c. 1934—all in MHS.

23. Phelps, diary, ISHD-HS; see also Margie Harger Davis, reminiscence, 1977, held by Dolores K. Gros-Louis, Indiana University, Bloomington; and Boylan, My Life Story, ISHD-HS.

24. For a description of antislavery campaigns by John Brown see anonymous, "Seventy Years in Iowa," *Annals of Iowa* 27, 2 (Oct. 1945): 97–118. For accounts of the effect of the border wars on women see William G. B. Carson, "Anne Ewing Lane," *Missouri Historical Society Bulletin* 21, 2 (Jan. 1965): 94–95; and Dorothy Brown Thompson, "A Young Girl in the Missouri Border War," *Missouri Historical Review* 58, 1 (Oct. 1963): 55–69.

25. Quoted in Mary Elizabeth Massey, *Bonnet Brigades: American Women and the Civil War* (New York: Knopf, 1966), p. 207.

26. Mary McCall to My Dear Thomas, 24 Jan., Mar., 19, 26, and 30 Dec. 1862; McCall Family Papers, Special Collections, Iowa State University Library, Ames; David Logan Hauser Letters, 1862, and J. W. Rice Letters, 1863–67, ISHD-HS.

27. Julia McMichael McCormick, letter to Dear Father, 8 Aug. 1861, UMWHMC and SHSMM.

28. Riley, *Frontierswomen*, pp. 110–35; Louisa Jane Phifer, "Letters from an Illinois Farm, 1864–1865," *Journal of the Illinois State Historical Society* 66, 4 (Winter 1973): 387–403; and Jane M. Johns, *Personal Recollections of Early Decatur* (Decatur, Ill.: Daughters of the American Revolution, 1912), pp. 151–56; see also Christian J. Eager-Young, "Ancestry and Recollections of Mrs. John Young, Rochelle, Illinois," *Journal of the Illinois State Historical Society* 6, 2 (Apr. 1913–Jan. 1914): 240–41.

29. Anonymous, "From New York to Iowa," *Palimpsest* 2, 10 (Oct. 1921): 315.

30. Nossaman, "Pioneering at Bonaparte and Near Pella," p. 441.

31. Sklar, *Catharine Beecher*, pp. 97–98, 102; John B. Newhall, *A Glimpse of Iowa in 1846* (Iowa City, Iowa: State Historical Society, 1957), p. 61. For two examples of women who never married see Carson, "Anne Ewing Lane," pp. 87–99; and Susan D. Vanarsdale, diary, 1847, UMWHMC and SHSMM.

32. Quoted in William J. Petersen, "Women in History," *Palimpsest* 38, 4 (Apr. 1957): 131; see also Geraldine Schwarz, "Family Cohesion in a Norwegian-American Settlement," in *Conversations with the Recent Past,* ed. Luis Torres (Decorah: Northeast Iowa Oral History Project, 1975), pp. 2–3.

33. See, e.g., *Iowa Historical and Comparative Census, 1836–1880* (Des Moines: n.p., 1883), pp. 190–91.

34. Lyon, "Grandmother's Story," p. 6, and "Prospecting for a New Home," pp. 225–32; Bartlett, letter to My Dear Children and Grandchildren, ISHD-MA.

35. Mary Alice Shutes, diary, 1962, ISHD-MA.

36. Florence Call Cowles, *Early Algona: The Story of Our Pioneers, 1854–1874* (Des Moines: Register & Tribune, 1929), p. 86. Other examples of family members' advising or imploring relatives to join them on the prairie are found in Herriott, "Seventy Years in Iowa," p. 98; Abby Fuller Abbe, Account of Trip West in 1854, n.d., Bernice P. Jenkins, Life of Jennie Atwood Pratt, 1949, and Sylvia Macomber Carpenter, letter to My Dear Aunt Ellen, 2 Dec. 1967, MHS; and Morse Family Letters, 1856–68, ISHD-HS.

37. Bartlett, letter to My Dear Children and Grandchildren, ISHD-MA; Emily Veblen Olsen, memoirs, 1941, MHS; Alice Evans, Some Reminiscences of Pioneer Days in Lura Township, n.d., MHS; Jenkins, Life of Jennie Atwood Pratt, and Gertrude Vandergon, reminiscences, 1940–41, MHS; and Marguerite Conroy, Helen Ross Hall, n.d., and Larissa J. Clark, Journal of Voyage to Indiana, 1823, MLCHS.

38. Michael J. O'Brien, *Grassland, Forest, and Historical Settlement* (Lincoln: University of Nebraska Press, 1984), pp. 211–14, 229–30; and Harriet L. Terhune, Reminiscences of Pioneer Days in LaSalle County, 1918, ISHL.

39. Vanarsdale, diary, UMWHMC and SHSMM; Johnson Brigham, "The Wedding of James Harlan," *Palimpsest* 4, 4 (Apr. 1923): 101–5; William J. Petersen, "Romancing in Pioneer Days" and "When Men Were Hard to Get," *Palimpsest* 50, 11 (Nov. 1969): 613–28, 629–36.

40. William G. Padgett, letter to Dear Miss, 28 Dec. 1853, in Ellen Smith Correspondence, 1852–57, MLCHS.

41. Bartlett, letter to My Dear Children and Grandchildren, ISHD-MA; and Peer Stromme, *Halvor: A Story of Pioneer Youth* (Decorah, Iowa: Luther College Press, 1960), pp. 22, 30.

42. *Waterloo* (Iowa) *Courier,* 3 Apr. 1860.

43. Ibid.

44. *Iowa News* (Dubuque), 2 Dec. 1837; and *Burlington* (Iowa) *Daily Hawk-Eye,* 24 Feb. 1859.

45. *Iowa News* (Dubuque), 16 Sept. 1837; and Vanarsdale, diary, UMWHMC and SHSMM.

46. *Fairfield* (Iowa) *Ledger,* 15 Dec. 1870. For other examples of similar advice see the *Dubuque* (Iowa) *Visitor,* 18 May 1836; *Waterloo* (Iowa) *Courier,* 5 June and 31 July 1861. For advice to men see William J. Petersen, "Boys, Keep away from Muslin," *Palimpsest* 50, 11 (Nov. 1969): 637–48.

47. O'Brien, *Grassland, Forest, and Historical Settlement,* p. 283. For a contemporary argument for early marriages see *Iowa News* (Dubuque), 21 Apr. 1838.

48. See, e.g., Frances M. Cockrell, letter to Mrs. Stapp, 7 June 1833, UMWHMC and SHSMM.

49. Phelps, Diary, ISHD-HS; and Ellen Smith, letter to Dear Carrie, 25 May 1857, MLCHS.

50. Mary Lynch, letter to Dear Sis, 12 June 1859, Joseph Marshall Family Papers, 1852–1909, UMWHMC and SHSMM; and Evans, Life History, MLCHS.

51. Mark E. Nackman and Darryl K. Paton, "Recollections of an Illinois Woman," *Western Illinois Regional Studies* 1, 1 (1978): 35.

52. Judith Bradner, Stories of the Old Time Folks of Sixty Years Ago, c. 1895; MLCHS; and Vandergon, reminiscences, MHS.

53. Mary Hedges Hubbard, letter to My Dear Girls, 5 May 1855, ISHL.

54. Nettie Sanford, *Early Sketches of Polk County* (Newton, Iowa: Chas. A. Clark, 1874), p. 33; see also George F. Parker, *Iowa Pioneer Foundations* (Iowa City: State Historical Society, 1940), p. 58.

55. *Iowa News* (Dubuque), 7 Oct. 1837; and *Waterloo* (Iowa) *Courier,* 9 Mar. 1864.

56. O'Brien, *Grassland, Forest, and Historical Settlement,* p. 283.

57. Nackman and Paton, "Recollections of an Illinois Woman," p. 36.

58. Leo E. Oliva, "Our Frontier Heritage and the Environment," *American West* 9, 1 (Jan. 1972): 45.

59. Conroy, Helen Ross Hall, MLCHS.

60. Moody, Territorial Days, MHS.

61. Lysander Patterson Foster, M.D., Reference Book, c. 1870, MHS; *Weekly Pantagraph* (Bloomington, Ill.), 22 Feb. 1854; and Frederick H. Falls, "Obstetrics and Gynecology," in *History of Medical Practice in Illinois,* ed. David J. Davis (Chicago: University of Illinois Press, 1955), pp. 211–44.

62. Ann Douglas Wood, " 'The Fashionable Diseases': Women's Complaints and Their Treatment in Nineteenth-Century America," *Journal of Interdisciplinary History* 4, 1 (Summer 1973): 26–27.

63. For a fuller discussion of these issues see Carroll Smith-Rosenberg and Charles Rosenberg, "The Female Animal: Medical and Biological Views of Woman and Her Role in Nineteenth-Century America," *Journal of American History* 60, 2 (Sept. 1973): 332–56; and Linda Gordon, *Woman's Body, Woman's Right: A Social History of Birth Control in America* (New York: Grossman, 1976).

64. *Fairfield* (Iowa) *Ledger,* 5 Dec. 1861. A similar work entitled "The Physical Life of Woman" was advertised in the *Fairfield* (Iowa) *Ledger* for 19 May 1870. A volume that claimed to be able to cure the ills resulting from masturbation by young men, but that also discussed masturbation by women, was F. C. Fowler's *Goods News for Weak, Debilitated Men* (1891), Mrs. Henry Hamilton Collection, 1885–97, UMWHMC and SHSMM.

65. *Wapello* (Iowa) *Intelligencer,* 27 Feb. 1854; *Iowa Capital Reporter* (Iowa City), 5 Apr. 1854; *Burlington* (Iowa) *Daily Hawk-Eye,* 4 and 6 Jan. 1859.

66. *Burlington* (Iowa) *Daily Hawk-Eye,* 6 Jan. 1859; and *Waterloo* (Iowa) *Courier,* 13 Dec. 1859 and 12 Feb. 1861.

67. Boylan, My Life Story, ISHD-HS.

68. James S. Ewing, Short Addresses, n.d., pp. 93–133, MLCHS.

69. Britania J. Livingston, reminiscences, 11 Dec. 1929, MHS.

70. Catherine Bissell Ely, diary, 1835–39, and Hibbard, reminiscences, MHS.

71. Margaret Stout Davis, The Story of My Life, 1952, UMWHMC and SHSMM.

72. *Burlington* (Iowa) *Daily Hawk-Eye,* 5 Jan. 1859.

73. Ellen R. Fenn, "Sweepin' out the Fabled Ghosts," *Iowan* 14, 1 (Fall 1965): 50; see also Janet Bogdan, "Care or Cure? Childbirth Practices in Nineteenth Century America," *Feminist Studies* 4, 2 (June 1978): 92–99; Pamela S. Eakins, ed., *The American Way of Birth* (Philadelphia: Temple University Press, 1986); and Richard W. Wertz and Dorothy C. Wertz, *Lying-in: A History of Childbirth in America* (New York: Schocken Books, 1979).

74. Fred W. Lorch, "Molly Clemen's Note Books," *Palimpsest* 10, 10 (Oct. 1929): 361.

75. Kitturah Penton Belknap, diary, IHSD-HS; Mary Parsons Christie, letter to My Dear Sister Julia, May 1840, ISHD-HS; and Mary E. Carpenter, letter, n.d., MHS.

76. Elizabeth Black, " 'Took Tea at Mrs. Lincoln's': The Diary of Mrs. William M. Black," *Journal of the Illinois State Historical Society* 48, 1 (Spring 1955): 62.

77. Paul, recollections, ISHS; and Kitturah Penton Belknap, reminiscences, c. 1839, ISHD-HS.

78. Priscilla J. Brewer, " 'The Little Citizen': Images of Children in Early Nineteenth-Century America," *Journal of American Culture* 7, 4 (Winter 1984): 45–62. For the importance of children as laborers see Marion Drury, *Early Days in Iowa* (Toledo, Iowa: Toledo Chronicle Press, 1931), p. 12.

79. Abby Bucklin, Just Indians, n.d., MHS; and Matie Ward James, Dr. James A. Ward, 23 Apr. 1938, UMWHMC and SHSMM.

80. Boylan, My Life Story, ISHD-HS; E. May Lacey Crowder, "Pioneer Life in Palo Alto County," *Iowa Journal of History and Politics* 46, 2 (Apr. 1948): 176; and Drury, *Early Days in Iowa*, p. 45.

81. To contrast these practices with those in other societies see Lloyd deMause, ed., *The History of Childhood* (New York: Harper Torchbooks, 1975).

82. Terhune, Reminiscences, ISHL.

83. Ellen Strang, diary, 1861, ISHD-MA.

84. Vigen, reminiscences, MHS; and Crowder, "Pioneer Life in Palo Alto County," p. 160.

85. Kolshorn, My Parents, MHS.

86. Sallie Abbott, diary, 1865, ISHL. For other descriptions of children's work see Murray, "Memoir of the William Archer Family," p. 364; Lucia B. Johnson, memoir, 28 Aug. 1963, MHS; Mary Walters Randall, Personal Recollections of Pioneer Life, n.d., in Adda A. Lawyer Papers, ISHD-HS; Paul, recollections, ISHD-HS.

87. Hibbard, reminiscences, MHS.

88. Burris, Patsy the Pioneer, UMWHMC and SHSMM.

89. Evans, Life History, MLCHS.

90. Davis, The Story of My Life, UMWHMC and SHSMM; Sarah Fuller, letters to Dear Lizzie, 31 Oct. 1861, in Abby Fuller Abbe, Family Papers, 1840–1928, MHS; Susan Short May, "The Story of Her Ancestry and of Her Early Life in Illinois," *Journal of the Illinois State Historical Society* 6, 1 (Apr. 1913–Jan. 1914): 126; and Nackman and Paton, "Recollections of an Illinois Woman," p. 33; and Amelia Murdock Wing, "Early Days in Clayton County," *Annals of Iowa* 27, 4 (Apr. 1946): 283.

91. Charlotte A. Scott, recollections, 1915, MLCHS; Eaton, reminiscences, MHS; Jenkins, Life of Jennie Atwood Pratt, MHS; and Sloan, reminiscences, MHS; Paul, recollections, ISHD-HS.

92. James, Dr. James A. Ward, UMWHMC and SHSMM; see also Elizabeth Crowley, in Illinois Women, 1893, ISHL; J. H. Burnham, "Subscription and Semi-Subscription Schools," in *Transactions of the McLean County Historical Society* (Bloomington, Ill.: Pantagraph Printing & Stationery Co., 1903), pp. 25–31; and May, "The Story of Her Ancestry," pp. 124–25.

93. Ruth A. Gallaher, *Legal and Political Status of Women in Iowa, 1838–1918* (Iowa City, Iowa: State Historical Society, 1918), p. 39; and Louis B. Wright, *Culture on the Moving Frontier* (New York: Harper Torchbook, 1961), p. 225; see also Wayne Edison Fuller, *The Old Country School: The Story of Rural Education in the Middle West* (Chicago: University of Chicago Press, 1982).

94. Strang, diary, ISHD-MA.

95. Described by John Plumbe, Jr., in "Plumbe's Sketches of Iowa in 1839," *Annals of Iowa* 14, 8 (Apr. 1925): 599; and a Pioneer, *Northern Iowa: Containing Hints*

and Information of Value to Emigrants (Dubuque, Iowa: Nonpareil Publishing House, 1858), pp. 29, 33–34.

96. Evans, Life History, MLCHS.

97. Julie Roy Jeffrey, *Frontier Women: The Trans-Mississipi West, 1840–1880* (New York: Hill & Wang, 1979), pp. 3–24.

98. Maxine Van De Wetering, "The Popular Concept of 'Home' in Nineteenth-Century America," *Journal of American Studies* 18, 1 (Apr. 1984): 5–28.

99. Bartlett, letter to Dear Children and Grandchildren, ISHD-MA; see also Bucklin, Just Indians, MHS; Fladager, Memoir of My Mother, MHS; and Ida Skordahl, reminiscence, n.d., MHS.

100. Shutes, diary, ISHD-MA; and Benedict, "My Early Days in Iowa," p. 341.

101. Belknap, reminiscences, ISHD-HS.

102. Lyon, "Grandmother's Story," p. 6; see also Shutes, diary, ISHD-MA; Paul, recollections, ISHD-HS; and Murray, "Memoir of the William Archer Family," p. 472.

103. Ruth A. Gallaher, "Around the Fireplace," *Palimpsest* 8, 1 (Jan. 1927): 18–23; William J. Petersen, "The Pioneer Cabin," *Iowa Journal of History and Politics* 36, 4 (Oct. 1938): 387–409; Mildred Sharp, "Early Cabins in Iowa," *Palimpsest* 2, 1 (Jan. 1921): 16–29; and Ezra M. Prince, John and Jane Hendrix, 5 June 1906, MLCHS. For other descriptions see Cowles, *Early Algona,* p. 97; Crowder, "Pioneer Life in Palo Alto County," p. 164; Davidson, "An Autobiography and a Reminiscence," pp. 247–48; Susan I. Dubell, "A Pioneer Home," *Palimpsest* 12, 12 (Dec. 1931): 445–53. Hibbard, reminiscences, MHS; and Horack, "In Quest of a Prairie Home," p. 255. For a discussion of variety in regional housing styles see James M. Denny, "Early Southern Domestic Architecture in Missouri, 1810–1840: The 'Georgianization' of the Trans-Mississippi West," *Pioneer America Society Transactions* 8 (1985): 11–25.

104. Benedict, "My Early Days in Iowa," pp. 342–43. For other descriptions see Petersen, "Pioneer Cabin," pp. 402–4.

105. Bonebright-Closz, *Reminiscences of Newcastle,* p. 33.

106. Faulkner, "Letters from Algona," p. 186.

107. Mary Burns, The Bright Side of Homesteading, 1923, MHS.

108. See., e.g., Bucklin, Just Indians, MHS; Hibbard, reminiscences, MHS; Sloan, reminiscences, MHS; anonymous, "From New York to Iowa," p. 317; and Riley, *Frontierswomen,* pp. 41–44.

109. Jeffrey, *Frontier Women,* pp. 53–54, 59–60; Sandra L. Myres, *Westering Women and the Frontier Experience, 1800–1915* (Albuquerque: University of New Mexico Press, 1982), pp. 141–46; and Riley, *Frontierswomen,* pp. 57–58.

110. "The Managing Woman," *Fairfield* (Iowa) *Ledger,* 21 Jan. 1869; "The Wife," ibid., 21 Jan. 1869; "Idyll of a Western Wife," *Waterloo* (Iowa) *Courier,* 10 July 1860; and "A Domestic Chat," *Burlington* (Iowa) *Daily Hawk-Eye,* 31 July 1845.

111. See, e.g., Carpenter, diary, MHS; and Mary St. John, diary, 1858, ISHD-HS. For an excellent case study of the extensive nature and difficulty of women's work see John Mack Faragher, *Sugar Creek: Life on the Illinois Prairie* (New Haven, Conn.: Yale University Press, 1986).

112. Kolshorn, My Parents, MHS.

113. Mrs. E. W. Logan, in Illinois Women, 1893, ISHL; and Hulda C. Deems, Making Maple Syrup and Sugar in Blooming Grove, n.d., MLCHS; Sanborn, Life Story, MHS; Vandergon, reminiscences, MHS.

114. Mrs. Andrew McCormick, in Illinois Women, 1893; ISHL; Terhune, reminiscences, ISHL; and Mary S. Ellis, letter to Dear Mother, 7 Nov. 1856, in John Kenyon Papers, ISHD-HS.

115. Wing, "Early Days in Clayton County," p. 380; see also Claude E. Simmonds, George Davies—Wright County Pioneer, 1946, MHS.

116. Kolshorn, My Parents, MLCHS; Prince, John and Jane Hendrix, MLCHS; Belknap, diary, ISHD-HS; Paul, recollections, ISHD-HS.

117. Anonymous, *Buckeye Cookery* (Minneapolis: Buckeye Publishing, 1887); and Mary B. Welch, *Mrs. Welch's Cookbook* (Des Moines, Iowa: Mills, 1884).

118. Belknap, diary, ISHD-HS.

119. Murray, "Women of North Tama," pp. 298–99; Benedict, "My Early Days in Iowa," p. 327; Paul, recollections, ISHD-HS; Wing, "Early Days in Clayton County," p. 280; B. F. Gue, "Early Iowa Reminiscences," *Iowa Historical Records* 16 (July 1900): 110; Bonebright-Closz, *Reminiscences of Newcastle,* p. 39; Murray, "Memoir of the William Archer Family," p. 3; Kolshorn, My Parents, MHS; Moody, Territorial Days, MHS; Farnham, *Life in Prairie Land,* pp. 64–5; Susan I. Dubell, "Rural Pioneering," *Palimpsest* 22, 8 (Aug. 1941): 233–35.

120. Bonebright-Closz, *Reminiscences of Newcastle,* pp. 185–86; Lucinda Casteen, letter to Dear Mother, 1830, ISHL; Elizabeth Crowley, Mrs. Andrew McCormick and Mrs. E. W. Logan, in Illinois Women, ISHL; anonymous, Dye Book, c. 1833, ISHL; Crowder, "Pioneer Life in Palo Alto County," pp. 179–80; Hibbard, reminiscences, MHS; Murray, "Memoir of the William Archer Family," p. 361; Riley, *Frontierswomen,* pp. 67–69.

121. Kolshorn, My Parents, MHS; Vandergon, reminiscences, MHS.

122. Lula Gillespie Lentz, "The Reminiscences of Lula Gillespie Lentz," pts. 1 and 2, *Journal of the Illinois State Historical Society* 68, 3 and 4 (1975): 271–73, 276–82, 356–57; see also William D. Andrews and Deborah C. Andrews, "Technology and the Housewife in Nineteenth-Century America," *Women's Studies* 2, 3 (1974): 309–28; and Susan Strasser, *Never Done: A History of American Housework* (New York: Pantheon, 1981), especially pp. 3–10.

123. Gladys Blair, "The Prairie Woman," *Prairie Farmer* 113 (11 Jan. 1941): 162.

124. *Fairfield* (Iowa) *Ledger,* 31 Mar. 1864.

125. *Burlington* (Iowa) *Daily Hawk-Eye,* 7 Jan. and 1 Apr. 1859; *Fairfield* (Iowa) *Ledger,* 14 Mar. 1861; *Waterloo* (Iowa) *Courier,* 18 Sept. 1860; and *Fairfield* (Iowa) *Ledger,* 2 July 1863.

126. Mrs. H. C. Johns, "The Farmer's Home," *Transactions of the Illinois State Agricultural Society* (Springfield: Baker, Bailhache, 1868), pp. 292–99.

127. *Davenport* (Iowa) *Gazette,* 14 June 1855; *Burlington* (Iowa) *Daily Hawk-Eye,* 1 and 31 Jan. 1859; *Fairfield* (Iowa) *Ledger,* 5 Dec. 1861; and *Waterloo* (Iowa) *Courier,* 17 Dec. 1868.

128. See, e.g., Davis, The Story of My Life, UMWHMC and SHSMM; and Johnson, memoir, MHS.

129. Floy Lawrence Emhoff, "A Pioneer School Teacher in Central Iowa: Alice Money Lawrence," *Iowa Journal of History and Politics* 33, 4 (Oct. 1935): 378–79.

130. Hibbard, reminiscences; Kolshorn, My Parents; and Dorothy St. Arnold, reminiscences—all in MHS.

131. See, e.g., *Business Directory and Review of the Trade, Commerce and Manufactories of the City of Burlington, Iowa, for the Year Ending May 1, 1856* (Burlington, Iowa: Hawk-Eye Power Press, 1856); John Kennedy, *Iowa City Directory and Advertiser, for 1857* (Iowa City, Iowa: A. G. Tucker, 1857); and J. H. Stevenson, *History and Business Directory of Wright County* (Des Moines, Iowa: Mills, 1870). For descriptions of the many Jewish peddlers see Simon Glazer, *Jews of Iowa* (Des Moines, Iowa: Koch Brothers, 1904), pp. 173–75, 179, 183–84; see also Florence Shuman Sher,

reminiscences, 1976, MHS; and Elizabeth Fickes, diary, 1856–57, Beinecke Collection, Yale University, New Haven, Conn.

132. *Missouri Intelligencer and Boon's Lick Advertiser* (Franklin, Missouri Territory), 13 Aug. 1819.

133. *Minnesota Pioneer* (St. Paul), 2 May 1850; see also *Iowa Sentinel* (Fairfield), 26 Feb. 1857; and *Waterloo* (Iowa) *Courier,* 9 Apr. 1861. For a description of the oyster suppers that often resulted see Edith H. Hurlbutt, "Pioneer Experiences in Keokuk County, 1858–1874," *Iowa Journal of History,* 52, 4 (Oct. 1954): 335.

134. *Iowa Sentinel* (Fairfield), 11 Jan. 1855.

135. Kolshorn, My Parents, MHS.

136. *Dubuque* (Iowa) *Visitor,* 6 July and 14 Sept. 1836; *Iowa News* (Dubuque), 1 and 15 July 1837; *Iowa Territorial Gazette and Advertiser,* 1 July 1844; *Burlington* (Iowa) *Daily Hawk-Eye and Telegraph,* 23 July 1855, 5 Apr. 1859, 18 June and 4 Jan. 1859.

137. Custer, Recollections of Mrs. Charlotte A. Scott, MLCHS.

138. *Frontier Guardian* (Council Bluffs, Iowa), 17 Oct. 1849; *Weekly Observer* (Mt. Pleasant, Iowa), 20 Apr. 1854; *Fairfield* (Iowa) *Ledger,* 24 Sept. 1863.

139. Sarah Ann Davidson, account books, 1854–59, ISHL; see also Adaline C. Clark, diaries, 1851–1911, ISHL.

140. Alice L. Longley, handwritten notation, n.d., Alice L. Longley Papers, ISHD-MA.

141. Natalie W. Kuemmel, day book, 1861, UMWHMC and SHSMM.

142. Lydia M. Sprague Scott, diary, 1878–1910, MHS.

143. Janet Vespa, "Pioneer Girl Tells of Early Peoria," *Peoria* (Ill.) *Journal Star,* 29 Dec. 1868; and Vandergon, reminiscences, MHS.

144. Clara Dodge, letter to My Dear Husband, 12 Dec. 1848, ISHD-HS.

145. See also Faye E. Dudden, *Serving Women: Household Service in Nineteenth-Century America* (Middletown, Conn.: Wesleyan University Press, 1983); David M. Katzman, *Seven Days a Week: Women and Domestic Service in Industrializing America* (New York: Oxford University Press, 1978); and Judith Rollins, *Between Women: Domestics and Their Employers* (Philadelphia: Temple University Press, 1985).

146. Sara Brooks Sundberg, "A Study of Farmwomen on the Minnesota Prairie Frontier, 1850–1900" (Master's thesis, University of Wisconsin–Eau Claire), pp. 86–87; Skordahl, reminiscence, n.d., MHS; and Mary Johnstone Powers, A Pioneer Woman's Reminiscences in Minnesota and Montana, 1947, MTHS.

147. Phelps, diary, ISHD-HS. For examples of women who helped with farm work see Baily, "Prairie Homesteading," p. 233; Crowder, "Pioneer Life in Palo Alto County," p. 173; Sarah Kenyon, letter to Dear Mother, 29 Aug. 1856 and 10 Oct. 1860, John Kenyon Papers, ISHD-HS; and Murray, "Memoir of the William Archer Family," p. 363. For the women who became involved in family businesses see Evans, Life History, MLCHS; and Davis, The Story of My Life, UMWHMC and SHSMM. For army women see Willa G. Cramton, *Women beyond the Frontier: A Distaff View of Life at Fort Wayne* (Fort Wayne, Ind.: Historic Fort Wayne, Inc., 1977); Mary Ellen McElligott, ed. " 'A Monotony Full of Sadness': The Diary of Nadine Turchin, May 1863–April, 1864," *Journal of the Illinois State Historical Society* 70, 1 (Feb. 1977): 27–89; Charlotte Van Cleve, *"Three Score Years and Ten": Life-Long Memories of Fort Snelling, Minnesota, and Other Parts of the West* (Minneapolis, Minn.: Harrison & Smith, 1888).

148. Patricia G. Harpole, ed., "The Black Community in Territorial St. Anthony: A Memoir," *Minnesota History* 49, 2 (Summer 1984): 42–55.

149. Eva Neal, Family Papers, 1881–1963, MHS.

150. See David V. Taylor, "The Blacks," in *They Chose Minnesota: A Survey of the State's Ethnic Groups*, ed. June Drenning Holmquist (St. Paul: Minnesota Historical Society Press, 1981), pp. 73–91; Myres, *Westering Women*, pp. 5, 86, 208; and Riley, *Frontierswomen*, pp. 89–99. For views of black women's lives on other frontiers see Sue Armitage, Theresa Banfield, and Sarah Jacobus, "Black Women and Their Communities in Colorado," *Frontiers* 2, 2 (1977): 45–51; and Lawrence B. de Graaf, "Race, Sex, and Region: Black Women in the American West, 1850–1920," *Pacific Historical Review* 49, 2 (May 1980): 285–314.

151. For urban/rural migration patterns on the prairie frontier see Michael P. Conzen, "Local Migration Systems in Nineteenth-Century Iowa," *Geographical Review* 64, 3 (July 1974): 340; and Richard C. Wade, *The Urban Frontier: Pioneer Life in Early Pittsburgh, Cincinnati, Lexington, Louisville and St. Louis* (Chicago: University of Chicago Press, 1964), pp. 305–42. For the types of people who were drawn to towns see Farnham, *Life in Prairie Land*, p. 163; anonymous, *Pioneer Settlers of Louisa County* (Wapello, Iowa: John Jenkins, 1859–60), p. 3; Harley Ransom, comp., *Pioneer Recollections* (Cedar Rapids, Iowa: Historical Publishing, 1941), p. 93; broadside, Western Stage Company, c. 1855 (Dubuque, Iowa: Express & Herald Job Print, n.d., and Rock Island, Ill., Raymond's Printing House, 1855); Alice Schlenker, Asahel Gridley, 1980, MLCHS; Frank I. Herriott, memoranda, n.d., in Alice L. Longley Papers, ISHD-MA; Vandergon, reminiscences, MHS; Farnham, *Life in Prairie Land*, p. 226.

152. For comments on the advantages of towns see Harriet Connor Brown, *Grandmother Brown's Hundred Years, 1827–1927* (Boston, Mass.: Little, Brown, 1929); and Virginia Ivins, *Yesterdays: Reminiscences of Long Ago* (Keokuk, Iowa: n.p., n.d.), pp. 35, 51.

153. Vespa, "Pioneer Girl Tells of Early Peoria."

154. Ellen Bigelow, "Letters Written by a Peoria Woman in 1835," *Journal of the Illinois State Historical Society* 22, 2 (Apr. 1929–Jan. 1930): 350.

155. Mellisa Stockdale, in Illinois Women and Hubbard, letter to My Dear Girls, ISHL; Miriam M. Worthington, ed., "Diary of Anna R. Morrison, Wife of Isaac L. Morrison," *Journal of the Illinois State Historical Society* 7, 1 (Apr. 1914–Jan. 1915): 43.

156. Mary Byram Wright, "Personal Recollections of the Early Settlement of Carlinville, Illinois," *Journal of the Illinois State Historical Society* 18, 4 (Oct. 1925–Jan. 1926): 668–85.

157. Henry L. Norton, "The Travels of the Marstons," *Journal of the Illinois State Historical Society* 58, 3 (Autumn 1965): 288; see also Fredrika Bremer, "Fredrika Bremer in Chicago in 1850," *Swedish Pioneer Historical Quarterly* 19, 4 (Oct. 1968): 238.

158. Katherine Clinton, "Pioneer Women in Chicago, 1833–1837," *Journal of the West* 12, 2 (Apr. 1973): 318. For a contrasting view of Chicago in later years see anonymous, "The Gay Nineties in Chicago: A French View," *Chicago History* 7, 11 (Spring 1966): 341–48.

159. *Bloomington* (Ill.) *Bulletin*, 26 Jan. 1899.

160. Justin G. Turner and Linda Levitt Turner, *Mary Todd Lincoln: Her Life and Letters* (New York: Alfred A. Knopf, 1972), p. 22.

161. Abby Fuller Abbe, letters, 1848–62, MHS.

162. Clinton, "Pioneer Women in Chicago," pp. 319–21; and Abbe, letters, MHS.

163. Glenda Riley, "The 'Female Frontier' in Early Illinois," *Mid-America* 67, 2 (Apr./July 1985): 69–81.

164. Mrs. E. A. Hadley, journal, 1851, ISHS-MS.

165. Julian E. McFarland, *A History of the Pioneer Era on Iowa Prairies* (Lake Mills, Iowa: Graphic, 1969), p. 145.

166. Burns, The Bright Side of Homesteading, MHS; and anonymous, "Some Letters of James Mathews, and Caroline Mathews Stone," *Iowa Journal of History* 45, 3 (July 1947): 311–20.

167. Brown, *Grandmother Brown's Hundred Years,* pp. 103, 111.

168. Nossaman, "Pioneering at Bonaparte and Near Pella," p. 450.

169. Jeffrey, *Frontier Women,* pp. 10–12.

170. Burris, Patsy the Pioneer, UMWHMC and SHSMM.

171. Bradner, Stories of the Old Time-Folks, MLCHS; and Simmonds, George Davies, MHS.

172. Mildred Freburg Berry, "Memories of a Swedish Christmas," *Palimpsest* 59, 1 (Jan./Feb. 1978): 20–23; see also Matie L. Baily, "Christmas of a Pioneer Family," *Annals of Iowa* 3, 31 (Oct. 1951): 152–53; and Philip Pacey, "Family Art: Domestic and Eternal Bliss," *Journal of Popular Culture* 18, 1 (Summer 1984): 43–52.

173. Mary Parsons Christie, letter to Beloved Home Friends, Jan. 1839, ISHD-HS; and Augusta Parks Smith, The Trip from Kentucky, n.d., MLCHS.

174. Van Cleve, *"Three Score Years and Ten,"* pp. 38–39.

175. See Esther Pillsbury, A Pioneer to the Lake Region Describes Trip Here in Diary, 1863, ISHD-HS, for various societies; and Kolshorn, My Parents, MHS, for a German school.

176. C. A. Moore and Jacob Moore, in Illinois Women, 1893, ISHL.

177. For discussions of the importance of female bonding to nineteenth-century women see Carroll Smith-Rosenberg, "The Female World of Love and Ritual: Relations between Women in Nineteenth Century America," *Signs* 1 (Aug. 1975): 1–29. Also helpful are Joel D. Block and Diane Greenberg, *Women and Friendship* (New York: Franklin Watts, 1985); Pauline Nestor, *Female Friendships and Communities: Charlotte Bronte, George Eliot, Elizabeth Gaskell* (New York: Oxford University Press, 1985); Janice G. Raymond, *A Passion for Friends: Toward A Philosophy of Female Affection* (Boston, Mass.: Beacon Press, 1986).

178. Casteen, letter to Dear Mother, ISHL.

179. Bucklin, Just Indians, MHS.

180. For descriptions of quilting bees see Eliza Ann Bartlett, diary, 1854–64, ISHD-MA; May, "The Story of Her Ancestry," p. 126; and Vanarsdale, diary, UMWHMC and SHSMM. For descriptions of wool pullings see Belknap, diary, ISHD-HS; and Eager-Young, "Ancestry and Recollections of Mrs. John Young," p. 238.

181. See, e.g., Davis, The Story of My Life, UMWHMC and SHSMM; and Vandergon, reminiscences, MHS.

182. Sallie F. Ellis, Papers, 1864–1932, UMWHMC and SHSMM; see also Moody, Territorial Days, MHS; and Riley, *Frontierswomen,* pp. 77–79.

183. *Waterloo* (Iowa) *Courier,* 17 and 3 Feb. 1864; see also ibid., 2 Dec. 1862, 30 Dec. 1863, 20 Jan. and 3 Aug. 1864, 29 Oct. 1868.

184. Moody, Territorial Days, MHS; Scott, diary, MHS; Bartlett, diary, ISHD-MA.

185. See, e.g., Burris, Patsy the Pioneer, UMWHMC and SHSMM; Clara Ann Dodge, letters, ISHD-HS; Hibbard, reminiscences, MHS; Mor Hetteen of Roseau County, in Minnesota American Mothers Committee Biographies, 1975, MHS.

186. Hibbard, reminiscences, MHS.

187. Fladager, Memoir of My Mother, MHS.

188. Sylvia Macomber Carpenter, letter to Dear Aunt, Apr. 1863, MHS; Bartlett, diary, ISHD-MA; Irving B. Richman, *Ioway to Iowa: The Genesis of a Corn and Bible Commonwealth* (Iowa City: State Historical Society, 1931), p. 317.

189. Anonymous, "From New York to Iowa," p. 320.

190. Rebecca Burlend and Edward Burlend, *A True Picture of Immigration* (New

York: Citadel Press, 1968), pp. 71, 152–53; see also John Willeford, Biography of Susannah Willeford, 1880, and Randall, Personal Recollections of Pioneer Life, ISHD-HS; Eager-Young, "Ancestry and Recollections of Mrs. John Young," pp. 237–39.

191. For descriptions of circuses see Paul, recollections, ISHD-HS; Evans, Some Reminiscences of Pioneer Days, and Olsen, memoirs, MHS. For detailed advertisements of these elaborate circuses see *Burlington* (Iowa) *Daily Hawk-Eye and Telegraph*, 20 and 21 July, 28 Sept., 3 Oct. 1855, 1 July 1866; *Fairfield* (Iowa) *Ledger*, 1 July 1869, 7 Sept. 1860, 13 Aug. 1863, 28 May 1868, 11 June 1863, and 25 June 1868; *Waterloo* (Iowa) *Courier*, 5 June 1861, 25 June 1862, and 27 July 1864; see also Peter T. Harstad, "The Spirit of '76 in Iowa," *Palimpsest* 57, 3 (May/June 1976): 66–75; and Bruce E. Mahan, "Frontier Fun," ibid., 8 (Jan. 1927): 38–41.

192. Gladys Scott Thomson, *A Pioneer Family: The Birkbecks in Illinois, 1818–1827* (London: Jonathan Cape, 1953), pp. 54, 76–77.

193. Price, Recollections of My Father, UMWHMC and SHSMM; and Johns, *Personal Recollections*, p. 26.

194. For a typical advertisement for a bowling saloon see *Minnesota Pioneer* (St. Paul), 2 May 1850.

195. Mary J. Mason Remey, diary, 1862–68, ISHD-MA; and Sarah Irwin Bunn, diary, 1870, ISHL; see also invitation to Fourth of July Ball, Fort Madison, Iowa, 1859, Graff Collection, Newberry Library, Chicago. See, e.g., Donald F. Carmony, ed., "Frontier Life: A Case of Loneliness and Hope," *Indiana Magazine of History* 61, 1 (1965): 53–57; Livingston, reminiscences, MHS; Carolyn Johnston Tucker, diary, 1833–49, MHS; Lenora Scholte, "A Stranger in a Strange Land: Romance in Pella History," *Iowa Journal of History* 37, 2 (Apr. 1939): 146–49. A case of female insanity is described by John B. Orendorff in Sketch of Omen and Zena Olney, n.d., MLCHS.

196. See, e.g., Catharine Bissell Ely, diary, 1835–39, and Edmund F. Ely, diary, 1838/39, MHS; John Kenyon Family Papers, letters of John and Sarah Kenyon and Mary S. Ellis; McCall Family Papers, letters of Mary and Thomas McCall, Special Collections, Iowa State University Library, Ames; and Joseph Marshall Family Papers, assorted letters, 1852–1909, UMWHMC and SHSMM.

Chapter 4. Home and Hearth on the Plains

1. Gilbert C. Fite, "Daydreams and Nightmares: The Late Nineteenth-Century Agricultural Frontiers," *Agricultural History* 40, 4 (Oct. 1966): 285–93; Harold E. Briggs, "The Settlement and Development of the Territory of Dakota, 1860–70," *North Dakota Historical Quarterly* 7 (1933): 114–49; Rupert N. Richardson, "Some Historical Factors Contributing to the Problems of the Great Plains," *Southwestern Social Science Quarterly* 18, 1 (June 1937): 1–14; Robert M. Finley, "A Budgeting Approach to the Question of Homestead Size on the Plains," *Agricultural History* 42, 2 (Apr. 1968): 109–14; and Gilbert C. Fite, "The United States Army and Relief to Pioneer Settlers, 1874–1875," *Journal of the West* 6, 1 (Jan. 1967): 99–107.

2. Louise Pound, *Pioneer Days in the Middle West: Settlement and Racial Stocks* (Lincoln: Nebraska State Historical Society, n.d.); Mary W. M. Hargreaves, "Homesteading and Homemaking on the Plains: A Review," *Agricultural History* 47, 2 (Apr. 1973): 156–63; Lillian Schlissel, "Women's Diaries on the Western Frontier," *American Studies* 18, 1 (Spring 1977): 87–100, and "Mothers and Daughters on the Western Frontier," *Frontiers* 3, 2 (1979): 29–33; Christine Stansell, "Women on the Great Plains, 1865–1900," *Women's Studies* 4, 1 (1976): 87–98; and John Mack Faragher and Christine Stansell, "Women and Their Families on the Overland Trail

to California and Oregon, 1842–1867," *Feminist Studies* 2, 2 and 3 (1975): 150–66.

3. Myra Waterman Bickel, Lydia Burrows Foote, Eleanor Schubert, and Anna Warren Peart, PDC, SDSHRC; Abbie Bright, diary, 1870/71, KSHS; Barbara Levorsen, "Early Years in Dakota," *Norwegian-American Studies* 21 (1962): 167–69; Kathrine Newman Webster, "Memories of a Pioneer," in *Old Timer's Tales*, vol. 2, pt. 1 (Lincoln: Nebraska State Historical Society, 1971); Bertha Scott Hawley Johns, Pioneer Memories, 1975, WSAMHD; and Emma Crinklaw (interview of Mary A. Thon), One Brave Homesteader of '89, 1939, WSAMHD. For a discussion of the problems revolving around scarce water see Everett Dick, "Water: A Frontier Problem," *Nebraska History* 49, 3 (Autumn 1968): 215–45; Herbert S. Schell, "Drought and Agriculture in Eastern South Dakota during the Eighteen Nineties," *Agricultural History* 5, 4 (Oct. 1931): 168–80; Walter Prescott Webb, "The West and the Desert," *Montana, the Magazine of Western History* 8, 1 (Jan. 1958): 2–12. For the solutions sought see Martin E. Carlson, "William E. Smythe: Irrigation Crusader," *Journal of the West* 7 (Jan. 1968): 41–47; Marc M. Cleworth, "Artesian-Well Irrigation: Its History in Brown County, South Dakota, 1889–1900," *Agricultural History* 15, 4 (Oct. 1941): 195–201; Donald F. Danker, "Nebraska's Homemade Windmills," *American West* 3, 1 (Winter 1966): 13–19; A. Bower Sageser, "Editor Bristow and the Great Plains Irrigation Revival of the 1890s," *Journal of the West* 3, 1 (Jan. 1964): 75–89, and "Windmill and Pump Irrigation on the Great Plains, 1890–1910," *Nebraska History* 48, 2 (Summer 1967): 107–18; Henry Nash Smith, "Rain Follows the Plow: The Notion of Increased Rainfall for the Great Plains," *Huntington Library Quarterly* 10, 2 (Feb. 1946): 169–93; and Walter Prescott Webb, "The Story of Some Prairie Inventions," *Nebraska History* 34, 4 (Dec. 1953): 229–43.

4. Ellen Stebbins Emery, letter to Dear Sister, 31 Dec. 1889, SHSND; see also Mabel Lorshbough, "Prairie Pioneer: Some North Dakota Homesteaders," *North Dakota History* 43, 2 (Spring 1976): 22, for a description of the menace of fire in towns.

5. Florence Marshall Stote, Of Such Is the Middle West, n.d., KSHS; and Meri Reha, PDC, SDSHRC.

6. Amanda Sayle Walradth, PDC, SDSHRC.

7. Jennie Larson, Mary Louise Thomson, and Ida Kittelson Gullikson, PDC, SDSHRC; Carolyn ("Carrie") Strong Robbins, Journal, 1887/88, KSHS; Venola Lewis Bivans, ed., "The Diary of Luna E. Warner, a Kansas Teenager of the Early 1870s," *Kansas Historical Quarterly* 35, 3 (Autumn 1969): 296; and Mrs. R. O. Brandt, "Social Aspects of Prairie Pioneering: The Reminiscences of a Pioneer Pastor's Wife," *Norwegian-American Studies* 7 (1933): 5, 9, 26–30; see also Alec. H. Paul, "Across the 49th: Thunderstorms in the Northern Great Plains," *Great Plains Quarterly* 3 (Fall 1983): 195–205.

8. Mrs. Mary C. Hembree, Pioneer Days in Kansas, c. 1949, KSHS.

9. Luna Kellie, memoirs, n.d., NSHS; and Anne E. Bingham, "Sixteen Years on a Kansas Farm, 1870–1886," Kansas State Historical Society *Collections* 15 (1919–22): 516; see also Joanna L. Stratton, "Making the Best of Hard, Hard Times," *Redbook*, Oct. 1980, p. 198; Mary Duneava Tellefson, Pioneer Days in Cass County, n.d., SHSND; Mary (Mrs. A. S.) Raymond, My Experiences as a Pioneer, 1929, 1933, NSHS; Lydia Burrows Foote and Lena Aaker Johnson, PDC, SDSHRC. Also useful are J. A. Munro, "Grasshopper Outbreaks in North Dakota, 1808–1948," *North Dakota History* 16, 3 (July 1949): 143–64; and Robert N. Manley, "In the Wake of the Grasshoppers: Public Relief in Nebraska, 1874–1875," *Nebraska History* 44, 4 (Dec. 1963): 255–75.

10. Chestina B. Allen, diary, 1854–57, KSHS; Bertha Josephson Anderson, autobiography, c. 1940, MTHS; Mary Paddock Berthold, MAMBP, MTHS; Miriam D. Colt, *Went to Kansas: Being a Thrilling Account of an Ill-Fated Expedition* (Water-

town, N.Y.: L. Ingalls, 1862), pp. 119–38; Mary Peachy Cox, interview, 1957, MTHS; Ella M. Edsall (Mrs. E. J.), autobiography, 1919, MSULSC; Hembree, Pioneer Days in Kansas, KSHS; Susanna Larson Bergh and Lydia Burrows Foote, PDC, SDSHRC; Emily Lindstrom, Reminiscence, n.d., SHSND; Darlene Ritter, "Mary Louise Ritter: The Pioneer Woman in Fact and Fiction," in *Women and Western American Literature,* ed. Helen Winter Stauffer and Susan J. Roswski (Troy, N.Y.: Whitston, 1982), p. 20; Martha Roe, diary, 4 May 1864–8 Sept. 1864, MSULSC; Elsie Carlson Stokes, "A History of the AU7," *Bits and Pieces* 7, 1 (1971): 22; Webster, Memories of a Pioneer, NSHS; Laura Ingalls Wilder, *The First Four Years* (New York: Harper & Row, 1971), pp. 31–33; and Walker D. Wyman, *Frontier Woman: The Life of a Woman Homesteader on the Dakota Frontier* (River Falls: University of Wisconsin/River Falls Press, 1972), pp. 20–21, 71–72; see also Glenda Riley, *Women and Indians on the Frontier, 1825–1915* (Albuquerque: University of New Mexico Press, 1984), and "The Specter of a Savage: Rumors and Alarmism on the Overland Trail," *Western Historical Quarterly* 15, 4 (Oct. 1984): 427–44.

11. Sara Tappan Doolittle Robinson, *Kansas: Its Interior and Exterior Life* (Freeport, N.Y.: Books for Libraries Press, 1856), pp. 85, 249–69, 347; see also Allen, diary, KSHS; Jane G. Carruth and Lucy A. Carruth, letters, n.d., KSHS; John R. Everett and Sarah M. C. Everett, "Letters of John and Sarah Everett, 1854–1864, Miami County Pioneers," *Kansas Historical Quarterly* 8, 1 (Feb. 1939): 3–34, 8, 2 (May 1939): 143–74, and 8, 4 (Nov. 1939): 350–83; Julia Louisa Lovejoy, "Letters of Julia Louisa Lovejoy, 1856–1864," *Kansas Historical Quarterly* 15, 2 (May 1947): 127–42, 15, 3 (Aug. 1947): 277–319, 15, 4 (Nov. 1947): 368–403, 16, 1 (Feb. 1948): 40–75, and 16, 2 (May 1948): 175–211; and Julia Louisa Lovejoy, Lovejoy Family Papers, 1828–1864, KSHS.

12. Georgiana Packard, Leaves from the Life of a Kansas Pioneer, 1914, KSHS.

13. Marian Lawton Clayton, Reminiscences: The Little Family, 1961, KSHS.

14. Mollie Dorsey Sanford, *Mollie: The Journal of Mollie Dorsey Sanford in Nebraska and Colorado Territories, 1857–1866* (Lincoln: University of Nebraska Press, 1976), p. 54.

15. Brandt, "Social Aspects of Prairie Pioneering," p. 30; see also Eva Klepper, Memories of Pioneer Days, n.d., in May Avery Papers, NSHS; Emma Boe Odegaard, PDC, SDSHRC; Mrs. W. M. Lindsay, My Pioneer Years in North Dakota, 1933, SHSND; Wilder, *First Four Years,* p. 1; and Wyman, *Frontier Woman,* pp. 103–6. For a discussion of changes and improvements in the Plains experience, particularly that associated with homesteading, see William H. Beezley, "Homesteading in Nebraska, 1862-1872," *Nebraska History* 53, 1 (Spring 1972): 58–75; Henry Frawley and Anne Frawley, "Agriculture, Dairying, Ranching," in *Lawrence County for the Dakota Territory Centennial, 1861–1961,* ed. Mildred Fielder (Deadwood/Lead, S.Dak.: Lawrence County Centennial Committee, 1960), p. 105; C. Barron McIntosh, "Forest Lieu Selections in the Sand Hills of Nebraska," Association of American Geographers *Annals* 64, 1 (Mar. 1974): 87–89; Mamie J. Meredith, "The Importance of Fences to the American Pioneer," *Nebraska History* 32, 2 (June 1951): 94–107; C. Howard Richardson, "The Nebraska Prairies: Dilemma to Early Territorial Farmers," *Nebraska History* 50, 4 (Winter 1969): 358–72; Homer E. Socolofsky, "Success and Failure in Nebraska Homesteading," *Agricultural History* 42, 2 (Apr. 1968): 103–7, and "Land Disposal in Nebraska, 1854–1906: The Homestead Story," *Nebraska History* 48, 3 (Autumn 1976): 225–48; H. L. Walster, "The Evolution of Agriculture in North Dakota," Soil Science Society of America *Proceedings* 19 (Apr. 1955): 118–24; and Edwin H. Webster, "Fifty Years of Kansas Agriculture," Kansas State Historical Society *Collections* 12 (1911/12): 60–64.

16. Allen, diary, KSHS; and Lucy Horton Tabor, An Old Lady's Memories of the Wyoming Territory, n.d., WSAMHD.

17. Blaine T. Williams, "The Frontier Family: Demographic Fact and Historical Myth," in *Essays on the American West,* ed. Harold M. Hollingsworth and Sandra L. Myres (Austin: University of Texas Press, for the University of Texas at Arlington, 1969), p. 51; and John C. Hudson, "The Study of Western Frontier Populations," in *American West: New Perspectives, New Dimensions,* ed. Jerome O. Steffen (Norman: University of Oklahoma Press, 1979), pp. 44–45.

18. Williams, "Frontier Family," pp. 57–59; Hudson, "Study of Western Frontier Populations," pp. 49–50; Sarah Jane Price, Diaries, 1878–95, NSHS; Paul Corey, "Bachelor Bess: My Sister," *South Dakota Historical Collections* 37 (1974): 1–101; and Enid Bern, ed., "They Had a Wonderful Time: The Homesteading Letters of Anna and Ethel Erickson," *North Dakota History* 45, 4 (Fall 1978): 4–31.

19. Susan Hallgarth, " 'No One Should Dictate as to Ways and Means': Single Women on the Frontier," unpublished paper in my possession, p. 14.

20. Williams, "Frontier Family," pp. 57–59. For case studies see Cora D. Babcock, reminiscences, 1880–1885, SDSHRC; Frances Huntress Carruthers, and Mary Fox Howe, MAMBP, MTHS; Ethel Hamilton, Mrs. Ethel Hamilton of Mountain View, 1936, WSAMHD; Mary Jane Gray, letters, 1858–94, KSHS; Lindsay, My Pioneer Years in North Dakota, SDSHRC; Fanny Achtnes Malone, The Experience of a Michigan Family on a Government Homestead in South Dakota, n.d., SDSHRC; Walker, *Frontier Woman,* p. 90; and Serena J. Washburn, autobiography, 1838–1904, MSULSC.

21. Wilson Cape, "Population Changes in the West North Central States, 1900–1930," *North Dakota Historical Quarterly* 6, 4 (1932): 290–91.

22. Brett Harvey Vuolo, "Pioneer Diaries: The Untold Story of the West," *Ms. Magazine* 3, 11 (May 1975): 32–34.

23. Dorothy Towe Tester, MAMBP, MTHS.

24. Donna M. Lucey, "The Intimate Vision of Evelyn Cameron," *Geo* 5, 1 (Jan. 1983): 72. For other examples of divorced plainswomen see Nellie M. Barker, PDC, SDSHRC; Jane Burr, *Letters of a Dakota Divorcee* (Boston, Mass.: Roxburgh, 1909); Katherine Grant, MAMBP, MTHS; Henry Killian Goetz, "Kate's Quarter Section: A Woman in the Cherokee Strip," *Chronicles of Oklahoma* 61, 2 (Fall 1983): 246–67; Charley O'Kieffe, *Western Story: The Recollections of Charley O'Kieffe, 1884–1898* (Lincoln: University of Nebraska Press, 1960), pp. 3–4; Cynthia Richards Pringle, PDC, SDSHRC; and Tellefson, Pioneer Days in Cass County, SHSND.

25. Paula Petrik, "If She Be Content: The Development of Montana Divorce Law 1865–1907," paper presented at the Western History Association meeting in Sacramento, Calif., in Oct. 1985, p. 1; idem, "If She Be Content," *Western Historical Quarterly* 18, 3 (July 1987): 261–92.

26. Lonnie E. Underhill and Daniel F. Littlefield, "Women Homeseekers in Oklahoma Territory 1889–1901," *Pacific Historian* 17, 3 (Summer 1973): 36–47. For a contemporary description of Sioux Falls, S.Dak., known in the 1890s as a mecca for those seeking divorces, see Harry Hazel and S. C. Lewis, *The Divorce Mill* (New York: Mascot, 1895).

27. Mary Johnstone Powers, A Pioneer Woman's Reminiscences, 1947, MTHS.

28. Allen, diary, KSHS; Bivans, "Diary of Luna E. Warner," p. 300; Clayton, Reminiscences: The Little Family, KSHS; Phyllis A. Dinkel, "Old Marriage Customs in Herzog (Victoria), Kansas," *Western Folklore* 19, 2 (Apr., 1960): 99–105; Orleantha Gravel Kellogg, *Bloom on the Land: A Prairie Pioneer Experience,* (Henderson, Nebr.: Service Press, 1982), pp. 281–312; Pat Kuehl, "Lebanese Immigrants in Southeast Kansas," *Heritage of the Great Plains* 17 (Fall 1984): 23–24; Jennie Larson,

PDC, SDSHRC; Lucie Emma Dickinson Lott, Reminiscences: Lucie Emma Dickinson Lott, Her Story, n.d., SDSHRC; Sanford, *Mollie,* pp. 109–12; Robbins, journal, KSHS; and James L. Thane, Jr., ed., "Love from All to All: The Governor's Lady Writes Home to Ohio," *Montana, the Magazine of Western History* 24, 3, (Summer 1974): 19.

29. Raymond, My Experiences as a Pioneer, NSHS; and Woodie Howgill, "Honeymoon across the Plains: The Ellen Bell Tootle Diary," *Heritage of the Great Plains* 16, 3 (Summer 1983): 11–17.

30. Webster, Memories of a Pioneer, NSHS.

31. Kellie, memoirs, NSHS. For an example of contemporary material urging women to have children see Pye Henry Chavasse, *Advice to a Wife on the Management of Her Own Health* (Chicago: R. G. Badoux, 1887), pp. 16–21.

32. Hudson, "Study of Western Frontier Populations," p. 47; and Cape, "Population Changes," pp. 281–86.

33. Anderson, autobiography, MTHS; Martha Suckow Packer, memoirs, 20 Sept. 1880–21 Jan. 1970, MSULSC; Julia Amsden, PDC, SDSHRC; Frances Huntress Carruthers and Carrie Roberts, MAMBP, MTHS.

34. Elizabeth Hampsten, *Read This Only to Yourself: The Private Writings of Midwestern Women, 1880–1910,* (Bloomington: Indiana University Press, 1983), p. 104.

35. Flora Moorman Heston, " 'I Think I Will Like Kansas': The Letters of Flora Moorman Heston, 1885–1886," *Kansas History* 6, 2 (Summer 1983): 86, 93–94.

36. Hempsten, *Read This Only to Yourself,* pp. 105–7; see also Elizabeth Jameson, "Women as Workers, Women as Civilizers: True Womanhood in the American West," *Frontiers* 7, 3 (1984): 4; Mary R. Melendy, *Perfect Womanhood for Maidens, Wives, Mothers: A Complete Medical Guide for Women* (n.p.: K. T. Boland, 1903), pp. 263–65; and Prudence B. Sauer, M.D., *Maternity: A Book for Every Wife and Mother* (Chicago: L. P. Miller, 1889). For an example of a husband's expectations that his wife control contraception see Cynthia Richards Pringle, PDC, SDSHRC.

37. Tellefson, Pioneer Days in Cass County, SHSND; see also Stote, Of Such Is the Middle West, KSHS; and Nellie Sinclair Maclay, MAMBP, MTHS.

38. Mrs. R. O. Andrews, in Frances Jacobs Alberts, ed., *Sod House Memories* (Hastings, Nebr.: Sod House Society, 1972), p. 99. For other accounts of births see Emma Boe Odegaard and Roxanne Heffelfinger-Mehner, PDC, SDSHRC; Mary Francis Baltzly, autobiography, 1942, WSAMHD; Martha Thal, "Early Days: The Story of Sarah Thal, Wife of a Pioneer Farmer of Nelson County, N.D.," *American Jewish Archives* 23, 1 (Apr. 1971): 53. To understand the historical development of childbirth practices see Sue Berkman, "Through Centuries of Childbirth," *American Baby,* Jan. 1979, pp. 48–49, 54; Janet Bogdan, "Care or Cure? Childbirth Practices in Nineteenth Century America," *Feminist Studies* 4, 2 (June 1978): 92–99; Richard W. Wertz and Dorothy C. Wertz, *Lying-in: A History of Childbirth in America* (New York: Schocken Books, 1979). Descriptions of unusual obstetrical cases are found in Francis A. Long, *A Prairie Doctor of the Eighties* (Norfolk: Nebraska Home Publishing Co., 1937), pp. 95–102.

39. Brandt, "Social Aspects of Prairie Pioneering," pp. 6–7; Emma Waterman Bickel, Jennie Larson, Emma Boe Odegaard, Eleanor Schubert, and Mary Louise Thomson, PDC, SDSHRC; Nelly Sinclair Maclay and Mary Frances Huntress, MAMBP, MTHS; May E. Murphy, Our Pioneer Mother, 1917, KSHS.

40. Heston, "I Think I Will Like Kansas," pp. 81, 87; Kellie, Memoirs, NSHS; and Anderson, autobiography, MTHS.

41. Anderson, autobiography, MTHS; Eva Urban, Early Days in Spring Brook, 1964, SHSND; Stella Tanner Fowler, The Tanner Family, c. 1960, MTHS; Laura Brown

Zook, Sketches of Laura Brown Zook's Early Life, 1869–1944, MSULSC; Ada Martin, interview, 15 Mar. 1980, KSHS; Lillie Goodrich, interview, 29 Sept. 1979, Laramie; Tone Saur Bramble, Anna Warren Peart, and Sarah Ann Cooper, PDC, SDSHRC.

42. Emily Butcher, diary, 1896–99, KSHS; Bivans, "Diary of Luna E. Warner," p. 284; Mable Cheney Moudy, Through My Life, n.d., UWAHC; see also Lloyd deMause, "The Evolution of Childhood," in *The History of Childhood,* ed. Lloyd deMause (New York: Harper Torchbook, 1975), pp. 1–74.

43. Elsie North Allison, "A One-Room School in Labette County," *Kansas Quarterly* 8, 2 (Spring 1976): 6–8; Minnie Rundall Delimont, I Lived in Soddies, n.d., NSHS; Marguerite Deming, Pioneer Life in Jackson County, S.Dak., 1899, SDSHRC; Minnie Doehring, Kansas One Room Public School, 1981, KSHS; Lindstrom, reminiscence, SHSND; Emma Stone Moss, memoirs, 1865–78, MSULSC; Moudy, Through My Life, UWAHC; Amelia Bruner Munroe, Some Happenings in the Early Days, c. 1856, NSHA; Raymond, My Experiences as a Pioneer, NSHS; Webster, Memories of a Pioneer, NSHS; and Zook, Sketches of Laura Brown Zook's Early Life, MSULSC.

44. For examples of children's doing a wide variety of jobs see Richard Carroll, "Mary Nash Mear, Pioneer," *Colorado Magazine* 11 (1934): 215–18; Evelyn Bradley, "The Story of a Colorado Pioneer: Mrs. Charles A. Finding," *Colorado Magazine* 2 (1925): 52–53; Roxanne Heffelfinger-Mehner and Ida Kittelson Gullikson, PDC, SDSHRC; Vera Holding, "A Heritage to Share," *Chronicles of Oklahoma* 42, 1 (1964): 4–5; Julia Wentworth Steele, PDC, SDSHRC; Munroe, Some Happenings in the Early Days, NSHS; Clayton, Reminiscences: The Little Family, KSHS; Olive B. Deahl, Interview, 13 Oct. 1979, UWAHC; Delimont, I Lived in Soddies, NSHS; Lucie Dickinson Lott, PDC, SDSHRC; Lillian Ouderkirk, "A Story of the Ganser Family," in *Pioneer Tales of the North Platte Valley,* ed. A. B. Wood (Gering, Nebr.: Courier Press, 1938), p. 91; and Eva Putnam, Reminiscences of Pioneer Women, 1936, WSAMHD.

45. Clayton, Reminiscences: The Little Family, KSHS. For accounts of children's hiring out see Sanford, *Mollie,* pp. 71–72, 82; Pauline Neher Diede, *Homesteading on the Knife River Prairies* (Bismarck, N.Dak.: Germans from Russia Heritage Society, 1983; 2d ed., 1984), pp. 74–75; see also Jessie Wentworth Steele, PDC, SDSHRC. For work done by urban children see Lucie Dickinson Lott, Robertina Macdonald, and Roxanne Heffelfinger-Mehner, PDC, SDSHRC; and Sanford, *Mollie,* pp. 68–69.

46. Myrtle Carter, diary, 1887, 1891, SDSHRC.

47. Della M. Todd, daily journal, 5 July 1911–5 July 1912, UWAHC.

48. Todd, journal, UWAHC.

49. Butcher, diary, KSHS.

50. Donald Mahoney, ed., "End of an Era: The Travel Journal of Mary Mahoney," *Nebraska History* 47, 3 (Sept. 1966): 333; and Sanford, *Mollie,* p. 25.

51. Estelle Crisman Laughlin, "Early Days in Banner County," in *Pioneer Tales of the North Platte Valley,* p. 18; and Raymond, My Experiences as a Pioneer, NSHS.

52. Clayton, Reminiscences: The Little Family, KSHS; see also Bivans, "Diary of Luna E. Warner," p. 433; Mathilda C. Engstad, The White Kid Glove Era, n.d., SHSND; Florence Hughes, Interview, 30 Sept. 1979, UWAHC; Eliza R. Lythgoe, Pioneer Blood, WSAMHD; Alice Richards McCreary, Various Happenings in the Life of Alice Richards McCreary, n.d., WSAMHD; Carrie Roberts, MAMBP, MTHS; and Sanford, *Mollie,* p. 125.

53. Raymond, My Experiences as a Pioneer, NSHS; see also Muriel H. Wright, "Mrs. John Williams: A Pioneer in the Indian Territory," *Chronicles of Oklahoma* 30 (Winter 1952/53): 378; and Schlissel, "Mothers and Daughters on the Western Frontier," pp. 31–32.

54. Sanford, *Mollie,* pp. 20, 39, 73.

55. Carrie Roberts, MAMBP, MTHS.
56. Paula Petrik, "Mothers and Daughters of Eldorado: The Fisk Family of Helena, 1867–1902," *Montana, the Magazine of Western History* 32, 3 (Summer 1982): 50–63; see also idem, *No Step Backward: Women and Family on the Rocky Mountain Mining Frontier, Helena, Montana, 1865–1900* (Helena: Montana Historical Society Press, 1986).
57. Kellie, Memoirs, NSHS.
58. Lucie Dickinson Lott, PDC, SDSHRC.
59. Mrs. George W. Snow, memoirs, n.d., WSAMHD; Kellogg, *Bloom on the Land,* pp. 45–86; John C. Hudson, "Frontier Housing in North Dakota," *North Dakota History* 42, 4 (Fall 1975): 4–15; William C. Sherman, "German-Russia House Forms in North Dakota: Distribution, Changing Patterns, and Survival," paper read at the Germans from Russia Immigration Centennial Conference, Bismarck, N.Dak., 29 Sept. 1984; and Fred W. Peterson, "Norwegian Farm Homes in Steele and Traill Counties, North Dakota: The American Dream and the Retention of Roots, 1890–1914," *North Dakota History* 51 (Winter 1984): 4–13.
60. Sarah Lindsay, Pioneer Memories, 1975, WSAMHD; see also Dorothy Pearson Williams, Pioneer Memories, 1975, WSAMHD; Fern Spencer Dumbrill, "A Woman's Memories of Homesteading," in *Wyoming Homestead Heritage,* ed. Charles F. Spencer (Hicksville, N.Y.: Exposition Press, 1975), p. 188; and Clara Field McCarthy, Clara's Episodes: A Reflection of Early Wyoming, 1901–1911, 1964, WSAMHD.
61. Lythgoe, Pioneer Blood, WSAMHD; Eva Putnam, in Reminiscences of Pioneer Women, 1936, WSAMHD; Ellen Throop, Reminiscences of Pioneer Days, n.d., NSHS; and Ella Davis Fox, Interview: A Pioneer Child, 1939, WSAMHD.
62. Diede, *Homesteading on the Knife River Prairies,* pp. 22–23; and Addie Osborn Stewart, Mother's Story, n.d., MTHS.
63. Allen, diary, KSHS; Tellefson, Pioneer Days in Cass County, SHSND; Crinklaw, Interview with Thon: One Brave Homesteader of '89, WSAMHD; and Brandt, "Social Aspects of Prairie Pioneering," p. 5.
64. Alice E. Lee, Sod House Letters, 1957/58, and Klepper, Memories of Pioneer Days, NSHS.
65. Baltzly, autobiography, WSAMHD.
66. Sallie Davenport Davidson, memoirs, 1928, MTHS; see also Gladys Iris Crouch Clark, "Sod House Pioneer," *American West* 21, 5 (Sept./Oct. 1984): 53; Mrs. Clifford Jencks, letter to Dear Maybel and All, 24 Mar. 1910, SDSHRC; Kenneth Hammer, "The Prairie Sod Shanty," *North Dakota History* 35 (Winter 1968): 57–61; Roger L. Welsch, "Sod Construction on the Plains," *Pioneer America* 1, 2 (July 1969): 13; Lee, Sod House Letters, NSHS; and John I. White, "That Zenith of Prairie Architecture— The Soddy," *American Heritage* 24, 5 (Aug. 1973): 33–35.
67. Baltzly, autobiography, WSAMHD; Kellogg, *Bloom on the Land,* pp. 137–80; Lee, Sod House Letters, NSHS; and Kate Roberts Pelissier, "Reminiscences of a Pioneer Mother," *North Dakota History* 24, 3 (July 1957): 132.
68. Lorna B. Herseth, ed., "A Pioneer's Letter," *South Dakota History* 6, 3 (Summer 1976): 309; Thomas D. Clark, "Starting Life at Ground Level on a Nebraska Homestead," in idem, *The Great American Frontier* (Indianapolis: Bobbs-Merrill, 1975), p. 115; and Barbara Levorsen, "Early Years in Dakota," p. 162.
69. Klepper, Memories of Pioneer Days, NSHS; Marshall, Of Such Is the Middle West, KSHS; Fannie Forbes Russel, My First Year in Montana, 1864–1865, 1920, MTHS; Packer, memories, MSULSC; and Angel Kwolek-Folland, "The Elegant Dugout: Domesticity and Moveable Culture in the United States, 1870–1900," *American Studies* 25, 2 (Fall 1984): 21–37.
70. Mrs. W. W. Diamond, diaries, 1870–73, KSHS; Anne Jones Davies, diary,

246 Notes to Pages 89–91

1882–88, KSHS; Grace Mandeville Gregory, Adventuring, 1936, WSAMHD; and Susan H. Armitage, "Household Work and Childrearing on the Frontier: The Oral History Record," *Sociology and Social Research* 63, 3 (Apr. 1979): 467–74.
  71. Addie M. Thompson Sinclair, My Story: An Autobiography Covering the Years 1880 to 1961, 1961, KSHS.
  72. Clayton, Reminiscences: Little Family, KSHS; see also Allen, diary, KSHS; Anderson, autobiography, MTHS; Herseth, "Pioneer's Letter," pp. 310–11; Faye C. Lewis, *Nothing to Make a Shadow* (Ames: Iowa State University Press, 1971), p. 40; Ada Robinson, Wyoming Homesteaders, n.d., UWAHC; Mari Sandoz, *Old Jules Country* (New York: Hastings House, 1965), p. 297; Tellefson, Pioneer Days in Cass County, SHSND; Webster, Memories of a Pioneer, NSHS; Mary Willard, MAMBP, MTHS; and Wyman, *Frontier Woman*, pp. 19–21, 27.
  73. Lindsay, My Pioneer Years in North Dakota, SHSND; see also Alice Conitz, "Prairie Pioneers: Some North Dakota Homesteaders," *North Dakota History* 43, 2 (Spring 1976): 52–54.
  74. Anderson, autobiography, MTHS; Julia Baptist, letter to Dear Sister, 10 Apr. 1885, NSHS; Clayton, Reminiscences: Little Family, KSHS; Ellen Calder DeLong, Memories of Pioneer Days in Cavalier County, n.d., SHSND; Lindstrom, reminiscence, SHSND; Moudy, Through My Life, UWAHC; anonymous, "One of the Knitters," *American-Scandinavian Review* 6, 4 (July/Aug. 1918): 215; Ingeborg Aaker Simons, PDC, SDSHRC; Anna Caldwell Stiefvater, reminiscence, 1954, MTHS; and Sigri Watnaas-Gronseth, PDC, SDSHRC.
  75. Myra Waterman Bickel, PDC, SDSHRC; and Clayton, Reminiscences: Little Family, KSHS.
  76. Mary W. M. Hargreaves, "Women in the Agricultural Settlement of the Northern Plains," *Agricultural History* 50, 1 (Jan. 1976): 187.
  77. Throop, Reminiscences of Pioneer Days, NSHS; see also William D. Andrews and Deborah C. Andrews, "Technology and the Housewife in Nineteenth-Century America," *Women's Studies* 2, 3 (1974): 309–28; W. F. Kumlien, *Basic Trends of Social Change in South Dakota: II: Rural Life Adjustments,* South Dakota Agricultural Experiment Station Bulletin no. 11 (Brookings: South Dakota State College, 1941), p. 19; and Susan Strasser, *Never Done: A History of American Housework* (New York: Pantheon, 1981), pp. 2–10.
  78. Julia Baptist, letter to Lizzie, 5 Dec. 1886, NSHS; Ellen McGowan Biddle, *Reminiscences of a Soldier's Wife* (Philadelphia: J. B. Lippincott, 1907); Bingham, "Sixteen Years on a Kansas Farm," p. 511; Isabel White Brenner, MAMBP, MTHS; Fleming Fraker, Jr., ed., "To Pike's Peak by Ox-Wagon: The Harriet A. Smith Day-Book," *Annals of Iowa* 35, 2 (Fall 1959): 112–48; Edna Fay Kaiser, MAMBP, MTHS; Kellie, memoirs, NSHS; James T. King, ed., "Fort McPherson in 1870: A Note by an Army Wife," *Nebraska History* 45, 1 (Mar. 1964): 101; Susan Leaphart, ed., "Montana Episodes: Frieda and Belle Fligelman: A Frontier-City Girlhood in the 1890s," *Montana, the Magazine of Western History* 32, 3 (Summer 1982): 85–92; Moudy, Through My Life, UWAHC; and Thane, "Love from All to All," p. 20.
  79. Colt, *Went to Kansas,* p. 125; and Allen, diary, KSHS; see also Riley, *Women and Indians,* pp. 170–72.
  80. Olivia Holmes, diary, Mar.–Aug. 1872, KSHS.
  81. Clayton, Reminiscences: The Little Family, KSHS; Kellie, memoirs, NSHS; Heston, " 'I Think I Will Like Kansas,' " p. 96; Levorsen, "Early Years in Dakota," p. 170; Elizabeth Cox Fabrick, letter to Granddaughter, 1937, MTHS; Leaphart, "Montana Episodes," p. 92; and Todd, journal, UWAHC.
  82. Moudy, Through My Life, UWAHC; Roe, diary, MSULSC; Josephine Windecker

Fitzgerald, Huntley Project Homesteading, 1968, MSULSC; Davidson, memoirs, MTHS; Susan Howells, Recollections of a Busy Life, 1972, MTHS; advertisement in *Grand Island* (Nebr.) *Daily Press,* 28 Apr. 1903; Kellogg, *Bloom on the Land,* pp. 181–252; Stella (no last name given), letter to My Dear Little Sister, 28 Jan. 1866, NSHS; H. G. Reynolds, "Early Day Trading in Bayard," in *Pioneer Tales of the North Platte Valley,* p. 150; Elizabeth J. Tallman, interviewed by James R. Harvey, "Pioneer Experiences in Colorado," *Colorado Magazine* 13 (July 1936): 143. For a discussion of the rapidity with which merchants and material culture arrived on the Plains see Deborah J. Hoskins, "Brought, Bought, and Borrowed: Material Culture on the Oklahoma Farming Frontier, 1889–1907," in *At Home on the Range, Essays on the History of Western Social and Domestic Life,* ed. John R. Wunder (Westport, Conn.: Greenwood Press, 1985), pp. 121–36; and John C. Hudson, *Plains Country Towns* (Minneapolis: University of Minnesota Press, 1985), pp. 104–20.

83. Nannie T. Alderson and Helena Huntington Smith, *A Bride Goes West* (Lincoln: University of Nebraska Press, 1969), p. 231.

84. Mary Lowman, letter to Respected Bro (Joseph C. Foster), 14 May 1861, NSHS; Mrs. Joe C. Horton, diary, 1874, KSHS; Ellen Payne Paullin, ed., "Etta's Journal, January 2, 1874–July 25, 1875," pt. 2, *Kansas History* 3, 4 (Winter 1980): 275; anonymous, household account book, Jan.–July 1880, SDSHRC; Ida McPherren, Sheridan Market Report, 1890, taken from the *Sheridan* (Wyo.) *Post,* 8 May 1890, WSAMHD; and Anna Gillespie, "Coxville, Nebraska, to Fay, Oklahoma, by Wagon (1899): The Journal of Anna Gillespie," *Nebraska History* 63, 3 (Fall 1984): 361.

85. Kellie, memoirs, NSHS; see also Bingham, "Sixteen Years on a Kansas Farm," p. 523; Holmes, diary, KSHS; McCreary, Various Happenings, WSAMHD; Sarah Bessey Tracy, diary, 1 Apr.–9 July 1869, MSULSC; see also Sandra L. Myres, *Westering Women and the Frontier Experience, 1800–1915* (Albuquerque: University of New Mexico Press, 1982), pp. 164–65. For an opposing view see Lillian Schlissel, *Women's Diaries of the Westward Journey* (New York: Schocken Books, 1982), pp. 91–92.

86. Kellie, memoirs, NSHS. For farm women see Mrs. Robert W. (Elsie) Allinson, biography based on interview, 11 Nov. 1980, MSULSC; Anderson, autobiography, MTHS; anonymous, Mr. and Mrs. James Casto, n.d., WSAMHD; Howells, Recollections of a Busy Life, MTHS; Louise Miller Kriepie, reminiscences, 1856, KSHS; Malone, The Experience of a Michigan Family, SDSHRC; Mrs. Mary Matovich, letter to Children, 1956, MSULSC; Pelissier, "Reminiscences of a Pioneer Mother," p. 132; Mary C. Smith, Huntley Project Homesteading, 1968, MSULSC; Nella Aldrich Stoddard, Events in the Life of a Nebraska Pioneer, n.d., in Benton Aldrich Papers, NSHS; Lillie Badgley, interview, 1982, MTHS. For the importance of women's farm work see John Mack Faragher, "History from the Inside-out: Writing the History of Women in Rural America," *American Quarterly* 33, 5 (Winter 1981): 537–57; and Glenda Riley, "Farm Women's Roles in the Agricultural Development of South Dakota," *South Dakota History* 13, 1 and 2 (Spring/Summer 1983): 55–62. For the importance of land to these women, see Gilbert C. Fite, " 'The Only Thing Worth Looking For': Land and Its Meaning for Pioneer Dakotans," *South Dakota History* 15, 1 and 2 (Spring/Summer 1985): 2–25. For plainswomen other than rural ones see Martha Babcock, PDC, SDSHRC; Brandt, "Social Aspects of Prairie Pioneering," pp. 1–46; Margaret Ronan, ed., *Frontier Woman: The Story of Mary Ronan* (Helena: University of Montana Publications in History, 1973), pp. 85–95; Thane, "Love from All to All," pp. 12–25; and Fanny McGillycuddy, diary, 1877/78, SDSHRC.

87. Fairfax Downey, *Indian-Fighting Army* (New York: Charles Scribner's Sons, 1941), pp. 96–112; Matt Lagerberg, Army Life at Fort Lincoln, 1935, SHSND; Nellie Sliney Rankin, A Pioneer Family, 1936, WSAMHD; John R. Sibbald, "Army Women

of the West," *American West* 111, 2 (Spring 1966): 56–67; and Miller J. Stewart, "Army Laundresses: Ladies of the 'Soap Suds Row,' " *Nebraska History* 61, 4 (Winter 1980): 421–36.

88. Thomas R. Buecker, ed., "Letters of Caroline Frey Winne from Sidney Barracks and Fort McPherson, Nebraska, 1874–1878," *Nebraska History* 62, 1 (Spring 1981): 1–14; Sarah Elizabeth Canfield, diary, 1866/67, SHSND; Margaret I. Carrington, *Ab-sa-ra-ka, Home of the Crows: Being the Experience of an Officer's Wife on the Plains* (Philadelphia: J. B. Lippincott, 1868), p. 141; King, "Fort McPherson in 1870," pp. 99–107; Elizabeth Van Ziegel Grosscurth, Some Experiences of an Early Pioneer, 1938, WSAMHD; Minnie Dubbs Millbrook, ed., "Rebecca Visits Kansas and the Custers: The Diary of Rebecca Richmond," *Kansas Historical Quarterly* 43, 4 (Winter 1976): 366–402; McGillycuddy, diary, SDSHRC; Sandra L. Myres, "The Ladies of the Army: Views of Western Life," in *The American Military on the Frontier*, USAF Academy Symposium, Colorado Springs, 1976, pp. 135–53, and "Romance and Reality on the American Frontier: Views of Army Wives," *Western Historical Quarterly* 13, 4 (Oct. 1982): 409–28; Alice Mathews Shields, "An Army Wife on the Wyoming Frontier," *Annals of Wyoming* 13 (Oct. 1941): 331–43; Sherry L. Smith, "Officers' Wives, Indians and the Indian Wars," *Order of the Indian Wars Journal* 1, 1 (Winter 1980): 35–46; Susie P. Van De Wiele, Travels and Experiences in America with Army and Indian Reminiscences, c. 1890, Graff Collection, Newberry Library, Chicago, pp. 8–29; Robert M. Utley, ed., "Campaigning with Custer: Letters and Diaries Sketch Life in Camp and Field during the Indian Wars," *American West* 14, 4 (July/Aug. 1977): 4–9, 58–60; see also Elizabeth Custer, *"Boots and Saddles": or Life in Dakota with General Custer* (Norman: University of Oklahoma Press, 1961), and *Tenting on the Plains: or General Custer in Kansas and Texas*, 3 vols. (Norman: University of Oklahoma Press, 1971).

89. Ada Adelaide (Adams) Vogdes, journal, 1868–72, Huntington Library, San Marino, Calif.; Robert C. Carriker and Eleanor R. Carriker, eds., *An Army Wife on the Frontier: The Memoirs of Alice Blackwood Baldwin, 1867–1877* (Salt Lake City: Tanner Trust Fund, University of Utah Library, 1975), pp. 27–38; Canfield, diary, SHSND; Frances C. Carrington, *My Army Life and the Fort Phil Kearney Massacre* (1910; reprint, Freeport, N.Y.: Books for Libraries Press, 1971); Kate Hogan, letter to Dear Sister, 12 July 1868, SHSND; Joan Ingalles, "Family Life on the Southwest Frontier," *Military History Texas Southwestern* 14, 4 (1978): 203–13; Sandra L. Myres, ed., *Cavalry Wife: The Diary of Eveline M. Alexander, 1866–1867* (College Station: Texas A & M University Press, 1977); Minnie Dubs Millbrook, ed., "Mrs. General Custer at Fort Riley, 1866," *Kansas Historical Quarterly* 40, 1 (Spring 1974): 63–71; and Frances M. A. Roe, *Army Letters from an Officer's Wife, 1871–1888* (New York: D. Appleton, 1909), pp. 90–119. A particularly good account by an army child is Mrs. G. W. Wales, reminiscences, 1866–77, SHSND.

90. Cape, "Population Changes in the West North Central States," p. 286; Alderson and Smith, *A Bride Goes West*, p. 251; Abbie Ann Jarvis and Lydia Burrows Foote, PDC, SDSHRC; and Webster, Memories of a Pioneer, NSHS.

91. Susanna Brown Bergh, MAMBP, MTHS; Mrs. Ashby Howell, biographical sketch, 1936, WSAMHD; and Corey, "Bachelor Bess," p. 10; see also Grosscurth, Some Experiences of an Early Pioneer, WSAMHD; McCreary, Various Happenings, WSAMHD; Martha Waln, The Life of Martha Waln, Pioneer of Tensleep, Wyo., 1939, WSAMHD. For a media image of western boom towns see E. W. Howe, "Provincial Peculiarities of Western Life," *Forum* 14 (Sept. 1892): 91–94. For scholarly descriptions of Plains towns see John C. Hudson, "The Plains Country Town," in *The Great Plains: Environment and Culture*, ed. Brian W. Blouet and Frederick C. Luebke (Lin-

coln: University of Nebraska Press, 1979), pp. 99–118; Lawrence H. Larsen, *The Urban West at the End of the Frontier* (Lawrence: Regents Press of Kansas, 1978); and John W. Reps, *The Forgotten Frontier: Urban Planning in the American West before 1890* (Columbia: University of Missouri Press, 1981).

92. Jesse Minard, PDC, SDSHRC; McCarthy, Clara's Episodes, WSAMHD; Stella, letter to My Dear Little Sister, 28 Jan. 1866, NSHS; Mrs. Lee A. Jones, Reminiscences of Early Days in Havre, n.d., MTHS; and Richard C. Wade, *The Urban Frontier: Pioneer Life in Early Pittsburgh, Cincinnati, Lexington, Louisville and St. Louis* (Chicago: University of Chicago Press, 1964), pp. 304–41.

93. Amelia C. Glecker, PDC, SDSHRC; Homer E. Socolofsky, ed., "The Private Journals of Florence Crawford and Arthur Capper, 1891–1892," *Kansas Historical Quarterly* 30, 2 (Summer 1964): 163–208. The Dobbins Collection, WSAMHD, contains many turn-of-the-century woman's invitations, dance cards, theater programs, and other memorabilia that document the many social opportunities available in frontier times. For descriptions of life in general in Plains towns see Seletha A. Brown, "Eliza Buford Rothcock, Colorado Pioneer," *Colorado Magazine* 23 (Sept. 1946): 214; Hudson, *Plains Country Towns*, pp. 121–30; Engstad, The White Kid Glove Era, SHSND; and Edna LaMoore Waldo, *Dakota* (Bismarck, N.Dak.: Capital, 1932), pp. 198–213; Alderson and Smith, *A Bride Goes West*, p. 150; Lucie Dickinson Lott, PDC, SDSHRC; Kate E. Glaspell, *Incidents in the Life of a Pioneer* (Davenport, Iowa: Baeden Bros., c. 1940), pp. 188–89; Gordon L. Iseminger, "Christina Hillius: Learning to Read at 62," paper presented at the Northern Great Plains History Conference, Bismarck, N.Dak., 28 Sept. 1984; Julia Lovejoy, letter to Mr. Editor, 13 Mar. 1865, KSHS; Raymond, My Experiences as a Pioneer, NSHS; Harriet Peck Fenn Sanders, MAMBP, MTHS; and Webster, Memories of a Pioneer, NSHS.

94. Howells, Recollections of a Busy Life, MTHS; Leaphart, "Montana Episodes," p. 92; and Sally Gammon Peck, "Memories of a Pioneer Minister's Daughter," in Wood, *Pioneer Tales of the North Platte Valley*, p. 180.

95. Allen, diary, KSHS; Alderson and Smith, *A Bride Goes West*, p. 266; Aunt Tish, MAMBP, MTHS; Lela Barnes, ed., "North Central Kansas in 1887–1889: From the Letters of Leslie and Susan Snow of Junction City," *Kansas Historical Quarterly* 29, 4 (Winter 1963): 424; Sarah L. Bernson and Robert J. Eggers, "Black People in South Dakota History," *South Dakota History* 7, 3 (Summer 1977): 252; Buecker, "Letters of Caroline Frey Winne," pp. 5, 10; Anne M. Butler, *Daughters of Joy, Sisters of Misery: Prostitutes in the American West, 1865–1890* (Champaign: University of Illinois Press, 1985), pp. 4–5, 109–12; Holmes, diary, KSHS; Bertha Meyers, Reminiscences of Pioneer Women, 1936, WSAMHD; Zook, Sketches of Laura Brown Zook's Early Life, MSULSC; Clara Frost, letter to Joseph Snell, 25 May 1978, KSHS; Sarah Schulyer Lawrence, reminiscence, 1929, KSHS; Packard, Leaves from the Life of a Kansas Pioneer, KSHS; and Porter, Sunday School Houses and Normal Institutes, KSHS. For a discussion of black women in the entire West see Lawrence B. de Graaf, "Race, Sex, and Region: Black Women in the American West, 1850–1920," *Pacific Historical Review* 49, 2 (May 1980): 285–313.

96. Ava Day, letter to Dear Mrs. Walker, 28 Mar. 1964, and letter to Dear Mr. Schmidt, 23 May 1964, NSHS; and Kathie Ryckman Anderson, "Era Bell Thompson: A North Dakota Daughter," *North Dakota History* 49, 4 (Fall 1982): 11–18.

97. Helen Johnson Downing, Interview, 16 Sept. 1976, State Historical Society of North Dakota, Oral History Project, Bismarck.

98. Sarah Ettie Armstrong, Pioneer Days, n.d., WSAMHD.

99. Armstrong, Pioneer Days, WSAMHD; and Waln, The Life of Martha Waln, WSAMHD; see also Alderson and Smith, *A Bride Goes West*, pp. 126–28, 169, 174,

213, 243; Mrs. Ole Battalfson, PDC, SDSHRC; Mary Jane Cowan, diary, 1895, MSULSC; Jones, Reminiscences of Early Days in Havre, MTHS; Hargreaves, "Women in the Agricultural Settlement of the Northern Plains," pp. 179–89; Max S. Lale, ed., "Letters From a Bride in Indian Territory, 1889," *Red River Valley Historical Review* 6, 1 (Winter 1981): 12–24; Lovejoy, "Letters of Julia Louise Lovejoy," 15, 2 (May 1947): 127–42, 15, 3 (Aug. 1947): 277–319, 15, 4 (Nov. 1947): 368–402, 16, 1 (Feb. 1948): 40–75, and 16, 2 (May 1948): 172–211; McCarthy, Clara's Episodes, WSAMHD; Reminiscences of Pioneer Women, 1936, WSAMHD; and Tabor, An Old Lady's Memories of the Wyoming Territory, WSAMHD. For the recurrence of these problems and complaints from plainswomen of all decades see Pioneer Memories Collection, 1975, WSAMHD. For the effects of climate see Richard Maxwell Brown, "The Enduring Frontier: The Impact of Weather on South Dakota History and Literature," *South Dakota History* 15, 1 and 2 (Spring/Summer 1985): 26–57. That women settlers on the Canadian Plains frequently made similar adjustments is demonstrated by Sandra L. Myres in " 'I Have Deliberately Chosen Hard Work and Plenty of It': Women Homesteaders on the Canadian Prairies, 1880–1920," paper read at the Conference on Women on the Great Plains, Lincoln, Nebr., 12 Mar. 1987.

100. Heston, "I Think I Will Like Kansas," p. 92; see also Carruth, letters, KSHS; Herseth, "Pioneer's Letter," p. 308; Mrs. LeFrench, letter to Hattie, 1886, SDSHRC; Flora Gardner, letter to Dear Mack and Mary, 11 June 1879, MSULSC; Lillian Hohnholz Hein, interview, 19 Aug. 1979, UWAHC; Luella Moyer, Campbell County Pioneer, 1936, WSAMHD; Ronan, *Frontier Woman,* p. 81; Wilder, *First Four Years,* p. 6; Eliza Wyckoff, "Early Days in Kansas," *South Kansas Tribune* (Independence), 16 July 1930.

101. *Laramie* (Wyo.) *Sentinal,* 10 Oct. 1885.

102. Faragher, "History from the Inside-out," pp. 537–57; John Mack Faragher, *Women and Men on the Overland Trail* (New Haven, Conn.: Yale University Press, 1979), p. 181; Melody Graulich, "Violence against Women in Literature of the Western Family," *Frontiers* 7, 3 (1984): 14–20; Michael F. Shaughnessy, "Psychological Violence of Men toward Women," paper presented at the Midwest Regional Women's Association meeting, 4 Oct. 1981; Stansell, "Women on the Great Plains," pp. 87–98; and U.S., Commissioner of Agriculture, *Annual Report,* 1862, pp. 462–70.

103. Stote, Of Such Is the Middle West, KSHS; Bingham, "Sixteen Years on A Kansas Farm," p. 517; Alderson and Smith, *A Bride Goes West,* pp. 206, 233–34; and Lewis, *Nothing to Make a Shadow,* pp. 33–34.

104. For descriptions of social events see Alderson and Smith, *A Bride Goes West,* p. 269; Mary Baillie and George Baillie, Recollections in the Form of a Duet, 1939, WSAMHD; Enid Bennetts, Rural Pioneer Life, 1939, WSAMHD; Doehring, Kansas One Room Public School, KSHS; W. H. Elznic, PDC, SDSHRC; Lottie Holmberg, recorder, Laura Ingraham Bragg, recollections, n.d., WSAMHD; Lena Carlile Hurdsman, Mrs. Lena Hurdsman of Mountain View, 1939, WSAMHD; Levorsen, "Early Years in Dakota," p. 161; McCreary, Various Happenings, WSAMHD; Millbrook, "Rebecca Visits Kansas and the Custers," pp. 366–402; and Graphia Mewhirter Wilson, Pioneer Life, 1939, UWAHC.

105. Mrs. Charles Robinson, Pioneer Memoires, 1975, WSAMHD. For the social effects of the railroad see S. C. Bassett, "The Soldiers' Free Homestead Colony," Nebraska Historical Society *Proceedings and Collections* 1, 2 (1894/95): 87–102; Barry B. Combs, "The Union Pacific Railroad and the Early Settlement of Nebraska 1868–1880," *Nebraska History* 50, 1 (Spring 1969): 1–26; Ross R. Cotroneo, "Northern Pacific Officials and the Disposition of the Railroad's Land in North Dakota after 1888," *North Dakota History* 37, 2 (Spring 1970): 77–103; John L. Harnsberger,

"Land Speculation, Promotion and Failure: The Northern Pacific Railroad, 1870–1873," *Journal of the West* 9, 1 (Jan. 1970): 33–45; Hudson, *Plains Country Towns,* pp. 54–85; Ronald Ridgley, "The Railroads and Rural Development in the Dakotas," *North Dakota History* 36, 2 (Spring 1969): 164–78; Mari Sandoz, "The Look of the West–1854," talk to the Nebraska State Historical Society's Territorial Centennial Dinner, 25 Sept. 1954, NSHS. For two opposing views from the time on women's isolation see Charles Moreau Harger, "The Prairie Woman: Yesterday and To-Day," *Outlook* 70, 17 (26 Apr. 1902): 1008–12; and E. V. Smalley, "The Isolation of Life on Prairie Farms," *Atlantic,* Sept. 1893, pp. 378–82.

106. Catherine E. Berry, Pioneer Memories, 1975, WSAMHD; see also Althea Boss, The Inheritance of Alice Robertson, 1955, in Boss Papers, 1847–1955, WHCUO. For discussion of women who reconstructed their known patterns on the Plains see James I. Fenton, "Critters, Sourdough, and Dugouts: Women and Imitation Theory on the Staked Plains, 1875–1910," in *At Home on the Range,* pp. 19–38; and Jacqueline S. Reinier, "Concepts of Domesticity on the Southern Plains Agricultural Frontier," ibid., pp. 57–70.

107. Wales, reminiscences, SHSND; Florence McKean Knight, "Anecdotes of Early Days in Box Butte County," *Nebraska History* 14, 2 (Apr.–June 1933): 142; and Alderson and Smith, *A Bride Goes West,* p. 89; see also Margaret Bohrnsen Luthje, MAMBP, MTHS; Cox, interview, MTHS; DeLong, Memories of Pioneer Days in Cavalier County, SHSND; Philip Pacey, "Family Art: Domestic and Eternal Bliss," *Journal of Popular Culture* 18, 1 (Summer 1984): 43–52.

108. Margaret Johnson, in "Prairie Pioneers: Some North Dakota Homesteaders," *North Dakota History* 43, 2 (Spring 1976): 40; Walter F. Peterson, "Christmas on the Plains," *American West* 1, 4 (Fall 1965): 53–57; Anna Warren Peart, PDC, SDSHRC; and Moudy, Through My Life, UWAHC.

109. Hannah Birkley, Mrs. Iver O. Birkley, 1957, NSHS. For the importance and widespread nature of the non-English press see Paul Schach, "German-Language Newspapers in Nebraska, 1860–1890," *Nebraska History* 65, 1 (Spring 1984): 84–107.

110. Sarah Raymond Herndon, *Days On the Road: Crossing the Plains in 1865* (New York: Burr Printing House, 1902), p. 5.

111. W. F. Kumlien, *Basic Trends of Social Change in South Dakota: II: Community Organization,* South Dakota Agricultural Experiment Station Bulletin no. 356 (Brookings: South Dakota State College, 1941), pp. 4–17.

112. Frawley and Frawley, "Agriculture, Dairying, Ranching," p. 105. The "four corner" phenomenon is also described in Kate Bouzek, PDC, SDSHRC.

113. Mrs. LeFrench, letter to Hattie, 1886, SDSHRC.

114. Lindsay, Pioneer Years, SHSND.

115. Leola Lehman, "Life in the Territories," *Chronicles of Oklahoma* 41 (Fall 1963): 373; see also Tabor, An Old Lady's Memories of the Wyoming Territory, WSAMHD; and Emma Vignal Borglum, The Experience at Crow Creek: A Sioux Indian Reservation at South Dakota, 1899, SDSHRC.

116. Lehman, "Life in the Territories," p. 373.

117. McGillycuddy, diary, SDSHRC.

118. Lillian Shumway Brown, Pioneers Arrive in Dakota, n.d., SHSND.

119. *Bozeman* (Mont.) *Chronicle,* 10 Aug. 1954; see also Mrs. Wm. H. (Sarah Jane) Tracy, The Brides of Pioneers, 1898, MSULSC; Russel, My First Year in Montana, MTHS; and unidentified newspaper clipping, "Journey from Missouri to Montana in 1880 Great Adventure According to Mrs. Mary Myer," n.d., MSULSC.

120. Mrs. Henry (Anna) Crouse, reminiscence, 13 Jan. 1939, MSULSC; DeLong, Memories of Pioneer Days in Cavalier County, SHSND; Agnes Henberg, interview,

6 Sept. 1979, UWAHC; Holms, diary, KSHS; and Tracy, diary, MSULSC; see also Elaine Hedges, "The Nineteenth-Century Diarist and Her Quilts," *Feminist Studies* 8, 2 (Summer 1982): 293–308.

121. *Nebraska Farmer,* 8 Dec. 1934.

122. Thal, "Early Days," p. 59; see also Knight, "Anecdotes of Early Days in Box Butte County," p. 142.

123. Raymond, My Experiences as a Pioneer, NSHS; see also Mrs. E. J. Farlow, Life of Mrs. E. J. Farlow, 1932, WSAMHD; Kitty McGrew, Women of Territorial Nebraska, n.d., NSHS; and Murphy, Our Pioneer Mother, KSHS.

124. Allen, diary, KSHS; Lindsay, My Pioneer Years in North Dakota, SHSND; Eleanor Schubert and Mary Louise Thomson, PDC, SDSHRC; see also Robert Kammen, ed., "Herbal Treatments Using Plants Found on the Northern Plains: Pioneer Remedies and Folk Medicines," *North Dakota History* 52, 1 (Winter 1985): 13–23.

125. Alderson and Smith, *A Bride Goes West,* pp. 205–6.

126. Lewis, *Nothing to Make a Shadow,* pp. 71–72.

Chapter 5. Employment and Income Production on the Prairie

1. See, e.g., Hjelm-Hansen, *Business Directory of Scandinavians in Minnesota* (Minneapolis, Minn.: P. Hjelm-Hansen, 1878); and J. H. Stevenson, *History and Business Directory of Wright County* (Des Moines, Iowa: Mills, 1870); E. H. Annewalt, *Mount Pleasant City Directory: Containing a Catalogue of Inhabitants* (Burlington, Iowa: Daily Gazette 1870); and John Kennedy, *Iowa City Directory and Advertiser, for 1857* (Iowa City, Iowa: A. G. Tucker, 1857).

2. Iowa, Territorial Census, 1836, ISHD-MA.

3. Greg Koos, comp., Census of Bloomington, Illinois, 1850, MLCHS.

4. *Weekly Pantagraph* (Bloomington, Ill.), 25 Jan. 1858.

5. James Hair, comp., *Iowa State Gazetteer* (Chicago: Bailey & Hair, 1865), pp. 518, 577–79, 596, 606, 610; see also John B. Newhall, *A Glimpse of Iowa in 1846* (Iowa City, Iowa: State Historical Society, 1957), p. 61; and Mary Allison Farley, "Iowa Women in the Workplace," *Palimpsest* 67, 1 (Jan./Feb. 1986): 2–27. For a discussion of American women who entered jobs and professions during this era see Claudia Golden, "The Economic Status of Women in the Early Republic: Quantitative Evidence," *Journal of Interdisciplinary History* 16, 3 (Winter 1986): 375–404.

6. Jennie McCowen, "Women in Iowa," *Annals of Iowa* 3 (Oct. 1884): 96–113.

7. Benjamin F. Gue, *History of Iowa,* 4 vols. (New York: Century History Co., 1903), 1: 396; idem, "Early Iowa Reminiscences," *Iowa Historical Records* 16 (July 1900): 110; Leonard F. Parker, "Teachers in Iowa before 1858," *Lectures upon Early Leaders in the Professions in the Territory of Iowa, Delivered at Iowa City, 1894* (Iowa City, Iowa: State Historical Society, 1894), p. 30.

8. *Ninth Census,* vol. 1: *The Statistics of the Population of the United States* (Washington, D.C.: Government Printing Office, 1872), pp. 450, 731; *Statistics of the Population of the United States at the Tenth Census, 1880,* vol. 1 (Washington, D.C.: Government Printing Office, 1883), p. 792; and *Comparative of the Tenth Census,* pt. 2, rev. ed. (Washington, D.C.: Government Printing Office, 1888), p. 1640.

9. Koos, comp., Census of Bloomington, Ill., MLCHS; and Glen Schwendemann, "Nicodemus: Negro Haven on the Soloman," *Kansas Historical Quarterly* 34 (Spring 1968): 14, 26.

10. J. H. Burnham, "Subscription and Semi-Subscription Schools," and Richard Edwards, "Education in McLean County"—both in *Transactions of the McLean County*

Historical Society (Bloomington, Ill.: Pantagraph Printing & Stationery Co., 1903), pp. 24–41; see also Maude Baumann Arney, Earliest History of School District Number 64, n.d., MHS; and Claude E. Simmonds, George Davies—Wright County Pioneer, 1946, MHS; and George Carroll, *Pioneer Life in and around Cedar Rapids, Iowa, from 1839 to 1849* (Cedar Rapids, Iowa: Iowa Printing & Binding House, 1895), p. 195.

11. Maria Louisa Sloan, reminiscences, 1926, MHS.

12. Mor Heteen of Roseau County, biography, in Minnesota American Mothers Committee, Inc., 1975, MHS; Arozina Perkins, "Letters of a Pioneer Teacher," *Annals of Iowa* 35, 8 (Spring 1961): 617; and anonymous, *Women of Montgomery County, Iowa* (Red Oak, Iowa: Nishna Valley Printing Co., 1982), pp. 44, 69.

13. Hattie Roberts Eaton, reminiscences, c. 1934, MHS; Mrs. E. E. Cox, Chenoa's First School, 1949, MLCHS; Edward D. Jervey and James E. Moss, eds., "From Virginia to Missouri in 1846: The Journal of Elizabeth Ann Cooley," *Missouri Historical Review* 60, 2 (Jan. 1966): 162–206; and *Women of Montgomery County, Iowa*, pp. 41, 43, 65, 69.

14. Kathryn Kish Sklar, *Catharine Beecher: A Study in American Domesticity* (New York: Norton, 1976), pp. 113–15, 168–83; *Burlington* (Iowa) *Weekly Hawk-Eye*, 6 Apr. 1849; Catharine Beecher, *Suggestions Respecting Improvements in Education* (Hartford: Packard & Butler, 1829), p. 12, and *The Evils Suffered by American Women and Children* (New York: Harper & Brothers, 1846), p. 12. The attitude toward such missionary teachers is described by Abigail Raymond Smith, letter to My Dear Mrs. Jenks, 21 Oct. 1836, Beinecke Collection, Yale University Library, New Haven, Conn. For discussions of the Board of National Popular Education teachers see Polly Welts Kaufman, "A Wider Field of Usefulness: Pioneer Women Teachers in the West, 1848–1854," *Journal of the West* 21, 2 (Apr. 1982): 16–25, and *Women Teachers on the Frontier* (New Haven, Conn.: Yale University Press, 1984).

15. Katherine Clinton, "Pioneer Women in Chicago, 1833–1837," *Journal of the West* 12, 2 (Apr. 1973): 322.

16. Smith, letter to My Dear Mrs. Jenks; anonymous, *Pioneer and Personal Reminiscences* (Marshalltown, Iowa: Marshall Printing Co., 1893), p. 47; Ellen Strang, diary, 1863, ISHD-MA; Rufus Blanchard, *Hand-book of Iowa* (Chicago: Rufus Blanchard, 1869), p. 71.

17. Floy Lawrence Emhoff, "A Pioneer School Teacher in Central Iowa: Alice Money Lawrence," *Iowa Journal of History and Politics* 33, 4 (Oct. 1935): 385; Agnes Briggs Olmstead, "Recollections of a Pioneer Teacher of Hamilton County," *Annals of Iowa* 28, 2 (Oct. 1946): 101; Perkins, "Letters of a Pioneer Teacher," pp. 616–17.

18. Sarah Gillespie Huftalen, "School Days of the Seventies," *Palimpsest* 28, 4 (Apr. 1947): 123; see also Delilah Mullin-Evans, "McLean County's First School Teacher," in *Transactions of the McLean County Historical Society* 2: 20; Arney, Earliest History of School District Number 64, MHS; Rebecca Z. Carse, Our Trip out West in 1842, 1920, ISHL; and Maud Bell Burton, Recollections, n.d., UMWHMC and SHSMM.

19. Mary S. Ellis, letter to Dear Mother, 15 Nov. 1857, in Kenyon Family Letters, ISHD-HS; Emhoff, "Pioneer School Teacher," pp. 385, 392; see also "School Government," in *Illinois Teacher*, ed. C. E. Hovey (Peoria, Ill.: Nason & Hill, 1856), pp. 136–37. For further discussion of discipline and problems faced by teachers see Julie Roy Jeffrey, *Frontier Women: The Trans-Mississippi West, 1840–1880* (New York: Hill & Wang, 1979), pp. 90–94.

19. Arney, Earliest History of School District Number 64, MHS.

20. Burton, recollections, UMWHMC and SHSMM; and Emhoff, "Pioneer School Teacher," p. 393.

21. Nellie Burchfield, Teacher's Certificate, 16 Feb. 1873, ISHL; Hovey, *Illinois Teacher,* pp. 180–81; and Sarah Raymond, *Rules and Regulations: Manual of Instruction to Teachers* (Bloomington, Ill.: Daily Leader Steam Printing House, 1877), p. 31. For descriptions of curricular innovations see Burton, recollections, UMWHMC and SHSMM; Strang, diary, ISHD-HS; and Marie Haefner, "An American Lady," *Palimpsest* 12, 5 (May 1931): 169–78.

22. Julia Barnard Strong, letter to My Ever Dear Aunt H., 15 Feb. 1838, UMWHMC and SHSMM.

23. *Hawk-Eye* and *Iowa Patriot* (Burlington), 5 Sept. 1839 and 1 Oct. 1850.

24. *Burlington* (Iowa) *Tri-Weekly Telegraph,* 1 Oct. 1850; *Gate City* (Keokuk, Iowa), 28 May 1857; *Burlington* (Iowa) *Daily Hawk-Eye,* 20 Apr. 1859, 9 and 10 Aug. 1866; and *Fairfield* (Iowa) *Ledger,* 24 August 1860 and 15 July 1869.

25. Charles L. Capen, Sarah E. Raymond Fitzwilliam, n.d., MLCHS; and Raymond, *Rules and Regulations.* For another example see Eleanor Gordon, *A Little Bit of a Long Story for the Children* (Humboldt, Iowa: n.p., 1934), pp. 11–12.

26. Anna Howell Clarkson, "A Beautiful Life: A Biographical Sketch," *Annals of Iowa* 11, 2/3 (July–Oct. 1913): 188–99; and Alvin Guttag, Margaret Jane Evans Huntington, n.d., MHS; and Matilda Jane Wilkin, autobiography, 1923, MHS.

27. Address of President A. S. Welch, 1870, Iowa State College, Mary B. Welch Papers, Special Collections, Iowa State University Library, Ames.

28. Welch Papers; Clarence R. Aurner, *History of Education in Iowa,* 4 vols. (Iowa City, Iowa: State Historical Society, 1916), 4:337; Mary B. Welch, *Mrs. Welch's Cookbook* (Des Moines, Iowa: Mills, 1884).

29. Quoted in M. Romdall Williams, "From Mount Pleasant: Nation's First Woman Lawyer," *Iowan* 15 (Summer 1967): 23.

30. Ibid., pp. 23–24, 54; and "Arabella Mansfield," in Edward T. James, ed., *Notable American Women, 1607–1950: A Biographical Dictionary,* 3 vols. (Cambridge, Mass.: Belknap Press of Harvard University Press, 1971), 2:492–93. For a discussion of prairie women who eventually pursued careers in law see Teresa Opheim, "Portias of the Prairie: Early Women Graduates of the University Law Department," *Palimpsest* 67, 1 (Jan./Feb. 1986): 28–36.

31. Gue, *History of Iowa,* 4:257; see also "Pauline Given Swalm," in Clarence A. Andrews, *A Literary History of Iowa* (Iowa City: University of Iowa Press, 1972), pp. 45–52; Henry S. Wood, A Woman of the Frontier, n.d., MHS; and for an example of a woman's writing, *Burlington* (Iowa) *Daily Hawk-Eye,* 2 May 1863.

32. Alma F. Vaughan, "Pioneer Women of the Missouri Press," *Missouri Historical Review* 64, 4 (July 1970): 289–305.

33. Paula A. Treckel, "Jane Grey Swisshelm and Feminism in Early Minnesota," *Midwest Review* 2 (Spring 1980): 1–17; and Alice Felt Tyler, "Jane Grey Swisshelm," in *Notable American Women,* 3:415–17.

34. *Weekly Missouri Statesman* (Columbia), 17 Mar. 1854; and Elizabeth C. Smith, Mexican War Service, 1848, UMWHMC and SHSMM.

35. Albert Cashier, Pension Papers, 1891–1915; clippings, c. 1960–78; and Central States Threshermen's Reunion, The Story of Jennie Hodgers alias "Albert Cashier," n.d.—all in MLCHS.

36. For further discussion of these issues see Jeanette C. Lauer and Robert H. Lauer, "The Language of Dress: A Sociohistorical Study of the Meaning of Clothing in America," *Canadian Review of American Studies* 10, 3 (Winter 1979): 305–23; idem, "The Battle of the Sexes: Fashion in Nineteenth Century America," *Journal of Popular Culture* 8, 4 (Spring 1980): 581–89.

37. For descriptions of women's apparel see Gertrude Vandergon, reminiscences,

1940/41, MHS; Alice Longley, handwritten notation, n.d., Alice L. Longley Papers, ISHD-MA; Emhoff, "Pioneer School Teacher," pp. 383, 387; and Harriet Bonebright-Closz, *Reminiscences of Newcastle, Iowa, 1848* (Des Moines: Historical Department of Iowa, 1921), p. 124.

38. *Population of the United States in 1860; Compiled from the Returns of the Eighth Census* (Washington, D.C.: Government Printing Office, 1864), pp. 131, 157; and *Statistics of the Population of the United States at the Tenth Census: 1880*, vol. 1 (Washington, D.C.: Government Printing Office, 1883), pp. 797, 799.

39. Mattie V. Rhoads, Family Papers, 1968, MHS.

40. Mary Parsons Christie, letter to Dear Brother Lyman, June 1839, ISHD-HS; Daisy Barncard Schmidt, History of the Jacob Zed Barncard Family, 2 July 1960, MHS; Bernice P. Jenkins, Life of Jennie Atwood Pratt, 10 Apr. 1949, MHS; Marguerite Conroy, Helen Ross Hall, n.d., MLCHS; Dorothy St. Arnold, The Pages and the Steinkamps, c. 1926, MHS.

41. *Weekly Observer* (Mt. Pleasant, Iowa), 20 Apr. 1856; and *Daily Pantagraph* (Bloomington, Ill.), 20 Apr. 1859. For other advertisements and descriptions of women's fashions see *Minnesota Pioneer* (St. Paul), 24 Oct. 1850; *Burlington* (Iowa) *Hawk-Eye*, 18 June 1859 and 16 Nov. 1866; *Fairfield* (Iowa) *Ledger*, 27 Aug. 1863 and 31 Mar. 1870; *Waterloo* (Iowa) *Courier*, 30 Aug. 1866; Amelia Murdock Wing, "Early Days in Clayton County," *Annals of Iowa* 27, 4 (Apr. 1946): 282; Judith Bradner, Stories of the Old Time Folks of Sixty Years Ago, c. 1895, MLCHS; Emily Veblen Olsen, memoirs, 1941, MHS; Janette Stevenson Murray, "Women of North Tama," *Iowa Journal of History and Politics* 41, 3 (July 1943): 289; Abbie T. Griffin, diary, 1882–85, MHS; Ramona Evans, "Fashions in the Fifties," *Palimpsest* 10, 1 (Jan. 1929): 16–29; and Amanda M. Thayer, Early Milliners and Dressmakers in Bloomington, Ill., 1912, MLCHS.

42. *Burlington* (Iowa) *Daily Hawk-Eye*, 3 Apr. 1863.

43. *Iowa Territorial Gazette and Advertiser* (Burlington), 1 June 1844; *Minnesota Pioneer* (St. Paul), 5 Feb. 1852; *Fairfield* (Iowa) *Ledger*, 24 Sept. 1863; *Illinois Statesman* (Bloomington), 30 Mar. 1860; and advertising post card, 1874, MLCHS.

44. Julia K. S. Hibbard, reminiscences, 1856–68, MHS; Thayer, Early Milliners and Dressmakers, MLCHS; Sloan, reminiscences, MHS; and Christie Daily, "A Woman's Concern: Milliners in Central Iowa, 1870–1880," *Journal of the West* 21, 2 (Apr. 1892): 26–27.

45. Daily, "Woman's Concern," p. 26.

46. *Women of Montgomery County, Iowa*, p. 11; *Missouri Intelligencer* (Fayette), 7 Mar. 1828; William Richard Gentry, Jr., Ann Hawkins Gentry, 1960, UMWHMC and SHSMM; *Daily Pantagraph* (Bloomington, Ill.), 25 Feb. 1859; and Sandra L. Myres, *Westering Women and the Frontier Experience, 1880–1915* (Albuquerque: University of New Mexico Press, 1982), pp. 244–45.

47. *Population of the United States in 1860*, pp. 105, 131, 157, 303; and *Statistics of the Population of the United States at the Tenth Census*, 1:793.

48. Edmund Flagg, *The Far West: or, A Tour beyond the Mountains*, 2 vols. (New York: Harper & Brothers, 1838), 2:204; Paul M. Angle, "The Hardy Pioneer: How He Lived in the Early Middle West," in *History of Medical Practice in Illinois*, ed. David J. Davis, 3 vols. (Chicago: University of Illinois Press, 1955), 2:26–35; William J. Petersen, "Doctors, Drugs, and Pioneers," *Palimpsest* 30, 3 (Mar. 1949): 93–96; and idem, "Diseases and Doctors in Pioneer Iowa," *Iowa Journal of History* 49, 2 (Apr. 1951): 97–116.

49. Mary Warren, interview, c. 1943, MHS; see also Sue Berkman, "Through Centuries of Childbirth," *American Baby*, Jan. 1979, pp. 48–49, 54. See, e.g., *Business*

Directory (Burlington: Iowa Hawk–Eye Power Press, 1856), p. 35; see also Frederick H. Falls, "Obstetrics and Gynecology," in *History of Medical Practice in Illinois,* 2:211–44.

50. Ezra M. Prince, John and Jane Hendrix, 5 June 1906, MLCHS; Abby Bucklin, Just Indians, n.d., MHS; Schmidt, History of the Jacob Zed Barncard Family, MHS; and Florence Nightingale, *Notes on Nursing* (London: Harrison, 1859), p. 1.

51. Mary Elizabeth Massey, *Bonnet Brigades: American Women and the Civil War* (New York: Knopf, 1966), p. 49; see also Cordelia Chester, Recollections of Hospital Life, n.d., ISHL; and Mary Ellen McElligott, " 'A Monotony Full of Sadness': The Diary of Nadine Turchin, May, 1863–April, 1864," *Journal of the Illinois State Historical Society* 70, 1 (Feb. 1977): 27–89.

52. Barbara Melosh, *"The Physician's Hand": Work, Culture, and Conflict in American Nursing* (Philadelphia: Temple University Press, 1982), pp. 3–7.

53. May Lacey Crowder, "Pioneer Life in Palo Alto County," *Iowa Journal of History and Politics* 46, 2 (Apr. 1948): 183; and Bonebright-Closz, *Reminiscences of Newcastle,* pp. 227–29.

54. Wing, "Early Days in Clayton County," p. 293; *Women of Montgomery County, Iowa,* p. 34; Nellie N. Barsness, M.D., Highlights in Careers of Women Physicians in Pioneer Minnesota, 1947, MHS; Winton U. Solberg, "Martha G. Ripley: Pioneer Doctor and Social Reformer," *Minnesota History* 39, 1 (Spring 1964): 1–17; "Martha George Rogers Ripley," in *Notable American Women,* 3:162–63.

55. Barsness, Highlights in Careers of Women Physicians, MHS; see also Herbert G. Kramer, Elizabeth Kramer, n.d., UMWHMC and SHSMM; Myres, *Westering Women,* pp. 252–53; and Daniel C. Eddy, *Daughters of the Cross: or, Woman's Mission* (Boston, Mass.: Wentworth, 1856).

56. *Ninth Census,* vol. 1: *The Statistics of the Population of the United States* (Washington, D.C.: Government Printing Office, 1872), pp. 692–95; and *Statistics of the Population of the United States at the Tenth Census,* 1:797, 799; Gordon, *Little Bit of a Long Story,* p. 12; and Wing, "Early Days in Clayton County," p. 261.

57. Fay E. Dudden, *Serving Women: Household Service in Nineteenth-Century America* (Middletown, Conn.: Wesleyan University Press, 1983), p. 101.

58. *Ninth Census,* vol. 1: *The Statistics of the Population of the United States,* pp. 686–87; and *Statistics of the Population of the United States at the Tenth Census,* 1:793.

59. Mark E. Nackman and Darryl K. Paton, "Recollections of an Illinois Woman," *Western Illinois Regional Studies* 1, 1 (1978): 32–33; see also Bernice P. Jenkins, Life of Jennie Atwood Pratt, 10 Apr. 1949, MHS; and Dudden, *Serving Women,* pp. 48, 149–50, 152–54.

60. Sarah Welch Nossaman, "Pioneering at Bonaparte and Near Pella," *Annals of Iowa* 13, 6 (Oct. 1922): 446; and Abby Fuller Abbe, letter to Dear Aunt Trotwood, 30 Dec. 1860, MHS.

61. Manuscript Census of Cooper County, Mo., 1851, UMWHMC and SHSMM; Georgiana Packard, Leaves from the Life of a Kansas Pioneer, 1914, KSHS; and Phillip T. Drotning, *A Guide to Negro History in America* (New York: Doubleday, 1968), p. 67.

62. David E. Schob, *Hired Hands and Plowboys: Farm Labor in the Midwest, 1815–60* (Urbana: University of Illinois Press, 1975), p. 191; and Mrs. A. M. Gridley, interview, *Bloomington* (Ill.) *Bulletin,* 26 Jan. 1899.

63. Henry L. Norton, "The Travels of the Marstons," *Journal of the Illinois State Historical Society* 58, 3 (Autumn 1965): 298–99.

64. Dudden, *Serving Women,* pp. 62, 200–201.

65. Anna Ramsey, letters to My Darling Children, 31 Mar. 1876, and to My Dear

Daughter, 2 Feb. and 8 Dec. 1876; see also Gridley interview, *Bloomington* (Ill.) *Bulletin,* 26 Jan. 1899.

66. Adrienne Christopher, The Story of Daniel Yoacham, Westport Innkeeper, n.d., UMWHMC and SHSMM; and "Louisa Warner's Diary as Hotel Chamber Maid in Tintah, Minnesota," in *To All Inquiring Friends: Letters, Diaries, and Essays in North Dakota, 1880–1910,* comp. Elizabeth Hampsten (Grand Forks: Department of English, University of North Dakota, 1979), pp. 275–83.

67. Clinton, "Pioneer Women in Chicago," p. 318; and Odd S. Lovoll, *The Promise of America: A History of the Norwegian American People* (Minneapolis: University of Minnesota Press, 1984), p. 167.

68. Joseph Payne, letter to Dear Sir, 22 July 1859, privately held by Howard S. Miller, University of Missouri–St. Louis.

69. *The Charter and Revised Ordinances of the City of Bloomington, Illinois* (Bloomington: Illinois Statesman Book & Job Printing House, 1861), p. 41; and *Journal of Proceedings of the City Council of the City of Bloomington, Illinois, for 1884* (Bloomington, Ill.: Pantagraph Printing, 1884), p. 25.

70. James E. Davis, *Frontier America, 1800–1840: A Comparative Demographic Analysis of the Settlement Process* (Glendale, Calif.: Arthur H. Clark, 1977), pp. 135–64; and Mrs. H. B. Halsted, "Essay on Women's Influence on Agriculture," in *Transactions of the Illinois State Agricultural Society* (Springfield, Ill.: Baker, Bailhache, 1868).

71. *Ninth Census,* vol. 1: *The Statistics of the Population of the United States,* pp. 686–87; and *Statistics of the Population of the United States at the Tenth Census,* 1:716, 724, 730.

72. Emhoff, "Pioneer School Teacher," p. 379.

73. Clarence R. Aurner, "Story of an Iowa Woman," *Palimpsest* 28, 6 (June 1947): 167; and Alma Amalie Guttersen, The Youth of Alma Amalie Guttersen, n.d., MHS.

74. Bertha Martinson Sonsteby, biography, in Minnesota American Mothers Committee, Inc., 1975, MHS.

75. Matie L. Baily, "Prairie Homesteading," *Palimpsest* 23, 7 (July 1942): 236; Kramer, Elizabeth Kramer, UMWHMC and SHSMM; Tildy Keist Heitman, reminiscences, c. 1840s–1860s, ISHL; Jefferson E. Kimler, Estate Papers, 1862, MLCHS; and Maria Van Kerkove, Papers, 1848–59, ISHD-HS. For examples of female property owners see *Missouri Intelligencer* (Fayette), 26 Oct. 1826; *Missouri Statesman* (Columbia), 14 July 1843; and Manuscript Census, Cooper County, Mo., 1850, UMWHMC and SHSMM.

76. Gilbert C. Fite, *The Farmers' Frontier, 1865–1900* (New York: Holt, Rinehart & Winston, 1966), p. 47.

77. Crowder, "Pioneer Life in Palo Alto County," p. 181.

78. Margaret Murray Archer, "Memoir of the William Archer Family," *Annals of Iowa* 39, 5 (Summer 1968): 362, 370.

79. Cora M. Anderson, PDC, SDSHRC.

80. Kitturah Belknap, reminiscences, 1839, ISHD-HS; Parthenia Lockwood, "Original Letters," *Journal of the Illinois State Historical Society* 9, 1 (Apr. 1916–Jan. 1917): 195–97; and William Oliver, *Eight Months in Illinois* (Chicago: Walter M. Hill, 1924), pp. 108–9.

81. Vandergon, reminiscences, MHS; and Crowder, "Pioneer Life in Palo Alto County," p. 178.

82. Emery S. Bartlett, letter to My Dear Children and Grandchildren, Dec. 1911, ISHD-HS.

83. Matilda Peitzke Paul, recollections, 1938, ISHD-HS.

84. Edith H. Hurlbutt, "Pioneer Experiences in Keokuk County, 1858–1874," *Iowa Journal of History* 52, 4 (Oct. 1954): 331.

85. Margaret Stout Davis, The Story of My Life, 1952, UMWHMC and SHSMM.

86. An interesting demonstration of this point is found in the family of a LaSalle County, Illinois, woman, whose sons pursued an extremely wide variety of jobs and professions while her daughters were typed into women's work: see James E. Armstrong, *Life of a Woman Pioneer* (Chicago: John F. Higgins Printing, 1931), pp. 9, 25–39. For examples of male mobility see Jerome Dutton, "Across the Plains in 1850," *Annals of Iowa* 3 (Oct. 1910): 447–83; and John Evans, letter to My Dear Sarah, 3 June 1848, MHS.

Chapter 6. Employment and Income Production on the Plains

1. Guidebooks written for women during the latter part of the nineteenth century encouraged them to prepare themselves for employment in a variety of jobs and professions: see, e.g., Mrs. M. L. Rayne, *What Can a Woman Do: or, Her Position in the Business and Literary World* (Detroit: F. B. Dickerson, 1884); and Frances E. Willard, *Occupations for Women* (Cooper Union, N.Y.: Success Co., 1897).

2. *Ninth Census*, vol. 1: *Population and Social Statistics* (Washington, D.C.: Government Printing Office, 1872), pp. 725, 734, 744, 745, 765; and *Thirteenth Census of the United States Taken in the Year 1910*, vol. 4: *Population, Occupation Statistics* (Washington, D.C.: Government Printing Office, 1910), pp. 462–63, 484–86, 501–2, 518, 534.

3. *Ninth Census*, vol. 1, pp. 725, 734, 744, 745, 765; *Thirteenth Census*, vol. 4, pp. 462–63, 484–86, 501–2, 518, 534.

4. Wayne E. Fuller, "Country Schoolteaching of the Sod-House Frontier," *Arizona and the West* 17, 2 (Summer 1975): 121–40.

5. Lila Gravatt Scrimsher, ed., "The Diary of Anna Webber: Early Day Teacher of Mitchell County," *Kansas Historical Quarterly* 38, 3 (Autumn 1972): 320–37.

6. Laura Brown Zook, Sketches of Laura Brown Zook's Early Life, 1869–1944, MSULSC.

7. Elizabeth Hampsten, comp., *To All Inquiring Friends: Letters, Diaries, and Essays in North Dakota, 1880–1910* (Grand Forks: University of North Dakota, Department of English, 1979), pp. 47–48. For other descriptions see Madge Yoder Smith, interview, 13 Oct. 1979, UWAHC; Bertha Wheeler Eustler, History of Churchill School, n.d., KSHS; Minnie Doehring, Kansas One Room Public School, 1981, KSHS; Addie M. Thompson Sinclair, My Story: An Autobiography Covering the Years 1880 to 1961, KSHS; and Olive Pickering Rankin, MAMBP, MTHS.

8. Gretchen Stoecker Norby, First Trip to South Dakota, 1961, privately held by Gretchen Stoecker Jacobson, Cedar Falls, Iowa; see also Mrs. Asby Howell, biographical sketch, 1936, WSAMHD.

9. Clara S. Conron, diary, 1884/85, KSHS; and Sarah Jane Price, Diaries, 1878–95, NSHS.

10. Catherine Wiggins Porter, Sunday School Houses and Normal Institutes: Pupil and Teacher in Northern Kansas, 1886–1895, KSHS; and Mrs. Lewis Gray, A Pioneer Teacher's Experiences, n.d., KSHS.

11. For accounts of full-time teachers see Scrimsher, "Diary of Anna Webber," pp. 302–37; Dora Moore Anderson, letters to Lawrence K. Fox, 1889–1935, SDSHRC; and Minnie Rundall Delimont, I Lived in Soddies, n.d., NSHS. For teachers with

other jobs see Price, diaries, NSHS; Susan Ophelia Carter, diary, 1887, NSHS; Elizabeth Rath Tyler, reminiscence, 1954, MTHS; Anne Wright, Mary Alice Davis, Pioneer Woman Educator, 1957, WSAMHD; Abbie Bright, diary, 1870/71, KSHS; Paul Corey, "Bachelor Bess: My Sister," *South Dakota Historical Collections* 37 (1974); Mrs. William Bangs, My Homesteading Days, n.d., MTHS; Norby, First Trip to South Dakota, privately held; Enid Bern, ed., "They Had a Wonderful Time: The Homesteading Letters of Anna and Ethel Erickson," *North Dakota History* 45, 4 (Fall 1978): 4–31; and Mary Hethy Bonar, diary, 1885, SHSND.

12. List of County Superintendents, in Park County Women, 1977, MSULSC; and Mary Johnstone Powers, A Pioneer Woman's Reminiscences, 1947, MTHS; see also My Mother, MAMBP, MTHS; and Adelia B. F. Spohr, in Five Came West, compiled by the Epsilon Sigma Alpha Sorority, MTHS.

13. Spohr, in Five Came West, MTHS.

14. Grace Reed Porter, Twenty-Five Years in South Dakota, SDSHRC. For another example of a woman who combined an active and lifelong career in education with marriage see "Emma Mott, 'Lady Instructor,'" in Elizabeth Hampsten, *Read This Only to Yourself: The Private Writings of Midwestern Women, 1880–1910* (Bloomington: Indiana University Press, 1983).

15. Thisba Hutson Morgan, "Reminiscences of My Days in the Land of the Ogallala Sioux," South Dakota Department of History *Report and Historical Collections* 29 (1969): 21–62; see also Elizabeth H. Hunt, ed., "Two Letters from Pine Ridge Mission," *Chronicles of Oklahoma* 50, 2 (Fall 1972): 219–25. For a discussion of adult education for female Indians see Rebecca J. Herring, "The Creation of Indian Farm Women: Field Matrons and Acculturation on the Kiowa-Comanche Reservation, 1895–1906," in *At Home on the Range: Essays on the History of Western Social and Domestic Life*, ed. John R. Wunder (Westport, Conn.: Greenwood Press, 1985), pp. 39–56.

16. Morgan, "Reminiscences," pp. 21–62.

17. Kay Graber, ed., *Sister to the Sioux: The Memoirs of Elaine Goodale Eastman* (Lincoln: University of Nebraska Press, 1978), pp. 29, 43, 64–65.

18. Morgan, "Reminiscences," pp. 41–46; and Graber, *Sister to the Sioux,* pp. 78–79, 85–86, 172–74.

19. Mary C. Collins, autobiography, Collins Family Papers, SDSHRC; see also Richard L. Clow, "Autobiography of Mary C. Collins, Missionary to the Western Sioux," *South Dakota Historical Collections* 41 (1982): 1–64; idem, "Mary Clementine Collins: Missionary at Standing Rock," *North Dakota History* 52, 2 (Spring 1985): 10–17; Mary Clementine Collins, *Winona: The Autobiography of Reverend Mary C. Collins* (New York: American Missionary Association, 1918); and Louise P. Olsen, "Mary Clementine Collins: Dacotah Missionary," *North Dakota History* 19 (Winter 1982): 58–81.

20. Susan C. Peterson, "Religious Communities of Women in the West: The Presentation Sisters' Adaptation to the Northern Plains Frontier," *Journal of the West* 21, 2 (Apr. 1982): 65–70; idem, "From Paradise to Prairie: The Presentation Sisters in Dakota, 1880–1896," *South Dakota History* 10, 3 (Summer 1980): 210–22.

21. Susan C. Peterson, "Challenging the Stereotypes: The Adaptation of the Sisters of St. Francis to South Dakota Indian Missions, 1885–1910," *Upper Midwest History* 4 (1984): 1–10; idem, " 'Holy Women' and Housekeepers: Women Teachers on South Dakota Reservations, 1880–1910," *South Dakota History* 13, 3 (Fall 1983): 245–60; idem, "Doing 'Women's Work': The Grey Nuns at Fort Totten Indian Reservation, 1874–1900," *North Dakota History* 52, 2 (Spring 1985): 18–25; and idem, "A Widening Horizon: Catholic Sisterhoods on the Northern Plains, 1874–1910," *Great Plains Quarterly* 5, 2 (Spring 1985): 125–32.

22. Grace Fitzgerald West, MAMBP, MTHS; and Maurine Hoffman Beasley, "Life as a Hired Girl in South Dakota, 1907–1908: A Woman Journalist Reflects," *South Dakota History* 12, 2 and 3 (Summer/Fall 1982): 147–62.

23. *Ninth Census,* 1:686; and *Thirteenth Census,* 4:463, 486. In Hall County, Nebraska, in 1870, 27 of the 33 working women were domestic servants, while 2 were seamstresses, 2 were laundresses, 1 was a schoolteacher, and 1 was a stewardess on a steamship (Charles G. Robbins, *A Physicist Looks at the 1860 and 1870 Hall County Census* [Grand Island, Nebr.: Prairie Pioneer Press, 1983], pp. 60–109).

24. Ellen Payne Paullin, ed., "Etta's Journal January 2, 1874–July 25, 1875," *Kansas History* 3, 3 (Autumn 1980): 201–2, 209, 217; see also Emma Crinklaw, interview of Mary A. Thon, One Brave Homesteader of '89, 1939, WSAMHD; Corey, "Bachelor Bess," pp. 8–9; Anna Warren Peart, PDC, SDSHRC; and Kathrine Newman Webster, "Memories of a Pioneer," in *Old Timer's Tales,* vol. 2, pt. 1, 1971, NSHS. For a discussion of the demographic characteristics of domestic workers see Sylvia Lea Sallquist, "The Image of the Hired Girl in Literature: The Great Plains, 1860 to World War I," *Great Plains Quarterly* 4, 3 (Summer 1984): 166–77. To place domestic service on the Plains in the context of national developments see Faye E. Dudden, *Serving Women: Household Service in Nineteenth-Century America* (Middletown, Conn.: Wesleyan University Press, 1983); David M. Katzman, *Seven Days a Week: Women and Domestic Service in Industrializing America* (Urbana: University of Illinois Press, 1981); and Judith Rollins, *Between Women: Domestics and Their Employers* (Philadelphia: Temple University Press, 1985).

25. Mrs. Glenys Wilkinson, Fannie—Pioneer Woman, 1936, WSAMHD; Carter, diary, NSHS; Katherine Grant, MAMBP, MTHS; Jessie Proud Minard, Robertina MacDonald, and Ethel Heffelfinger Mehner, PDC, SDSHRC; Susan Howells, Recollections of a Busy Life, 1972, MTHS; and Emma Lynchburg, Pioneer Memories, 1975, WSAMHD.

26. Mary Dunlava Tellefson, Pioneer Days in Cass County, n.d., SHSND; and Mary Althoff McLaughlin, Pioneer Memories, 1975, WSAMHD.

27. Sarah L. Bernson and Robert J. Eggers, "Black People in South Dakota History," *South Dakota History* 7, 3 (Summer 1977): 250; D. Cheryl Collins, "Women at Work in Manhattan, Kansas, 1890–1910," *Journal of the West* 21, 2 (Apr. 1982): 40; Tish Nevins, PDC, SDSHRC; Sallquist, "Image of the Hired Girl in Literature," p. 168; Sherman Savage, "The Negro in the Westward Movement," *Journal of Negro History* 25, 4 (Oct. 1940): 532–33; and Dorothy Sterling, "Washwomen, Maumas, Exodusters, Jubileers," in *We Are Your Sisters: Black Women in the Nineteenth Century* (New York: Norton, 1984), pp. 355–94.

28. Sarah Millard Schultz and Percie Matheson Knowles, in Park County Women, MSULSC; see also Jette Petterson, PDC, SDSHRC.

29. Aunt Tish, MAMBP, MTHS; see also Stella Tanner Fowler, The Tanner Family, c. 1960, MTHS.

30. Madam Bulldog, in Park County Women, MSULSC.

31. Paul Frizon, The Life of Martha Waln, Pioneer of Tensleep, Wyoming, 1939, WSAMHD; see also W. H. Elznic, PDC, SDSHRC; Myra Danile, interview, 1982, MTHS; Estella Trotter Peterson and Jessie E. Mudgett, Pioneer Memories Collection, WSAMHD; and Mary Peachy Cox, interview, 1957, MTHS. Lebanese women peddlers are described in Pat Kuehl, "Lebanese Immigrants in Southeast Kansas," *Heritage of the Great Plains* 17 (Fall 1984): 19–20.

32. *Ninth Census,* 1:692–95.

33. Christie Daily, "A Woman's Concern: Milliners in Central Iowa, 1870–1880,"

Journal of the West 21, 2 (Apr. 1982): 26–27; and Marian Lawton Clayton, Reminiscences: The Little Family, 1961, KSHS.

34. Fannie Forbes Russel, My First Year in Montana, 1864/65, MTHS.

35. Hazel Reeder, letter to Dear Sister, 4 Sept. 1884, NSHS; and Inez Thompson Peterson, PDC, SDSHRC. For a description of the importance of fashion for nineteenth-century women see Jeanette C. Lauer and Robert H. Lauer, "The Language of Dress: A Sociohistorical Study of the Meaning of Clothing in America," *Canadian Review of American Studies* 10, 3 (Winter 1979): 305–23.

36. Collins, "Women at Work in Manhattan, Kansas," p. 37; and Mary Baillie and George Baillie, Recollections in the Form of a Duet, 1939, WSAMHD; see also Lizzie Elliot Holmes, PDC, SDSHRC; and Lucie Emma Dickinson Lott, reminiscences, n.d., SDSHRC.

37. Donna M. Lucey, "The Intimate Vision of Evelyn Cameron," *Geo* 5, 1 (Jan. 1983): 68–78; Delores J. Morrow, "Female Photographers on the Frontier: Montana's Lady Photographic Artists, 1886–1900," *Montana, the Magazine of Western History* 32, 3 (Summer 1982): 76–84; and Peter E. Palmquist, "Photographers in Petticoats," *Journal of the West* 21, 2 (Apr. 1982): 58–64.

38. Jeannie L. Wuillemin, A Homesteader's Letter, n.d., SDSHRC; Edith Eudora Ammons Kohl, *Land of the Burnt Thigh* (New York: Funk & Wagnalls, 1938), pp. 38–39; and Lott, reminiscences, SDSHRC.

39. Walter E. Kaloupek, "Alice Nelson Page: Pioneer Career Woman," *North Dakota Historical Quarterly* 13 (1946): 71–79. For other discussions of women writers see Sondra Van Meter, "Pioneer Women," *Wichita State University Magazine* 2, 1 (Winter 1976): 19; Dorothy K. Gray, *Women of the West* (Millbrook, Calif.: Les Femmes, 1976), pp. 135–40; Elizabeth Cochran, "Hatchets and Hoopskirts: Women in Kansas History," *Midwest Quarterly* 2, 3 (Apr. 1961): 240; Mary Long Alderson, A Half Century of Progress for Montana Women, 1934, MTHS; and Eunice G. Anderson, Women's Accomplishments in Wyoming, n.d., WSAMHD. For examples of women writers see Bright, diary, KSHS; Julia Louise Lovejoy, "Letters of Julia Louise Lovejoy, 1856–1864," *Kansas Historical Quarterly* 15, 2 (May 1947): 127–42, 15, 3 (Aug. 1947): 277–319, 15, 4 (Nov. 1947): 368–403, 16, 1 (Feb. 1948): 40–75, and 16, 2 (May 1948): 175–211; Adelaide Jewett Skinner, poetry, n.d. (probably c. 1880–85), NSHS; State Historical Society, "The First Ladies of South Dakota," *South Dakota History* 3, 2 (Spring 1973): 162; and Miriam D. Colt, *Went to Kansas: Being a Thrilling Account of an Ill-Fated Expedition* (Watertown, N.Y.: L. Ingalls, 1862).

40. Richard B. Roeder, "Crossing the Gender Line: Ella L. Knowles, Montana's First Woman Lawyer," *Montana, the Magazine of Western History* 32, 3 (Summer 1982): 64–75; and information from catalog card on Wyoming professional women, WSAMHD.

41. Half-sheet notation concerning Sarah E. Gardinier, Woman Suffrage File, WSAMHD.

42. Mrs. W. D. B. Gray, unidentified newspaper clipping, UWAHC.

43. Maren Michelet, "Agnes Mathilde Wergeland," *American Scandinavian Review* 2, 4 (July 1914): 32; and Agnes Mathilde Wergeland, clippings and miscellaneous items, UWAHC.

44. Jean Todd, PDC, SDSHRC; and Ellen Allen Robinson, in Park County Women, MSULSC.

45. Ava Day, letters to Nebraska Historical Society, 28 Mar. and 23 May 1964, NSHS; Hannah Ropes, *Six Months in Kansas: By a Lady* (Freeport, N.Y.: Books for Libraries Press, 1972); Cochran, "Hatchets and Hoopskirts," p. 235; and anony-

mous, "Black Women in Colorado: Two Early Portraits," *Frontiers* 7, 3 (1984): 21.

46. Crinklaw, interview of Thon, One Brave Homesteader of '89, WSAMHD; Martha V. Shaw, diary, 1893, KSHS; Clara Haight, in Five Came West, 1976, compiled by the Epsilon Sigma Alpha Sorority, MTHS; Isabella Diehl and Cynthia Richards Pringle, PDC, SDSHRC. For the larger historical context in which Plains nursing developed see Barbara Melosh, *"The Physician's Hand": Work, Culture, and Conflict in American Nursing* (Philadelphia: Temple University Press, 1982).

47. Friede Van Dalsem and Abbie Jarvis, PDC, SDSHRC; see also Estelle Chrisman Laughlin, "Dr. Georgia Arbuckle Fix: Pioneer," in *Pioneer Tales of the North Platte Valley*, ed. A. B. Wood (Gering, Nebr.: Courier Press, 1938), pp. 188–89.

48. Anonymous, "Prostitutes," *Heritage of the Great Plains* 16, 3 (Summer 1983): 10.

49. Elliott West, "Scarlet West: The Oldest Profession in the Trans-Mississippi West," *Montana, the Magazine of Western History* 31, 2 (Spring 1981): 18; and Paula Petrik, "Capitalists with Rooms: Prostitution in Helena, Montana, 1865–1900," ibid., p. 33.

50. Bernson and Eggers, "Black People in South Dakota History," p. 247; and Tish Nevins, MAMBP, MTHS.

51. Carol Leonard and Isidor Walliman, "Prostitution and Changing Morality in the Frontier Cattle Towns of Kansas," *Kansas History* 2, 1 (Spring 1979): 37–39; and Joseph W. Snell, *Painted Ladies on the Cowtown Frontier* (Kansas City, Mo.: Lowell Press, 1965), pp. 3–5, 11–12.

52. Leonard and Walliman, "Prostitution and Changing Morality," pp. 27–40; and Snell, *Painted Ladies,* pp. 7–10.

53. Anne P. Diffendal, "Prostitution in Grand Island, Nebraska, 1870–1913," *Heritage of the Great Plains* 16, 3 (Summer 1983): 1–5.

54. Petrik, "Capitalists with Rooms," pp. 29–30, 34.

55. Rex C. Myers, "An Inning for Sin: Chicago Joe and Her Hurdy-Gurdy Girls," *Montana, the Magazine of Western History* 27, 2 (Apr. 1977): 24–33; see also Burton S. Hill, "A Girl Called Nettie," *Annals of Wyoming* 37, 2 (1965): 147–56.

56. Paula Petrik, "Strange Bedfellows: Prostitution, Politicians and Moral Reform in Helena, Montana, 1885–1887," *Montana, the Magazine of Western History* 35, 3 (Summer 1985): 2–13.

57. Mary Murphy, "The Private Lives of Public Women: Prostitution in Butte, Montana, 1878–1917," *Frontiers* 7, 3 (1984): 30–35. For an excellent and thorough discussion of prostitution in the American West see Anne M. Butler, *Daughters of Joy, Sisters of Misery: Prostitutes in the American West, 1865–1890* (Champaign: University of Illinois Press, 1985); see also West, "Scarlet West," pp. 16–27. For a discussion of the changes in American prostitution during this period see Leslie Fishbein, "Harlot or Heroine? Changing Views of Prostitution, 1870–1920," *Historian* 43, 1 (Nov. 1980): 23–35; and for the early twentieth century, Ruth Rosen, *The Lost Sisterhood: Prostitution in America, 1900–1918* (Baltimore, Md.: Johns Hopkins University Press, 1982).

58. *Ninth Census,* 1:725, 734, 744–45, 765; and *Thirteenth Census,* 4:461–62, 484–86, 501–2, 517–18, 533–34. All statistics were compiled by my research assistant, Rebecca L. Wheeler.

59. *Ninth Census,* 1:699.

60. *Thirteenth Census,* 4:462, 486.

61. Laura Ingalls Wilder, *The First Four Years* (New York: Harper & Row, 1971), p. 17; see also idem, *These Happy Golden Years* (New York: Harper & Brothers, 1943),

pp. 114–22; Dorothy Kimball, "Alone on That Prairie: The Homestead Narrative of Nellie Rogney," *Montana, the Magazine of Western History* 33, 4 (Autumn 1983): 55, 57; Bruner Family Papers, Mother's Trip West in 1856 to Omaha, n.d., NSHS; and Mae Waterman, Huntley Project Homesteading, 1968, MSULSC.

62. Evelyn King, "Women on the Cattle Trail and in the Roundup," *Buckskin Bulletin* 18 (Spring 1984): 3–4; see also idem, *Women on the Cattle Trail and in the Roundup* (Bryan, Tex.: Brazos Corral of the Westerners, 1983); Nannie T. Alderson and Helena Huntington Smith, *A Bride Goes West* (Lincoln: University of Nebraska Press, 1969), pp. 271–73; Fowler, The Tanner Family, MTHS; Gray, *Women of the West,* pp. 109–19; Georgia Kelley, a Courageous Homesteader—Edna N. Eaton, interview, 1936, WSAMHD; Lucey, "Intimate Vision of Evelyn Cameron," pp. 69, 78; Eva Putnam, Reminiscences of Pioneer Women, 1936, WSAMHD; and Emily J. Shelton, "Lizzie Johnson: A Cattle Queen of Texas," *Southwestern Historical Quarterly* 50, 3 (Jan. 1947): 349–66. For examples of women who farmed or ranched while their husbands did housework see Lillie Goodrich, Reminiscing on Her Father, n.d., WSAMHD; and Walker D. Wyman, ed., *Frontier Woman: The Life of a Woman Homesteader on the Dakota Frontier* (River Falls: University of Wisconsin/River Falls Press, 1972), pp. 57–58; see also Florence Lanchbury Sumpter and Jessie E. Mudgett, Pioneer Memories Collection, WSAMHD. Sumpter farmed because her husband was ill, and Mudgett because her husband worked as a bridge builder.

63. Lottie Holmberg, interviewer, Early Experiences of Miss Lucy Wells in Wyoming, 1936, WSAMHD.

64. Mrs. W. M. Lindsay, My Pioneer Years in North Dakota, 1933, SHSND; Frances Huntress Carruthers, MAMBP, MTHS; and Mary Jane Gray, Letters, 1858–94, KSHS; see also Julia Brown Brock, Mrs. May V. Gardner, 1936, WSAMHD; Howells, Recollections of a Busy Life, MTHS; Fowler, The Tanner Family, MTHS; and James T. King, ed., "Fort McPherson in 1870: A Note by an Army Wife," *Nebraska History* 45, 1 (Mar. 1964): 106.

65. Sheryll Patterson-Black, "From Pack Trains to Publishing: Women's Work in the Frontier West," in *Western Women in History and Literature,* ed. Sheryll Patterson-Black and Gene Patterson-Black (Crawford, Nebr.: Cottonwood Press, 1978), pp. 5–6; idem, "Women Homesteaders on the Great Plains Frontier," ibid., pp. 15–31; idem, "Women Homesteaders on the Great Plains Frontier," *Frontiers* 1, 2 (Spring 1976): 67–88. For additional data on Wyoming see Paula M. Bauman, "Single Women Homesteaders in Wyoming, 1880–1930," *Annals of Wyoming* 58 (Spring 1986): 52–53.

66. Everett Dick, *The Sod-House Frontier, 1854–1890* (New York: D. Appleton-Century, 1937), p. 129; see also ibid., pp. 36, 232–43, and 303; idem, "Free Homes for the Millions," *Nebraska History* 43, 4 (Dec. 1962): 221; and Mary W. M. Hargreaves, "Women in the Agricultural Settlement of the Northern Plains," *Agricultural History* 50, 1 (Jan. 1976): 182.

67. Mari Sandoz, *Old Jules Country* (New York: Hastings House, 1965), p. 292.

68. Enid Bern, "The Enchanted Years on the Prairie," *North Dakota History* 40, 4 (Fall 1973): 11.

69. Serena J. Washburn, Autobiography, 1836–1904, MSULSC; and Cora D. Babcock, reminiscences, 1880–85, SDSHRC; see also Mary Fox Howe, MAMBP, MTHS; Mrs. Ethel Hamilton, Mrs. Ethel Hamilton of Mountainview, 1936, WSAMHD; Fanny Achtnes Malone, The Experience of a Michigan Family on a Government Homestead in South Dakota, n.d., SDSHRC; Margaret Matilda Mudgett, Pioneer Memories Collection, WSAMHD; Martha Ferguson McKeown, *Them Was the Days: An American Saga of the '70s* (Lincoln: University of Nebraska Press, 1961) p. 129; Walker, *Fron-*

tier Woman, p. 90; and Kate Roberts Pelissier, "Reminiscences of a Pioneer Mother," *North Dakota History* 24, 3 (July 1957): 138.

70. Katherine Grant, MAMBP, MTHS; Henry Killian Goetz, "Kate's Quarter Section: A Woman in the Cherokee Strip," *Chronicles of Oklahoma* 61, 2 (Fall 1983): 246–67; Tellefson, Pioneer Days in Cass County, SHSND; and Charley O'Kieffe, *Western Story: The Recollections of Charley O'Kieffe, 1884–1898* (Lincoln: University of Nebraska Press, 1960), pp. 3–4. For women who hung onto their claims despite marriage see Jennie Williams Duret, in Park County Women, 1977, MSULSC; Mary Willard, MAMBP, MTHS; Frances Jacobs Alberts, ed., *Sod House Memories* (Hastings, Nebr.: Sod House Society, 1972), p. 61; Emma Lanchbury, memories, 1975, WSAMHD; Grace Fitzgerald West, MAMBP, MTHS; and Elinore Pruitt Stewart, *Letters of a Woman Homesteader* (Lincoln: University of Nebraska Press, 1961), pp. 7, 77, 216.

71. Bern, "Enchanted Years on the Prairie"; and Kohl, *Land of the Burnt Thigh,* pp. 6–7; see also Winifred Erdman, "Prairie Pioneers: North Dakota Homesteaders," *North Dakota History* 43, 2 (Spring 1976): 40.

72. Bright, diary, KSHS.

73. Ella Martfeld, Homesteading Days, n.d., WSAMHD.

74. Norby, First Trip to South Dakota, privately held; see also Sarah Schooley Randall, "My Trip West in 1861," in *Collection of Nebraska Pioneer Reminiscences* (Cedar Rapids, Iowa: Torch Book Press, 1916), p. 211; Mary Price Jeffords, "The Price Girls Go Pioneering," in *Pioneer Stories of Custer Country, Nebraska,* ed. E. R. Purcell (Broken Bow, Nebr.: Custer County Chief, 1936), p. 74. The complete words and music to "Dakota Land" can be found in John A. Lomax and Alan Lomax, eds., *Cowboy Songs and Other Frontier Ballads* (New York: Macmillan, 1938), pp. 410–12.

75. Carter, diary, NSHS; Bern, "They Had a Wonderful Time," pp. 15, 17, 19; and Bangs, My Homesteading Days, MTHS.

76. Carter, diary, NSHS; and Bright, diary, KSHS; see also Babcock, reminiscences, 1880–85, SDSHRC.

77. Corey, "Bachelor Bess," pp. 15, 18; and Bangs, My Homesteading Days, MTHS. For other examples see Ada Glayner Clarke, "Pothook Pioneer: A Reminiscence," ed. Monroe Billington, *Nebraska History* 39, 1 (Mar. 1958): 45, 50–52; and Martfeld, Homesteading Days, WSAMHD.

78. Bright, diary, KSHS.

79. Babcock, reminiscences, 1880–85, SDSHRC; and Washburn, autobiography, 1836–1904, MSULSC.

80. Bangs, My Homesteading Days, MTHS; and Martfeld, Homesteading Days, WSAMHD.

81. Corey, "Bachelor Bess," p. 16; Clarke, "Pothook Pioneer," p. 54; and Norby, First Trip to South Dakota, privately held.

82. Clarke, "Pothook Pioneer," pp. 46, 48–49; see also Alberts, *Sod House Memories,* pp. 6, 51.

83. Bess Cobb, letter to Dear Helen, 31 July 1907, SHSND.

84. Bern, "They Had a Wonderful Time," pp. 6, 8, 28.

85. O'Kieffe, *Western Story,* p. 26; and Roger L. Welsch, *Shingling the Fog and Other Plain Lies* (Chicago: Swallow Press, 1972), p. 126.

86. Clarke, "Pothook Pioneer," p. 5.

87. Bern, "They Had A Wonderful Time," p. 28.

88. Corey, "Bachelor Bess," p. 65; Martfeld, Homesteading Days, WSAMHD; and Bern, "They Had a Wonderful Time," pp. 6, 10–11, 14, 17, 25.

89. Myrtle Yoeman, letter to Dear Grace, 24 June 1905, SDSHRC; and Mrs. Lottie Holmberg, Experiences of Mary Culbertson, 1939, WSAMHD; Howell, biographical sketch, WSAMHD; see also Martha Suckow Packer, memoirs, 20 Sept. 1880–21 Jan. 1970, MSULSC.

90. Kohl, *Land of the Burnt Thigh,* pp. 2–7, 12–13, 21–23, 33, 38–39, 88–89, 120. For another example of a woman homesteader who became a printer to support her homestead claim see Idah E. McComsey, "Story by Early Woman Resident of the Hull Section," in *Pioneer Tales of the North Platte Valley,* pp. 59–65.

91. Kohl, *Land of the Burnt Thigh,* pp. 27, 38, 65, 84; see also pp. 22–23.

92. Katherine Llewellyn Hill Harris, "Women and Families on Northeastern Colorado Homesteads, 1873–1920" (Ph.D. diss., University of Colorado, Boulder, 1983), pp. 257–64; and idem, "Sex Roles and Work Patterns among Homesteading Families in Northeastern Colorado, 1873–1920," *Frontiers* 7, 3 (1984): 43–49; and Lonnie E. Underhill and Daniel F. Littlefield, "Women Homeseekers in Oklahoma Territory, 1889–1901," *Pacific Historian* 17, 3 (Summer 1973): 36–47. For other descriptions of women in land runs see Goetz, "Kate's Quarter Section," pp. 246–67; Lynnette Wert, "The Lady Stakes A Claim," *Persimmon Hill* 6, 2 (Spring 1976): 18–23; B. B. Chapman, "The Land Run of 1893, as Seen at Kiowa," *Kansas Historical Quarterly* 31, 1 (Spring 1965): 67–75; and Charles Moreau Harger, "The Prairie Woman: Yesterday and To-Day," *Outlook* 70, 17 (26 Apr. 1902): 1009.

93. Harriet Joor, "The Winning of a Homestead," *Craftsman* 27 (Jan. 1915): 436–40; and "Women Farmers," *Breeder's Gazette* 67 (29 Apr. 1915): 853–54; see also H. W. Doyle, "She Farms Alone," *Country Gentleman* 83, 32 (10 Aug. 1918): 36–37; and A. May Holoday, "The Lure of the West for Women," *Sunset* 38, 2 (Mar. 1917): 61.

94. Price, diaries, NSHS; Bright, diary, KSHS; and Corey, "Bachelor Bess," pp. 17, 60; see also Bern, "They Had a Wonderful Time," pp. 14, 57.

95. Anne Jones Davies, diary, 1882–88, KSHS.

96. Crinklaw, Interview of Thon, One Brave Homesteader of '89, WSAMHD; Lindsay, My Pioneer Days in North Dakota, SHSND; Julia Louisa Lovejoy, "Letters of Julia Louisa Lovejoy, 1856–1864," pt. 2, *Kansas Historical Quarterly* 15, 3 (Aug. 1947): 277–319; Tellefson, Pioneer Days in Cass County, SHSND; Wyman, *Frontier Woman,* pp. 21, 27; Frances Huntress Carruthers and Margaret Bohrnsen Luthje, MAMBP, MTHS; Chestina B. Allen, diary, 1854–57, KSHS; Luna Kellie, memoirs, n.d., NSHS; Sadie Jones Krause, Pioneer Memories, 1975, WSAMHD; Kimball, "Alone on That Prairie," pp. 55, 58; Babcock, reminiscences, SDSHRC; and Bessie N. Eder, interview, 1971, WSAMHD.

97. Colt, *Went to Kansas;* Julia Louisa Lovejoy, letters, 1828–64, in Lovejoy Family Papers, KSHS; and Bright, diary, KSHS; and C. O. Stout, Huntley Project Homesteading, 1968, MSULSC.

98. Holmberg, Early Experiences of Miss Lucy Wells, WSAMHD.

99. Gusta Anderson Chapin, PDC, SDSHRC.

100. For examples of the many jobs pursued by plainsmen and the tremendous choice of employment available to them see Michael J. Brodhead and John D. Unruh, Jr., eds., "Isaiah Harris' 'Minutes of a Trip to Kansas Territory' in 1855," *Kansas Historical Quarterly* 35, 4 (1969): 373–85; Byron N. McKinstry, *The California Gold Rush Overland Diary of Byron N. McKinstry* (Glendale, Calif.: Arthur H. Clarke, 1975); James E. Potter, ed., "The Missouri River Journal of Leonard W. Gilchrist, 1866," *Nebraska History* 58, 3 (1977): 267–300; J. F. Triplett, "The Scout's Story from the Journal of a Cattleman," *Atlantic Monthly,* Apr. 1925, pp. 493–500; Donald K. Watkins, ed., "A Dane's View on Frontier Culture: 'Notes on a Stay in the United

States,' 1872–1874, by Wilhelm Dinesen," *Nebraska History* 55, 2 (Summer 1974): 264–89; and Wood, "Story of Early Irrigation Promoter and Merchant" and "A Story of the Ewing Family," in *Pioneer Tales,* pp. 50–52, 70–78.

Chapter 7. Community Participation on the Prairie

1. *Godey's Lady's Book,* 14 (Jan. 1857): 5; see also Glenda Riley, "The Subtle Subversion: Changes in the Traditionalist Image of the American Woman," *Historian* 32, 2 (Feb. 1970): 210–27.

2. For further discussion of the domestic novelists see Ann Douglas, *The Feminization of American Culture* (New York: Knopf, 1979); Mary Kelley, "The Sentimentalists: Promise and Betrayal in the Home," *Signs* 4, 3 (Spring 1979): 434–36; idem, *Private Woman, Public Stage: Literary Domesticity in Nineteenth-Century America* (New York: Oxford University Press, 1984).

3. Elisha D. Ely, *The Ely and Weare Families: Pioneers of Michigan and Iowa* (Cedar Rapids, Iowa: Privately printed at the Torch Press, 1926), p. 46.

4. Julia Barnard Strong, letter to My Dear Aunt H, 26 Dec. 1836, UMWHMC and SHSMM.

5. Elizabeth Crowley, in Illinois Women, 1893, ISHL.

6. Gertrude Vandergon, reminiscences, 1940/41, MHS; Harriet Connor Brown, *Grandmother Brown's Hundred Years, 1827–1927* (Boston, Mass.: Little, Brown, 1929), p. 111; Amelia Murdock Wing, "Early Days in Clayton County," *Annals of Iowa* 27, 4 (Apr. 1946): 275; Sarah Davis, letter to My Dear Husband, 15 Mar. 1868, MLCHS; and Clara Rieger Berens, letter to Dear Mama, 12 Oct. 1878, MHS.

7. Annis Marshall, letter to Dear Sis, 12 Jan. 1860, in Joseph Marshall Family Papers, UMWHMC and SHSMM.

8. Quoted in Julian Sargent, "Fuller Girls," *St. Paul* (Minn.) *Dispatch,* Jan. 1928.

9. *Burlington* (Iowa) *Daily Hawk-Eye,* 11 Feb. 1859.

10. *Missouri Statesman* (Columbia), 20 Jan. 1843; and *Minnesota Pioneer* (St. Paul), 19 May 1849 and 26 June 1851.

11. For an example of an etiquette book that sold widely on the prairie see Charles E. Sargent, *Our Home; or, The Key to a Nobler Life* (Des Moines, Iowa: King, Richardson, 1889).

12. Esther Pillsbury, diary, 1863, and Louisa Gelhorn Boylan, My Life Story, 1867–83, ISHD-HS; John Evans, letter to My Dear Sarah, 3 June 1848, MHS; and Sarah Withers, diary, 1860/61, MLCHS.

13. Ann E. Page, diary, 1855/56, ISHL; Catherine Bissell Ely, diary, 1835–39, MHS; Withers, diary, MLCHS; Edward D. Jervey and James E. Moss, eds., "From Virginia to Missouri in 1846: The Journal of Elizabeth Ann Cooley," *Missouri Historical Review* 60, 2 (Jan. 1966): 189; and Mary E. Murtfeldt, "Agricultural Literature," *Transactions of the Illinois State Agricultural Society* (Springfield, Ill.: Baker, Bailhache, 1861), pp. 378–82.

14. Philomathian Society, Minutes, 1880, MLCHS.

15. Withers, diary, MLCHS; Daryl E. Jones and James H. Pickering, ed., "A Young Woman in the Midwest: The Journal of Mary Sears, 1859–1860," *Ohio History* 82, 3 and 4 (Summer/Autumn 1973): 227–28; and Sarah Fuller, letter to Dear Lizzie, 23 Jan. 1853, MHS.

16. Jervey and Moss, "From Virginia to Missouri in 1846," pp. 195, 205; and Miriam M. Worthington, ed., "Diary of Anna R. Morrison, Wife of Isaac L. Morrison," *Journal of the Illinois State Historical Society* 7, 1 (Apr. 1914–Jan. 1915): 49–50.

17. Glenda Riley, "Origins of the Argument for Improved Female Education," *History of Education Quarterly* 9, 4 (Winter 1969): 455–70.

18. Robert E. Belding, "The Dubuque Female Seminary," *Palimpsest* 63, 2 (Mar./Apr. 1982): 34–41; *Burlington* (Iowa) *Weekly Hawk-Eye,* 20 Apr. 1848 and 6 Apr. 1849; Nathan Parker, *Iowa Handbook for 1856* (Boston, Mass.: John P. Jewett, 1856), p. 170; Thomas Woody, *History of Women's Education* (New York: Science Press, 1929), vol. 1, pp. 324–25.

19. Kathryn Kish Sklar, "The Founding of Mount Holyoke College," in *Women of America: A History,* ed. Carol Ruth Berkin and Mary Beth Norton (Boston, Mass.: Houghton Mifflin, 1979), pp. 177–202, 378; and Iowa Female Collegiate Institute, Address and Poem, 1853, ISHD-HS, pp. 5–6. For another example claiming to follow an eastern model see handwritten announcement, Young Ladies' School of Alton, Ill., 1836, Samuel Willard Papers, 1783–1913, ISHS.

20. Patricia Vertinsky, "Sexual Equality and the Legacy of Catharine Beecher," *Journal of Sport History* 6, 1 (Spring 1979): 38–49.

21. *Missouri Intelligencer* (Fayette), 25 Jan. 1827.

22. *Frontier Guardian* (Council Bluffs, Iowa), 7 Feb. 1851; and Mrs. H. C. Johns, "On the Education of Farmers' Daughters," *Transactions of the Illinois State Agricultural Society* (Springfield, Ill.: Baker, Bailhache, 1868), pp. 273–78.

23. Robert E. Belding, "Academies and Iowa's Frontier Life," *Annals of Iowa* 44, 5 (Summer 1978): 335–58.

24. *Burlington* (Iowa) *Daily Hawk-Eye,* 25 Dec. 1851, 12 Jan. and 20 Apr. 1859, 10 Aug. 1866; *Burlington* (Iowa) *Weekly Hawk-Eye,* 4 Sept. 1845; *Burlington* (Iowa) *Tri-Weekly Telegraph,* 1 Oct. 1850; *Hawk-Eye and Iowa Patriot* (Burlington), 5 Sept. 1839; *Davenport* (Iowa) *Gazette,* 8 Feb. 1855; *Democratic Banner* (Davenport, Iowa) 7 Apr. 1854; *Eddyville* (Iowa) *Free Press,* 6 Apr. 1854; *Fairfield* (Iowa) *Ledger,* 24 Aug. 1860, 13 Apr. 1854, 5 July 1869; *Gate City* (Keokuk, Iowa), 28 May 1857; and *Iowa Territorial Gazette and Advertiser* (Burlington, Iowa), 17 Feb. 1844.

25. *Missouri Statesman* (Columbia), 14 Apr. 1843; and *Eddyville* (Iowa) *Free Press,* 30 Mar. 1855; see also *Gate City* (Keokuk, Iowa), 25 Aug. 1857; and *Waterloo* (Iowa) *Courier,* 30 Apr. 1862.

26. *Iowa News* (Dubuque), 6 Jan. 1838; and Jean-Jacques Rousseau, *Emile: or, On Education,* trans. Allan Bloom (New York: Basic Books, 1979), pp. 386–87.

27. Harriet Martineau, *Retrospect of Western Travel,* vol. 1 (London: Saunders & Otley, 1838), p. 24; and idem, letter to My Dear Sir, n.d., UMWHMC and SHSMM.

28. Fredrika Bremer, *America of the Fifties: Letters of Fredrika Bremer* (New York: American-Scandinavian Foundation, 1924), p. 245.

29. E. H. Annewalt, *Mount Pleasant City Directory: Containing a Catalogue of Inhabitants* (Burlington, Iowa: Daily Gazette, 1870), pp. 5, 15–18.

30. John Nollen, *Grinnell College* (Iowa City: State Historical Society of Iowa, 1953), pp. 55–65; anonymous, *Poweshiek County, Iowa: A Descriptive Account* (Montezuma, Iowa: W. C. Condit, 1865), pp. 25–28; anonymous, "Seventy Years in Iowa," *Annals of Iowa* 27, 2 (Oct. 1945): 111; *Burlington* (Iowa) *Hawk-Eye,* 9 Aug. 1866.

31. Clarence Ray Aurner, *History of Education in Iowa* (Iowa City, Iowa: State Historical Society, 1916), pp. 2–23, 40–45; Woody, *History of Women's Education,* 2:238, 296; Ruth A. Gallaher, *Legal and Political Status of Women in Iowa, 1838–1918* (Iowa City, Iowa: State Historical Society, 1918), pp. 40–41; Benjamin F. Shambaugh, *Iowa City: A Contribution to the Early History of Iowa* (Iowa City: State Historical Society of Iowa, 1893), pp. 80–84; circular, State University of Iowa, 1856 (Iowa City: Published by the University, 1856); and Mary B. Welch Papers, Special Collections, Iowa State University Library, Ames; see also Earle Dudley Ross, *The Land-Grant*

Idea at Iowa State College: A Centennial Trial Balance, 1858–1958 (Ames: Iowa State University Press, 1958).

32. Aurner, *History of Education in Iowa,* p. 337; Maud Burton Bell, recollections, n.d., UMWHMC and SHSMM; and chart, First Women Graduates from the University of Missouri, n.d., UMWHMC and SHSMM.

33. Ibid; chart, Enrollment at the University of Missouri, 1839–1925, n.d., UMWHMC and SHSMM; Earl Leon Heck, The Rise of Higher Education in the Missouri Valley, 1818–1900, 1965, UMWHMC and SHSMM; see also H. Warren Button, *History of Education and Culture in America* (Englewood Cliffs, N.J.: Prentice-Hall, 1983); and William Fraser Connell, *A History of Education in the Twentieth Century World* (New York: Teacher College Press, 1980). For cases of women who were honored in various ways by colleges and universities see *Winona* (Minn.) *Daily Republican,* 9 June 1875; *Minneapolis* (Minn.) *Mail,* 10 June 1875; chart, First Women Graduates of the University of Missouri, UMWHMC and SHSMM; and Alvin Guttag, Margaret Jane Evans Huntington, n.d., MHS.

34. Broadside, Illinois College, 1859, MLCHS; and Rules for the Boarding Pupils of Howard Female College, 1859, UMWHMC and SHSMM; see also Ruth Ferris, Bettie Raglan at Adelphai College, 1854/55, n.d., UMWHMC and SHSMM.

35. Ferris, Bettie Raglan at Adelphai College, UMWHMC and SHSMM; Allean Lemmon Hale, *Petticoat Pioneer* (St. Paul, Minn.: North Central Publishing Co., 1968), pp. 1–17; A. L. Chapin, Historical Sketch of Rockford Female Seminary, 1861, Rockford College Archives, Rockford, Ill.; and C. Hal Nelson, ed., *Rockford College: A Retrospective Look* (Rockford, Ill.: Rockford College, 1980), pp. 31–52. The supplying of secondary education was also sometimes done by universities: see Merle Curti and Vernon Carstenson, *The University of Wisconsin: A History, 1848–1925* (Madison: University of Wisconsin Press, 1949).

36. Chapin, Historical Sketch of Rockford Female Seminary, Rockford College Archives, Rockford, Ill.

37. Ian R. Tyrrell, "Women and Temperance in Antebellum America, 1830–60," *Civil War History* 28, 2 (June 1982): 128–32.

38. Mrs. Gordon H. Read, The Temperance Movement in McLean County, n.d., MLCHS; and John Magoun, biography, 1902, MLCHS.

39. Barbara Leslie Epstein, *The Politics of Domesticity: Women, Evangelism, and Temperance in Nineteenth-Century America* (Middletown, Conn.: Wesleyan University Press, 1981), especially pp. 135–38.

40. Tyrrell, "Women and Temperance," pp. 133–34.

41. Daughters of Temperance, broadside, Seal of Bloomington Union No. 1, Daughters of Temperance, Muscatine, Iowa, 4 Feb. 1850, Graff Collection, Newberry Library, Chicago. For other examples of public support of women's efforts see *Burlington* (Iowa) *Daily Hawk-Eye,* 9 Jan. 1851 and 2 Feb. 1859.

42. Jack S. Blocker, Jr., *"Give to the Winds Thy Fears": The Women's Temperance Crusade* (Westport, Conn.: Greenwood Press, 1985), pp. 3–5, 209–38; and idem, ed., "Annie Wittenmyer and the Women's Crusade," *Ohio History* 88, 4 (Autumn 1979): 419–22; see also Annie Turner Wittenmyer, *History of the Woman's Temperance Crusade* (Philadelphia: Office of the Christian Woman, 1878); Frances E. Willard, *Woman and Temperance* (New York: Arno Press, 1972), pp. 160–67; and Judith Papachristou, "WCTU: They Were Fighting More Than Demon Rum," *Ms. Magazine* 4, 12 (June 1976): 74.

43. WCTU, Columbia, Mo., chapter, minute book, 1884–88, UMWHMC and SHSMM.

44. WCTU, St. Paul, Minn., chapter, minute book, 1885, MHS; WCTU, Minnesota

WCTU, n.d., in Records, 1862–1983, MHS; Read, The Temperance Movement in McLean County, MLCHS; and anonymous, The Story of the National Colony, c. 1943, MHS.

45. For examples of eastern female abolitionists see Philip S. Foner and Josephine F. Pacheco, *Three Who Dared: Prudence Crandall, Margaret Douglass, Myratilla Miner—Champions of Antebellum Black Education* (Westport, Conn.: Greenwood Press, 1984), pp. 3–54.

46. Anonymous, "Seventy Years in Iowa," *Annals of Iowa* 27, 2 (Oct. 1945): 98–100, 114–15. That even abolitionist Grinnell could experience dissension over slavery is illustrated by Sarah Parker, letter to My Dear Mother, 10 Mar. 1860, ISHD-HS. For a description of the underground railroad see Nettie Sanford, *Early Sketches of Polk County* (Newton, Iowa: Chas. A. Clark, 1874), p. 134; and Abbie Mott Benedict, "My Early Days in Iowa," *Annals of Iowa* 17, 5 (July 1930): 331.

47. Mrs. Laurence C. Jones, "The Desire for Freedom," *Palimpsest* 7, 5 (May 1927): 153–63.

48. For more about women abolitionists see Blanche G. Hersh, *The Slavery of Sex: Feminist-Abolitionists in Nineteenth-Century America* (Urbana: University of Illinois Press, 1978); Gerda Lerner, *The Grimke Sisters from South Carolina: Pioneers for Woman's Rights and Abolition* (New York: Schocken Books, 1971); and Gerda Lerner, "The Political Activities of Antislavery Women," in her *The Majority Finds Its Past* (New York: Oxford University Press, 1979), pp. 112–28.

49. *Iowa News* (Dubuque), 26 Aug. 1837; see also Julie Roy Jeffrey, *Frontier Women: The Trans-Mississippi West, 1840–1880* (New York: Hill & Wang, 1979), pp. 128–29, 135–39, 186–90; and Sandra L. Myres, *Westering Women and the Frontier Experience, 1800–1915* (Albuquerque: University of New Mexico Press, 1982), pp. 206–12.

50. Jane M. Johns, *Personal Recollections of Early Decatur* (Decatur, Ill.: Daughters of the American Revolution, 1912), pp. 40–41; and Diderikke Brandt, Papers, Luther College Library, Decorah, Iowa.

51. Anne M. Boylan, "Evangelical Womanhood in the Nineteenth Century: The Role of Women in Sunday Schools," *Feminist Studies* 4, 3 (Oct. 1978): 62–80; Page Putnam Miller, "Women in the Vanguard of the Sunday School Movement," *Journal of Presbyterian History* 58, 4 (Winter 1980): 311–25; Mrs. E. E. Cox, Chenoa Methodist Church, 1949, MLCHS; and Mattie Lykins-Bingham, "Recollections of Old Times," *Westport Historical Quarterly* 7, 2 (1971): 20.

52. First Congregational Church, Marine (Minn.) Sewing Society, minutes, 1857, MHS; Helen E. Howie, The Historical Background of the Dundas Methodist Church, 1955, MHS; Lykins-Bingham, "Recollections of Old Times," p. 20; and Bonnie Blue Gee, The Auxvasse Church, 1959, UMWHMC and SHSMM; see also Daniel C. Eddy, *Daughters of the Cross: or, Woman's Mission* (Boston: Wentworth, 1856).

53. Adda Patterson Wertz, Civil War Reminiscence, 1911; Mary P. Evans, Reminiscence, 1904, MLCHS; and Springfield Ladies Soldiers' Aid Society, memorial, 1887, ISHL.

54. Ely, *Ely and Weare Families,* pp. 47–48; Mary Parke Evans, life history, n.d., MLCHS; and interview, Margaret Funk, c. 1943, MHS.

55. Anonymous, "Mrs. Ann E. Harlan," *Annals of Iowa* 2, 7 (Oct. 1896): 496.

56. Sarah Gregg, War Time Diary, 1863–65, and Cordelia Chester, Recollections of Hospital Life, n.d., ISHL; Eugenia B. Farmer, A Voice from the Civil War, 1918, MHS; Martha Turner Searle, Personal Experience and Reminiscence of the Civil War, 1861–65, n.d., ISHD-HS; and Ladies Union Aid Society of Missouri, reports, 1862/63, UMWHMC and SHSMM.

57. Ruth A. Gallaher, "Annie Turner Wittenmyer," *Iowa Journal of History and*

Politics 29, 4 (Oct. 1931): 518–69; and L. O. Cheever, "Annie Wittenmyer," *Palimpsest* 48, 6 (June 1967): 249–52; see also Annie Turner Wittenmyer, *Under the Guns: A Woman's Reminiscences of the Civil War* (Boston, Mass.: E. B. Stillings, 1895).

58. Ruth A. Gallaher, "Annie Turner Wittenmyer," *Palimpsest* 38, 4 (Apr. 1957): 150.

59. Gallaher, "Annie Turner Wittenmyer," *Iowa Journal of History and Politics,* p. 558.

60. Mary E. Shelton, diary, 1864, Shelton Family Papers, Manuscript Collection, University of Iowa Library, Iowa City.

61. "Annie Turner Wittenmyer," in *Notable American Women: A Biographical Dictionary,* ed. Edward T. James (Cambridge, Mass.: Belknap Press, 1971), pp. 636–37; see also Johns, *Personal Recollections of Early Decatur,* pp. 157, 168–69; and Harvey C. DeMotte, "Illinois Soldiers' Orphans' Home," *Transactions of the McLean County Historical Society* (Bloomington, Ill.: McLean County Historical Society, 1903), pp. 187–200.

62. M. A. Rogers, "An Iowa Woman in Wartime," pt. 1, *Annals of Iowa* 35, 7 (Winter 1961): 523–48, and pt. 2, ibid., 35, 8 (Spring 1961): 600–609.

63. Rogers, "Iowa Woman in Wartime," pt. 2, pp. 610–11, and pt. 3, *Annals of Iowa* 36, 9 (Summer 1961): 16–24, 30.

64. *Burlington* (Iowa) *Daily Hawk-Eye,* 28 Jan. 1863, 6 Jan. 1864. For an account of a sanitary fair see *Waterloo* (Iowa) *Courier,* 6 Apr. 1864. For a fuller discussion of war relief work in Iowa see Earl S. Fullbrook, "Relief Work in Iowa during the Civil War," *Iowa Journal of History and Politics* 16, 2 (Apr. 1918): 155–274.

65. Woman's Christian Association of Minneapolis, records, 1866/67, MHS.

66. See, e.g., First Universalist Church, Bylaws of the Social Circle, 1878, MHS; and "Mrs. M. E. Huntington's Biography," *St. Paul* (Minn.) *Pioneer Press,* 18 Oct. 1925.

67. Alice Schlenker, The Literary Clubs, 1893, MLCHS; Zylpha Morton, A Brief History of the Schubert Club, 1882–1962, n.d., MHS; anonymous, The Woman's Club of Fergus Falls, 1897–1925, n.d., MHS; and Mrs. E. L. Lowe, Accounts of Various Clubs, MHS.

68. Eva Neal, Family Papers, 1881–1963, MHS.

69. Anonymous, Pilgrim Baptist Church, c. 1977, MHS; and Patricia C. Harpole, ed., "The Black Community in Territorial St. Anthony: A Memoir," *Minnesota History* 49, 2 (Summer 1984): 44.

70. Neal, Family Papers, MHS; and Harpole, "Black Community in Territorial St. Anthony," p. 44.

71. Mount Zion Hebrew Congregation of St. Paul, Records, 1857–72, MHS; Hebrew Ladies Benevolent Society, minutes, 1881, MHS; and B. Marx, Address at Twenty-fifth Anniversary of Jewish Welfare Association of St. Paul, 12 Apr. 1937, MHS.

72. Mrs. A. W. Danielson, Some Special Dates and Events, 1954, Federation of Women's Clubs, MHS.

73. Mary D. Taylor, "A Farmers' Wives' Society in Pioneer Days," *Annals of Iowa* 3, 13 (July 1921): 22–31.

74. For more on women's voluntary associations during the nineteenth century see Anne Firor Scott, *Making the Invisible Woman Visible* (Urbana: University of Illinois Press, 1984), pp. 259–94; idem, "On Seeing and Not Seeing: A Case of Historical Invisibility," *Journal of American History* 71, 1 (June 1984): 7–21; Anne M. Boylan, "Women in Groups: An Analysis of Women's Benevolent Organizations in New York and Boston, 1797–1840," *Journal of American History* 71, 3 (Dec. 1984): 497–523; and Naomi Rosenthal et al., "Social Movements and Network Analysis: A Case Study of Nineteenth-Century Women's Reform in New York State," *American*

Journal of Sociology 90, 5 (Mar. 1985): 1022–54. The tie between women's voluntary associations and the emergence of women's rights is discussed by Jean V. Matthews in " 'Woman's Place' and the Search for Identity in Ante-Bellum America," *Canadian Review of American Studies* 10, 3 (Winter 1979): 289–304; and Jack S. Blocker, Jr., "Separate Paths: Suffragists and the Women's Temperance Crusade," *Signs* 10, 3 (Spring 1985): 460–75.

75. *Burlington* (Iowa) *Hawk-Eye,* 26 Dec. 1850: *Waterloo* (Iowa) *Courier,* 15 Apr. 1869; anonymous, "Iowa Suffrage Memorial Association," *Annals of Iowa* 45, 4 (Spring 1980): 1–2; anonymous, "Political Equality in Iowa," ibid., 26, 3 (Jan. 1945): 197; and Edith H. Hurlbutt, "Pioneer Experiences in Keokuk County, 1858–74," *Iowa Journal of History* 52, 4 (Oct. 1954): 342.

76. *Burlington* (Iowa) *Hawk-Eye,* 8 Aug. 1866; Iowa House, Journal, Eleventh General Assembly, Jan. 1866, pp. 188, 442; and Susan B. Anthony, letter to Dear Friend, 22 June 1868, MHS; and idem, letter to My Dear Sir, 25 June 1902, ISHL.

77. Horace Austin, letter to My Dear Madam, 14 Mar. 1870, MHS. For discussions of support for woman suffrage by non-American-born Minnesotans see H. Arnold Barton, "Scandinavian Immigrant Women's Encounter with America," *Swedish Pioneer Historical Quarterly* 25 (1974): 40–42; Susie Stageberg, Papers, 1881–1938, MHS; and Rolf Waldemar Stageberg, Biography of Susie W. Stageberg of Red Wing, Minnesota American Mothers Committee, Inc., 1975, MHS.

78. Gallaher, *Legal and Political Status of Women in Iowa,* p. 238; and Frank E. Horack, "Equal Suffrage in Iowa," in *Applied History,* ed. Benjamin Shambaugh, vol. 2 (Iowa City, Iowa: State Historical Society, 1914), pp. 293–96.

79. Paula A. Treckel, "Jane Grey Swisshelm and Feminism in Early Minnesota," *Midwest Review* 2 (Spring 1980): 11; and Jane Grey Swisshelm, "Letters to 'Dear Journal,' " *Woman's Journal,* 2 Apr. and 27 Oct. 1870.

80. Louise Noun, "Amelia Bloomer: A Biography," pt. 1: "The Lily of Seneca Falls," *Annals of Iowa* 47, 7 (Winter 1985): 575–617, and pt. 2: "The Suffragist of Council Bluffs," ibid., 47, 8 (Spring 1985): 575–621.

81. Louise R. Noun, *Strong-Minded Women: The Emergence of the Woman Suffrage Movement in Iowa* (Ames: Iowa State University Press, 1969), pp. 12–13; and Ruth S. Beitz, "Amelia Bloomer's Own Emancipation Proclamation," *Iowan* 14, 2 (Winter 1965/66): 40. For reactions to bloomers see *Daily Pantagraph* (Bloomington, Ill.), 1 Apr. 1859.

82. Noun, *Strong-Minded Women,* pp. 20, 264–65; Philip D. Jordan, "Amelia Jenks Bloomer," *Palimpsest* 37, 4 (Apr. 1957): 143–48; and "Amelia Jenks Bloomer," in *Notable American Women,* pp. 179–81. Collections of Bloomer's letters and other papers are at the Seneca Falls Historical Society in New York and the Council Bluffs Free Public Library in Iowa.

83. Noun, *Strong-Minded Women,* pp. 113–15; Mary Newbury Adams, letters, in Austin Adams Family Papers, Special Collections, Iowa State University Library, Ames, Iowa; and Louise Moede Lex, "Mary Newbury Adams: Feminist Forerunner from Iowa," *Annals of Iowa* 43, 5 (Summer 1976): 323–41.

84. Mrs. I. N. Taylor, "The Grange: Its Advantages, Social and Educational," *Iowa Yearbook of Agriculture* (Des Moines: Iowa Department of Agriculture, 1910), pp. 646–48; and Mrs. William Rhodes, The Grange, n.d., MLCHS; see also W. A. Anderson, "The Granger Movement in the Middle West with Special Reference to Iowa," *Iowa Journal of History* 221 (Jan. 1924): 3–51; Charles M. Gardner, *The Grange: Friends of the Farmer* (Washington, D.C.: National Grange, 1949); and D. Sven Nordin, *Rich Harvest: A History of the Grange, 1867–1900* (Jackson: University Press of Mississippi, 1974).

85. For more on the women's-rights movement on the prairie see Mari J. Matsuda, "The West and the Legal Status of Women: Explanations of Frontier Feminism," *Journal of the West* 24, 1 (Jan. 1985): 47–56. For more detailed discussions of suffrage in prairie states see Beverly Beeton, "Woman Suffrage in the American West, 1869–1896" (Ph.D. diss., University of Utah, 1976); Steven Michael Buechler, "Social Change and Movement Transformation: The De-radicalization of the Illinois Women's Rights/WomanSuffrage Movement" (Ph.D. diss., State University of New York, Stony Brook, 1982); Ethel Edgerton Hurd, *Woman Suffrage in Minnesota: A Record of the Activities on Its Behalf since 1847* (Minneapolis: Minnesota Woman Suffrage Association 1916); Catherine Mambretti, "The Battle against the Ballot: Illinois Women Antisuffragists," *Chicago History* 9, 2 (1980): 168–77; Adade Mitchell Wheeler, "Conflict in the Illinois Suffrage Movement of 1913," *Journal of the Illinois State Historical Society* 76, 2 (1983): 95–114; and Marilyn Ziebarth, "Women's Rights Movement," *Minnesota History* 42, 6 (1971): 225–30.

86. Wing, "Early Days in Clayton County," pp. 281–82.

87. See, e.g., Emery S. Bartlett, letter to My Dear Children and Grandchildren, Dec. 1911, ISHD-MA.

Chapter 8. Community Participation on the Plains

1. For articles that urge women to read see Charles E. Sargent, *Our Home: or, Influences Emanating from the Hearthstone* (Springfield, Mass.: King-Richardson, 1900), pp. 152–66; Samuel Smiles, *Mothers and Nations* (Chicago: American Publishing House, 1897), pp. 544–56; and Richard A. Wells, *Manners, Culture and Dress of the Best American Society* (Springfield, Mass.: King, Richardson & Co., 1891), pp. 205–14.

2. Marian Lawton Clayton, Reminiscences: The Little Family, 1961, KSHS; Edna Jewett Allen, PDC, SDSHRC; and Faye C. Lewis, *Nothing to Make a Shadow* (Ames: Iowa State University Press, 1971), p. 76; see also Alice E. Barrett, Reminiscences of Mrs. Alice E. Barrett, Montana Pioneers Collection, MTHS; Alice E. Lee, Sod House Letters, 1857/58, NSHS; Clara Field McCarthy, Clara's Episodes: A Reflection of Early Wyoming, 1909–1911, 1964, WSAMHD; and Fannie Forbes Russel, My First Year in Montana, 1864/65, 1920, MTHS.

3. Hannah Birkley, Mrs. Iver O. Birkley, 1957, NSHS; and Anne E. Bingham, "Sixteen Years on a Kansas Farm, 1870–1886," Kansas State Historical Society *Collections* 15 (1919/20): 520; see also Mary S. Kerlee and Grace Fitzgerald West, MAMBP, MTHS.

4. Anonymous, household account book, Jan.–July 1880, SDSHRC; Ellen Payne Paullin, ed., "Etta's Journal, January 2, 1874–July 25, 1875," pt. 2, *Kansas History* 3, 4 (Winter 1980): 275; Mary S. Kerlee, MAMBP, MTHS; Eva Neal, Papers, 1881–1963, MHS; and Kathie Ryckman Anderson, "Era Bell Thompson: A North Dakota Daughter," *North Dakota History* 49, 4 (Fall 1982): 11–18.

5. Round Table Club of Crete, Nebr., records, 1885–1935, NSHS; and Shakespeare Club of Cheyenne, records, 1899–1941, WSAMHD.

6. A. P. Libby, Pioneer Memories Collection, 1975, WSAMHD; see also Cora M. Beach, *Women of Wyoming* (Casper, Wyo.: Commercial Printing Co., 1925); Jane Rooker Breeden, PDC, SDSHRC; Mary Paddock Berthod, MAMBP, MTHS; Mathilda C. Engstad, The White Kid Glove Era, n.d., SHSND; Lewis, *Nothing to Make a Shadow*, p. 75; Sedona F. Nelson and Estelle Peterson, Pioneer Memories Collection, 1975, WSAMHD; and Mrs. Ed W. Sayre, "Organization of First Women's Club in the

Valley," in *Pioneer Tales of the North Platte Valley*, ed. A. B. Wood (Gering, Nebr.: Courier Press, 1938), pp. 43–45.

7. Sarah Elizabeth Canfield, Diary, 1866/67, SHSND. For other listings of books see Venola Lewis Bivans, ed., "The Diary of Luna E. Warner, a Kansas Teenager of the Early 1870s," *Kansas Historical Quarterly* 35, 3 (Autumn 1969): 289, 302, 304, and 35, 4 (Winter 1969): 414; Edna LaMoore Waldo, *Dakota* (Bismarck, N.Dak.: Capital Publishing Co., 1932), p. 205; Fern Spencer Dumbrill, "A Woman's Memories of Homesteading," in *Wyoming Homestead Heritage*, ed. Charles F. Spencer (Hicksville, N.Y.: Exposition Press, 1975), p. 189; and Susan Leaphart, ed., "Montana Episodes: Frieda and Belle Fligelman: A Frontier-City Girlhood in the 1890s," *Montana, the Magazine of Western History* 32, 3 (Summer 1982): 87.

8. See, e.g., Alice Richards McCreary, Various Happenings in the Life of Alice Richards McCreery, n.d., WSAMHD; Nannie T. Alderson and Helena Huntington Smith, *A Bride Goes West* (Lincoln: University of Nebraska Press, 1969), p. 38; Marian Fowler, *The Embroidered Tent* (Toronto: House of Anansi Press, 1982), pp. 8–9; Clayton, Reminiscences: The Little Family, KSHS; and Elizabeth Hampsten, *Read This Only to Yourself: The Private Writings of Midwestern Women, 1880–1910* (Bloomington: Indiana University Press, 1983), p. 65.

9. Unidentified clipping, c. 1915, found in *Godey's Lady's Book;* see also Mrs. John A. Logan, *The Home Manual: Everybody's Guide in Social, Domestic and Business Life* (n.p.: n.p., 1889); Mary R. Melendy, *Perfect Womanhood for Maidens, Wives, Mothers: A Complete Medical Guide for Women* (n.p.: K. T. Boland, 1903); Sidney Morse, *Household Discoveries: An Encyclopedia of Practical Recipes and Processes* (Petersburg, N.Y.: S. L. Morse, 1908); anonymous, *The Housekeepers' Companion* (Chicago: Mercantile Pub. & Adv. Co., 1883); Margaret E. Sangster, *Good Manners for All Occasions* (New York: Christian Herald, 1904); Woman's Home Companion, *The Woman's Book* (New York: Crowell, 1907); and John H. Young, *Our Deportment: or, The Manners, Conduct and Dress of the Most Refined Society* (Harrisburg: Pennsylvania Publishing Co., 1881). There were also a number of guidebooks directed partially or wholly to men: see anonymous, *Good Manners* (New York: Butterick, 1889), pp. 39–44, 182–88.

10. For accounts for women seeking education see Becky Berry, "Grandma Berry's Ninety Years in Oklahoma," *Chronicles of Oklahoma* 45, 1 (Spring 1967): 58–67; Ida W. Fearnall, Olive Pickering Rankin, and Ella Wheeler Turpin, MAMBP, MTHS; Gertrude B. Gunderson, PDC, SDSHRC; Elizabeth Hampsten, comp., *To All Inquiring Friends: Letters, Diaries, and Essays in North Dakota, 1880–1910* (Grand Forks: University of North Dakota, Department of English, 1979), pp. 31–40; Gordon L. Iseminger, "Christina Hillius: Learning to Read at 62," paper presented at the Northern Great Plains History Conference, Bismarck, N.Dak., 28 Sept. 1984; Myrtle Taylor Kemplin, "Homesteading in Garden County," in *Pioneer Tales of the North Platte Valley*, pp. 184–87; Martha Suckow Packer, memoirs, 20 Sept. 1880–21 Jan. 1970, MSULSC; Grace Reed Porter, Twenty-Five Years in South Dakota, SDSHRC; and State Historical Society, "The First Ladies of South Dakota," pp. 156–64. For a discussion of teacher-training opportunities see Wayne E. Fuller, "Country Schoolteaching of the Sod-House Frontier," *Arizona and the West* 17, 2 (Summer 1975): 129–35.

11. Inez Thompson Peterson, PDC, SDSHRC; Catherine Wiggins Porter, Sunday School Houses and Normal Institutes: Pupil and Teacher in Northern Kansas, 1886–95, KSHS; and Mable Cheney Moudy, Through My Life, n.d., UWAHC.

12. Elizabeth Cochran, "Hatchets and Hoopskirts: Women in Kansas History," *Midwest Quarterly* 2, 3 (Apr. 1961): 232.

13. Helen Siampos, "Early Education in Nebraska," *Nebraska History* 29, 2 (June 1948): 113–33; Phyllis Key Wilke, "Physical Education for Women at Nebraska University, 1879–1923," ibid., 56, 2 (Summer 1975): 192–220; and Nellie Snyder Yost, "Nebraska's Scholarly Athlete: Louise Pound, 1872–1958," ibid., 64, 4 (Winter 1983): 476–90. For other distinguished women academics on the Plains see Eunice G. Anderson, "Woman's Accomplishments in Wyoming," WSAMHD; Maren Michelet, "Agnes Mathilde Wergeland," *American Scandinavian Review* 2, 4 (July 1914): 23; and Agnes Mathilde Wergeland, obituaries, 1914, UWAHC.

14. Martha Call Farnworth, diaries, 1882–97, 1899, 1903–14, KSHS; and Dorothy Kimball, "Alone on That Prairie: The Homestead Narrative of Nellie Rogney," *Montana, the Magazine of Western History* 33, 4 (Autumn 1983): 58–62.

15. Mary Long Alderson, A Half Century of Progress for Montana Women, 1934, MTHS; and *Abilene* (Kans.) *Chronicle,* 14 Sept. 1871. For a discussion of the anti-prostitution campaign on the Plains see Anne M. Butler, *Daughters of Joy, Sisters of Misery: Prostitutes in the American West, 1865–1890* (Champaign: University of Illinois Press, 1985), pp. 63–69, 81–92; Robert R. Dykstra, *The Cattle Towns* (New York: Atheneum, 1974), pp. 216, 243–45, 258, 272–74, 286–92; and Carol Leonard and Isidor Walliman, "Prostitution and Changing Morality in the Frontier Cattle Towns of Kansas," *Kansas History* 2, 1 (Spring 1979): 44–53.

16. Cochran, "Hatchets and Hoopskirts," pp. 241–44; Paul R. Messbarger, "Carry Nation," in Edward T. James, ed., *Notable American Women, 1607–1950: A Biographical Dictionary* (Cambridge, Mass.: Belknap Press of Harvard University Press, 1971), pp. 609–11; Robert S. Bader, "Mrs. Nation," *Kansas History* 7, 4 (Winter 1984/85): 247–62; and idem, *Prohibition in Kansas: A History* (Lawrence: University Press of Kansas, 1986).

17. Porter, Sunday School Houses and Normal Institutes, KSHS; and Clayton, Reminiscences: The Little Family, KSHS.

18. Anonymous, A Partial History of the Bismarck WCTU, n.d., and Elizabeth Preston Anderson, Two Weeks in the Lobby of the North Dakota Legislature, n.d.—both in the WCTU Records, SHSND.

19. Grand Forks Scandinavian WCTU, 1898–1938, in the WCTU Records, SHSND; and History of the Women's Christian Temperance Union of Bottineau, N.Dak., n.d., in WCTU Records, SHSND.

20. For the argument that women were reacting against the freedom of men see Barbara Leslie Epstein, *The Politics of Domesticity: Women, Evangelism, and Temperance in Nineteenth-Century America* (Middletown, Conn.: Wesleyan University Press, 1981), p. 4; see also Julie Roy Jeffrey, *Frontier Women: The Trans-Mississippi West, 1840–1880* (New York: Hill & Wang, 1979), pp. 180–89; and Ian R. Tyrrell, "Women and Temperance in Antebellum America, 1830–1860," *Civil War History* 28, 2 (June 1982): 128–52.

21. Ada M. Bittenbender, History of the Women's Christian Temperance Union in Nebraska, c. 1893, WCTU Records, NSHS; see also Jack S. Blocker, Jr., "Annie Wittenmyer and the Women's Crusade," *Ohio History* 88 (Autumn 1979): 420–21.

22. McCreary, Various Happenings in the Life of Alice Richards McCreary, WSAMHD.

23. Mrs. R. O. Brandt, "Social Aspects of Prairie Pioneering: The Reminiscences of a Pioneer Pastor's Wife," *Norwegian-American Studies* 7 (1933): 16–17. For descriptions of other societies and their work see Lydia Burrows Foote, Inez Thompson Peterson, and Sarah Wood Ward, PDC, SDSHRC; Josephine Grahm, Huntley Project Homesteading, 1968, MSULSC; Laura Kammann Mann and Jessie E. Mudgett, Pioneer Memories Collection, 1975, WSAMHD; Ella Martfeld, Homesteading Days,

n.d., WSAMHD; and Mae Waterman, Huntley Project Homesteading, 1968, MSULSC; see also Darlene Ritter, "The Faith of Pioneer Women," *Nebraska Humanist* 6, 2 (Fall 1983): 26–30.

24. For a contemporary account of women's clubs and their work see Helen M. Winslow, *The Woman of Tomorrow* (New York: James Pott & Co., 1905), p. 115–38.

25. Engstad, The White Kid Glove Era, SHSND.

26. Marilyn Hoder-Salmon, "Myrtle Archer McDougal: Leader of Oklahoma's 'Timid Sisters,'" *Chronicles of Oklahoma* 60 (Fall 1982): 332–43.

27. Alderson, A Half Century of Progress for Montana Women, MTHS.

28. Ibid., Anderson, "Woman's Accomplishments in Wyoming," WSAMHD; Beach, Women of Wyoming, UWAHC; Jane Rooker Breeden, Amelia C. Glecker, Ellen Agnes Feeney Hughes, and Eleanor Schubert, PDC, SDSHRC; McCarthy, Clara's Episodes, WSAMHD; State Historical Society, "The First Ladies of South Dakota," pp. 156–63; Esther Thornberg, Pioneer Memories Collection, 1975, WSAMHD; and Ella Wheeler Turpin, MAMBP, MTHS.

29. Cochran, "Hatchets and Hoopskirts," p. 235; letter to L. O. Jones from the president of the Nebraska Epworth League, 20 Apr. 1915, Nebraska WCTU Records, NSHS; Ella Irvine Mountjoy, reminiscences, 1911, 1942, MTHS; and Porter, Twenty-Five Years in South Dakota, SDSHRC; see also June O. Underwood, "Civilizing Kansas: Women's Organizations, 1880–1920," *Kansas History* 7, 4 (Winter 1984/85): 219–306; and Stephenie Ambrose Tubbs, "Montana Women's Clubs at the Turn of the Century," *Montana, the Magazine of Western History* 36, 1 (Winter 1986): 27–34.

30. Lora Foster, interview, 1982, MTHS. For comments on the development and importance of extension clubs during the World War I era see Myra Daniel, interview, 9 Apr. 1982, MTHS; Louella Hardie, interview, 24 Sept. 1981, MTHS; Ruth Miller, interview, 29 Sept. 1979, UWAHC; and Hattie Usher, interview, 2 Oct. 1979, MTHS.

31. Sudie Rhone, interview, 8 Nov. 1979, UWAHC.

32. Ronald J. Quinn, "The Modest Seduction: The Experience of Pioneer Women on the Trans-Mississippi Frontier" (Ph.D. diss., University of California at Riverside, 1977); and Glenda Riley, *Women and Indians on the Frontier, 1825–1915* (Albuquerque: University of New Mexico Press, 1984), pp. 13–16; see also Nancy B. Black and Bette S. Weidmen, eds., *White on Red: Images of the American Indian* (Port Washington, N.Y.: Kennikat, 1976); and Roy Harvey Pearce, *The Savages of America: A Study of the Indian and the Idea of Civilization* (Baltimore, Md.: Johns Hopkins Press, 1965).

33. Lois L. Murray, *Incidents of Frontier Life* (Goshen, Ind.: Evangelical United Mennonite Publishing House, 1880), p. 92.

34. Miriam P. Colt, *Went to Kansas: Being a Thrilling Account of an Ill-Fated Expedition* (Watertown, N.Y.: L. Ingalls, 1862), p. 67; Frances M. A. Roe, *Army Letters from an Officer's Wife, 1871–1888* (New York: D. Appleton, 1909), pp. 96–97; and Frances C. Carrington, *My Army Life and the Fort Phil Kearney Massacre, with an Account of the Celebration of "Wyoming Opened"* (Philadelphia: Lippincott, 1910), p. 45.

35. Virginia Wilcox Ivins, *Pen Pictures of Early Western Days* (Keokuk, Iowa: n.p., c. 1905); and Carrie A. Strahorn, *Fifteen Thousand Miles By Stage* (New York: G. P. Putnam's Sons, 1911), p. 316.

36. Sandra L. Myres, "Romance and Reality on the American Frontier: Views of Army Wives," *Western Historical Quarterly* 13, 4 (Oct. 1982): 414; and Sherry L. Smith, "Officers' Wives, Indians and the Indian Wars," *Order of the Indian Wars Journal* 1, 1 (Winter 1980): 42–43.

37. Murray, *Incidents of Frontier Life*, p. 92; and Ada Adelaide Adams Vogdes, journal, 1866–72, Huntington Library, San Marino, Calif.

38. Margaret I. Carrington, *Ab-sa-ra-ka, Home of the Crows: Being the Experience of an Officer's Wife on the Plains* (Philadelphia: Lippincott, 1868), p. 75; and Thomas R. Buecker, ed., "Letters of Caroline Frey Winne from Sidney Barracks and Fort McPherson, Nebraska, 1874–1878," *Nebraska History* 62, 1 (Spring 1981): 24–25.

39. America Elmira Collins, letter to Dear Edith, 29 Mar. 1891, SHSND; see also Riley, *Women and Indians on the Frontier,* pp. 20–21, 172–75, 180–84, 226–27.

40. See Robert Clark, *Ellen Swallow: The Woman Who Founded Ecology* (Chicago: Follett, 1973); Vera L. Norwood, "Heroines of Nature: Four Women Respond to the American Landscape," *Environmental Review* 8, 1 (Spring 1984): 37–40; Ann LaBastille, *Women and Wilderness: Women in Wilderness Professions* (San Francisco, Calif.: Sierra Club Books, 1980), pp. 45–46, 72–74; and Maxine Benson, *Martha Maxwell: Rocky Mountain Naturalist* (Lincoln: University of Nebraska Press, 1986).

41. Annie D. Tallent, *The First White Woman in the Black Hills* (Mitchell, S.Dak.: Educator Supply Co., 1923); idem, *The Black Hills: or, The Last Hunting Ground of the Dakotahs* (Sioux Falls, S.Dak.: Brevet Press, 1974).

42. Bright, diary, KSHS; Martfeld, Homesteading Days, WSAMHD; Jessie E. Mudgett, Pioneer Memories Collection, 1975, WSAMHD; Elinore Pruitt Stewart, *Letters on an Elk Hunt* (Lincoln: University of Nebraska Press, 1979), pp. 34–35, 57–58, 82–83, 97–99; and Grace Fitzgerald West, MAMBP, MTHS.

43. Mary Hetty Bonar, diary, 1885, SHSND; Alderson, A Half Century of Progress for Montana Women, MTHS; Carolyn Merchant, "Women of the Progressive Conservation Movement, 1900–1916," *Environmental Review* 8, 1 (Spring 1984): 61, 69–73; and Richard Slotkin, *The Fatal Environment: The Myth of the Frontier in the Age of Industrialization, 1800–1890* (New York: Atheneum, 1985), pp. 242–43, 358–64.

44. Donna M. Lucey, "The Intimate Vision of Evelyn Cameron," *Geo* 5, 1 (Jan. 1983): 76–78; and Peter E. Palmquist, "Photographers in Petticoats," *Journal of the West* 21, 2 (Apr. 1982): 60–64.

45. Colt, *Went to Kansas*, p. 65; and Lucey, "Intimate Vision of Evelyn Cameron," p. 78.

46. Sandra L. Marburg, "Women and the Environment: Subsistence Paradigms, 1850–1950," *Environmental Review* 8, 1 (Spring 1984): 7–22; Janice Monk, "Approaches to the Study of Women and Landscape," *Environmental Review* 8, 1 (Spring 1984): 23–33; Sandra L. Myres, *Westering Women and the Frontier Experience, 1800–1915* (Albuquerque: University of New Mexico Press, 1982), pp. 12–36; Frederick Turner, "The Terror of the Wilderness," *American Heritage* 28, 2 (Feb. 1977): 58–65; and Peg Wherry, "At Home on the Range: Reactions of Pioneer Women to Kansas Plains Landscape," *Kansas Quarterly* 18, 3 (1986): 79–91. For a discussion of the impact of wilderness on institutions and thought see Mary W. M. Hargreaves, "Space: Its Institutional Impact in the Development of the Great Plains," in *The Great Plains: Environment and Culture*, ed. Brian W. Blouet and Frederick C. Luebke (Lincoln: University of Nebraska Press, 1979), pp. 205–23; and Roderick Nash, *Wilderness and the American Mind* (New Haven, Conn.: Yale University Press, 1982).

47. Luna Kellie, memoirs, n.d., NSHS; Douglas A. Bakken, ed., "Luna E. Kellie and the Farmers' Alliance," *Nebraska History* 50 (Summer 1969): 201–2; Marilyn Dell Brady, "Populism and Feminism in a Newspaper by and for Women of the Kansas Farmers' Alliance, 1891–1894," *Kansas History* 7, 4 (Winter 1984/85): 280–90; Dorothy K. Gray, *Women of the West* (Millbrook, Calif.: Les Femmes, 1976), p. 144; and Cochran, "Hatchets and Hoopskirts," p. 246.

48. Quoted in Gray, *Women in the West,* p. 143.

49. O. Gene Clanton, "Intolerant Populist? The Disaffection of Mary Elizabeth Lease," *Kansas Historical Quarterly* 34, 1 (Summer 1968): 189–200; Katherine B. Clinton, "What Did You Say, Mrs. Lease?" *Kansas Quarterly* 1, 4 (Fall 1969): 52–59; Cochran, "Hatchets and Hoopskirts," pp. 244–46; and Gray, *Women in the West,* pp. 140–45; see also Richard Stiller, *Queen of the Populists: The Story of Mary Elizabeth Lease* (New York: Crowell, 1970).

50. Alderson, A Half Century of Progress for Montana Women, MTHS; and Richard B. Knowles, "Crossing the Gender Line: Ella L. Knowles, Montana's First Woman Lawyer," *Montana, the Magazine of Western History* 32, 2 (Summer 1982): 64–75.

51. Carlos A. Schwantes, "Western Women in Coxey's Army in 1894," *Arizona and the West* 26, 1 (Spring 1984): 5–20.

52. Olive Pickering Rankin, MAMBP, MTHS; see also Jennie Williams Duret, Park County Women, MSULSC; Georgia L. McRoberts, "Pioneer Ranch Life Near Sterling," *Colorado Magazine* 11 (1934): 68; and State Historical Society, "The First Ladies of South Dakota," p. 163.

53. Cochran, "Hatchets and Hoopskirts," p. 232; and Porter, Twenty-Five Years in South Dakota, SDSHRC.

54. Kellie, memoirs, NSHS.

55. Porter, Sunday School Houses and Normal Institutes, KSHS; see also Bingham, "Sixteen Years on a Kansas Farm," p. 502; and Mrs. Elias Jacobsen, PDC, SDSHRC.

56. Beverly Beeton and G. Thomas Edwards, "Susan B. Anthony's Woman Suffrage Crusade in the American West," *Journal of the West* 21, 1 (Apr. 1982): 5.

57. For a discussion of this issue see Virginia Scharff, "The Case for Domestic Feminism: Woman Suffrage in Wyoming," *Annals of Wyoming* 56 (Fall 1984): 29–37.

58. Bill Nye's Humorous Report, n.d., Woman Suffrage Collection, WSAMHD.

59. Beach, Women of Wyoming, UWAHC; Dr. Grace Raymond Hebard, How Woman Suffrage Came to Wyoming, n.d., WSAMHD; T. A. Larson, "Dolls, Vassals, and Drudges: Pioneer Women in the West," *Western Historical Quarterly* 3, 1 (Jan. 1972): 5–7; and Katharine A. Morton, "A Historical Review of Women's Suffrage," *Annals of Wyoming* 12 (Apr. 1940): 23–25. Other relevant sources include Grace Raymond Hebard, Esther Hobart Morris, Woman Suffrage Collection, WSAMHD; House Joint Resolution, 1923, Woman Suffrage Collection, WSAMHD; Sadie Bristol Jensen, letter, n.d., Woman Suffrage Collection, file no. 1, WSAMHD; Gray, *Women of the West,* pp. 75–80; T. A. Larson, "Woman Suffrage in Wyoming," *Pacific Northwest Quarterly* 56, 2 (Apr. 1965): 58–61; Larson, "Dolls, Vassals, and Drudges," pp. 8–9; Katharine A. Morton, How Woman Suffrage Came to Wyoming, n.d., Woman Suffrage Collection, WSAMHD; Staff of the Library of the University of Wyoming, Esther Hobart Morris and Suffrage, n.d., Woman Suffrage File, UWAHC; Mary Lee Stark, One of the First Wyoming Women Voters Tells How Franchise Was Granted, n.d., UWAHC; *Casper* (Wyo.) *Morning Star,* 3 Feb. 1955; and letter from Esther Hobart Morris to My Dear Mrs. Hooker, 21 Jan. 1871, Woman Suffrage Collection, WSAMHD. For other women who aided the suffrage cause in Wyoming see Larson, "Woman Suffrage in Wyoming," pp. 57–59; Jeffrey, *Frontier Women,* pp. 190–93; T. A. Larson, "Home Rule on the Range," in *Western America in the Seventies,* ed. Daniel Tyler (Fort Collins, Colo.: Robinson Press, 1973), pp. 77–82; Mari J. Matsuda, "The West and the Legal Status of Women: Explanations of Frontier Feminism," *Journal of the West* 24, 1 (Jan. 1985): 51; and Myres, *Westering Women and the Frontier Experience,* pp. 220–21.

60. Mrs. S. I. Hooker, The Part Women Had in the Growth of Wyoming, 1933, WSAMHD.

61. Women's First Ballot Here Was "Shot Heard 'Round World," n.d., WSAMHD; Lottie Holmberg, Experiences of Mary Culbertson, 1939, WSAMHD; and Agnes Mathilde Wergeland, obituary, UWAHC. For more on the impact of woman suffrage in Wyoming see *Cheyenne* (Wyo.) *Weekly Sun*, 24 Oct. 1889; *Revolution*, 16 Dec. 1869; *Nation*, 3 Mar. 1870; Larson, "Dolls, Vassals, and Drudges," pp. 7–8; Bruce Noble, "The Quest for Settlement in Early Wyoming," *Annals of Wyoming* 55 (Fall 1983): 19–24; and *Frank Leslie's Illustrated Newspaper*, 24 Nov. 1888, pp. 233–34.

62. Larson, "Woman Suffrage in Wyoming," p. 63.

63. Clarice Whittenburg, "Portrait of an 'Ordinary' Woman: Eliza Stewart Boyd," *Annals of Wyoming* 29, 1 (Apr. 1957): 33–37; quoted in *Laramie* (Wyo.) *Republican*, 8 Dec. 1922; and quoted in *Cheyenne* (Wyo.) *Daily Sun Leader*, 28 Nov. 1895; Esther Morris, Justice of the Peace Docket, 14 Feb. to 20 Oct. 1870, WSAMHD.

64. *South Pass* (Wyo.) *News*, reported in the *Rocky Mountain Herald* (Denver), 7 Mar. 1914; *Oswego* (N.Y.) *Gazette*, 24 Mar. 1870; and *San Francisco* (Calif.) *Chronicle*, 16 Feb. 1872.

65. Maude B. Ingham, A Woman of Achievements: Mary G. Bellamy, n.d., Woman Suffrage file, WSAMHD; Laramie Women's Club, Mary Godot Bellamy, 1940, UWAHC; and *Rawlins* (Wyo.) *Republican*, 13 Sept. 1913.

66. Anonymous, Wyoming First State to Give Women Right to Vote, n.d., Hebard Collection, Laramie.

67. Donald B. Marti, "Sisters of the Grange: Rural Feminism in the Late Nineteenth Century," *Agricultural History* 58, 3 (July 1984): 247–61; quoted in Judith Papachristou, "WCTU: They Were Fighting More Than Demon Rum," *Ms. Magazine* 4, 12 (June 1976): 105; and Anderson, Two Weeks in the Lobby of the North Dakota Legislature, SHSND; see also Jack S. Blocker, Jr., "Separate Paths: Suffragists and the Women's Temperance Crusade," *Signs* 10, 3 (Spring 1985): 460–76.

68. Cochran, "Hatchets and Hoopskirts," p. 230; Joseph G. Gambone, ed., "The Forgotten Feminist of Kansas: The Papers of Clarinda I. H. Nichols, 1854–1885," *Kansas Historical Quarterly* 39, 3 (Fall 1973): 392–444, 39, 4 (Winter 1973): 515–63, 40, 1 (Spring 1974): 72–135, 40, 2 (Summer 1974): 241–92, 40, 3 (Fall 1974): 410–59, 40, 4 (Winter 1974): 503–62; and Martha B. Caldwell, "The Woman Suffrage Campaign of 1912," *Kansas Historical Quarterly* 12, 3 (Aug. 1943): 300–318.

69. Broadside, The Celebrated Platte Circus, c. 1870/71, NSHS.

70. Grace Mason Wheeler to Dear Mrs. [Mary Ware] Dennett, 15 Dec. 1910; *Headquarters Message*, May 1910; report, Oct. 1911; Resolutions of State Suffrage Convention, 1912; Mary H. Williams to Anna Howard Shaw, 10 Dec. 1912; Minutes of the Thirty-third Annual Convention of the Nebraska Woman Suffrage Association, 6 Nov. 1913—all in the Woman Suffrage Collection, NSHS; see also Ann L. Wiegman Wilhite, "Sixty-five Years till Victory: A History of Woman Suffrage in Nebraska," *Nebraska History* 49, 2 (Summer 1968): 149–63.

71. Billie Barnes Jensen, "Let the Women Vote," *Colorado Magazine* 41 (Winter 1964): 13–19; idem, "Colorado Woman Suffrage Campaign of the 1870s," *Journal of the West* 12, 2 (Apr. 1973): 254–71; and Myres, *Westering Women and the Frontier Experience*, pp. 223–29.

72. Dorinda Riessen Reed, *The Woman Suffrage Movement in South Dakota* (Pierre: South Dakota Commission on the Status of Women, 1975), pp. 5–7, 11–14, 18–113; Ruth B. Hipple, History of Women Suffrage in South Dakota, 1920, Woman Suffrage Movement Papers, SDSHRC; and Mary Kay Jennings, "Lake County Woman Suffrage Campaign in 1890," *South Dakota History* 5, 4 (Fall 1975): 390–401. For a detailed discussion of Susan B. Anthony's role in the 1889/90 campaign see Cecelia M. Wittmayer, "The 1889–90 Woman Suffrage Campaign: A Need to Organize," *South*

Dakota History 11, 3 (Summer 1981): 199–225. For accounts of later suffrage crusades see Jane Rooker Breeden, PDC, SDSHRC; and Jane Rooker Breeden Papers, 1886–1946, SDSHRC; Mrs. John (Mamie I. Shields) Pyle Papers, Richardson Archives, I. D. Weeks Library, University of South Dakota, Vermillion; and the Woman Suffrage Movement Papers, 1890–1925, SDSHRC. Of particular interest are Request to the NWSA for Funds, n.d.; Minutes of the first Meeting of the Organization of Fort Pierre Political Equality Club, 1894; Minutes of the Ft. Pierre Equal Suffrage Club, 15 Jan. 1910; letter from Anna Howard Shaw to My Dear Mrs. Hipple, 19 Dec. 1913; letter from Adele M. Nelson to My Dear Mrs. Hipple, 14 May 1913.

73. Alderson, A Half Century of Progress for Montana Women, MTHS.

74. An account of the fight for woman suffrage in Oklahoma is found in James R. Wright, "The Assiduous Wedge: Woman Suffrage and the Oklahoma Constitutional Convention," *Chronicles of Oklahoma* 51, 4 (Winter 1973/74): 421–43. For Texas see Frances Edward Abernethy, ed., *Legendary Ladies of Texas* (Dallas, Tex.: E. Heart Press, 1981).

75. Scott G. McNall and Sally Allen McNall, *Plains Families: Exploring Sociology through Social History* (New York: St. Martin's Press, 1983), pp. 146–47.

76. Jean V. Matthews, " 'Woman's Place' and the Search for Identity in Ante-Bellum America," *Canadian Review of American Studies* 10, 3 (Winter 1979): 289–304; and June O. Underwood, "Western Women and True Womanhood: Culture and Symbol in History and Literature," *Great Plains Quarterly* 5, 2 (Spring 1985): 93–106.

77. For examples of men who opposed alcohol and saloons see George W. Spivey, letter to My Dear Father, Sir, 22 Jan. 1855, UMWHMC and SHSMM; and anonymous, "History of a Pioneer Newspaper," in *Pioneer Tales,* pp. 142–44. For men who supported bands and choirs see Spivey, letter to My Dear Father, Sir, 22 Jan. 1855; and anonymous, "Music of Half Century Ago," in *Pioneer Tales,* pp. 114–16. For men who served on church and school boards and in political capacities see Susan Baird, The Low Road Home, n.d., Effie Conwell Collection, KSHS; Henry A. R. Martinson, ed., "Homesteading Episodes," *North Dakota History* 40, 2 (Spring 1973): 28; William F. Schmidt, ed., "The Letters of Charles and Helen Wooster: The Problems of Settlement," *Nebraska History* 46, 2 (June 1965): 121–37; "Early Resident Now in Gering," in *Pioneer Tales,* pp. 93–94.

*Chapter 9. The Female Frontier
on the Prairie and on the Plains*

1. Mary Huntress Carruthers, MAMBP, MTHS. For other similar cases see Mrs. Iver O. Birkley, NSHS; Hattie Daughtery Place, PDC, SDSHRC; and Nannie T. Alderson and Helena Huntington Smith, *A Bride Goes West* (Lincoln: University of Nebraska Press, 1942).

2. Lillie Goodrich, reminiscences, n.d., WSAMHD.

3. Jean Todd and Abbie Ann Jarvis, PDC, SDSHRC; and Muriel B. Scott, interview, 13 Oct. 1979, UWAHC.

4. Donna M. Lucey, "The Intimate Vision of Evelyn Cameron," *Geo* 5, 1 (Jan. 1983): 65–79.

5. Grace Reed Porter, Twenty-Five Years in South Dakota, n.d., SDSHRC.

6. Francis A. Long, "The Prairie Doctor's Wife," in her *Prairie Doctor of the Eighties* (Norfolk: Nebraska Home Publishing, 1937).

7. Mrs. John Van Cleve, diaries, 1859–63, ISHL; Sarah Wood Ward, PDC, SDSHRC; Julia Lovejoy, letters, 1828–64, KSHS; and Mrs. W. B. D. (the Rev. Annette B.) Gray, 1918, UWAHC.

8. Caroline Phelps, diary, 1832, ISHD-HS; Mrs. R. H. Hall, Mrs. Noyes Baldwin, Mother of Lander, 1932, WSAMHD; Margaret Ronan, ed., *Frontier Woman: The Story of Mary Ronan* (Helena: University of Montana Publications in History, 1973); and Coraline Saxton Boesl, PDC, SDSHRC.

9. Mathilda C. Engstad, The White Kid Glove Era, n.d., SHSND.

10. James L. Thane, Jr., ed., "The Governor's Lady Writes Home to Ohio," *Montana, the Magazine of Western History* 24, 3 (July 1974): 12–25; see also Bertha M. H. Shambaugh, "The Scrap-Books of a Quiet Little Lady with Silvery Hair," *Palimpsest* 4, 12 (Dec. 1923): 401–27; Ruth A. Gallaher, "From Connecticut to Iowa," ibid., 22, 3 (Mar. 1941): 65–78; Ben H. Wilson, "Amelia Smith Hay," ibid., 28, 7 (July 1947): 218–22; Mrs. C. S. Amsden, Martha Babcock, Amelia C. Gleckler, and Eleanor Schubert, PDC, SDSHRC; and Martha Call Farnsworth, diary, 1882–97, 1899, 1903–14, KSHS.

11. Roxanne Heffelfinger-Mehner, PDC, SDSHRC.

12. Susan Carter, diary, 1887, NSHS.

13. Sarah Ann Cooper and Ellen Feeney Hughes, PDC, SDSHRC; and Ida W. Fearnall, MAMBP, MTHS.

14. Ellen Strang, diary, 1859–72, ISHD-HS; and Clara Conron, diary, 1884/85, KSHS.

15. Lottie Holmberg, Early Experiences of Miss Lucy Wells in Wyoming, 1936, WSAMHD; and Lizzie Elliot Holmes, PDC, SDSHRC.

16. Madge Yoder Smith, interview, 13 Oct. 1979, UWAHC.

17. Rufus W. Payne, letter to Dear Brother, 12 Dec.. 1858, MHS; and Fanny Achtnes Malone, The Experience of a Michigan Family on a Government Homestead in South Dakota in 1905, n.d., SDSHRC.

18. For general accounts of men's lives on the prairie and the Plains see Susan Baird, The Low Road Home, n.d., KSHS; Alvin J. Bowman, Huntley Project Homesteading, 1968, MSULSC; Florence M. Edwards, Richard Edwards, 1908, MLCHS; E. Duis, *The Good Old Times in McLean County, Illinois* (Bloomington, Ill.: Leaders Publishing and Printing House, 1874); Mary Jane Gray, letters, 1869, KSHS; Charles V. Kegley, interview, 31 Dec. 1934, MHS; Henry R. Martinson, ed., "Homesteading Episodes," *North Dakota History* 40, 2 (Spring 1973): 20–33; Ray H. Mattison, "Life at Roosevelt's Elkhorn Ranch: The Letters of William W. and Mary Sewall," *North Dakota History* 27, 3 and 4 (Summer/Fall 1960): 105–41; Mrs. William J. Rhodes, William J. Rhodes, n.d., MLCHS; A. B. Wood, ed., *Pioneer Tales of the North Platte Valley* (Gering, Nebr.: Courier Press, 1938). For accounts of men's travel see George C. Anderson, "Touring Kansas and Colorado in 1871," *Kansas Historical Quarterly* 22, 3 (Autumn 1956): 193–219; Louise Barry, ed., "Scenes in (and en route to) Kansas Territory, Autumn, 1854: Five Letters by William H. Hutter," *Kansas Historical Quarterly* 35, 3 (1969): 312–36; Emery S. Bartlett, letter to My Dear Children and Grandchildren, Dec. 1911, ISHD-MA; Michael J. Brodhead and John D. Unruh, Jr., eds., "Isaiah Harris' 'Minutes of a Trip to Kansas Territory' in 1855," *Kansas Historical Quarterly* 35, 4 (1969): 373–85; Ruth Seymour Burmester, ed., "Jeffries Letters," *South Dakota History* 6, 3 (Summer 1976): 316–23; Truman W. Camp, ed., "The Journal of Joseph Camp, 1859," *Nebraska History* 46, 1 (1965): 29–38; W. W. Chapman, "Diary," *Wyoming State Historian Quarterly Bulletin* 1, 2 (15 Sept. 1923): 7–9; Caspar Weaver Collins, letters, 1844–65, Beinecke Collection, Yale University, New Haven, Conn.; Edmund F. Ely, diary, 1838/39, MHS; John Evans, letter to My Dear Sarah, 3 June 1848, MHS; Noah M. Glatfelter, "Letters from Dakota Territory," *Bulletin of the Missouri Historical Society* 18, 2 (Jan. 1962): 104–34; R. Douglas Hurt, "Davis H. Waite: Travels in Kansas, 1878," *Kansas Historical Quarterly*

42, 1 (Spring 1976): 66–72; Betty Littleton, ed., "Touring the Southeast Kansas Area in 1896: From the Diary of Thomas Butcher," *Kansas Historical Quarterly* 35, 2 (Summer 1969): 143–54; Charles W. Martin, ed., "Joseph Warren Arnold's Journal of His Trip to and from Montana, 1864–66," *Nebraska History* 55, 4 (1974): 463–552; Spencer H. Mitchell, letter to Dear Mother and Father, 30 Jan. 1863, UMWHMC and SHSMM; Watson Parker, "An Illinois Greenhorn in Bismarck, D.T.," *North Dakota History* 35, 1 (Winter 1968): 20–27; William F. Schmit, ed., "The Letters of Charles and Helen Wooster: The Problems of Settlement," *Nebraska History* 46, 2 (June 1965): 121–37; George W. Spivey, letter to My Dear Father, Sir, 22 Jan. 1855, UMWHMC and SHSMM; Donald K. Watkins, ed., "A Dane's View on Frontier Culture: 'Notes on a Stay in the United States,' 1872–74, by Wilhelm Dinesen," *Nebraska History* 55, 2 (Summer 1974): 264–89; William E. Wilson, "Hoboing in the West in the 1880s," *Montana, the Magazine of Western History* 18, 2 (1968): 36–51.

19. Edmund F. Ely, diary, 1838/39, MHS.

20. Glatfelter, "Letters from Dakota Territory," p. 106.

21. David Davis, letter to My Dear Wife, 2 Mar. 1868, ISHL.

22. Heffelfinger-Mehner, PDC, SDSHRC; and Fred W. Lorch, "Molly Clemen's Note Books," *Palimpsest* 10, 10 (Oct. 1929): 357–63.

23. Catharine Bissell Ely, diary, 1835–39, and Edmund F. Ely, diary, 1838/39, MHS. For another interesting comparison see Susan E. Newcomb, diary, 1869, 1873, and Samuel P. Newcomb, diary, 1 Jan.–21 Dec. 1865, Barker Texas History Center, University of Texas, Austin.

Note on the Sources

The most important sources for this study are the writings of prairie women and plainswomen themselves, describing their experiences, work, thought, feelings, and actions. These documents include journals, diaries, daybooks, letters, memoirs, and reminiscences. Transcriptions of oral-history interviews were also utilized. Women's sources are found in state and local libraries and archives scattered across the prairie and Plains states. Some of them catalog women's sources separately, but many still do not do so. The excellent and willing staffs of these institutions are usually pleased to search, sort, and unearth whatever they can that might be of use.

Some of the major collections that include prairie and plainswomen's source materials are the Barker Texas History Center at the University of Texas in Austin; the Denver Public Library; the Historical Society of Iowa in Iowa City; the Illinois State Historical Library in Springfield; the Iowa Museum and Archives in Des Moines; the Kansas State Historical Library in Topeka; the Minnesota Historical Society Archives in St. Paul; the Montana State Historical Society Library in Helena; the Montana State University Library Special Collections Department in Bozeman; the Nebraska State Historical Society Library in Lincoln; the Newberry Library in Chicago; the South Dakota State Historical Resource Center in Pierre; the State Historical Society of Missouri Library in Columbia; the State Historical Society of North Dakota in Bismarck; the University of Missouri Western History Manuscript Collection in Columbia; the University of Oklahoma Western History Collection in Norman; the Wyoming American Heritage Center in Laramie; and the Wyoming State Archives, Museum, and Historical Department in Cheyenne.

Some determination of available sources can be made in advance of travel to these institutions by perusing Andrea Hinding and Clark Chambers, eds., *Women's History Sources*, 2 vols. (New York: Bowker, 1979); and Cynthia E. Harrison, ed., *Women in American History: A Bibliography*, vol. 1 (Santa Barbara, Calif.: Clio Press, 1979), and vol. 2 (Santa Barbara: ABC-Clio Information Services, 1985).

Many guides also include listings of the numerous women's writings that are available in regional, state, and local historical journals and in book form. The latter were often privately printed and can be found in rare-book collections. Two helpful guidebooks are Sheryll Patterson-Black and Gene Patterson-Black, *Western Women: In History and Literature* (Crawford, Nebr.: Cottonwood Press, 1978); and Carol Fairbanks and Sara Brooks Sundberg, *Farm Women on the Prairie Frontier: A Sourcebook for Canada and the United States* (Metuchen, N.J.: Scarecrow Press, 1983). Useful bibliographical articles are Joan M. Jensen and Darlis A. Miller, "The Gentle Tamers Revisited: New Approaches to the History of Women in the American West," *Pacific Historical Review* 49, 2 (May 1980): 173–212; and Glenda Riley, "Suggestions for Further Reading," *Journal of the West* 21, 2 (Apr. 1982): 82–88.

Other materials that were used in this study include nineteenth-century women's prescriptive literature, particularly domestic and other novels, poetry, speeches, sermons, newspaper and journal articles, travelers' commentaries, fashion plates, paintings, census data, and court, tax, and police records. The writings of a number of men were also utilized for contrast. In all cases, an attempt was made to ensure the representation of all groups and classes—the literate to those barely so, young and old, single and married, upper and lower class, and members of diverse racial and ethnic stocks.

Finally, the rich and burgeoning secondary literature that deals with women's history in general and western women's history in particular was incorporated throughout. Papers and reports given at rural and western women's conferences, associations, and extension-service organizations were also drawn upon. I hope not only that this study has benefited from the rapidly growing scholarship on women but also that it will suggest ideas and theories that will generate even more research in the near future.

Index